"A great book on legal English skills for lawyers, law students, and legal English trainers; full of real-life situations and practical exercises. Highly recommended."

Elisabeth Staels, *President European Legal English Teachers' Association (EULETA), Legal English trainer and consultant*

"Combining language for specific purposes acquisition with much sought after real-world legal skills, which elsewhere are frequently treated cursorily or as a background or secondary topic, this new publication moves away from the traditional teaching of Legal English by 'legal theme' to place skills development right at the centre of the reader-learner's focus. This is a highly practical resource book by two of the most dynamic and innovative instructors-materials developers in the Legal English field today with whom I have had the pleasure and privilege to work."

David Albert BEST (PhD), *Lecturer in English for Legal Purposes at the Université Libre de Bruxelles and former President of EULETA (2016-2021)*

"Two aspects of this well-structured and clearly written book put it ahead of the pack: its use of realistic and modern legal scenarios and the detailed and practical guidance it offers. It will be an invaluable resource for lawyers and law students who wish to improve their English language skills."

Rupert Haigh, *Author of* Legal English *(6th edn., Routledge 2021) and the* Oxford Handbook of Legal Correspondence *(2006)*

"Natasha Costello and Louise Kulbicki have effectively integrated deep legal knowledge and student-centered language learning pedagogy to create a work that is a rare combination in the field of legal English. Their love of law, of language teaching, and of their students shows through in all of their work and will be well appreciated by both students and teachers."

Stephen Horowitz, *Professor of Legal English at Georgetown Law, Co-Host of the USLawEssentials Law & Language Podcast*

"This excellent coursebook provides ideal soft-skills training in English for lawyers working in international contexts. Rather than focussing on a more traditional four-skills approach to Legal English, it concentrates on the professional skills attorneys need to best represent their clients. It has filled a long-standing gap in the market, and will provide enjoyable and effective training for practicing lawyers. Highly recommended!"

Matt Firth, *University of St. Gallen, Switzerland, co-author of* Introduction to International Legal English, *co-founder of EULETA*

"A brilliant legal English resource book suitable for class study, full of real-life insights, useful phrases, engaging roleplays and hands-on tasks."

Mgr. Kateřina Chudová, *Department head, Language Centre, Faculty of Law Division, from Masaryk University*

Practical English Language Skills for Lawyers

A high level of English remains essential for any lawyer wishing to work internationally, but transferring language skills from the classroom to the workplace can be challenging. This book shows non-native, English-speaking lawyers how to apply their English language skills to everyday legal situations and contexts, providing essential guidance to ensure they can work confidently in different settings and mediums.

Including activities based on real-life scenarios, the book will allow lawyers and law students to practise their English in key areas of working life, from networking and client meetings, to telephone and conference calls, contract drafting and contract negotiations, presentations, and using social media. Written by two highly experienced legal English language tutors, both former legal professionals, it also features online support material that includes listening exercises to complement those based on writing and reading comprehension.

Designed to hone skills required in working life, *Practical English Language Skills for Lawyers* is practical, accessible, and fun. Including guidance on job applications and interview practice, this book is an invaluable resource not only for current legal professionals but also for those students considering their first career step.

Natasha Costello is English, a solicitor (non-practising), and former senior lecturer in law at Manchester Metropolitan University. She currently works as an independent teacher in Paris, France and teaches legal English to practising French lawyers and to law students at various universities in the Paris area.

Louise Kulbicki is a legal English teacher and founder of Study Legal English, which provides online legal English resources to language learners in over 140 countries. Louise gained practical experience in the field of international environmental law before turning to legal English teaching.

Practical English Language Skills for Lawyers

Improving Your Legal English

Natasha Costello and Louise Kulbicki

Routledge
Taylor & Francis Group
LONDON AND NEW YORK

Designed cover image: © Getty Images

First published 2023
by Routledge
4 Park Square, Milton Park, Abingdon, Oxon OX14 4RN

and by Routledge
605 Third Avenue, New York, NY 10158

Routledge is an imprint of the Taylor & Francis Group, an informa business

British Library Cataloguing-in-Publication Data
A catalogue record for this book is available from the British Library

ISBN: 978-0-367-69050-2 (hbk)
ISBN: 978-0-367-69046-5 (pbk)
ISBN: 978-1-003-14020-7 (ebk)

DOI: 10.4324/9781003140207

Typeset in The Sans
by Deanta Global Publishing Services, Chennai, India

Support Material (including Audio Tracks, Audio Notes and Teacher Notes) can be accessed from the Support Material section at www.routledge.com/9780367690465

About the Authors

Both authors are board members of the European Legal English Teachers' Association. They have significant experience teaching legal English and understand the language needs of the modern lawyer. They are well aware of the resource requirements of legal English teachers and have expertise in resource development both on and offline.

Natasha Costello

Natasha Costello LLB PGCE is English, a solicitor (non-practising), and former senior lecturer in law at Manchester Metropolitan University. She currently works as an independent teacher in Paris, France, and teaches legal English to practising French lawyers and to law students at various universities in the Paris area.

Natasha has over 20 years' experience teaching legal skills, both to native and non-native English speakers. She enjoys creating fun and practical activities for the classroom to encourage student participation and interaction.

contact@natashacostello.com | www.natashacostello.com | www.linkedin.com/in/natasha-costello

Louise Kulbicki

Louise Kulbicki, LLB, LLM, is a British legal English teacher and founder of Study Legal English, which provides online legal English resources to language learners around the world. Louise gained practical experience working in the legal field on the development of international environmental law before turning to legal English teaching. Since 2013 she has been teaching legal English to lawyers and law students from around the world, specialising in online teaching and online resources development.

louise@studylegalenglish.com | www.studylegalenglish.com | @legalenglisher | www.linkedin.com/in/louisekulbicki

To Neil, Adam, and Zoe
To Matteo

Contents

Introduction

What is this book?

This book gives you the opportunity to combine learning legal English with developing legal skills through highly practical and realistic exercises.

Who is this book for?

This book is for lawyers and law students who want to learn legal English and practise and improve their legal skills. The book can be used for self-study or with a teacher. If you are using the book on your own, we recommend finding a study buddy for some activities.

What is the English level of this book?

This book is aimed at students with an intermediate level of English (B1 and above). It is not suitable for beginners.

How is this book structured?

Following this introduction, there are 11 chapters in the book. Each chapter provides an introduction to one main skill that lawyers need: *networking; telephoning and conference calls; client meetings; legal writing; presentations; social media marketing; job applications and interviews; contract drafting and review; contract negotiation; alternative dispute resolution; and advocacy.*

You can study the chapters in any order. However, we recommend following the chapters as they are set out. This is because each chapter builds on skills and vocabulary acquired in previous chapters. For example, small talk skills acquired in Networking are used in Client meetings. Writing techniques acquired in Legal writing are used in Contract drafting and review. You may find it helpful to consult previous chapters when working on activities in later chapters.

At the back of the book, you can find:

- Appendices:
  - *Appendix A*: Self-assessment questions and peer-assessment questions
  - *Appendix B*: Legalese to plain English quick reference
- *Transcripts* for all of the audio recordings.
- An *Answer key* containing answers to exercises.

- A *Glossary* of key legal terms in British English (BrE) with American English (AmE) equivalents. We recommend you complete this with translations of words in your own language as you work through the book.

How are chapters structured?

Each chapter begins with an *About* section giving an *Overview* of the contents and setting *Learning objectives* to achieve. This is followed by an *Introduction* encouraging students to consider what this skill means to them and their experience using it.

There are then a number of exercises for language and skill acquisition and practice. Exercises only relate to legal areas which are common for international lawyers, such as contracts, corporate, employment, real estate, and intellectual property. Exercises do not focus on areas of law which are not common for international lawyers, such as tort or criminal law.

Each chapter ends with a *Test yourself* section to check whether you have achieved the learning objectives.

What type of exercises are there?

Each chapter has a range of exercises to learn language. Helpful language is contained in *Phrase banks, Vocabulary notes, Grammar notes,* and *Pronunciation notes.* There are many highly practical and realistic exercises which combine language and soft skills.

Example activities:

Speaking: role-plays to network at a legal event, advise clients on legal matters, conduct international conference calls, and negotiate commercial contracts.

Reading: client emails requesting advice, blog articles giving legal tips, social media posts marketing law firms, contract clauses setting out rights and obligations, job adverts inviting applications, and court documents setting out claims.

Writing: emails of legal advice, presentation slides, CVs and covering letters, social media profiles, contract clauses.

Listening: formal conversations between lawyers, law podcast episodes, court hearings. You can identify listening exercises by this symbol:

Improving language and legal skills involves practising, making mistakes, becoming aware of mistakes, and trying to avoid repeating mistakes. Therefore, in some activities, students are encouraged to carry out a reflection activity to self-assess their performance and take note of what they did well and what can be improved. The *Self-assessment questions* are contained in *Appendix A.*

Are the listening activities with native speakers?

International lawyers must be able to understand a range of accents from both native and non-native speakers. To reflect the reality of working as an international lawyer, the listening activities contain international lawyers who speak with a slight accent and native English speakers.

Are the exercises realistic?

The exercises in this book are based on real-life situations that international lawyers face at work. They have been developed based on our own experience teaching international lawyers and understanding the language and skills needed. We have also consulted a range of experts working in the legal field to ensure that these exercises reflect what lawyers really do.

Are the exercises up to date?

International lawyers need to stay up to date with the law and the latest trends in order to be successful. This book is fully up to date as of 2023 with the latest trends and developments in the legal sector. While many exercises relate to familiar topics such as contracts and intellectual property, some exercises refer to modern developments such as *fintech, legal tech, and online courts*. The contract drafting and alternative dispute resolution chapters both have specific exercises on future developments in these areas.

Is this book based on the English legal system?

The chapters focus on skills, not the substantive law of any jurisdiction. While some activities in the book refer to English law, most of the activities use scenarios that international lawyers face. The default language is the legal English of England; however, where possible, the legal English of America is given.

What do these words mean?

References to:

- the *laws of England* or *English law* mean the *laws of England and Wales* and *English and Welsh law*.
- legal proceedings in *America*, the *USA*, or *US* mean the *federal legal system of the USA*, not the legal system of a specific state.
- *they/their/theirs/them/themselves* are used traditionally as third person plurals and also in a gender-inclusive manner for the third person singular.
- *it/its* and *they/their/theirs* are used as pronouns for companies.
- *AmE* refers to American English and *BrE* refers to British English.

A note about language

The authors of this book are not language purists. We see language as evolving. And while legal terms of art and legal terminology take specific meanings and should be used accurately, many aspects of language are subjective and determined by culture and preference. Where relevant, we have tried to reflect that there is not always a right or wrong answer. Regarding our default spelling and grammar usage, we use BrE not AmE.

Disclaimer

Please note that all of the scenarios, characters, companies, and law firms in exercises are fictitious unless stated otherwise. This book is a language-learning resource. It does not constitute legal advice and should not be used as a basis to give legal advice.

This book refers to these social media platforms:

- LinkedIn™
- Instagram™
- Twitter™
- WhatsApp™
- YouTube™

The authors do not have a relationship or affiliation with, sponsorship, or endorsement of any of these companies, and the content of this book is not authorised by and does not represent the views or opinions of any of these companies or their personnel.

For teachers

Throughout the book, there are open discussion questions to facilitate conversation. Encourage your students to speak about their own experience of each skill. Teacher notes are available in the online support material.

Support Material (including Audio Tracks, Audio Notes and Teacher Notes) can be accessed from the Support Material section at www.routledge.com/9780367690465

Acknowledgements

We have many people to thank for making this book possible.

We would like to thank the following people.

For reviewing chapters and providing helpful feedback on exercises, we would like to thank:

Štěpánka Bilová, Barbora Chovancová, Alena Hradilová, Kateřina Chudová, Hana Kallus, Radmila Doupovcová, Věra Hromádková from Masaryk University. Małgorzata Chmielewska from the Maria Curie-Skłodowska University. Mark Brophy, owner of English Training SAS. Myriam Seers, partner at Savoie Laporte LLP. Fábio Machado Baldissera of Souto Correa Advogados, PhD in Law and specialist in real estate law. Anton Osminkin, comparative jurilinguist. Elisabeth Staels, Sandrine Boisset, Dmitry Martynov.

Thank you to our American colleagues for reviewing exercises and answering our questions on American legal English terminology:

Stephen Horowitz, Professor of Legal English at Georgetown Law, co-host of the USLawEssentials Law & Language Podcast. Daniel Edelson, founder of USLawEssentials and Director of Academic Success at Seton Hall Law School. Jonah Perlin, Associate Professor of Law, Legal Practice, Georgetown University Law Center and host of the How I Lawyer Podcast.

Thank you to these people for helping us with exercises, resources, answering questions, and connecting us to people in the know:

Richard Hill of the University of Nottingham. Gordon Lingard, Retired District Judge. Sarah Fox of 500 Words Ltd. Alex Woods, founder of Court Wingman. Rupert Haigh, legal English specialist. Dr Deborah Brewis, Senior Lecturer, School of Management, University of Bath. Mark Anderson, Stefano Motta, Thaís Darahem, Regiane Gurski, Ashley Roughton, Caroline Hanratty. Solongo Marneur, Dawid Sztuwe, Bea Bento, Nichole Bird.

Thank you to EULETA for providing such a supportive network and for being the reason we connected to write this book. Thank you to our students for giving us insights into what learners really need.

Thank you to current and former employees at Routledge: Russell George for accepting our book proposal, Emily Kindleysides as our editor, and Chloe James and Chloe Herbert for assisting us with questions.

And finally, a huge thank you to our family and friends, especially: Matteo Bertola, Liz, Alex, Helen, and Will Kulbicki, Neil, Adam, and Zoe Costello, for standing by us through a challenging time.

1 Networking

About this chapter

Overview

This chapter is about networking for legal professionals. The first part introduces the topic. The second part looks at preparing for a networking event, including how to identify people you could talk to and what to say. The third part looks at what you can do when you attend an event, including how to join people, make small talk, talk about your work, keep a conversation going, bring others into a conversation, and end a conversation politely. The final part looks at how to follow up in writing after a networking event to continue to build relationships with your new contacts.

Learning objectives

By the end of the chapter, you should be able to:

- understand the benefits of networking for lawyers
- prepare for networking events
- engage with people at networking events
- deliver an elevator pitch about your work
- follow up appropriately with new contacts

Test yourself at the end of the chapter to check that you have achieved the learning objectives.

1. Introduction

1.1 Read Text 1.1 and choose the correct preposition to complete each gap. You may use each preposition more than once.

in	on	with	at	for	to

Text 1.1 Networking for lawyers

Networking is the activity of meeting, connecting, and interacting (a)_______ people to exchange information and develop professional relationships. As a lawyer, you can network online (b) _______ social media platforms and face-to-face (c) _______ events such as law conferences and business networking events.

DOI: 10.4324/9781003140207-1

Networking is one of the most important soft skills (d) ________ lawyers. If done well, it can lead (e) ________ new clients, open up new opportunities, and even help you land your dream job.

But nowadays, when you can simply log in to a networking event (f) ________ your computer, why should you spend more time and money to physically attend?

Industry leaders have suggested that in-person communication is better (g) ________ many instances, including when you need to start a new relationship, build trust, and strengthen connections.[1]

Therefore, while physically attending a networking event can be time-consuming and expensive, those who make the extra effort are sure to reap the rewards.

1.2 Read Text 1.1 again and answer the following questions:

a. What is networking?
b. Where can lawyers network?
c. Why is networking important for lawyers?
d. How is networking online different from networking in real life?

1.3 Review the expressions for talking about your networking experience in Phrase bank 1.1:

Phrase bank 1.1	
When and where *I attended/am going to attend a networking event about [topic] in [month, year]. The networking event took/will take place in [city, country].* **Meeting and talking** *At this event, I made some/hope to make some new connections. We talked/will talk about [topic].* **Exchanging contact details** *We exchanged/I will make sure we exchange contact details so that we could/can stay in touch.*	**Following up** *I didn't follow up with my new contacts because [reason].* *After the event, I followed up/will follow up by sending an email/a message on social media to my new contacts.* **Feeling** *Before the event I felt/feel [feeling, e.g. scared/excited] because [reason].* *After the event, I felt/hope that I will feel [feeling] because [reason].*

Vocabulary note: *experience* or *experiences*

Experience can be a countable or an uncountable noun.

Experience as an uncountable noun is more common. It is used to talk about the process of acquiring knowledge or skills. For example, '*I gained work experience during my internship*' or '*I have experience in commercial litigation*'.

Experience as a countable noun is less common. It is used to talk about important events which have an emotional effect. For example, '*Julie had many positive experiences during her year studying abroad including making new friends and travelling to new places*'.

1.4 Use the language from Phrase bank 1.1 to discuss your own networking experience. If you are talking about a particular event in the past, use the past simple tense, and if you are talking about a future event, use the future tense. Include the following information:

- when and where the event took place or will take place
- who you met or who you hope to meet
- what you talked about or what you will talk about
- if you exchanged or plan to exchange contact details
- if you followed up or plan to follow up
- how you felt or may feel before and after the event

2. Preparing for a networking event

2.1. There are many ways you can prepare for a networking event to make it a success. Read Text 1.2 and answer these questions:

a. What items on the checklist would you do to prepare for a networking event?
b. Can you add anything to this list?

Text 1.2 Networking event preparation checklist

1. Research event topics
2. Research event participants
3. Identify people you want to meet
4. Connect with event participants online
5. Invite a colleague to come with you
6. Prepare your business card or contact details
7. Think of what you could say in English
8. Practise what you will say in English

2.2. Read the following statements about preparing for a networking event and choose the correct item from Text 1.2 Networking event preparation checklist to complete each gap. Each statement may have more than one item, and you may use each item more than once.

a. ______________________________

The first time I went to a networking event in English I was really scared about going. I practised some phrases about myself and my work as well as some small talk questions I could ask. It made me feel more confident!

b. ______________________________

I research the speakers and host before a networking event. This helps me understand who the most interesting people to meet could be, to identify what we have in common, and to think of questions I could ask them.

c. ____

Before a networking event I always check to see if a list of event participants is available. Then I try to connect with people online on LinkedIn™ or via email. I find this makes it easier to talk to them at the event as we're not total strangers.

d. ____

I hate going to networking events on my own, so I always ask a colleague to come with me. I find it easier to meet other people when I have someone by my side.

e. ____

I used to hand out business cards at events, but now I've prepared a virtual business card which is saved on my phone. It contains a QR code that people can scan to get my contact details immediately. I think this is the future of networking.

2.3. Audio 1.1

Listen to Anton, Leya, and Feven speaking about themselves and the type of networking events they would like to attend. Decide if these statements are true or false and correct any false statements.

Anton:	True	False
a. is currently a law student	O	O
b. is a job seeker	O	O
c. has secured a training contract	O	O
d. has many years' work experience	O	O
e. wants to meet other trainee lawyers	O	O

Leya:	True	False
a. works in a law firm	O	O
b. works for a company	O	O
c. works in London	O	O
d. wants to improve her contract drafting skills	O	O
e. wants to meet other contract lawyers	O	O

Feven:	True	False
a. is a partner at a law firm	O	O
b. is an in-house lawyer	O	O
c. is an M&A lawyer	O	O
d. wants to develop connections	O	O
e. needs to gain new clients	O	O

2.4. Read Texts 1.3 to 1.5, which are adverts for upcoming networking events. Refer to Exercise 2.3 and decide which event is suitable for Anton, Leya, and Feven, and why.

Text 1.3

The International Society for M&A Lawyers presents:
12th Annual Conference on Mergers and Acquisitions in the Technology Sector
25th–26th September 2022
Hotel Granada, London, N13ZQ

Now in its 12th year, we once again bring together leading legal and business professionals to share knowledge and debate the hottest topics in the M&A tech sector.

Topics include:

- M&A due diligence, avoiding unnecessary legal risks
- Structuring cross-border joint tech ventures
- Tech trends in a post-COVID-19 world
- Antitrust aspects of technology M&A

Book now at www.isltech-sec.com/conf032022
Fees

Before 14 August (Early bird discount 10% applied): £225
After 14 August: £250

Fees include

- Attendance at all sessions
- Conference materials and speakers' papers
- Lunch, and tea or coffee during breaks

Speaker opportunities

If you would like to be a speaker at this conference, please send your presentation abstract and bio, including information on your qualifications and expertise on the relevant topic, to info@isltech-sec.com.

Text 1.4

Bengal Jackman Open Day
7 March 2022
09:00–17:00

Our open day offers an insight into a career in law and what it is like to be a lawyer at our law firm, Bengal Jackman. The day will include talks from our trainee solicitors and senior partners, and participants will have the opportunity to network with other participants, lawyers, and our recruitment team during tea and coffee breaks.

If you are planning on submitting an application for a training contract with us, we strongly recommend that you attend this event. You will find out about our law firm's culture and get tips on how to complete our application form.

If you are currently studying law at university or have recently graduated, apply below to attend this free event. Please note that places are limited to 45 participants.

Text 1.5

Drafting International Contracts Five-Day Course
Hong Kong

Overview

Participants will learn how to understand and draft international commercial contracts in legal English using correct vocabulary and grammar. Throughout the course, we will take example provisions from authentic contracts, including real estate, employment, and sale of goods agreements, and do a range of reading, speaking, and drafting exercises to reinforce learning.

This course is suitable for lawyers who work in law firms and in-house, in addition to business people who draft contracts.

Cost and concessions

The standard fee is HK$7,500 and discounts are available for full-time students (ID required). Please contact Lucy Bobwell to register your interest and to be informed of upcoming course dates.

2.5. Refer to Exercise 2.4 and discuss the following questions:
   a. Have you been to any events which were similar to these?
   b. Which event would you be most interested in attending and why?

3. At a networking event

Joining people

3.1. When you enter a room at a networking event, you usually find people standing on their own, in couples, or in groups.

Look at the following images. If you were at a networking event, who would you join and why?

1. an individual

2. two people

3. a small group

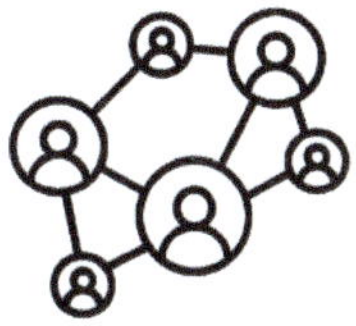

4. a large group

3.2. Audio 1.2

Listen to Anton, Leya, and Feven talk about their strategy for joining people at a networking event. Tick the option they would choose in the following table.

	an individual	two people	a small group	a large group
a. Anton	○	○	○	○
b. Leya	○	○	○	○
c. Feven	○	○	○	○

3.3. Listen to Audio 1.2 again and pay attention to the reasons why the speakers like or dislike joining an individual, couple, or group. Label the following statements with the correct option. You may use an option more than once. The first statement has been given a label as an example.

an individual	two people	a small group	a large group

With this option, you may:

a. have better conversations and make better connections

an individual

b. practise speaking

____

c. be interrupting someone who is busy

____

d. be interrupting a private or confidential conversation

____

e. listen to others

____

f. find it difficult to make strong connections

____

g. easily leave if the conversation is boring

____

3.4. Joining people and introducing yourself is a fundamental step in networking. But how you do it and what you say can depend on your personality and culture. Some people join others by making eye contact, smiling, and shaking hands, but this is not appropriate for everyone. Some people introduce themselves by saying their name and stating their job position, but not everyone is comfortable being so direct. Often a person will respond to your introduction by introducing themselves. If they do not do this, it is important to ask the other person their name, and to remember it.

What is an appropriate way to join someone and introduce yourself at a networking event in your culture?

3.5. Review the expressions for joining someone at a networking event in Phrase bank 1.2:

Phrase bank 1.2	
Politely joining	***Being direct***
Hi, I'm [your name]. Could I join you? ... What's your name?	*Hi, I'm [your name + job position]. Nice to meet you.*
Excuse me, are you busy? Do you mind if I join you? Thank you. Hi, my name is [your name].	*Hi everyone, [your name]. Pleased to meet you.*

3.6. Practise joining someone and introducing yourself at a networking event with a partner. You may use the expressions in Phrase bank 1.2.

Starting a conversation with small talk

3.7. Read Text 1.6 and discuss the following questions:

a. What is small talk?
b. Do lawyers use small talk in your culture?
c. What small talk topics are appropriate and inappropriate in your culture?

Text 1.6 Small talk for international lawyers

When you meet someone new, it is common to start the conversation with small talk. Small talk is conversation to help break the ice, build trust, and build relationships. It is becoming recognised as an essential skill for international lawyers and is even being taught in law schools.[2] But for many people, it is difficult to know what to talk about and how to keep the conversation going.

Find what to talk about

Try to find common interests. You may have both holidayed in the same destination, enjoy the same food, or share the same hobby. Talking about a shared interest will build your relationship. Typical small talk topics to explore are:

- weather
- food
- travel
- news
- interests
- work
- studies
- origins: where the person is from and where they live now
- the event: topic, speakers, location, reason for attending

Keep the conversation going

In small talk, it is important to ask both open and closed questions. Closed questions get a quick short answer such as yes or no. Open questions begin with *what, where, who, how, when*, or *why*, and invite the other person to speak freely on a topic. Actively listening and asking questions will help you develop your conversation.

Pay attention to culture

Building relationships and trust differs across cultures. In her book *The Culture Map*,[3] Erin Meyer explains that in task-based countries, such as the US, Denmark, Netherlands, Australia, and Germany, trust is based on a person's accomplishments, skills, and reliability. In these countries, talking about professional achievements may help build trust as this shows your credibility, whereas talking about your personal life, such as your family, may be considered unprofessional and inappropriate.

On the contrary, in relationship-based countries, such as Saudi Arabia, Nigeria, India, China, and Brazil, trust is based on building personal relationships. In these countries, talking about your personal life may be welcomed and lead to greater trust, whereas talking about your professional achievements may be considered arrogant and inappropriate.

3.8. 🔊 Audio 1.3

Anton, Leya, and Feven are each attending their networking events and are using small talk with the people they meet.

Listen to Audio 1.3 and tick the small talk topics mentioned in each conversation.

	Anton and Ingrid	Leya and Zul	Feven and Sudhvir
a. weather	○	○	○
b. food	○	○	○
c. travel	○	○	○
d. news	○	○	○
e. interests	○	○	○
f. work	○	○	○
g. studies	○	○	○
h. origins	○	○	○
i. the event	○	○	○

3.9. Listen to Audio 1.3 again and then read the transcript.

a. Identify the open and closed questions used by each speaker.

b. Write one open and one closed question that Leya and Feven could ask to keep the conversation going with their new contacts. Anton's questions are given as examples.

Anton could ask Ingrid:

Open: *How did you find out about the event?*

Closed: *Are you enjoying the event?*

Leya could ask Zul:

Open:

Closed:

Feven could ask Sudhvir:

Open:

Closed:

3.10. Review the expressions for making small talk at a networking event in Phrase bank 1.3:

Phrase bank 1.3	
Weather	**Work**
It's much hotter/colder here than where I live. What's the weather like now where you are from?	*It's great to see so many lawyers here. What do you do? What does your work involve?*
Food	**Studies**
This food looks really good. What do you recommend? What's the typical dish here?	*I graduated from [name of university] in [date]. Where did you study?*

Travel	The event
How did you get here? *How was your journey?* *Do you have any holidays planned?* **News** *I read in the news about [news story]. Did you hear about it? Does this affect your work?* **Interests** *I'm currently reading [name of book]. Have you read it? What are your interests?* *I really enjoyed your presentation. How did you become interested in that field?*	*Is this your first time at this conference?* *Are you a member of this organisation?* *The location's great. Have you been here before? What are the top places to visit or sights to see here?* *I'm really looking forward to seeing [name of speaker] present. What about you?* **Origins** *Where are you from? Have you always lived there?* *It didn't take me long to get here as I live close by. What about you, where do you live?*

3.11. Practise making small talk with a partner. Choose Scenario 1 or Scenario 2 and then choose a role. Only read the information for your role, do not read the others. In your role play, try to discover common interests by asking a range of open and closed questions to keep the conversation going. You may use the expressions in Phrase bank 1.3.

Scenario 1

Students at New York University meet in the snow, one is lost ...

Stephen Carter

You are a second-year law student at New York University and you are from New York. Next semester you will study abroad in Amsterdam, the Netherlands. You have never been to Europe before, but you love to travel. Last year you travelled around Asia where you discovered that you love the food, especially from India and Thailand. It's snowing and you are walking towards the law school to get lunch at the student café. Someone stops you ...

Elsa Andersson

You are an international exchange student. You are studying Law in New York for one year. You are from Stockholm, Sweden. You share a flat with another international student, Anita from the Netherlands. You like yoga and meditation and would like to visit India in the future to go on a yoga retreat. Today is your first day at university and you are lost. You are trying to find the law school as you have a class in one hour. You have been walking around for half an hour and are tired and hungry. It has just started snowing. You stop someone to ask for some help ...

Scenario 2

A lawyer and potential client are at a Japanese restaurant and are about to order. After lunch, they are going to see a Botafogo v Flamengo football game at Maracana stadium, Rio de Janeiro, Brazil ...

Regiane Flores

You are a Brazilian construction lawyer. You have been invited to a football game by the CEO of TáCasa, a large construction company in Brazil. You hope that this company will become a client of yours. You are originally from a small city outside São Paolo, but you've lived in Rio for over ten years. You, your husband, and two children all support the Botafogo football team. This will be the first time you have been to a big stadium. You like healthy living, and on Saturdays you do fitness training on the beach. Japanese is your favourite cuisine, especially sushi ...

Bruno Oswald

You are the CEO of TáCasa, a Brazilian construction company. You are a potential client interested in Regiane's law firm's services. You are a huge sports fan. You support the Botafogo football team and are so excited about the game! This year you started a new hobby; every morning, you wake up at 6 am to go jogging along the beachfront. You worked for five years in São Paolo before moving to Rio. You prefer Rio for the healthy living lifestyle. This is your first time eating Japanese food and you are not sure what to order ...

3.12. Reflect on your small talk role-play in Exercise 3.11 and tick the following options.

	I asked a question about:	Our common interests were:
a. weather	○	○
b. food	○	○
c. travel	○	○
d. news	○	○
e. interests	○	○
f. work	○	○
g. studies	○	○
h. origins	○	○
i. the event	○	○

3.13. Now read the information for your partner's role. Could you have found more things in common?

Talking about business

3.14. Read Text 1.7 and discuss the following questions:

a. What is an elevator pitch?
b. Have you ever given an elevator pitch?

Text 1.7 Elevate opportunities with your elevator pitch

Typically at a networking event, sooner or later, someone will ask you '*What do you do?*' Responding with '*I'm a lawyer*' does not give the other person a good idea about your role, and they might walk away thinking '*Oh great, another lawyer!*' without realising that you both have things in common and could help each other. To avoid missing out on opportunities, you should be prepared with your elevator pitch. An elevator pitch is a short persuasive speech that makes someone interested in an idea, person, or service. The concept behind an elevator pitch is this:

Imagine you get into an elevator (AmE), or a lift (BrE), with a stranger. You have a short amount of time before the door opens again. During this time, you must *pitch* yourself to the other person. To *pitch* means to present something in order to sell it or persuade people to do something. In your elevator pitch, you should briefly explain who you are as a legal professional in a way that the other person will want to continue speaking with you.

The next time someone asks you what you do, expand your answer into an elevator pitch and include:

- what your position is or what you are studying
- where you work or study
- who you help or who you would like to help

3.15. Audio 1.4

Anton, Leya, and Feven ask their new contacts about their work or studies. Listen to the responses and decide if these statements are true or false. Correct any false statements.

Ingrid:	True	False
a. says that IP law is a core module	○	○
b. studies three electives	○	○
c. studies music and entertainment law	○	○
d. makes films in her spare time	○	○
e. wants to represent celebrities	○	○

Zul:	True	False
a. is an employment lawyer	○	○
b. has clients from Singapore and abroad	○	○
c. only does contentious work	○	○
d. represents clients in online cases	○	○
e. owns some software called Robolawyer	○	○

Sudhvir:	True	False
a. is a tax lawyer	○	○
b. works at a regional law firm	○	○
c. advises on tax issues in mergers	○	○
d. finds his work boring	○	○
e. speaks some French and Mandarin	○	○

3.16. Listen to Audio 1.4 again. Write one open question and one closed question Anton, Leya, and Feven could ask in response to the elevator pitches to find out more about the work or studies of their new contact.

Anton could ask Ingrid:

Open:

Closed:

Leya could ask Zul:

Open:

Closed:

Feven could ask Sudhvir:

Open:

Closed:

3.17. Practise delivering your own elevator pitch with a partner using the following instructions. Take it in turns to be Student A and Student B.

Student A

Ask Student B '*What do you do?*' After Student B has answered this question try to keep the conversation going by asking more questions about their work or studies. Use the questions you thought of in Exercise 3.16 if they are appropriate.

Student B

Tell Student A about your work or studies. Include:

- what your position is or what you are studying
- where you work or study
- who you help or who you would like to help

Bringing others into a conversation

3.18. While you are networking, you may need to bring a person into a conversation you are having with your new contact. It is important to know the names of the people you are introducing, but sometimes we forget. Some people may feel comfortable asking for names directly and will explicitly ask. If you feel uncomfortable doing this, you can indirectly encourage the person to say their name without directly saying that you cannot remember it.

Read the following statements and decide if they are direct or indirect ways to ask for the new contact's name.

	Direct	Indirect
a. Can I ask, what's your name?	○	○
b. Could I have your business card?	○	○
c. Sorry, I can't remember your name. Could you remind me of it?	○	○
d. I'm afraid I didn't catch your name, what was it again?	○	○
e. [*Try to pronounce name*], am I pronouncing your name correctly?	○	○
f. How do you spell your name?	○	○

3.19. Read Text 1.8 about bringing someone into your conversation and answer these questions:

a. What is the difference between step one and step two?
b. What could you do if the person you are bringing into the conversation does not have something in common with your new contact?
c. If you want to change the topic of conversation, when could you do this?

Text 1.8 Bringing others into a conversation

If you need to bring someone into your conversation, follow these steps to make sure you do it effectively.

Step one

Introduce the person you want to bring into the conversation. State their name and some background information, such as how you know them. For example, '*Chris, I'd like you to meet my colleague, Jane. Jane and I work together at Hamzah Tann LLP in Dubai*'. Note that in highly formal contexts and in certain cultures, it may be more appropriate to use full names.

Step two

Introduce the person you are already talking to, to the person you are bringing into the conversation. State their name and some background information, such as where they are from or what they do. For example, '*Jane, this is Chris Bishop. I've just found out that Chris is a lawyer in Abu Dhabi*'. Note that if the person you are bringing into the conversation does not know you, you may need to introduce yourself as well. For example, '*Dr Javid, we enjoyed your presentation, I'm Alex and this is Rose*'.

Step three

Refer to something shared between the person you are bringing into the conversation and the person you are talking to. For example, '*Both of you work in oil and gas*'. If there is no shared interest, skip this step.

Step four

State what you were just talking about. For example, '*We were just talking about the news story that came out this morning about global oil prices plunging by 10%*'. Or, if you want to change the topic, this is your chance to introduce something new.

3.20. Imagine you are in a conversation with Sudhvir, the President of the International Society for M&A Lawyers. You have just been talking to Sudhvir about his work as a senior tax lawyer in London. Read the following descriptions of the people you want to bring into the conversation and write what you would say to introduce them to Sudhvir.

a. Jane, a former colleague of yours, who is a banking lawyer in London.
b. Someone you recognise from your university law course, who you have not seen since you graduated. You think his name is John.
c. A colleague who you should know the name of, but you have forgotten. She has expertise in tax law, which could be relevant for Sudhvir.
d. A speaker at the event who you have met once before. The speaker's name is Olaf. Both you and Sudhvir have questions to ask him, and you want to change the topic to these questions.

Ending a conversation

3.21. It is important to end a conversation politely as this will make a good impression on the person you have just met.

Read the following statements and decide if they are polite or impolite.

	Polite	Impolite
a. It was lovely meeting you [*their name*]. Now, if you'll please excuse me, I have just seen a colleague I would like to have a quick word with before the next session.	○	○
b. I've just seen someone I need to speak to. Bye.	○	○
c. Yeah, I'm not interested in that kind of work. Bye.	○	○
d. It was nice to meet you. I must quickly make a call. I hope we have a chance to speak again later on.	○	○
e. I gotta take a call. What was your name again? Catch you later.	○	○
f. Thank you so much for telling me about your work. It was really interesting. I hope to see you at another event.	○	○
g. I've gotta go. Let's meet again.	○	○
h. I'm afraid I have to rush off to catch my train, but I'd love to speak again. Could we exchange contact details?	○	○
i. I've really enjoyed speaking to you. I would like to catch that speaker quickly to ask about her research. I hope you enjoy the rest of the event.	○	○

3.22. Statement h. in Exercise 3.21 mentions exchanging contact details. This is an important part of networking and can be done at any time during your conversation. Why is exchanging contact details important?

3.23. Review the expressions for exchanging contact details and ending the conversation at a networking event in Phrase bank 1.4:

Phrase bank 1.4	
Exchanging contact details	**Ending the conversation**
Let's exchange contact details. Here's my business card. Do you have one? *Could we exchange contact details? My email address is [email], and my mobile number is [number]. Could I take yours?* *Do you have LinkedIn™? I have the app on my phone. Let me send you a connection request right now. What is your full name?*	*It was nice to meet you. Please excuse me, I must quickly make a call, but I hope we have a chance to speak again later.* *Thank you so much for telling me about your work. It was really interesting. I have to leave now. I hope to see you at another event.* *It really was a pleasure speaking with you. I'm going to try and talk to the host/speaker before they leave.*

3.24. Practise ending your conversation and exchanging details with a partner in the following situations:
   a. You are at a conference and the next speaker is about to present.
   b. Your phone rings and you can see it is a client. You have to take the call.
   c. You have to leave as you have a client meeting scheduled.

Practise networking

3.25. You are going to role play networking during the morning coffee break of a conference.

Instructions

Read the conference programme and the participant roles. You may choose a participant role or be yourself. If you choose a participant role, only read the information for your role, do not read the others. Role play networking, making sure that you:

- join people and introduce yourself
- start a conversation with small talk
- use open and closed questions to keep the conversation going
- talk about your work or studies
- bring others into a conversation
- end a conversation and exchange contact details

Conference programme

Hedwin House Attorneys presents
5th Annual Conference on International Commercial Law
1st March–2nd March 2023
Grand Waldorf Business Centre, Zurich Switzerland

More information on the Conference App | Social Media: #ACICL5

The 5th annual conference on international commercial law meets once again live in Zurich, after an online conference last year. This event brings together clients, business people, academics, students, and legal professionals for a practical and academic programme addressing the latest trends in international commercial law.

1st March	
18:00–19:00	Registration
19:30+	Welcome dinner
2nd March	
09:00–10:00	Elio Schmidt, Welcome address
10:00–11:00	Deborah Masley, Contract drafting for the modern world
11:00–11:30	**Coffee Break** *[Role play takes place here]*
11:30–12:30	Albert Choy, Arbitrating online: an arbitrator's perspective
12:30–14:00	Lunch
14:00–15:00	Zoltán Silvas, Learning from client feedback: improving our services
15:00–16:00	Leo Van de Berg, Law firm trends on social media
16:00–16:30	Coffee Break
16:30–17:30	Jenny Walsh, Pay attention to IP: five landmark cases
17:30–18:00	Majid Al Shamsi, Conference closing
19:30+	Closing dinner

Participant roles

Elio Schmidt

You are the managing partner at Hedwin House Attorneys, Zurich, and the event host. You want to find new ways to promote your law firm to gain clients. You love travelling and exploring new places on your motorbike.

Deborah Masley

You are a law professor at Novo University, New York. You have already presented. You want to find lawyers who could give you an industry perspective for another research project. You enjoy reading books and writing. You are currently writing a book about contract drafting.

Albert Choy

You are an arbitrator at the Singapore Arbitration Institute. You will present next. You want to promote your institute as a place to resolve commercial disputes. You are interested in psychology and watch YouTube videos about psychological well-being in your free time.

Zoltán Silvas

You are an associate at BudaLaw Centre, Budapest. You will present later today. You are interested in qualifying as an arbitrator and want to find out more about what the job involves. Last month you bought a puppy Labrador and you love posting photos of him on Twitter!

Leo Van de Berg

You are an independent social media expert and will present about social media later today. You want to help law firms with their social media marketing. You are addicted to checking the news on Twitter and read an interesting story this morning.

Majid Al Shamsi

You are the conference sponsor and CEO of Alva Industries, a solar energy company in Dubai. You are currently in a contractual dispute and are not satisfied with your lawyers. You are passionate about travelling and luxury hotels.

3.26. Reflect on your networking role play in Exercise 3.25. Use the self-assessment questions in Appendix A.

4. Following up after an event

This section looks at following up after a networking event with written messages.

4.1 Networking does not come to an end just because the networking event is over. In fact, this is just the beginning of the relationship with your new contact. Why is following up with new contacts important?

4.2 Audio 1.5

Listen to Anton, Leya, and Feven talk about who they met at the networking events they attended. Match each speaker to the method they will use to follow up.

Speaker	Method
a. Anton	1. LinkedIn™
b. Leya	2. WhatsApp™
c. Feven	3. Instagram™ direct message

4.3 Listen to Audio 1.5 again. Match each speaker to the reason for following up.

Speaker	Reason
a. Anton	1. To put themselves forward as a board member candidate
b. Leya	2. To send the other person a link to a helpful website
c. Feven	3. To inform the other person that their boss will be in touch

4.4 Read the following methods of contact you can use to follow up with a new contact and discuss the following questions:

a. Which method would you prefer to use and why?
b. How formal should your message be for each method?
c. Do you think it is appropriate to use emojis in your message?
d. How long should your message be for each method?

Social media	WhatsApp™ message	Email

4.5 Review the expressions for following up after a networking event in Phrase bank 1.5. These expressions are appropriate for writing informal messages on social media, WhatsApp™, and by SMS.

Phrase bank 1.5

Salutation

Hi/Hello/Dear [their name]

Previous contact

I enjoyed talking to you at [event] on [exact date] about [topic] ...

It was a pleasure to meet you at [event] ...

Reason for writing

I'm writing to share a link to the website/article/video I mentioned: [insert link].

I'm writing to connect with you and say thank you for answering my questions at the event.

Future contact

Let's stay in touch.

I hope to see you at the next event.

If you have time, could we arrange a meeting to discuss this further?

Closing

Best/Thanks/Thank you [your name]

4.6 Read Ingrid's follow-up message and rewrite it in a more appropriate style. Then write a response to Ingrid from Anton. You may use the expressions in Phrase bank 1.5 and the following structure:

- salutation
- previous contact
- reason for writing
- future contact
- closing

Test yourself

1. Explain how lawyers can benefit from networking.
2. Name five things you can do to prepare for a networking event.
3. How can you keep a conversation going?
4. What are some important points to include in your elevator pitch?
5. How could you structure a follow-up message to a new contact?

Notes

1 Forbes Coaches Council, '13 Times In-Person Communication is Better than Electronic Exchanges' (*Forbes*, 17 July 2020) <https://www.forbes.com/sites/forbescoachescouncil/2020/07/17/13-times-in-person-communication-is-better-than-electronic-exchanges> accessed 22 November 2021

2 'BPP University Introduces "Business Small Talk" Module to Help Students Prepare for World of Work' (*BPP Law*, 16 February 2021) <https://www.bpp.com/insights/business-small-talk> accessed 18 January 2022

3 Erin Meyer, *The Culture Map* (International edition, Public Affairs, 2015) 171

2 Telephoning and conference calls

About this chapter

Overview

This chapter is about making and answering telephone calls and participating in telephone and video conference calls with clients and other legal professionals. The first part introduces the topic. The second part includes useful expressions for making and answering telephone calls and recording and leaving voicemail messages. The third part looks at how you can prepare for a telephone call with a client and how you can ask for clarification during a call. The final part focuses on a conference call about an intellectual property dispute.

Throughout the chapter, there are exercises related to common business phrasal verbs which may feature in telephone and conference calls. The chapter ends with a role-play conference call scenario.

Learning objectives

By the end of this chapter, you should be able to:

- use appropriate expressions for making and answering telephone calls
- feel more confident when preparing for a telephone call
- ask for clarification and interrupt politely during a call
- understand some common phrasal verbs used in telephone calls
- participate in a conference call

Test yourself at the end of the chapter to check that you have achieved the learning objectives.

1. Introduction

1.1 Which of the following emojis describe how you feel when you have to make a telephone call or participate in a conference call in English?

1.2 Do you agree or disagree with these statements about English telephone and conference calls?

- I find it difficult when there is more than one other person on the call.
- I cannot follow the call because people talk too quickly.
- There is too much background noise during conference calls.
- I am not confident interrupting a speaker to ask for clarification.

DOI: 10.4324/9781003140207-2

- Native English speakers often use expressions which I do not understand.
- It is more difficult when there is a mix of native and non-native English speakers on the call.
- I need more legal vocabulary to be able to follow the call.
- I can understand what is being said, but I cannot find my words quickly enough to speak.
- It is hard to maintain concentration during long calls.

1.3 What is your experience of telephone and conference calls in English? Can you suggest any solutions for dealing with the difficulties identified in Exercise 1.2?

2. Making and answering telephone calls

Expressions for making and answering telephone calls

2.1 In an English law firm or company, it is usual to answer the telephone by giving your name or your department. For example:

- *Hello, Janice Brooks.*
- *Hello, Janice Brooks speaking.*
- *Hello, Legal Department.*
- *Hello, Commercial Litigation.*

How do you usually answer the telephone in your language? Does your law firm or company have a policy for how you should answer the telephone?

2.2 Read the following expressions. Which ones can you use for:

a. making a telephone call
b. answering a telephone call
c. taking a message
d. leaving a message

1. *Hello, this is Michelle Taylor.*	2. *Could you ask him to call me back?*
3. *Please can I speak to Mr Johnson?*	4. *Hello, Michelle Taylor speaking.*
5. *Could I leave a message?*	6. *I'm calling about ...*
7. *Can I ask who's calling?*	8. *How may I help you?*
9. *I'm calling in connection with ...*	10. *Can I take a message?*

2.3 Telephone conversations with native English speakers often contain informal language, such as contractions (*don't* instead of *do not*) and phrasal verbs.

A phrasal verb is a verb followed by a particle (a preposition or an adverb), which changes the verb's original meaning. The following box contains an example, using the verb *to hang*.

Verb/phrasal verb	Definition	Example sentence
to hang (verb)	to fix something at the top, leaving the lower part free	Can you hang that new picture in the meeting room?
to hang up (phrasal verb)	to end a telephone call	I'm going to hang up and try reconnecting.

Note that sometimes a pronoun or noun can come between the verb and the particle. For example, *I rang him up* but there was no answer. *To ring someone up* means to telephone someone.

2.4 Text 2.1 is a transcript of a short telephone conversation in which a lawyer, Michelle Taylor, calls Paul Johnson, the opposing lawyer in a case she is working on. Paul's assistant answers the telephone.

Read Text 2.1 and find examples of four contractions and three phrasal verbs. What is the meaning of each phrasal verb?

Text 2.1 A short telephone conversation

Janice: *Hello, Commercial Litigation; Janice Brooks speaking.*
Michelle: *Hello. Please can I speak to Mr Johnson?*
Janice: *Can I ask who's calling?*
Michelle: *This is Michelle Taylor.*
Janice: *And what matter does it relate to please?*
Michelle: *I'm calling about the Nemesis file.*
Janice: *Hold on a moment, I'll just put you through ...*
... Sorry, but Mr Johnson is on another call right now.
Michelle: *Could you ask him to call me back when he's free? He has my number.*
Janice: *Will do. Thanks for your call.*
Michelle: *Thank you. Bye.*

Vocabulary note: *to hold on* or *on hold*

To hold on is a phrasal verb which means to wait for a short time. For example, '*Hold on while I check if Mr Johnson is available*' or '*Hold on while I find my client's file*'.

The expression *on hold* means waiting to speak to someone on the telephone. For example, '*I have been on hold for 15 minutes*' or '*I am going to put you on hold for a few minutes*'.

Recording and leaving voicemail messages

2.5 Read Text 2.2 about how to say telephone numbers and email addresses.

Text 2.2 How to say telephone numbers and email addresses

Saying telephone numbers in English:

- *0* is usually pronounced *oh* in BrE and *zero* in AmE
- *+44* is pronounced *plus four four*
- each digit is usually pronounced separately

For example, +44 1204 78462 is pronounced: *plus four four, one two zero four, seven eight four six two.*

Saying email addresses in English:

- @ is pronounced *at*
- . is pronounced *dot*
- _ is pronounced *underscore*
- - is pronounced *dash*

For example, michelle_taylor@realestate-lawyers.com is pronounced: *michelle underscore taylor at real estate dash lawyers dot com*

2.6 Practise recording and leaving voicemail messages with a partner using the language from Exercise 2.5 and the following instructions. Take it in turns to be Student A and Student B.

Student A

Imagine you are recording the voicemail greeting on your telephone. Think about what you would include in this message and then when you are ready say it out loud. Here is an example message:

Hi, this is [name]. I'm not available to take your call right now. Please leave a message and I'll get back to you as soon as I can.

Student B

Imagine you are going to telephone someone and leave a message. Think about what you would include in this message. When you are ready, student A will read aloud a message, as if it was the voicemail message greeting on their telephone. You should then leave your message. Here is an example message:

Hi, this is [name]. Please could you contact me as soon as possible? My number is [telephone number] or you can email me at [email address]. Thank you.

Practise making and answering telephone calls

2.7 Review the expressions for making and answering telephone calls in Phrase bank 2.1:

Phrase bank 2.1	**Taking or leaving a message**
Making a call	*[name] is not available at the moment.*
Hello, this is [name].	*[name] is on another call right now.*
Please can I speak to [name]?	*Could you ask [name] to call me back?*
I'm calling about ...	*Could I leave a message?*
I'm calling in connection with ...	*Can I take a message?*
Answering a call	**Ending the call**
Hello, [name] speaking.	*Thanks for your call.*
Can I ask who's calling?	*Bye.*

How may I help you? *Hold on a moment.* *I'll put you through.* *I'll try to connect you.*	

2.8 Practise making and answering telephone calls with a partner. Use the following scenarios and the expressions in Phrase bank 2.1 and take it in turns to be the person making the call or the person answering the call.

Scenario 1

Person making the call

You are a lawyer. One of your clients would like advice on taking a lease of commercial premises in Berlin. You are part of a European network of real estate lawyers. You are calling Mr Schmidt, a German lawyer in your network, to see if he could act for your client.

Person answering the call

You are Mr Schmidt's assistant. Mr Schmidt is a lawyer at Schmidt Adenauer law firm in Berlin. Mr Schmidt is in a meeting at the moment.

Scenario 2

Person making the call

You are Lars Andersson. You have just been served with an injunction. You immediately call your lawyer, Ms Warner, to ask what you should do.

Person answering the call

You are Ms Warner's assistant. Ms Warner is a commercial litigation lawyer. Ms Warner is on holiday until next week, but her colleague, Mr Peters, is available.

3. Preparing for a telephone call

This section is about a client meeting on the telephone.

Telephone call scenario

3.1 Claire Monet, a junior associate specialising in intellectual property law at law firm Garniers, has just received an email from her client, Sophie Driscoll.

Read the email and answer the following questions:

a. What do you think *touch base* means?
b. Find two phrasal verbs in this email.

From: Sophie Driscoll sdriscoll@agiledesign.com
To: Claire Monet cmonet@garniers.com
Subject: Design right infringement

Dear Claire

Many thanks for agreeing to act for us in this matter. I suggest we touch base tomorrow morning so that I can fill you in. Can I call you at 10 a.m. UK time?

Kind regards

Sophie Driscoll
Group Legal Counsel, Agile Design

3.2 Audio 2.1

Claire is having a coffee at the office with Angela, another junior associate at Garniers. Listen to the first part of their conversation and then answer the following questions.

a. Why is Claire nervous?
b. What advice would you give Claire about preparing for this telephone call?

3.3 Audio 2.2

Listen to the second part of Claire and Angela's conversation. Compare the tips that Angela gives to Claire with your answers in Exercise 3.2.

3.4 Following Angela's advice, Claire asks her supervising partner, Marc, for more details. Claire has made a note of the following legal English words and phrases. She wants to check that she has understood this vocabulary before her telephone call with the client. What do these words and phrases mean? Check the Glossary for definitions:

Vocabulary to check

- *proprietor*
- *registered design*
- *infringement*
- *grant a licence*
- *assign a right*
- *letter before claim*

Dealing with problems on a call

3.5 Audio 2.3

Claire now feels ready for the telephone call with her client, Sophie. However, even if you are well prepared, problems can arise and you may have difficulties hearing or understanding what the other person is saying.

Listen to the telephone call between Claire and Sophie. What are the three problems that arise during this call? Write your answers in the following table:

Problem 1	
Problem 2	
Problem 3	

3.6 Claire uses a common technique for dealing with problems during a call. In each case, she explains the problem and then asks for clarification.

Listen to Audio 2.3 again and complete the following table with the expressions Claire uses. The first answer is given as an example.

	Explaining the problem	**Asking for clarification**
Problem 1	*Sorry, I'm not familiar with the expression 'rolled it out'.*	*What do you mean by that?*
Problem 2		
Problem 3		

3.7 Read the transcript for Audio 2.3 and complete the following table with the four phrasal verbs that Sophie uses during the call. The first answer is given as an example.

Phrasal verb	**Definition**
a. *to roll out*	To launch a new product on the market
b.	To start to lose connection on the telephone
c.	To break a telephone connection
d.	To tell someone something

3.8 Review the expressions for explaining the problem and asking for clarification in Phrase bank 2.2. Notice how using the word *sorry* is not always an apology and is a way of sounding more polite in English.

Phrase bank 2.2	
Explaining the problem	**Asking for clarification**
Sorry, I'm not familiar with the expression ...	*What do you mean by that?*
Sorry, I didn't hear what you said.	*Could you just repeat that, please?*
Sorry, that was a bit fast for me.	*Can I check that I've understood correctly?*
Sorry, I didn't follow that.	*Would you mind saying that again?*
I'm afraid I don't understand.	*Could you explain that in another way?*
I'm afraid I didn't catch all that.	*Please could you speak more slowly?*
Sorry, it is difficult to hear you.	*Could you speak more loudly, please?*
Sorry, I don't recognise that word.	*Could you spell that, please?*

3.9 Practise dealing with problems on a telephone call with a partner. Use the following scenario to role-play a telephone conversation between Claire and Marc. Use the expressions for explaining the problem and asking for clarification in Phrase bank 2.2. You can also create and deal with other problems on the call.

Scenario

Marc calls Claire. He wants Claire to summarise her telephone call with Sophie.

Marc

During your call with Claire, these problems arise:

- You are on the train and you keep losing connection.
- You need Claire to spell a word to be sure that you understand what she has said.

Claire

During your call with Marc, these problems arise:

- There are noisy works at your office and you cannot hear Marc.
- You cannot follow what Marc is saying.

4. Participating in conference calls

Different types of conference calls

4.1 The Cambridge dictionary defines a conference call as *'a work phone call that involves three or more people'*.[1]

When there are more than two people on a telephone call, it can be more difficult to follow what is being said and to participate in the conversation.

Refer to your discussions in Exercise 1.3 at the beginning of this chapter. What experience do you have of conference calls?

4.2 The Cambridge dictionary defines a video conference as *'a meeting at which two or more people who are in different places can talk to and see each other using electronic technology'*.[2] This is a meeting which is taking place remotely. You can also call this:

- a video meeting
- an online meeting
- a virtual meeting

a. What advantages are there in having a video conference rather than a telephone conference call?

b. During a virtual court hearing in Texas, a lawyer appeared as a cat after failing to realise that a filter setting had been changed. What problems have you experienced during video conferences?

Video conferences

4.3 Read Text 2.3 about improving your video conference experience and decide if these statements are true or false. Correct any false statements.

	True	False
a. Lawyers hold video conferences with both colleagues and clients.	○	○
b. You can attend video conferences when working from home.	○	○
c. Lawyers usually have one or two video meetings per week.	○	○
d. Video conferences are better than physical meetings.	○	○
e. It is a good idea to set some rules, such as requiring participants to turn off their microphones unless they are speaking.	○	○

Text 2.3 How to improve your video conference experience

Since the COVID-19 pandemic, the use of video conferencing has increased dramatically. Lawyers now hold video conferences on a daily basis for internal and client meetings, for negotiations, and even for arbitration and court hearings.

While there are many advantages to video conferences, such as the ability to have meetings with people all over the world without having to leave the comfort of your office or home, this new way of working has proved challenging in other ways.

Lawyers' diaries are now full of back-to-back video meetings, which means very intense and tiring days. Also, despite the surge in the development of video conference platforms, people still experience technical problems which can disrupt the flow of their meetings.

How can you improve your video conference experience? Here are a few ideas:

- Are you familiar with the video conferencing platform that will be used? Most platforms have similar functions but check the settings and the ability to share your screen.
- Have you checked that your equipment is working properly? Test your camera and microphone and preview your background.
- Have you set a start and finish time for your meeting? Try to keep video conferences short. In longer meetings, make sure that you take breaks.
- Do you have someone to lead the meeting? Appoint a chairperson so that the meeting stays on topic and on time.
- Have you established some basic rules? Consider requiring participants to have their cameras on, and to mute their microphones when they are not speaking.
- Is it an international video conference? Be aware of cultural differences: in some cultures it could be impolite to interrupt when someone else is speaking and more appropriate to wait until you are invited to speak.

4.4 Read Text 2.3 again and discuss these questions:
  a. Do you think that video conferencing is appropriate for arbitration or court hearings?
  b. Have you experienced any cultural differences in video conferences?
  c. Can you think of any other ways to improve your video conference experience?

Conference call scenario

4.5 At the end of Audio 2.3, Claire suggests sending a letter before claim to Ideal Home. A letter before claim is a preliminary step before commencing court proceedings. It includes a summary of the claim and the remedies sought.

Claire sent the letter before claim to Ideal Home and has just received an email from Marc. Read the email and then answer the following questions:
  a. *To set something up* is a phrasal verb. What does it mean?
  b. What is Marc asking Claire to do?

From: Marc Leblanc mleblanc@garniers.com
To: Claire Monet cmonet@garniers.com
Subject: Agile Design and Ideal Home conference call

Hi Claire

I've just heard from the lawyer acting for Ideal Home, Anya Marshall at Hatton Marshall. She's suggesting a video conference call this week to discuss the letter before claim.

Can you check everyone's availability and set up the call? Anya's email address is amarshall@hattonmarshall.llp.

Many thanks

Marc

4.6 After checking everyone's availability, Claire schedules a 30-minute video conference call, starting at 11:00 CET (Central European Time) on Tuesday 26th October 2022.

Write Claire's email to Anya with the invitation to the video conference call. Use the following template and this meeting link: http://web.conf./485723

Template for conference call invitation

From: [*sender's name and address*]
To: [*recipient's name and address*]
Subject: [*suitable subject line*]

Dear [*name*]

I am writing to invite you to a meeting to discuss [*describe the purpose of the meeting*].

The meeting will take place on [*name of video conference platform*] on [*date*], starting at [*time and time zone*] and finishing at [*time and time zone*]. Click on this link to join the meeting: [*insert meeting link*]

Please do not hesitate to contact me if you have any questions.

Kind regards

[sender's name]

4.7 Audio 2.4

Listen to the first part of the conference call in the Agile Design and Ideal Home case and answer the following questions:

a. What language indicates that this is a video conference call?
b. Who is leading this meeting?
c. Who is late and why?

4.8 Listen to Audio 2.4 again and complete the following table with details of the roles of the participants. The first answer is given as an example.

Name	Role
Claire Monet	a. *Associate at Garniers, acting for Agile Design*
Marc Leblanc	b.
Sophie Driscoll	c.
Philip Prescott	d.
Anya Marshall	e.
Paul Turner	f.

4.9 Audio 2.5

Listen to the second part of the conference call in the Agile Design and Ideal Home case and answer the following questions:

a. Is everyone polite during the call?
b. Do Agile Design and Ideal Home resolve their dispute?
c. What will Claire do next?

Conference call expressions

4.10 The following expressions were all used in the Agile Design and Ideal Home conference call. Match the expressions on the left with their functions on the right. There are two expressions which match with function 6. The first answer is given as an example.

Expressions	Functions
a. *In my view ...* →	1. Beginning the meeting
b. Just to recap what we said ...	2. *Giving an opinion*
c. I'm afraid we can't agree ...	3. Apologising for being late
d. Let's make a start.	4. Dealing with an interruption
e. Sorry to interrupt, but ...	5. Inviting someone to contribute
f. Could you just let Sophie finish her point?	6. Interrupting politely
g. Shall we wrap it up there?	7. Agreeing
h. Do you want to add something?	8. Disagreeing
i. Sorry for being late.	9. Ending the meeting
j. Yes, we can agree to that.	10. Summarising
k. Can I just come in here?	

4.11 All of the following phrasal verbs were heard in the Agile Design and Ideal Home conference call. Match each verb on the left with the correct particle on the right to form the phrasal verb. The first answer is given as an example.

Verb	Particle
a. *to run* →	1. back
b. to hand	2. *over*
c. to drop	3. with
d. to go	4. out
e. to wrap	5. in
f. to bear	6. ahead
g. to come	7. over
h. to get	8. up

4.12 Use your answers from Exercise 4.11 to complete the following table. The table gives the meanings of these phrasal verbs in the context of the conference call. The first answer is given as an example.

Phrasal verb	Definition
a. *to run over*	*to finish later than scheduled*
b.	to talk to someone again
c.	to finish something
d.	to lose connection
e.	to interrupt and make a point
f.	to give control to someone else
g.	to continue
h.	to wait a moment

Practise participating in a conference call

4.13 Review the expressions for participating in a conference call in Phrase bank 2.3

Phrase bank 2.3	
Interrupting	**Managing the call**
Sorry to interrupt, but ...	*[name] has just joined the call.*
It's [name]. Can I just come in here?	*Let's make a start.*
Could I just ask something?	*Could everyone introduce themselves?*
Technical problems	*The reason for this meeting is ...*
Can you see me and hear me?	*Could you just let [name] finish their point?*
I'm trying to share my screen.	*Do you want to add something?*
You're on mute.	*Shall we wrap it up?*
You've frozen.	*To recap ...*
We've lost [name].	*To summarise ...*
[name] has dropped out of the call.	

4.14 You are going to role-play the next conference call between Agile Design and Ideal Home. One group is Agile Design (client and lawyers) and the other group is Ideal Home (client and lawyers).

Read the instructions for your group. Appoint a person to lead the call and then role-play the call.

Agile Design instructions

In the call, Ideal Home will propose modifying its product to avoid infringement. It will only do this if Agile Design agrees not to take further legal action. You can choose whether to agree or disagree with Ideal Home's proposal. You can invent any other details, including other solutions to this dispute.

During the call, your group must use the following expressions:

- *Sorry I'm late, I ...*
- *Could I just ask ...*
- *I can't hear you. Could you just repeat that please?*
- *I'm afraid I don't understand. Please could you explain that in another way?*
- *I'm trying to share my screen.*
- *I'm afraid we can't agree to .../Yes we can agree to ...*

You can also use other expressions for participating in conference calls from Phrase bank 2.3.

Ideal Home instructions

In the call, you will propose modifying your product to avoid infringement. You will only do this if Agile Design agrees not to take further legal action. You can invent any other details, including other solutions to this dispute.

During the call, your group must use the following expressions:

- *You're on mute. I can see you, but I can't hear you.*
- *Who's speaking please?*
- *Can I just come in here?*
- *I'm afraid I didn't catch that. Would you mind saying that again?*
- *Can I check that I've understood correctly?*
- *I think we've lost [name].*

You can also use other expressions for participating in conference calls from Phrase bank 2.3.

4.15 Reflect on your conference call role-play in Exercise 4.14. Use the self-assessment questions in Appendix A.

Test yourself

1. How would you answer a telephone call in a professional context?
2. How can you prepare for a telephone call with an English-speaking client?
3. What expressions could you use if you do not understand what somebody says during a call?
4. What is a phrasal verb? Give three phrasal verbs examples from this chapter.
5. Explain how you could improve your video conference experience.

Notes

1 Conference call <https://dictionary.cambridge.org/dictionary/english/conference-call> accessed 18 April 2022

2 Video conference <https://dictionary.cambridge.org/dictionary/english/video-conference> accessed 18 April 2022

3 Client meetings

About this chapter

Overview

This chapter is about meetings between lawyers and their clients. The first part introduces the topic and looks at the types of meetings lawyers attend. The second part focuses on a lawyer's first meeting with a client. It looks at listening skills, questioning techniques, giving legal advice, and writing an attendance note after the meeting. It ends with a role-play first meeting with a client. The third part focuses on a meeting where a lawyer explains a legal procedure to a client.

Learning objectives

By the end of this chapter, you should be able to:

- use active listening to understand the client's matter
- use different questioning techniques to gather information
- understand expressions for giving legal advice
- compare the advantages and disadvantages of different courses of legal action
- explain a legal procedure to a client

Test yourself at the end of the chapter to check that you have achieved the learning objectives.

1. Introduction

1.1 Read Text 3.1 about the types of meetings that lawyers attend and answer these questions:

a. Who do lawyers have meetings with and what is the purpose of those meetings?
b. Where do meetings take place?
c. What cultural difference can have an impact on meetings?

Text 3.1 What types of meetings do lawyers attend?

Like many other business professionals, participating in meetings is part of a lawyer's daily work.

Lawyers spend most of their time attending client meetings, where they take instructions from or give advice to their clients. Lawyers also take part in meetings with the other side's lawyers, for example, to negotiate contracts or to try to settle disputes.

DOI: 10.4324/9781003140207-3

Lawyers also have internal meetings with colleagues, either to discuss cases that they are working on or to deal with the management of their law firm. And potential clients may invite lawyers to meetings for lawyers to pitch their legal services.

While lawyers often hold internal meetings face-to-face in the office, it is now common for lawyers to arrange other types of meetings by telephone or video conference. This is useful in an international environment where clients and lawyers may be based in other parts of the world.

When organising international meetings, it is important for lawyers to think about practical issues, such as participants being in different time zones, and also about cultural issues, such as different attitudes to punctuality.

1.2 What is your experience of meetings? Have you experienced any other cultural differences during meetings?

1.3 Text 3.1 contains a number of collocations with the word *meeting*. A collocation means words that go together. For example, *lawyers attend meetings*. The verb *attend* goes with the noun *meetings* to form a natural expression in English.

   a. Complete the following list with other verbs in Text 3.1 which go with the noun *a meeting*. Write the verb in the infinitive form. The first answer is given as an example.

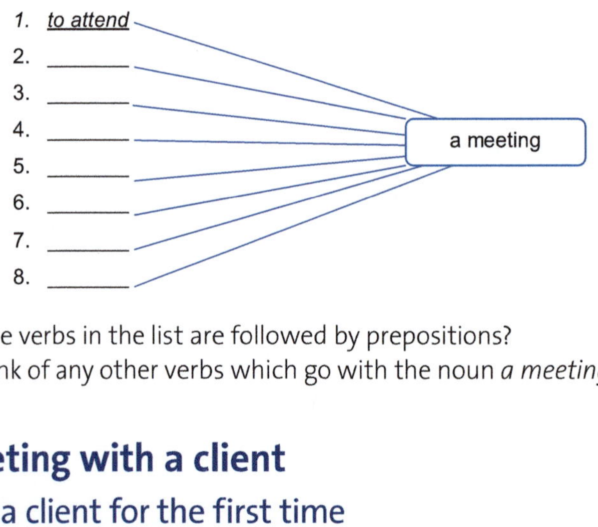

   b. Which of the verbs in the list are followed by prepositions?
   c. Can you think of any other verbs which go with the noun *a meeting*?

2. A first meeting with a client

Before meeting a client for the first time

2.1 Katie Thomas is a lawyer specialising in contract litigation. She had a brief telephone conversation yesterday with a potential client, Mike Jones. Mike said that he wanted some advice about a contract. Katie does not know Mike and has never acted for him before.

Katie has set up a face-to-face meeting with Mike at her office. To prepare for this meeting, Katie has made some notes on the following client meeting information sheet. Read her notes and discuss these questions:

   a. Who are the parties in this matter?
   b. What is the issue?
   c. What are Katie's objectives for this meeting?

Client meeting information sheet	Notes
Client contact details	Mike Jones, CEO of MPJ Limited Tel: 01625 73492 Email: mpj@mpj.co.uk MPJ Limited registered office: 398 Highcroft Road, London SE5 24B
Other party contact details	Organibars Limited Registered office: Tower City, Manchester, M1 67Q
Is there a conflict of interest?	Need to check
Brief details of the issue	The client's company makes packaging for the food industry He wants advice about a contract
Meeting objectives:	• Build a relationship with the client • Obtain more information about the issue from the client • Understand the client's objectives • Advise the client and discuss options • Explain the next steps

Vocabulary note

You can use different words for referring to the subject that the client wants to discuss. The word *problem* suggests that there is a dispute or conflict. The words *issue* or *matter* are more neutral.

2.2 The client meeting information sheet in Exercise 2.1 refers to a conflict of interest.

a. What is a conflict of interest?

b. What information can Katie use from her notes to check if a conflict of interest exists?

At the meeting

2.3 Audio 3.1

Listen to the beginning of the first meeting between Katie and Mike. Decide if the following statements are true or false and correct any false statements.

	True	False
a. Katie uses small talk about the weather to build a relationship with the client.	○	○
b. Organibars wants MPJ to make changes to the machine.	○	○
c. Mike's main objective is to take Organibars to court.	○	○
d. Katie has already read the contract between MPJ and Organibars.	○	○

Listening skills

2.4 Some people refer to the first meeting between a lawyer and a client as a client interview. In this meeting, the lawyer needs to ask the client a lot of questions to understand the facts of the case and the client's objectives. The lawyer needs to have good listening skills and good questioning techniques to conduct the meeting effectively.

Read the following comments about what makes a good listener. What would you add?

Someone who can summarise what you have said

Someone who turns their phone off

2.5 Practise your listening skills with a partner, using the following instructions:

Student A

Explain to Student B why you want to become a lawyer or, if you are already practising law, explain why you decided to become a lawyer. You must speak for two minutes.

Student B

Listen to Student A without making any sound, or using any body language, or making any interruptions.

2.6 Refer to Exercise 2.5 and discuss the following questions:

a. As the speaker, how did you feel during this exercise? Did you think that Student B was really listening to you?
b. As the listener, do you think that you were really listening to Student A? Can you summarise what they said?

2.7 In Exercise 2.5, by listening but not showing any verbal or non-verbal reactions, Student B was being a passive listener.

When interviewing a client, a lawyer needs to be an active listener. The lawyer needs to actively demonstrate that they are listening to the client, to encourage the client to continue speaking and to show that they have understood what the client has said.

Listen to Audio 3.1 again and complete the following table with examples of active listening techniques that Katie uses.

Active listening techniques	Examples
a. Using positive body language	She maintains eye contact and nods her head.
b. Using short expressions to show that you are listening	
c. Showing empathy	
d. Summarising what the client has said	

2.8 Practise your listening skills with a partner again, using the following instructions:

Student A

You are the listener. You must actively listen to Student B, using the active listening techniques in Exercise 2.7.

Student B

Explain to Student A why you want to become a lawyer, or if you are already practising law, why you decided to become a lawyer. You must speak for two minutes.

2.9 Refer to Exercise 2.8 and discuss the following questions:

a. As the speaker, how did you feel during this exercise? Did you think that Student A was really listening to you?
b. As the listener, do you think that you were really listening to Student B? Can you summarise what they said?

2.10 Practise your listening skills with a partner again, using the following instructions:

Student A

You are the listener. You must actively listen to Student B, using the active listening techniques in Exercise 2.7. You must also take notes while Student B is speaking.

Student B

You are the speaker. Talk about a recent meeting you had. If you are a practising lawyer, this could be a meeting with a client or another lawyer. If you are a student, this could be a meeting with a teacher or with a friend. You must speak for two minutes.

2.11 Refer to Exercise 2.10 and discuss the following questions:

a. As the speaker, how did you feel during this exercise? Did you think that Student A was really listening to you while they were taking notes?
b. As the listener, do you think that you were really listening to Student B while you were taking notes? Can you summarise what they said?

Questioning techniques

2.12 Katie uses a mixture of open and closed questions in her meeting with Mike. Read the transcript for Audio 3.1 and answer these questions:

a. Identify the open questions and the closed questions that Katie uses.
b. What question words does Katie use to form her open and closed questions?
c. Why does Katie use both open and closed questions in her meeting with Mike?

2.13 Katie also uses a question tag in her meeting with Mike. She says, '*It's awful weather today, isn't it?*' A question tag turns a statement into a question and it can be useful for asking for confirmation. For example, *We haven't met before, have we?*

Notice that if the statement is positive, then the question tag is negative. But if the statement is negative, the question tag is positive. There is a comma after the statement and before the tag:

Positive statement	Negative tag
It's awful weather today,	*isn't it?*

Negative statement	Positive tag
We haven't met before,	*have we?*

Complete the following questions by adding a question tag:

Statement	Tag
a. You didn't sign a contract with Organibars,	
b. I haven't sent you the contract,	
c. It's going to cost a lot of money to sue Organibars,	

2.14 Practise asking open questions by playing the following game with a partner:

Open questions game

Student A

You have two minutes to ask Student B as many open questions as you can on Topic 1. If Student B answers yes or no, it means you have asked a closed question. You lose the game! You can then change roles: Student B will ask you open questions for two minutes on Topic 2.

Student B

Student A has two minutes to ask you as many open questions as they can on Topic 1. If they ask you a closed question, you should answer yes or no, and Student A will lose the game! You can then change roles: You will ask Student A open questions for two minutes on Topic 2.

You can use these question words to help you ask open questions:

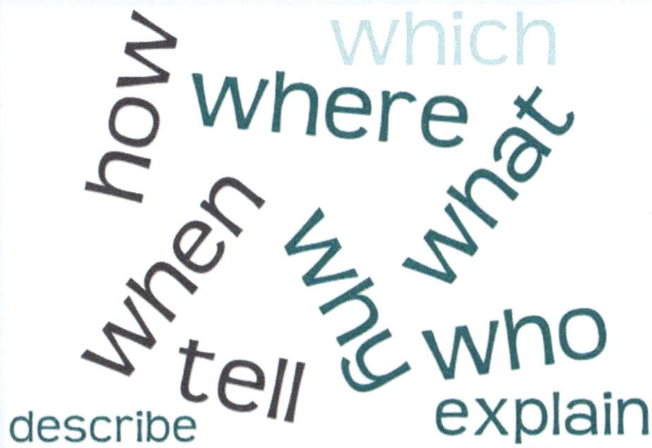

Topic 1

Reasons why clients come to see lawyers

Topic 2

Making a good impression in a first meeting with a client

Giving advice

2.15 🔊 Audio 3.2

After using good listening and questioning skills to establish the facts of the case, the lawyer needs to give the client some preliminary advice. Preliminary advice means the first piece of advice, which may not be complete and may require a follow-up. Giving preliminary advice can involve outlining how the relevant law applies to the facts of the case, understanding the client's objectives, and discussing options for further action.

Listen to the second part of the meeting between Katie and Mike. Decide if the following statements are true or false and correct any false statements.

	True	False
a. Katie advises Mike that he has a legally binding contract with Organibars	○	○
b. Katie outlines how the law applies to Mike's case	○	○
c. Katie advises Mike to use litigation to resolve his issue	○	○
d. Katie suggests different options for further action	○	○
e. Katie says that the next step is to negotiate a new contract with Organibars	○	○

Vocabulary note

When the parties have agreed on the main terms of a deal, they may record those terms in a document called *Heads of terms*. Other expressions are *Heads of agreement*, *Term sheet*, *Memorandum of understanding*, or *Letter of intent*. Usually, these documents are not intended to be legally binding; the aim is to show the main terms of the deal before the drafting and negotiation of the full contract.

2.16 Verbs for giving advice can take different forms.

The verbs *suggest, recommend, propose,* and *advise* can be followed by the -ing form of a verb or by a structure using the word *that:*

Verb for giving advice	Verb + -ing form	Verb + that
suggest	*I suggest suing Organibars*	*I suggest that you sue Organibars*
recommend	*I recommend negotiating with Organibars*	*I recommend that you negotiate with Organibars*
propose	*I propose organising a meeting with Organibars*	*I propose that you organise a meeting with Organibars*
advise	*I advise taking action against Organibars*	*I advise that you take action against Organibars*

The verb *advise* can also be followed by an object and a verb in the infinitive form:

Verb for giving advice	Verb + object + infinitive
advise	*I advise you to take action against Organibars*

Correct the following sentences:

a. I propose you to file a claim against Organibars.
b. I advise to enter into a new contract with Organibars.
c. I suggest to stop work on the packaging machine.

Grammar note

In spoken language, when using verbs for giving advice, the word *that* is often left out. For example, *I suggest you sue Organibars.*

In AmE, in formal spoken and written language, when using verbs for giving advice with the structure using the word *that*, the subjunctive mood is often used. For example, *I suggest that he sue Organibars.* Whereas in BrE the ordinary present tense is usually used. For example, *I suggest that he sues Organibars.*

2.17 Listen to Audio 3.2 again and complete the following sentences. These sentences all contain appropriate expressions for giving advice in a client meeting. Each space represents one word.

a. _______ _______ _______ *there are three possible outcomes in your case.*
b. *However, even without a formal contract,* _______ _______ _______ _______ *request a reasonable payment for the work you have already done.*
c. *... although* _______ _______ _______ *it would be difficult for Organibars to prove this.*
d. *I agree.* _______ _______ _______ *going to court should be a last resort.*
e. *And* _______ _______ _______ *if you do go to court and you lose your case, you might have to pay Organibars' legal costs ...*
f. *OK,* _______ _______ _______ *to reach an agreement*

2.18 In Audio 3.2, Katie says, '*The advantage of resolving this dispute amicably is that it could help maintain your commercial relationship with Organibars*'.

A for advantage, D for disadvantage

To express an advantage in English, you can use words beginning with *a*, such as:

- *the advantage of this is ...*
- *the attraction of this is ...*

To express a disadvantage, you can use words beginning with *d*, such as:

- *the disadvantage of this is ...*
- *the drawback of this is ...*
- *the downside of this is ...*

What other expressions can you use in English to explain advantages and disadvantages?

2.19 In Audio 3.2, Katie mentions the following advantages and disadvantages of using court action to resolve MPJ's dispute with Organibars:

It could help maintain their commercial relationship

It would put the parties in a confrontational situation

If MPJ loses the case it might have to pay Organibars' legal costs, in addition to its own costs

MPJ could demand payment for the work it has done

Practise comparing these advantages and disadvantages of using court action to resolve MPJ's dispute with Organibars using the following language:

A for advantage	Comparing	D for disadvantage
the advantage of this is ...	*on the other hand*	*the disadvantage of this is ...*
the attraction of this is ...	*however*	*the drawback of this is ...*
	but	*the downside of this is ...*

2.20 When giving advice to a client, the lawyer needs to use language that the client can understand. There may be words or expressions that the lawyer has to explain more clearly.

For example, in Audio 3.2, Katie says, '*To put it simply, a heads of terms document is a document which usually just sets out the main terms of your deal before negotiation of a full contract*'.

The following expressions were all used in Audio 3.2. Match the expressions on the left with their definitions on the right. The first answer is given as an example.

Expressions	Definitions
a. *a last resort*	1. The contract between a lawyer and their client, explaining the terms on which the lawyer will act for the client.
b. legal costs	2. *The only choice after trying other options.*
c. engagement letter	3. The method by which the client will pay the lawyer for their work. This could be on a fixed-fee or an hourly-rate basis.
d. billing arrangements	4. Information about the lawyers who will be responsible for the client's matter and details about the law firm's complaints procedure.
e. client care	5. Lawyers' fees and other expenses relating to a case, which could include court fees and experts' fees.

2.21 Practise explaining expressions to a client with a partner. Use the expressions and definitions from Exercise 2.20 and the following introductory language:

To put it simply …	What this means is …
In other words …	To explain that in another way ...

2.22 Katie's objectives for her meeting with Mike were to:

- build a relationship with the client
- obtain more information from the client about the issue
- understand the client's objectives
- advise the client and discuss options
- explain the next steps

Read the transcripts for Audios 3.1 and 3.2. Do you think that Katie has achieved these objectives?

After the meeting

2.23 Read the following attendance note that Katie has written after her meeting with Mike and answer these questions:

a. What is an attendance note?
b. Why has this attendance note been written?
c. What information does it include?
d. What does Katie need to do next?

Attendance note

Client file reference: To be allocated – new client
Date: 16 January 2022
Time: 10:00–11:00
Venue: At our offices
Present: Katie Thomas and Mike Jones, MPJ Limited

Background

- This was a first meeting with Mike Jones, CEO of MPJ Ltd. MPJ makes packaging for the food industry.
- MPJ had an order from Organibars to supply a machine for a new range of chocolate bars. Mike hoped that this would lead to more business as Organibars is part of a global group.

Issues

- MPJ started work on the machine and did a test run, but now Organibars is refusing to pay MPJ.
- Organibars wants to change the specifications of the machine because it has changed the dimensions of its chocolate bars. MPJ said they could do this for an increased price, but Organibars won't agree to a price increase.
- No formal contract has been signed. The parties agreed some heads of terms, including the specifications of the machine, the delivery date, and the price and then MPJ started work.

Preliminary advice given

- I advised the client that it is not clear whether MPJ has a legally binding contract with Organibars.
- I explained three possible outcomes:
  1) The court decides that there is no contract, but in this case MPJ could try to ask for reasonable payment for work already done;
  2) The court decides that there is a contract on the basis of the heads of terms, so MPJ has to supply the machine to the original specifications, and Organibars has to pay MPJ;
  3) Organibars shows that it was agreed they could make changes to the specifications without an increase in price. This would be difficult for Organibars to prove.
- Mike wants MPJ to be paid for the work it has done, but he also wants to resolve this dispute amicably, without going to court. I advised him to consider a meeting with Organibars, either on their own or with lawyers present.

Next steps

- Mike will send me a copy of the heads of terms and let me know how he wants to proceed.
- I will write to Mike with a summary of today's meeting.
- I will send Mike the firm's engagement letter.
- I need to check Mike's instructions and arrange a meeting with Organibars if necessary.

Katie Thomas

Practise a first meeting with a client

2.24 Review the objectives for a first meeting with a client in Exercise 2.1 and the expressions in Phrase bank 3.1

Phrase bank 3.1	
Build a relationship with the client	**Advise the client**
Pleased to meet you. I'm [name].	*I suggest [+ing/that]*
Would you like a coffee before we start?	*I recommend [+ing/that]*
Obtain information from the client	*I propose [+ing/that]*
I understand you'd like some advice about [a contract]?	*I advise [+ing/that/object + infinitive]*
What happened?	*In my view ...*
Perhaps you could explain what happened?	*In my opinion ...*
Use open questions	*I think that ...*
Who, what, which, where, why, when, how, explain, tell me, describe ...	*I must warn you that ...*
Use closed questions	**Discuss options**
Did ...?	*There are a number of options here:*
Do ...?	*You have the following options:*
Understand the client's objectives	*The advantage of ... is ...*
Can I just check that I have understood correctly?	*The attraction of ... is ...*
So what you're saying is ...?	*The disadvantage of ... is ...*
To summarise what you have told me ...	*The drawback of ... is*
	The downside of ... is
	On the one hand ...
	On the other hand ...
	Explaining the next steps
	After this meeting I will send you ...
	Please could you send me ...
	I will get back to you after I have ...

2.25 Practise a first meeting with a client. Choose whether you are going to play the role of the lawyer or the client. Then read your instructions and role-play the meeting using the expressions from Phrase bank 3.1.

Lawyer instructions

You recently took a call from a new client. The client said that they wanted advice about a contract. You have arranged a meeting with the client to discuss this in more detail. Use your own legal knowledge to advise the client or see the guidance on legal points below.

Make sure that you actively listen and ask open questions to obtain information and understand the client's objectives. Remember to advise the client and discuss options in language that the client can understand.

Guidance on legal points: it is usually possible to form a contract by email unless the law says that a specific form of contract is required. You will need to check that the email correspondence shows that the parties have agreed on the essential terms of the contract and that these terms are not too vague. You will need to see the emails that the client mentions.

Client instructions

You recently called a lawyer. You explained that you wanted advice about a contract. You have arranged a meeting with the lawyer to discuss your issue in more detail.

The facts of your case: you make jewellery and specialise in affordable pieces for young people. You were very excited because a high street retailer was interested in stocking your brand. After an exchange of emails, the retailer agreed to buy €500,000 of stock over a six-month period for sale in their largest stores. However, the retailer has just written to you to say that it has changed its mind and will not be placing any orders with you. Can it do this? You thought that you had a contract with the retailer.

2.26 Reflect on your client meeting role-play in Exercise 2.25. If you played the role of the lawyer, use the self-assessment questions in Appendix A. If you played the role of the client, use the peer-assessment questions in Appendix A

2.27 After your meeting, write an attendance note for your file. Use the attendance note in Exercise 2.23 as a guide.

3. Explaining a legal procedure

A lawyer often has to explain a legal procedure to a client. The lawyer may do this in writing or orally. This section focuses on an oral explanation of a procedure during a client meeting.

3.1 🔊 Audio 3.3

Listen to an extract from a client meeting where an English lawyer, Paul Fairley, is explaining a procedure to a client and answer the following questions:

a. What type of legal procedure is Paul explaining?
b. Do you think that Paul's explanation is effective? Why or why not?

3.2 Read Text 3.2 which contains some tips on explaining a legal procedure to a client. In Audio 3.3, did Paul use these tips?

Text 3.2 Explaining a procedure to a client

- Organise the information into a logical order, such as chronologically. For example, *firstly, secondly, thirdly, and finally ...*
- Use linking words to move from one part of the procedure to another. For example, *first, then, next, after that, the next step is ..., let's move on to the next point ...*
- Refer to written documents and images, such as diagrams or checklists. For example, *as you can see in this diagram ..., if we turn to the checklist ...*
- Explain any legal terminology in language that the client can understand. For example, *the claimant means the person who is making a claim.*

- Explain any acronyms or abbreviations. For example, *ADR stands for Alternative Dispute Resolution.*
- Make sure you explain who has responsibility for each step of the procedure. For example, *the claimant starts proceedings by filing a claim form at the court.*
- Be clear about any time limits. For example, *the time limit is [length of time], it will take [length of time], you must file this document no later than [date].*

3.3 Audio 3.4

Listen to Paul explaining the same procedure in a different way and discuss how Paul uses the tips from Text 3.2.

3.4 Listen to Audio 3.4 again and complete the gaps in the following diagram. Each space represents one word.

Step 1: Before starting proceedings

a. The lawyer checks the ________ ________
b. The claimant considers the________ of litigation.
c. The claimant sends a ________ ________ ________ to the defendant.
d. The claimant and the defendant try to ________ ________ ________

Step 2: Starting proceedings

e. The claimant sends a ________ ________ to the court.
f. The claimant ________ the claim form and the particulars of claim on the defendant.
g. The defendant files a ________
h. The court allocates the claim to one of three ________

Step 3: Going to trial

i. The court will give ________ and set a timetable.
j. The parties have to ________ documents and exchange ________ ________ and experts' reports
k. The ________ takes place.
l. The claimant might need to take action to ________ the judgment.

3.5 Practise explaining a legal procedure to a client using the tips and expressions in Text 3.2.

If you are a practising lawyer, you can explain a legal procedure you are familiar with. For example, how to register a company.

If you do not yet have experience in legal practice, research the litigation procedure in your jurisdiction and use the diagram in Exercise 3.4 to help explain it.

3.6 Reflect on your explanation of a legal procedure in Exercise 3.5. If you played the role of the lawyer, use the self-assessment questions in Appendix A. If you played the role of the client, use the peer-assessment questions in Appendix A

Test yourself

1. Explain the type of listening lawyers should use in a client meeting.
2. Why do lawyers use both open and closed questions in a client meeting?
3. Give two examples of expressions for giving legal advice.
4. What language can you use to compare the advantages and disadvantages of different courses of legal action?
5. Explain two tips a lawyer should follow when explaining a legal procedure.

4 Legal writing

About this chapter

Overview

This chapter is about different types of legal writing. The first part introduces the topic. The second part focuses on writing short emails, looking at different ways of starting and ending emails, different levels of formality, and the content of a short email. The third part looks at five key skills for legal writing: planning and organising your content, helping your reader navigate your document, improving your sentences, using plain English, and reviewing your writing. It includes exercises on writing an email of advice to a client and a memorandum.

Learning objectives

By the end of this chapter, you should be able to:

- write a short email to a client, colleague, or another lawyer, using the appropriate level of formality
- plan and organise the content of longer emails or legal documents
- use techniques to help your reader easily find the information they need
- write clearly and concisely by improving your sentence structure
- understand plain English alternatives to legalese

Test yourself at the end of the chapter to check that you have achieved the learning objectives.

1. Introduction

1.1 Read the following quote from Ruth Bader Ginsburg, who was being interviewed about how she wrote her United States Supreme Court decisions.[1] Then discuss these questions:

a. What do you think '*my eye is on the reader*' means?

b. This quote is about writing Supreme Court decisions. What other types of writing do lawyers do and who are their readers?

c. In addition to being clear and concise, how can lawyers help their readers?

> *'My eye is on the reader, and that's predominantly judges or other courts who must apply our decisions as precedent and lawyers who must account for them in their briefs. So I try to be clear and as concise as I can be.'*[1]

DOI: 10.4324/9781003140207-4

2. Writing short emails

Writing exercise

2.1 Anthony Long is an employment lawyer. He had a telephone conversation with a new client yesterday. The client's name is Jeff Walters, and he is a senior manager at a software company. Jeff is thinking of leaving the software company to set up his own business and he wants advice about the non-competition clause in his employment contract. Anthony has agreed to meet Jeff at Anthony's office next Tuesday to discuss this.

Write an email from Anthony Long to Jeff Walters in which you:

- include a subject line in the heading of the email
- refer to their telephone conversation
- confirm the meeting next Tuesday
- ask the client for a copy of his employment contract

Write your email before reading the following sections. You will refer to this email in some of the following exercises.

Email subject line

2.2 Emails include a subject line with a short description of the email content. Try to keep your subject line informative but concise, so that it is quickly and easily understandable. Which of the following would be the best subject line for the email to Jeff Walters?

a. Your phone call yesterday
b. Information required before our meeting on Tuesday 19th October
c. Meeting next Tuesday to discuss leaving your company and the non-competition clause in your employment contract

2.3 Check the answer to Exercise 2.2 in the Answer key, and then read the email you wrote to Jeff Walters. How does your subject line compare with the suggested answer? Is it longer or shorter? Does it contain the same information?

Starting and ending emails

2.4 Refer again to the email you wrote to Jeff Walters in Exercise 2.1. How did you start your email? Which of the following salutations are most appropriate for this email?

a. Hello
b. Jeff
c. Hi Jeff
d. Dear Jeff
e. Dear Jeff Walters
f. Dear Mr Jeff
g. Dear Mr Walters
h. Dear Sir
i. To whom it may concern

2.5 In emails, it can be difficult to choose a salutation if you do not know the name of the person you are writing to or if you know their name but not their gender. The language for salutations has evolved and continues to do so. The following tables list traditional salutations and more modern, gender-inclusive alternatives.

Read the salutations in the following tables. What are the appropriate salutations to address the following people?

a. A new client, who signs their name *Bryony Marsh* (*she, her, hers*).
b. A colleague you know very well, called Alice Foster.
c. The other party in an employment law dispute. You are writing to the Human Resources Manager at their company and you do not know their name.
d. The opposing lawyer in a litigation dispute. You know the name of the law firm, Pickfords, but not the name of the lawyer dealing with the matter.

Traditional salutations	Examples
Writing to a man	*Dear Mr [surname]* *Dear Mr Harrison*
Writing to a married woman	*Dear Mrs [surname]* *Dear Mrs Brown*
Writing to an unmarried woman	*Dear Miss [surname]* *Dear Miss Brown*
Writing to a woman when you do not know her marital status*	*Dear Ms [surname]* *Dear Ms Brown*
Very formal salutation to a man or where the man's name is unknown	*Dear Sir*
Very formal salutation to a woman or where the woman's name is unknown	*Dear Madam*
Very formal salutation when you do not know the person's gender	*Dear Sir or Madam* *Dear Sir/Madam*
Writing to a law firm or a company**	*Dear Sir or Madam*

*Some married women also prefer this neutral title.

**You might also see the expression *Dear Sirs* but this is outdated and we do not recommend that you use this.

Gender-inclusive salutations***	Examples
Writing to a person when you know their name	*Dear [name of person]* *Dear P. Harrison* *Dear Peter Harrison*
Writing to a person by their first name, if you know them well	*Dear [first name]* *Dear Peter* *Hi Peter* (informal) *Peter* (informal)
Writing to a person when you do not know their name but you know their position	*Dear [position]* *Dear Finance Director* *Dear Counsel*

Writing to a law firm or a company	*Dear [name of firm or company]* *Dear Goldings* *Dear [name of department]* *Dear Litigation Department*
Writing to a group of people	*Dear all* *Hi everyone* (informal)

***These salutations do not specify the gender of the person you are writing to. People who do not want to specify their gender or who do not identify as being male or female may also use the title *Mx*. For example, someone may sign their name *Mx Sam Tyler*. In this case, you could also use the salutation *Dear Mx Tyler*.

2.6 Read the following expressions that you can use in ending, also called closing, an email. Discuss when you would use each of these endings. Did you use an appropriate ending in your email to Jeff Walters?

a. Yours sincerely	b. Yours faithfully	c. Best regards	d. Kind regards
e. Respectfully yours	f. Yours truly	g. Best	h. Cheers

Punctuation note

In emails, there are no strict rules about the punctuation of salutations and closings.

In AmE, a full stop is used after someone's title, for example, *Dear Mr. Walters* and there may be a colon after the salutation, for example, *Dear Mr. Walters:*

In BrE, there is no punctuation mark after someone's title, but there may be a comma after the salutation, for example, *Dear Mr Walters,*

Some writers may include a comma after the closing, for example, *Best regards,*

Email tone

2.7 Tone refers to the sound of your writing. Depending on what language you use, your writing can sound formal or informal. The level of formality you use depends on why you are writing your email and who is going to read it.

Read Emails 1 to 4 and then answer the following questions:

a. Which email would be appropriate for Anthony Long to send to Jeff Walters?
b. Which email is the most similar to the email you wrote?
c. What aspects of the language in the emails make them sound more formal or more informal?
d. Discuss where each email would go on this scale:

too informal ←——— *just right* ———→ *too formal*

Email 1

Dear Mr Walters,

Following our telephone conversation yesterday, I am writing to confirm our meeting next Tuesday, 19th October, at 10:00 at my office.

Please could you send me a copy of your employment contract before the meeting, so that I can have a look at the non-competition clause?

If you have any other questions, please do not hesitate to contact me.

Kind regards

Anthony Long

Email 2

Jeff,

Thanks for reaching out. Happy to meet next Tues. at 10 to go over the non-compete stuff. Can you just ping over the contract ASAP – I'd like to check it out before the meeting.

Anything else, just let me know!

Cheers

Tony

Email 3

Dear Sir,

We write with reference to the above-mentioned matter, which was the subject of our telephone conversation yesterday. Please be advised that the forthcoming meeting has been organised for Tuesday 19th October at 10:00.

We respectfully request that a copy of your employment contract be sent in advance of the meeting.

The writer remains at your disposal should you have any further questions.

Yours faithfully

A. Long

Email 4

Dear Mr Walters,

I write further to our telephone conversation yesterday, when we discussed the matter of your employment contract. A meeting has duly been scheduled for next Tuesday, 19th October, at 10:00 at our offices.

I would be grateful if you could arrange to forward a copy of your employment contract for my perusal before the meeting.

Please do not hesitate to contact me if you require any further information regarding this matter.

Yours sincerely

A. Long

2.8 Abbreviations, acronyms, and buzzwords are indications of informal writing. It is important to understand these even if you do not use them in your own writing.

- An abbreviation is a shortened form of a word or phrase. It usually contains a punctuation mark to show that the word has been abbreviated. For example, *approx.* is an abbreviation of *approximately*.
- An acronym is formed from the first letters of each word in a phrase. It uses capital letters. For example, *ROI* means *return on investment*.
- A buzzword is a word or expression which is currently very popular. Business people often use buzzwords and commercial lawyers need to be able to understand their clients' language. For example, *deep dive* means a detailed analysis of a topic.

a. Read Email 2 in Exercise 2.7 again. Identify the abbreviations, acronyms, and buzzwords. What does each one mean?

b. Complete the following table with the meanings of some acronyms and abbreviations which are commonly used in emails. The first answer is given as an example.

Acronym	**Meaning**
BR	*1. Best regards*
COB	2.
FYI	3.
VM	4.
Abbreviation	**Meaning**
c.c.	5.
e.g.	6.
i.e.	7.

c. Match the following buzzwords on the left with their definitions on the right. The first answer is given as an example.

Buzzword	**Definition**
a. *ballpark figure* →	1. using something to your advantage
b. big picture	2. *approximate amount*
c. game changer	3. something unlikely to succeed
d. hands are tied	4. the wider context
e. kick off	5. something that significantly affects a situation
f. leverage	6. the main message

(Continues on the next page)

g. long shot	7. do something which upsets someone
h. on the same page	8. unable to act as you wish
i. rock the boat	9. being in agreement
j. takeaway	10. start

d. In the following email a client, Ray Brown, is writing to his lawyer, Nick Roche. Ray and Nick have a meeting tomorrow with one of Ray's customers concerning a breach of contract. Complete the gaps in the email with appropriate buzzwords from Exercise 2.8 c.

From: Ray Brown raybrown@brogan.com
To: Nick Roche nroche@turbins.llp
Subject: Horton's breach of contract

Hi Nick,

I think we should (a)__________ the meeting tomorrow by asking them what amount of compensation they had in mind. I need a (b)__________ before I can go any further.

I am hoping that they will settle for £50,000 although I know that's a (c)__________.

To give you the (d)__________, this is a long-standing customer, who gives us good business. I don't want to (e)__________ as we really don't want to lose them.

Best

Ray
Managing Director, Brogan Ltd.

e. What other abbreviations, acronyms, and buzzwords have you seen lawyers or clients use?

Email content

This section looks at the structure of a short email. For more information about organising the content of a longer email, see the five key writing skills in the next part of this chapter.

2.9 The purpose of a short email is usually to inform someone about something, to request something or to reply to someone's request. You can structure a short email like this:

- **Opening**
  This refers to previous contact and your reason for writing
- **Middle**
  This gives information or contains a request
- **Closing remarks**
  This refers to future contact or gives thanks

a. Refer to the email you wrote to Jeff Walters in Exercise 2.1. Did you follow this structure?
b. Read Email 1 in Exercise 2.7 again. Which expressions are used for the opening, the middle, and the closing remarks?

2.10 When making a request in an email, if you use the imperative form of a verb, your request could sound too direct and be considered impolite. For example, *Give me your contract.*

On the other hand, if your language is too indirect, the reader might think that you are making a suggestion rather than a request. For example, *Would you mind giving me your contract?*

It is important for lawyers to make their requests clear, while also being polite.

Read the following expressions and discuss where you would place them on this scale:

← *too direct* — *polite request* — *too indirect* →

a. Send me the contract.	*b. Please send me the contract.*
c. I would be grateful if you could send me the contract.	*d. Please could you send me the contract?*
e. I was wondering if you could send me the contract.	*f. I would appreciate it if you could send me the contract.*

Practise writing short emails

2.11 Review the expressions for writing short emails in Phrase bank 4.1

Phrase bank 4.1

Referring to previous contact

Thank you for your email of [date].

I refer to your email of [date].

Following our meeting yesterday ...

As discussed, ...

Reason for writing

I am writing [+ infinitive. For example, *I am writing to confirm*] ...

I am writing about [subject matter].

I understand that ...

I am acting for [client's name].

Making a request

Please [+ imperative. For example, *Please send ...*]

Please could you ...

**I would be grateful if you could ...*

**I would appreciate it if you could ...*

Giving information

I attach ...

Please see the attached document.

Here is [the website link/the email address]:

Please note that ...

I would like to inform you that ...

I am pleased to inform you that ...

Unfortunately ...

Closing remarks

Please let me know if you need any more information.

Please do not hesitate to contact me if you have any questions.

I look forward to hearing from you.

I will get back to you as soon as possible.

Thank you for your assistance in this matter.

Many thanks.

*Be careful with these expressions. They could be interpreted as suggestions rather than requests. Refer to Exercise 2.10.

2.12 The following phrases contain common mistakes that non-native speakers make when writing emails. Refer to Phrase bank 4.1 and choose the correct expression that a native speaker would use. The first answer is given as an example.

a. I revert to you about the sale of your company.

I am writing about the sale of your company.

b. I write to you this email to obtain some information.

____

c. Please see the enclosed document.

____

d. I attach the link: www.harrisonmiller.com.

____

e. I look forward to hear from you.

____

f. I remain at your disposal if you have any questions.

____

2.13 Read the following scenario and write the emails using the appropriate level of formality and the expressions from Phrase bank 4.1. Remember to include a subject line for each email.

Scenario

You had a meeting last week with an existing client, Sandip Singh, Real Estate Director at Singh Properties Limited. Sandip gave you instructions to sell one of the company's properties, known as Ramsford House. The buyer is Maxim Estates, and they are represented by Ms Murphy at the law firm Murphy Cotton.

a. Write an email to the buyer's lawyers, sending the draft sale contract.
b. Write an email to your client confirming that you have now sent the draft sale contract to Maxim Estates' lawyers.
c. Write an email to your colleague, Helen, in the tax law department at your firm. Your client has asked for some additional tax law advice regarding the sale of this property and you would like Helen's help with this. You know Helen well and you have already spoken briefly on the telephone with Helen about this matter.

2.14 Read the example emails for Exercise 2.13 in the Answer key. These contain other helpful expressions for writing emails.

3. Five key skills for legal writing

This part of the chapter focuses on five key skills for legal writing. These skills apply to any type of legal writing. The examples given in this section are an email of advice and a memorandum.

Introduction to legal writing skills

3.1 🔊Audio 4.1

Listen to Judith Freeman, an employment lawyer, talking about legal writing. Decide if these statements are true or false and correct any false statements.

Judith:	True	False
a. spends most of her time drafting complex legal documents	○	○
b. says that you should think about who will be reading your writing	○	○
c. always writes in a formal style	○	○
d. knows that she needs to be concise, but finds this difficult	○	○
e. thinks that you should use legal jargon so that you sound like a lawyer	○	○

Vocabulary note: *to write* or *to draft*

Usually in English we say that lawyers *write* emails or letters, but *draft* other legal documents. For example, the lawyer *drafted* the contract. This is not a strict rule as lawyers may write or draft reports.

Skill 1: Plan and organise your content

3.2 In Audio 4.1, Judith says that she has to '*think about how I'm going to organise all the information I want to include*'. Before you start writing, you need to think about the points that you want to make and then decide how you are going to organise those points.

Refer to the scenario in Exercise 2.1 at the beginning of this chapter. Anthony Long is acting for Jeff Walters, who is a senior manager in a software company. Jeff is thinking of leaving the company to set up his own business. He wants advice about the non-competition clause in his employment contract.

Anthony and Jeff have had their first meeting. Jeff provided Anthony with more information about his plans and they discussed the terms of Jeff's employment contract. Anthony made some notes at the meeting and he now needs to write an email to Jeff with a summary of his legal advice.

a. Read the following notes of the main points that Anthony is thinking of including in his email. Check the Glossary for definitions of any words that you do not know.

1. For the restrictions in Jeff's contract to be enforceable, they must be reasonable
2. In his position as a senior manager, Jeff has had access to confidential information and client data
3. There are different types of restrictions in Jeff's contract: a non-competition clause and a non-solicitation clause

4. There are risks in setting up his business sooner than six months after he leaves his existing job
5. Recent case law states that a restriction for six months after the end of employment is reasonable
6. The non-competition clause states that Jeff is prevented from being involved in any business or activity which competes with his employer's business
7. The restrictions in Jeff's contract last for six months after the end of his employment
8. The factors that the court will look at when deciding if clauses are reasonable include the length and scope of the restrictions and the seniority of the employee
9. Jeff has the option to wait six months or to try to negotiate a release from the restrictions
10. The non-solicitation clause states that Jeff is not allowed to solicit the business of any of his employer's customers
11. The risks are that Jeff's employer could try to obtain an injunction and compensation if Jeff does not comply with the restrictions in his contract
12. The restrictions in Jeff's contract are probably reasonable as they are limited to a six-month period
13. Jeff needs to decide how he wants to proceed

b. In short emails, each point can constitute one paragraph. You can see an example of this in Email 1 in Exercise 2.7. In longer emails and other types of legal writing, you need to arrange your points to form paragraphs.

Arrange points 1 to 13 into paragraphs. You should be able to make five paragraphs in total. Put related points together. For example, points 4 and 11 both relate to the risks of breaching the non-competition clause and could go together in one paragraph:

4. There are risks in setting up his business sooner than six months after he leaves his existing job
11. The risks are that Jeff's employer could try to obtain an injunction and compensation if Jeff does not comply with the restrictions in his contract

3.3 Once you have arranged your points, you have the outline of your paragraphs of text. Next you need to decide in what order to arrange those paragraphs.

Bryan Garner suggests that you '*Order your material in a logical sequence. Present facts chronologically. Keep related material together*'.[2]

The logical sequence for your material can depend on the type of document you are writing and your intended reader.

A sequence that lawyers usually use for an email or letter of advice is:

- summary of the facts of the client's case
- identification of the legal issue
- application of the relevant law to the facts
- the lawyer's advice
- next steps

Read the following outline paragraphs for your email to Jeff Walters. Arrange the paragraphs in a logical sequence:

a. There are risks in setting up his new business sooner than six months after he leaves his existing job. The risks are that Jeff's employer could try to obtain an injunction and compensation if Jeff does not comply with the restrictions in his contract.
b. For the restrictions in Jeff's contract to be enforceable, they must be reasonable. The factors that the court will look at when deciding if clauses are reasonable include the length and scope of the restrictions and the seniority of the employee. Recent case law states that a restriction for six months after the end of employment is reasonable.
c. Jeff has the option to wait six months or to try to negotiate a release from the restrictions. Jeff needs to decide how he wants to proceed.
d. There are different types of restrictions in Jeff's contract: a non-competition clause and a non-solicitation clause. The non-competition clause states that Jeff is prevented from being involved in any business or activity which competes with his employer's business. The non-solicitation clause states that Jeff is not allowed to solicit the business of any of his employer's customers. The restrictions in Jeff's contract last for six months after the end of his employment.
e. The restrictions in Jeff's contract are probably reasonable as they are limited to a six-month period. In his position as a senior manager, Jeff has had access to confidential information and client data.

Vocabulary note

The sequence referred to in Exercise 3.3 is similar to the *IRAC* method. The acronym *IRAC* stands for: *issue, rule, application, conclusion*. This is a method used by English and American law students to answer law exam questions. It involves identifying the legal issue, stating the relevant legal rules, applying the legal rules to the facts of the case, and concluding with an answer to the issue.

3.4 Review the expressions for an email of advice in Phrase bank 4.2:

Phrase bank 4.2	
Summarising the facts	**Giving advice**
You explained that ...	*In my opinion ...*
You told me that ...	*In my view ...*
We discussed ...	*I suggest [+ing/that] ...*
I understand that ...	*I recommend [+ing/that] ...*
Identifying the legal issue	*I propose [+ing/that] ...*
The legal issue is whether ...	*I advise [+ing/that/object + infinitive] ...*
The question is whether ...	*One option is to ...*
Referring to the relevant law	*The risk is that ...*
According to [case law/legislation] ...	*You risk [+ing] ...*
Under [name of legislation] ...	**Next steps**
The law is set out in [name of legislation].	*Please let me have your instructions.*
Recent case law states that ...	*Please could you send me [e.g. a copy of your contract]?*
In a previous case, the court decided that ...	
The factors that the court will look at include ...	*I will now [e.g. contact the other side's lawyers].*

3.5 Write Anthony's complete email to Jeff, using the notes and paragraph structure in Exercise 3.3 and the expressions in Phrase bank 4.2. Your email should also include a salutation, an opening, closing remarks, and a suitable ending.

Skill 2: Help your reader navigate your document

3.6 In Audio 4.1, Judith says, *'my clients are busy business people with decisions to make and deadlines to meet'*. You need to help your reader navigate your document so that it is easy for them to find the information they require.

Organising your content in a logical sequence is one way to help with this. What are some other ways?

3.7 Audio 4.2

Listen to a conversation between Judith and her trainee, Theo, and then answer the following questions:

a. What is redundancy?
b. What does Judith want Theo to do?
c. What points does Theo need to include in his memorandum?

3.8 A memorandum, or memo, is a type of note sent internally in a law firm. A lawyer might use a memorandum to update a colleague on a client's matter, or to ask a colleague for advice on a particular aspect of a client's case. In Audio 4.2, Theo is going to report on his legal research in a memorandum, but in some cases a supervisor might require a more formal legal research report in a specified format.

Do you use memoranda in your work? For what purposes?

Headings

3.9 Using headings can help a reader to navigate a document, particularly in memoranda and reports. Theo has identified the points that he is going to make in his memorandum. He has planned and organised his paragraphs, and he has started to write the memorandum.

Read what Theo has written so far and complete the headings. The first answer is given as an example.

MEMORANDUM

From: Theo Powell
To: Judith Freeman
Date: 24 April 2022
Subject: Overview of redundancy law

(a) *Introduction*
When restructuring a business, it is important to consider the law relating to redundancy. This memorandum gives an overview of English redundancy law.

(b)__________________________________
Redundancy is when you dismiss an employee because you no longer need someone to do their particular job. There must be a genuine redundancy situation and this is defined in the law as where your business is closing down, you are moving your business to another location, or you need fewer employees to do particular kinds of work.

(c) __________________________________
If you are proposing to make employees redundant, you have to follow a fair procedure. You must discuss your proposals with your employees through a procedure called consultation and use fair criteria to select the employees for redundancy. If you do not follow a fair procedure, an employee could bring a claim against you for unfair dismissal.

(d) __________________________________
Consultation involves a series of meetings with your employees in which you explain your redundancy proposals. If you propose to make 20 or more employees redundant at one site, you need to have collective consultation with trade union or staff representatives in addition to individual consultation with the employees at risk of redundancy. Your explanation should include your reasons for the redundancies, the number of employees you propose to dismiss, the selection criteria you will use, and how you will calculate the redundancy payments. You are not under an obligation to reach an agreement with the employees but you have to discuss ways of avoiding or reducing the number of redundancies and allow them to suggest counterproposals.

3.10 The Answer key gives alternative headings in the form of questions. Discuss the following questions:

a. Which type of heading do you prefer and why?
b. Which type of heading would help the client to navigate the information more easily and why?

Topic sentences

3.11 Read the following two example paragraphs. What is the difference between them?

Paragraph 1

If you propose to make 20 or more employees redundant at one site, you need to have 'collective' consultation with trade union or staff representatives in addition to 'individual' consultation with the employees at risk of redundancy. Your explanation should include your reasons for the redundancies, the number of employees you propose to dismiss, the selection criteria you will use, and how you will work out the redundancy payments.

Paragraph 2

Consultation involves a series of meetings with your employees in which you explain your redundancy proposals. If you propose to make 20 or more employees redundant at one site, you need to have 'collective' consultation with trade union or staff representatives in addition to 'individual' consultation with the employees at risk of redundancy. Your explanation should include your reasons for the redundancies, the number of employees you propose to dismiss, the selection criteria you will use, and how you will work out the redundancy payments.

3.12 Paragraph 2 in Exercise 3.11 contains a topic sentence to introduce the paragraph. It gives the reader an idea of what the paragraph is going to be about. This is another method of helping a reader navigate a document. If the reader quickly reads the topic sentence of each paragraph, they should be able to understand the main points being made in the document.

Write a heading and a topic sentence for the next paragraph of Theo's memorandum:

(a) Heading ______________________________
(b) Topic sentence ______________________________

____

If you are making fewer than 20 employees redundant, there is no minimum or maximum timescale for consultation. However, it is good practice to allow time for a meaningful consultation with the employees. If you are making 20 or more employees redundant, there is no maximum timescale, but consultation must start at least 30 days before dismissal where the number of redundancies is between 20 and 99 and must start at least 40 days before dismissal where the number of redundancies is 100 or more.

List format

3.13 A document will be easier to read if there is more white space, rather than dense text. Using headings is one way to help with this. Another way is using a list format.

Read the following paragraph of Theo's memorandum, which is written in list format:

How do I consult with the employees?

Consultation involves a series of meetings with your employees in which you explain your redundancy proposals. If you propose to make 20 or more employees redundant at one site, you need to have 'collective' consultation with trade union or staff representatives in addition to 'individual' consultation with the employees at risk of redundancy.

Your explanation should include:

- your reasons for the redundancies
- the number of employees you propose to dismiss
- the selection criteria you will use
- how you will calculate the redundancy payments.

You are not under an obligation to reach an agreement with the employees but you have to discuss ways of avoiding or reducing the number of redundancies and allow them to suggest counterproposals.

3.14 Write the next paragraph of Theo's memorandum using the following notes that Theo has made. You should use a list format and include a heading and a topic sentence.

Memorandum notes

I need to write about redundancy payments. I must explain that there are two different types of redundancy payments: statutory payments and contractual payments. The employer will have to make a statutory redundancy payment to any employee who has at least two years' continuous service. The statutory redundancy payment is based on the age of the employee, their length of service and their weekly salary. Also, there may be provision for an additional redundancy payment in the employee's employment contract.

Skill 3: Improve your sentences

3.15 In Audio 4.1, Judith says, '*I need to get my message across as accurately and efficiently as I can*'.

Here are three ways of improving your sentences to help with this:

1. Write short sentences.
2. Use the active voice.
3. Keep the subject, verb and object together.

Write short sentences

3.16 Read Text 4.1 about writing short sentences and answer these questions:

a. When should you think about making your sentence shorter?
b. What methods can you use to make your sentence shorter?
c. Which two methods of making your sentence shorter are illustrated in the text?

Text 4.1 How to write short sentences

Once your sentence becomes longer than two lines, or around 25 words, like this sentence you are reading now, you should think about making it shorter, by making two or more shorter sentences, or by removing surplus words, or by using a list format.

Here is an example with two shorter sentences:

Once your sentence becomes longer than two lines, or around 25 words, you should think about making it shorter. You could make two or more shorter sentences, remove surplus words, or use a list format.

And here is an example using the list format:

Once your sentence becomes longer than two lines, or around 25 words, you should think about making it shorter. You could:

- create two or more shorter sentences
- remove surplus words
- use a list format.

3.17 Rewrite the following sentence, either by creating two or more shorter sentences or by using a list format:

A contract of employment can be made orally or in writing, but even if the contract is made orally the law requires that some information be provided in writing to the employee, such information to include the names of the employer and employee, job title, amount of pay, hours and place of work, any other benefits and amount of notice to terminate the employment, all of which information is to be given to the employee no later than their first day of work.

3.18 Text 4.1 also suggests removing surplus words to make sentences shorter.

Read the following pairs of sentences. What technique is used in the revised versions of each pair to remove surplus words?

Sentence pair 1	
Original version	I attach a summary of the arguments of the parties.
Revised version	I attach a summary of the parties' arguments.
Sentence pair 2	
Original version	We have the intention of filing a claim.
Revised version	We intend to file a claim.

3.19 Rewrite the following text, removing surplus words:

On 15th February 2022, the Court of Appeal made the decision to dismiss the appeal of the respondents.

The appellants were food delivery drivers and claimed that they had the status of employees. The respondents argued that the drivers were independent contractors. The Employment Tribunal found in favour of the drivers, and the Employment Appeal Tribunal upheld the decision of the lower court.

The argument of the respondents in the Court of Appeal was that the drivers were free to work as much or as little as they wanted. They could also work for other delivery companies.

However, the Court of Appeal found that there was an expectation on the part of the respondents that the drivers would be available at all times, and if there was a refusal by a driver to make a delivery, that driver would be penalised.

The Court of Appeal therefore came to the conclusion that because the respondents had control over the drivers, the drivers were employees.

Use the active voice

3.20 English sentences can be written in the active voice or the passive voice.

a. Rearrange the following boxes to form an active voice sentence:

a memorandum (object)	the trainee (subject)	drafted (verb)

b. Rearrange the following boxes to form a passive voice sentence:

a memorandum (object)	by the trainee (subject)	was drafted (verb)

c. Read the following sentences. In each case, identify the subject, verb, and object in the sentence and decide whether it is written in the active or the passive voice:
   1. The employer must make a redundancy payment to the employee.
   2. A redundancy payment must be made to the employee by the employer.

d. Read the sentences in c. again. Which sentence do you prefer? Why?

3.21 Read Text 4.2 about the active and passive voice and discuss these questions:

a. Why is it preferable to use the active voice in most of your legal writing?

b. When is it appropriate to use the passive voice?

Text 4.2 Active or passive voice?

The active voice and the passive voice are both useful but should be used for different purposes.

Usually, it is better to use the active voice because the subject of the sentence can be identified more easily. This will help your reader to understand the core message of your sentence more effectively. Being clear about the subject of the sentence is particularly important in legal writing: you should use the active voice when you are imposing obligations on someone or explaining who has the responsibility for a certain action.

However, the passive voice is more appropriate where the focus of the sentence is on the object rather than the subject. This is because in a passive voice sentence the object comes first and the subject comes last. The subject can even be entirely removed. For example:

- *The company was fined for anti-competitive practices by the regulatory authority.*

The focus of this sentence is the action of being fined, which is more important than who imposes the fine. The words *'by the regulatory authority'* could be removed from the sentence.

The passive voice can also be useful when you want to avoid responsibility for an action. For example:

- *Mistakes were made and customers' personal data was stolen.*

The focus of this sentence is on the fact that there were mistakes and a data breach. It avoids saying who made the mistakes and who stole the data by removing the subject completely.

3.22 Decide whether the following sentences are in the active or passive voice. If they are in the passive voice, rewrite them in the active voice and if they are in the active voice, rewrite them in the passive voice.

a. Thank you for your email, which was received this morning.
b. The director was assaulted by the sales manager.
c. The claimant has filed a claim at the court.
d. A copy of the claim form is attached.
e. The employer has dismissed the sales manager.
f. The amount of compensation will be negotiated by the parties.

Keep the subject, verb and object together

3.23 The subject, verb, and object provide the core message of the sentence. Lawyers often have extra information that they need to include in a sentence but if you separate the subject, verb and object, it becomes more difficult for the reader to follow.

Read the following example sentence and answer these questions:

a. Identify the subject, verb and object in the sentence. How many words separate the subject from the verb?
b. Where would you place the extra information in this sentence?
c. Rewrite the sentence, keeping the subject, verb and object together. Make two sentences if you need to.

Example sentence
The employer, even if the contract is made orally and no later than the first day of work, must provide a written statement of the main employment terms to the employee.

Practise improving your sentences

3.24 Read the following paragraph from an email of advice from a lawyer to a client. Rewrite this paragraph making sure that you:

- write short sentences
- use the active voice
- keep the subject, verb, and object together.

> I understand that you were told on 31st March 2022 by your manager that there was going to be a relocation of the business and therefore this meant that your offices would be closing and so you would be made redundant, but, however, that you should not worry as a result of this because you would be paid a redundancy payment by your employer. Furthermore, you were offered some other positions by your employer to avoid redundancy, but you explained to your employer that because the hours were not suitable because you had to care for your young children and because you would have to travel too far from home and due to the fact that you had a medical condition which prevented you from undertaking complex tasks, those positions were not suitable.

Skill 4: Use plain English

3.25 What is plain English and how would you define it? Read the following definition of plain language from PLAIN (Plain Language Association International) and compare it with your definition:

> *'A communication is in plain language if its wording, structure, and design are so clear that the intended audience can easily find what they need, understand what they find, and use that information.'*[3]

3.26 Do you agree or disagree with these comments about using plain English in legal writing?

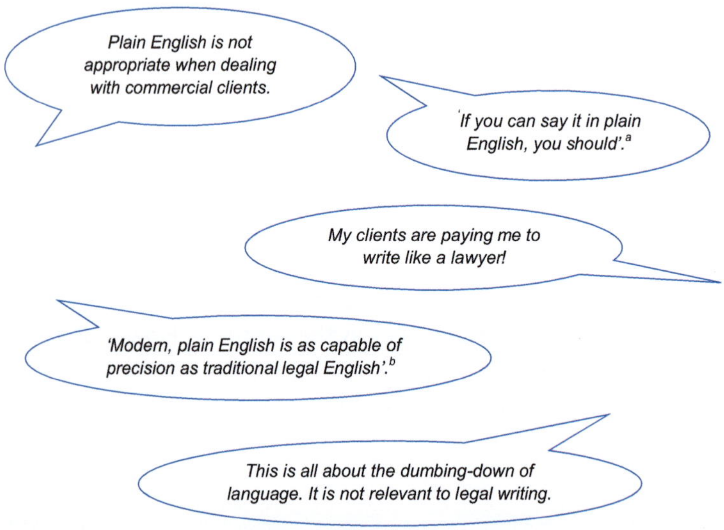

[a]Bryan A Garner, 'Interviews with United States Supreme Court Justices' (2010) 13 The Scribes Journal of Legal Writing 141. [b]Joseph Kimble, *Writing for Dollars, Writing to Please: The Case for Plain Language in Business, Government, and Law* (Kindle edn, Carolina Academic Press 2014) location 636 citing Peter Butt and Richard Castle, *Modern Legal Drafting: A Guide to Using Clearer Language* (2nd edn, Cambridge University Press 2006) 126.

3.27 Audio 4.3

Lawyers have their own jargon and a particular style of writing. We call this lawyerly language *legalese*.

Listen to the conversation between Janice and Sanjit and answer the following questions:

a. Make a note of all the legalese words and expressions that Janice uses.
b. Would you speak like this in real life? If not, then why do lawyers write like this?

3.28 Read the transcript for Audio 4.3 and identify all the legalese.

a. Replace the legalese in Audio 4.3 with plain English, using the words in the following boxes. You may use each word more than once:

this	the	under	despite	
immediately	to	details	if	remaining

b. With a partner, role-play the conversation in Audio 4.3 using your plain English version.

For more examples, see the Legalese to Plain English Quick Reference in Appendix B

Skill 5: Review your writing

3.29 Before you send your legal writing to your reader, remember to take time to review what you have written.

How would you review your writing? Discuss the advantages and disadvantages of the following methods:

a. asking a colleague to review your writing
b. asking a native English speaker to review your writing
c. reading aloud what you have written
d. using a spelling and grammar-checking tool

3.30 The following pairs of sentences show common mistakes in written English. Tick the correct sentence in each pair.

a. Using the wrong verb tense	
O	1. I am acting for this client for over five years (*present continuous tense*).
O	2. I have been acting for this client for over five years (*present perfect continuous tense*).
b. Incorrect agreement between subject and verb	
O	1. The main reason for the redundancies are that there is not enough demand for our products.

O	2. The main reason for the redundancies is that there is not enough demand for our products.
c. Misuse of countable noun	
O	1. I am writing to give you more information on discrimination and harassment claims.
O	2. I am writing to give you more informations on discrimination and harassment claims.
d. Confusing the noun and verb form of a word	
O	1. I am writing with my advise on your claim for damages.
O	2. I am writing with my advice on your claim for damages.
e. Incorrect preposition	
O	1. The quality control manager was responsible for ensuring that there were no defects in the product.
O	2. The quality control manager was responsible of ensuring that there were no defects in the product.

3.31 What mistakes do you make in your writing? Make a checklist of particular aspects of your writing that you need to take care to review.

Test yourself

1. Give an example of an appropriate salutation and closing in an email to a client.
2. How can you organise the points that you want to make in your email or legal document?
3. Explain what a topic sentence is.
4. Describe two techniques for writing shorter sentences.
5. Give one example of legalese and a plain English alternative.

Notes

1 Bryan A Garner, 'Interviews with United States Supreme Court Justices' (2010) 13 The Scribes Journal of Legal Writing 134.

2 Bryan A Garner, *Legal Writing in Plain English* (2nd edn, The University of Chicago Press 2013) 16.

3 Plain Language Association International, 'What is Plain Language?' (*Plain Language Association International)* <https://plainlanguagenetwork.org/> accessed 23 April 2022.

5 Presentations

About this chapter

Overview

This chapter is about giving presentations on a legal topic. The first part introduces the topic and looks at different types of presentations that lawyers give. The second part focuses on preparing a presentation. It contains sections on the introduction, main points, and conclusion of a presentation. It also includes exercises on preparing visual aids, giving feedback, and dealing with questions from the audience. The third part considers some tips for delivering a presentation. The scenario used in this chapter is the preparation of a webinar for clients, but the skills can be used for other types of presentations, including face-to-face presentations.

Learning objectives

By the end of this chapter, you should be able to:

- plan and prepare a presentation on a legal topic
- introduce and conclude a presentation effectively
- create and describe your main presentation slides
- deal with questions about a presentation
- deliver a presentation with confidence

Test yourself at the end of the chapter to check that you have achieved the learning objectives.

1. Introduction

1.1 What types of presentations do lawyers give? Discuss the following examples. What other examples can you add to this list?

1. An in-person seminar for clients	2. A presentation to a potential client in a tender process
3. An online webinar for clients	4. A training session for colleagues in a law firm
5. A presentation of a legal issue by in-house counsel to the company's board of directors	6. A talk on a legal subject at a conference

DOI: 10.4324/9781003140207-5

1.2 Refer to the examples in Exercise 1.1 and discuss your own experience of giving presentations.

You can use the following verbs to express the action of presenting: *to do, to give, to deliver, to present.*

Use the past simple tense to talk about presentations that you gave at a particular time in the past and use the present perfect tense to talk generally about presentations you have given. For example:

Past simple

- *Last week I did a presentation on force majeure in my contract law class.*
- *In April we presented a series of webinars for clients on current trends in commercial litigation.*

Present perfect

- *I have delivered lots of training sessions for the junior lawyers in our department.*
- *I have given elevator pitches at networking events.*

2. Preparing a presentation

Presentation planning

2.1 Angus Wilson is a senior associate in the corporate department at Riley Weaver LLP, an international law firm. Angus is based at the firm's London office. He has just received an email from Matt Hogan, the head of the department. Read the email and answer the following questions:

a. What types of presentations does Matt mention?
b. What does Matt want Angus to do?
c. Where can Angus find more information about giving presentations?

From: Matt Hogan m.hogan@rileyweaver.llp
To: Angus Wilson a.wilson@rileyweaver.llp
Subject: Corporate law presentation

Hi Angus,

As you know, we've created a dedicated team within the department to advise start-ups on all aspects of setting up their businesses. We'd like to launch a series of webinars on corporate law topics, such as funding, tax, regulatory matters, and so on.

I'd really like you to get involved and present the first webinar. I was thinking that you could do something about different types of business structures.

When you have a moment, perhaps we could have a chat about this? You could also speak to the marketing department. I think they have some guidance on giving presentations on behalf of the firm.

Many thanks.

Matt
Partner | Corporate

2.2 Angus has spoken to the marketing department about how to prepare for his webinar on common business structures. They told him he should think about the three Ws: who, what, why. Read his notes and discuss what you would do to prepare for this webinar. Would you add any more questions to this list?

> ***Angus's notes***
>
> ***Remember the 3 Ws: Who, What, Why***
>
> *a. **Who** are the presenters? Who is the intended audience?*
>
> *b. **What** content should I include?*
>
> *c. **Why** am I presenting? What is the aim of the webinar?*

2.3 Audio 5.1

Listen to the conversation between Angus and Matt. What answers does Matt give to Angus's questions in Exercise 2.2?

The introduction

2.4 A presentation usually comprises three sections: the introduction, the main points, and the conclusion.

The purpose of the introduction is to:

- welcome the audience
- introduce yourself
- give the topic of your presentation
- capture your audience's attention
- explain how your presentation is organised

Discuss a presentation you have seen and liked. What did the presenter do in the introduction that was effective?

2.5 Audio 5.2

Listen to Angus and Marcin discussing their webinar. Decide if these statements are true or false and correct any false statements.

	True	False
a. Angus is going to give the introduction to the webinar because he is more experienced than Marcin in corporate law.	O	O
b. The title of the webinar is '*Legal aspects of business organisations for start-ups*'.	O	O
c. Angus needs to plan something to capture the audience's attention.	O	O
d. The presentation will be divided into three main parts.	O	O
e. *Housekeeping* means making sure that the presenters dress appropriately for the webinar.	O	O

2.6 Angus has started preparing the first part of his introduction to the webinar. Read the following three introductions and discuss which introduction is the most appropriate for Angus and Marcin's presentation and why.

Introduction 1
Hello everyone. Thanks very much for joining us today for the first session in our series dedicated to start-ups. I'm Angus Wilson, senior associate at Riley Weaver, and with me is my colleague Marcin Wójcik. Today we're going to be talking about different business structures for start-ups ...

Introduction 2
Good morning, ladies and gentlemen. Thank you everybody for attending our presentation today. Let me start by introducing myself. My name is Angus Wilson and I am a senior associate here at Riley Weaver. Furthermore, I would like to introduce my colleague, Marcin Wójcik, who will be assisting me. The subject of our presentation is the different business structures which are available for start-ups ...

Introduction 3
Hi everyone. I'm Angus and you're watching Riley Weaver's latest webinar. I'll be your host today, and this is Marcin who'll be presenting with me. Stay tuned to hear more about business structures for start-ups ...

2.7 Audio 5.3

Angus has been thinking about how to capture the audience's attention in the introduction to the webinar. He wants to say something that relates to the audience's interests and to the aim of the webinar. Listen to Angus presenting four alternative ideas and answer the following questions:

a. What techniques does Angus use to try to capture the audience's attention?
b. Which idea do you prefer?
c. Can you suggest any other ideas?

2.8 Angus has prepared the last part of his introduction, explaining how the presentation will be organised. Match the first part of his sentences on the left to the second part of his sentences on the right. The first answer is given as an example.

a. *Our presentation is divided into*	1. please put them in the chat box
b. Marcin will start by	2. *three main parts*
c. He will then	3. questions at the end

(Continues on the next page)

d. And finally I will talk	4. we will be recording this webinar
e. Our presentation will last	5. about companies
f. And there will be time for	6. around 30 minutes
g. So, if you have any questions	7. look at partnerships
h. And don't worry if you miss anything as	8. I'll hand over to Marcin to get started
i. So, without further ado	9. explaining sole traders

2.9 Refer to Exercise 2.8. Which expression does Angus use to show that he is moving from the introduction to the main points in the presentation?

2.10 Review the expressions for the introduction to a presentation in Phrase bank 5.1:

Phrase bank 5.1

Welcome the audience

Hello/Good morning/good afternoon everyone/ladies and gentlemen.

Thank you all for being here/joining me today.

Thank you all for coming along to hear my presentation today.

Introduce yourself

So, just to introduce myself, I'm [name] and I'm [a senior associate] here at [law firm].

First, I'll introduce myself. My name is [name] and I'm [position].

I'll begin by introducing myself ...

Introduce someone else

And with me is [name].

And I would like to introduce [name].

Give the topic of your presentation

Today I'm going to talk about ...

The subject of my presentation is ...

Refer to your aim

The aim of this presentation is to ...

My aim today is to ...

Explain how your presentation is organised

My presentation will take [duration of time].

I'm going to talk about [three] main issues.

My presentation is divided into [three] main parts.

There are [three] key points that I would like to cover today.

I will start by ... then I will look at ... and finally I will talk about ...

If you have any questions, please feel free to interrupt me.

If you have any questions, please could you save these until the end of the presentation.

If you have any questions, please put these in the [chat/Q&A box] and I will answer these at the end of the presentation.

This presentation is being recorded.

Moving from the introduction to the main points

So, let me start by explaining [first main point].

I'll move on now to my first main point.

Without further ado, let's make a start.

I'll now hand over to [name] to get started.

2.11 Practise giving the introduction to a presentation using the expressions from Phrase bank 5.1. You can either practise the introduction to Angus and Marcin's webinar or you can choose your own topic. Some topic ideas are given in the following boxes:

Common business structures in your jurisdiction	A recent news story about business law
Intellectual property issues for new businesses	When do I need a non-disclosure agreement?

When giving your introduction, remember to:

- welcome the audience
- introduce yourself
- give the topic of your presentation
- capture your audience's attention
- explain how your presentation is organised

The main points

Signalling your main points

2.12 The middle section of your presentation is where you explain your main points. Angus and Marcin's presentation will include three main points:

- sole traders
- partnerships
- companies

They need to help the audience follow their presentation by signalling when they move between these points.

The following expressions can be used to signal the main points in a presentation. Match the situations on the left with the expressions on the right. There are two expressions for each situation. The first answer is given as an example.

Situation	Expression
a. *The presentation of Marcin's first point about sole traders* (→ 2) b. The end of Marcin's first point about sole traders c. The presentation of Marcin's second point about partnerships d. The presentation of Angus's point about companies	1. I will now hand over to [name] to talk about the next point ... 2. *The first point is ...* 3. This leads me to my next point ... 4. That's all I was going to say about [topic]. 5. Moving on to my next point ... 6. [Name] will now speak about [topic]. 7. The first topic I'm going to talk about is ... 8. That brings me to the end of my first point.

Visual aids

2.13 Depending on the type of presentation, try to vary how you present your main points to keep your audience engaged. One way of doing this is by changing speaker, like Angus and Marcin. Another way is to use visual aids.

Read the following boxes, which contain some examples of visual aids, and answer these questions:

a. Are you familiar with these visual aids?
b. Can you give any other examples of visual aids?

c. Refer to your discussion about the types of presentations that lawyers give in Exercise 1.1. Which visual aids could you use in those presentations?

slides	handout	flip chart	whiteboard	poll

2.14 Angus and Marcin have decided to use slides in their webinar. Read the following two slides that Marcin has prepared. Slide 1 is Riley Weaver LLP's standard title slide and Slide 2 is a slide that Marcin has written himself. What improvements could Marcin make to Slide 2?

Slide 1

Riley Weaver LLP

Which business structure is right for my start-up?

Angus Wilson
Senior associate
a.wilson@rileyweaver.llp

Marcin Wójcik
Senior associate
m.wojcik@rileyweaver.llp

Slide 2

Sole proprietorship

A sole proprietorship is an unincorporated business structure with an individual owner. A sole proprietor has full control of their business and is entitled to keep all of their profits after tax. On the other hand the business is not a separate legal entity from the owner and so the owner has unlimited liability for any debts of their business. Hence creditors may be able to seize the owner's personal assets and their home. However, this type of business organisation is the easiest to establish as there is no requirement to file any forms or accounts at Companies House.

2.15 Audio 5.4

Listen to Angus giving Marcin some feedback on the slides in Exercise 2.14 and answer the following questions:

a. What improvements does Angus suggest to Slide 2? Compare his suggestions with your answer in Exercise 2.14.

b. Rewrite Slide 2, using Angus and Marcin's suggestions and the following template:

RILEY WEAVER LLP

Sole trader

- Owns and runs a business alone
- Advantages
  -
  -
  -
- Disadvantages
  -
  -

Giving feedback

2.16 Giving feedback is an important skill for international lawyers working together. Listen to Audio 5.4 again and tick the expressions that Angus uses to give feedback to Marcin.

O	a. *This is a really good point.*
O	b. *I like the way you ...*
O	c. *Have you thought about ...?*
O	d. *It might be useful to ...*
O	e. *It might be a good idea to ...*
O	f. *Perhaps it would be better to ...*
O	g. *I wonder whether you should ...*
O	h. *You could ...*

2.17 Styles of feedback vary across cultures. Feedback can be direct, for example, '*Your presentation is too long*', or indirect, for example, '*Have you considered a shorter presentation?*'

Refer to Exercise 2.16 and discuss these questions:

a. Would you describe the style of Angus's feedback as direct or indirect?

b. How do you give feedback in your culture?

2.18 Practise writing slides and giving feedback with a partner.

Write a slide on a topic of your choice or use the following notes prepared by Marcin to write a slide on the topic of partnerships. Check the Glossary for definitions.
Remember to:

- summarise with bullet points and key words
- write in language that your audience can understand
- give feedback to your partner on their slide

Marcin's notes on partnerships

A partnership is another type of unincorporated structure but involves two or more people who own and run their business together.

The advantage of this business structure is that the partners can share the costs and the running of the business. They share the profits of the business but also have unlimited liability for the losses. The partners are jointly and severally liable which means that creditors may be able to seize one partner's personal assets and home even if debts were incurred by another partner.

Like sole traders, it is easy to form a partnership as there is no requirement to file any forms or accounts at Companies House. However, there is the potential for partnerships to lead to disagreements and so it is advisable for partners to enter into a partnership agreement to govern their relationship.

Describing a slide

2.19 Angus has found some interesting statistics[1] about different types of business structures and he would like to include these in his part of the presentation. He has created a chart in the following slide. According to the chart, which was the most popular type of business structure chosen by UK private sector businesses in 2021?

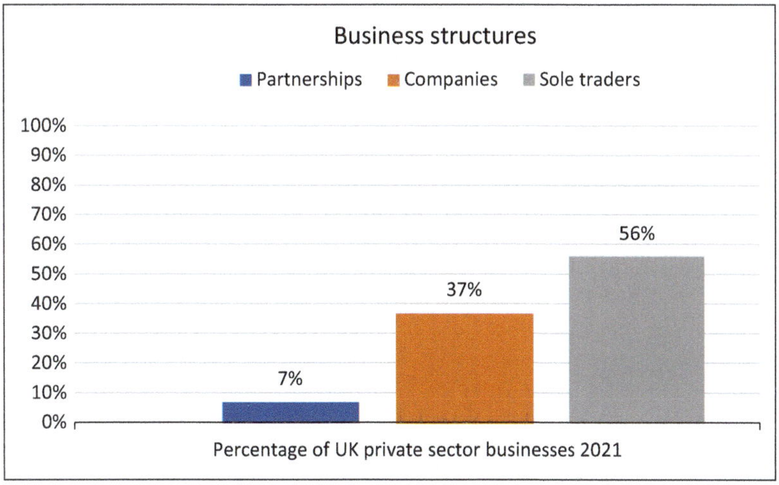

2.20 Review the expressions for describing a slide in Phrase bank 5.2:

Phrase bank 5.2	
Explaining the information on a slide	**Describing the different parts of a slide**
I'd like you to have a look at this chart/graph/ diagram. It shows ...	*At the top of the slide you can see ...*
According to this chart/graph/diagram ...	*At the bottom of the slide you can see ...*
I'd like to draw your attention to ...	*If you look on the left/right ...*
As you can see from the title, this slide is about ...	*On the left/right hand side, there is ...*
	In the middle/centre ...
	On the top left/right ...
	On the bottom left/right ...
	At the top in the middle/centre ...

2.21 Practise describing Angus's slide in Exercise 2.19, using the expressions from Phrase bank 5.2.

The conclusion

2.22 Make it clear when your presentation is over and remember to check that you have achieved the objectives that you set at the beginning.

A good conclusion will:

- indicate to the audience that the presentation is coming to an end
- refer to the objectives of the presentation
- summarise the key points that have been made
- thank the audience for attending
- invite the audience to ask questions

Discuss whether the following is a good conclusion to Angus and Marcin's webinar:

To conclude, the aim of this webinar was to help you understand more about the common types of structures chosen by start-ups. We have discussed three main types of legal structures today: sole traders, partnerships, and companies.

So, which business structure will you choose? As we have seen, most small businesses choose the sole trader structure, mainly because this is easy to set up and operate. It is more expensive to form a company, and your accounts will be public if you choose this structure. But remember that the advantage of a company is that it limits your personal responsibility for business debts.

In the next webinar, we will look at the tax implications of different types of business structures, so don't forget to sign up. You will find the link on our website and I will put it in the chat box.

Thank you everybody for listening. We now have 15 minutes for some questions.

Dealing with questions

2.23 Audio 5.5

Listen to Angus and Marcin talking about the Q&A part of their presentation and answer the following questions. The acronym Q&A stands for the question and answer session.

a. Why is the Q&A one of the most difficult parts of a presentation?
b. What can you do to prepare for the Q&A?
c. What expressions do Angus and Marcin use to give themselves time to think of an answer to a question?
d. Why does Marcin like Angus's Pharmaroo example?
e. What can you do if you do not know the answer to a question?

2.24 Review the expressions for dealing with questions in Phrase bank 5.3:

Phrase bank 5.3	
Giving yourself time to think	***Referring to an earlier point***
That's a good question. *Can I just check I've understood you correctly?* *I'm pleased you've asked that question.*	*As I said at the beginning/end of the presentation* *As [I/name] said earlier* *To echo what [name] said*
Saying that you don't know the answer	***Saying that you will respond later***
I will have to check the answer to that question and get back to you. *Sorry, that is not my area of expertise. I will ask one of my colleagues and get back to you.*	*I don't have enough time to answer that now. Could I contact you after the presentation?* *I'd be happy to talk to you separately about that. Please drop me an email. My contact details are on this slide.*

2.25 Practise dealing with questions with a partner. Read the following two questions that Angus and Marcin anticipate in their presentation and then take it in turns to ask and respond to the questions. When responding to the questions, use the expressions in Phrase bank 5.3 and refer to Angus's notes with some suggested answers.

Question 1 Can you explain some of the tax implications of the different business structures?
Question 2 One thing I'm concerned about is intellectual property rights. How do I protect the brand I have created?

> ***Angus's notes***
>
> *Question 1. Refer to the conclusion where I said that the next webinar will cover this topic.*
>
> *Question 2. This is outside our expertise. We will have to ask someone from our IP team to contact them.*

3. Delivering a presentation

3.1 Read the following quote from the introduction to Patrick Barry's book *Good with Words: Speaking and Presenting*.[2] Do you agree with what he says? In what other ways would you describe a good presenter?

> *Good speakers and presenters do something magical, valuable, and rare: they hold our attention.*

3.2 Marcin is nervous about presenting the webinar. Read Text 5.1 on top tips for delivering a presentation, written by Riley Weaver's marketing department. What tips would you add to this list?

Text 5.1 Top tips for delivering a presentation

Feeling nervous about giving a presentation on behalf of the firm? That's perfectly normal. Follow our top tips to success on the day:

1. **Be confident and enthusiastic.** It is a good idea to practise your opening lines until you know them by heart, so that you sound confident at the start of your presentation. Sound interested in what you are talking about. And remember to smile!
2. **Think about your body language and your gestures**. You could do a trial run and ask a colleague to comment on any annoying habits that you need to eliminate.
3. **Dress appropriately**. Even if you are presenting remotely, remember to dress professionally.
4. **Maintain eye contact with your audience**. It is OK to have a few notes but try not to look at them too much or you will lose the connection with your audience. On the other hand, do not stare too much at one person. Keep your gaze balanced around the room.
5. **Project your voice.** Make sure that you speak loudly and clearly enough so that your audience can hear you. Articulate your words correctly and check the pronunciation of any unfamiliar words.

Contact us if you need more assistance: marketing@rileyweaver.llp

3.3 Audio 5.6

Listen to Marcin practising part of his presentation with Angus. What three tips does Angus mention that can be added to Text 5.1?

3.4 Practise preparing and delivering a presentation to a partner. Choose whether you are going to be the presenter or the audience. Read your instructions and give the presentation. After you have finished, switch roles.

Presenter instructions

Prepare a presentation on business structures in your jurisdiction or choose another topic. In your presentation, make sure you:

- include an introduction, main points, and a conclusion
- use appropriate expressions to signal your main points
- describe visual aids
- include a Q&A

Use the tips that you discussed in Exercises 3.2 and 3.3 to deliver a successful presentation.

Audience instructions

Listen to your partner's presentation. Make sure that you:

- complete the peer-assessment questions in Appendix A while you are listening
- ask a question at the end of the presentation
- give feedback to the presenter after the presentation, using the expressions from Exercise 2.16

3.5 Reflect on your presentation in Exercise 3.4 using the self-assessment questions in Appendix A.

Test yourself

1. What three Ws should you think about when planning a presentation?
2. Give two ideas for capturing your audience's attention in your introduction.
3. Do you need to use complete sentences when writing presentation slides? Why?
4. Explain one expression you can use if you do not know the answer to a question in a presentation.
5. Give one tip for being more confident in a presentation.

Notes

1 Department for Business, Energy & Industrial Strategy, 'Business Population Estimates for the UK and the Regions 2021' (October 2021) <https://www.gov.uk/government/statistics/business-population-estimates-2021> accessed 27 April 2022.
2 Patrick Barry, *Good with Words: Speaking and Presenting* (Kindle edn, Michigan Publishing 2021) 2.

6 Social media marketing

About this chapter

Overview

This chapter is about using legal English for marketing yourself and your law firm on social media.

The first part introduces how lawyers use social media. The second part looks at setting up a profile on different social media platforms, using SEO, and building your network. The third part looks at ways to engage with your connections and includes practical activities to stay active on social media. It first looks at simple engagement techniques, such as writing short posts and commenting on content. It then looks at the more advanced engagement techniques of creating your own content, including podcast episodes and blog posts. The chapter ends with an exercise to plan your social media strategy.

Learning objectives

By the end of this chapter, you should be able to:

- create a social media profile optimised for search engines
- recognise how language and style reflects a brand
- use techniques to build your social media network and find content to follow
- understand legal issues which can arise on social media
- explain different ways of engaging on social media

Test yourself at the end of the chapter to check that you have achieved the learning objectives.

1. Introduction

1.1 Discuss the following questions about social media:

a. What is social media?

b. How many social media platforms can you name?

c. In what ways can lawyers use social media?

1.2 The American Bar Association carried out a survey asking over 10,000 US lawyers about their social media usage.[1] The results showed that 80% of both law firms and individual lawyers have a presence on social media, with LinkedIn™ being the most popular. 31% of individual lawyers said they got clients as a result of social media.

DOI: 10.4324/9781003140207-6

Discuss the following questions:

a. Would you get the same survey results in your country? Why?
b. Which social media platforms do you use for professional purposes? Why?

1.3 Read Text 6.1 and choose the correct preposition to complete each gap. You may use each preposition more than once.

with	in	to	on	of	as

Text 6.1 Social media marketing for lawyers

Nowadays, one (a)_______ the most popular ways to market yourself or your law firm is social media marketing. Social media marketing is the activity of using social media platforms to encourage people or companies to buy your products or services. For example, you could use social media to promote:

- yourself, to get work opportunities
- your law firm, to gain clients.

The first step towards marketing yourself or your law firm is to create a profile (b)_______ a social media platform. A strong social media profile tells people who you are, what you do, and how you can help them.

The next step is to build your network. Connect (c)_______ people and companies that post content relevant (d)_______ your legal practice area. This will help you stay up to date (e)__ legal developments and business news. You should also connect with your target audience. If you are looking for work, your target audience could be recruiters who may hire you. If you are looking for clients, your target audience could be people or companies who may be interested (f)_______ your legal services.

Once you have set up your social media profile and begun building your network, there is still another important part of social media marketing to consider. You must raise awareness (g)_______ and build trust (h)_______ your services. A simple way to do this is to like, comment on, and share your connection's content, as well as write your own short posts. Another effective way, which requires more effort, is to create and share your own quality content, such as blog posts and podcasts.

Staying active and engaging with your connections can establish you (i)_______ an expert in your legal field and is key to marketing yourself or your law firm successfully on social media.

2. Creating your profile and building your network

LinkedIn™

LinkedIn™ is a social network focusing on professional networking and career development where you can create a personal profile or company page. This section focuses on creating a personal profile.

Different profile sections

2.1 A LinkedIn™ profile contains the following sections. Read the following profile sections and discuss what information you would include in each one.

a. Personal information	b. About	c. Experience	d. Education
e. Licenses & certifications*	f. Volunteer experience	g. Interests	
h. Skills & endorsements	i. Recommendations	j. Accomplishments	

***Vocabulary note:** *licence* or *license*

In AmE, *license* as a noun and a verb is spelt with an *s*. This is what LinkedIn™ uses. In BrE, *licence* as a noun is spelt with a *c* and *license* as a verb is spelt with an *s*.

2.2 Audio 6.1

Listen to the conversation between two students, Ethan and Sofia, who are studying for a master's degree in law. They have just attended a seminar given by Linda Hughes, a careers adviser. She spoke to them about the importance of having a LinkedIn™ profile and tips for improving it.

Decide if these statements are true or false and correct any false statements:

	True	False
a. Ethan and Sofia have completed all sections in their profiles.	○	○
b. Sofia will add some law-firm voluntary experience to her profile.	○	○
c. Non-legal work positions should not be included on your profile.	○	○
d. Updating your current position can lead to more profile views.	○	○
e. Ethan and Sofia will help each other update and proofread their profiles.	○	○

2.3 In Audio 6.1, the students mentioned *transferable skills*. What are *transferable skills*? What transferable skills does Ethan mention?

Making your profile stand out

2.4 Read Text 6.2 about SEO and answer the following questions:

a. What does the acronym *SEO* stand for?
b. How does a search engine choose which results to show a user?
c. How can you improve the search engine ranking of your LinkedIn™ profile?

Text 6.2 SEO for lawyers

People use the internet to search for things. When a user searches for '*Commercial lawyer in Beijing*', the search engine will provide results which it considers will be helpful. But how does the search engine choose which results to show? There are many different factors that the search engine takes into account, including whether or not the keywords the user is searching for are present in the online content.

If your LinkedIn™ profile states, '*I am a commercial lawyer in Beijing specialising in complex commercial litigation*' the search engine is more likely to display your profile in the search results than if it said, '*Chinese lawyer*'. This is because the search terms *commercial, lawyer,* and *Beijing* are present in the profile.

SEO stands for search engine optimisation. It refers to the way of improving your online content so that you increase your chances of appearing in relevant search results.

For your LinkedIn™ profile to rank highly in search results, you must have a complete and up-to-date profile which contains keywords. In practical terms, this means that your target audience – be it clients, recruiters, or other professionals – will be able to find you more easily.

2.5 Think about your own LinkedIn™ profile and discuss the following questions:

a. Who is your target audience?
b. What search terms do you think your target audience would use to find you?
c. What is your job position, location, and specialisation? If you are a student, where are you studying and what is your course?
d. What five keywords could you include in your profile to ensure that your target audience can find you?

Headline

2.6 Your LinkedIn™ Headline tells people what you do in a few words. It is one of the first things someone will see when:

- they visit your profile page
- you post on the home feed
- you feature in the search results on LinkedIn™

Ethan has updated his Headline. Do you prefer his original or updated Headline? Why?

Original Headline	**Updated Headline**
Ethan Mowry	**Ethan Mowry**
Law student	Job seeker, training contract in law firm • LLB LLM • Participant in international mooting competition • Interested in privacy & data protection law
London, United Kingdom	London, United Kingdom

2.7 Write your own Headline. If you already have a LinkedIn™ profile, rewrite your Headline to improve it. Remember to include information about:

- what you do
- how you can help your target audience
- keywords to boost SEO

If you are a student, use Ethan's updated example in Exercise 2.6 as a guide. If you are a practising lawyer, use the following examples as a guide.

Tim Hubble

Data protection lawyer | CEO of Express Law | Helping companies achieve compliance with privacy laws

London, UK

Mia Tremblay

White collar crime lawyer with 10+ years' experience representing companies in corruption and fraud cases seeks new full-time position

Toronto, Canada

About section

2.8 Your LinkedIn™ About section comes after the Headline. This is your chance to summarise who you are as a legal professional. Completing this part allows recruiters or potential clients to find out more about you.

Read the following example About sections. Which example do you prefer and why?

Example 1

Tim is a UK and US qualified lawyer and after making partner in a large law firm he went on to found Express Law. Tim is a data protection lawyer focused on helping businesses achieve compliance with privacy laws.

Example 2

My work

I am the CEO of Express Law, the award-winning NewLaw firm. Since 2015 Express Law has been helping businesses with legal issues in the fields of information technology, cyber security, and privacy and data protection.

In my position as leader of the Data Protection Team, I advise businesses and corporations on all core aspects of data privacy, including:

- compliance with the General Data Protection Regulation (GDPR)
- maintaining data security
- responding to data breaches

My credentials

- Qualified lawyer: UK qualified solicitor and US qualified attorney
- Previously partner at magic circle law firm Wallace Clunes LLP
- Winner of the International Legal Innovator prize

My contact details

If you are interested in legal tech or need help with data protection:

- connect with me: on LinkedIn™
- email me: tim.hubble@express-law.ai
- visit: www.express-law.ai

2.9 Write your own About section using Example 2 in Exercise 2.8 and the following template. If you already have a LinkedIn™ profile, rewrite your About section to improve it. Remember to include keywords to boost SEO and if you do not have much legal experience include information about your transferable skills.

Template About section

Heading 1: My work/What do I do?

Lawyer: I am a [*type of lawyer*]. I help [*type of clients*] achieve [*goal*] by providing [*service*].
Student: I am currently studying [*course*] at [*university*]. Modules include:

- [*course modules*]

Heading 2: My credentials/What are my credentials?

Lawyer: In my position as [*job title*], I [*advise clients on/represent clients in*] the following matters:

- [*specific areas of expertise*]

Student: Throughout university I have gained experience and transferable skills relevant to a legal career. For example:

- [*how you developed transferable skills*]

Heading 3: My contact details/How can we connect?

Lawyer and Student: I am interested in connecting with [*target audience*]. Reach out to me on:

- Email: [*email address*]
- Website: [*website link*]

Experience section

2.10 Audio 6.2

Your LinkedIn™ Experience section showcases your past and present work experience. Each position can include:

- job title
- name of employer
- job location
- work responsibilities

Listen to Ethan and Sofia discussing Ethan's work experience and complete his Experience section. Each space represents one word. The first answer is given as an example.

Experience

Job title
(a) *Receptionist*

Employment type (full-time, part-time, self-employed, freelance, contract, internship)
(b) _______ - _______

Company name
(c) _______ and _______ LLP

Location
(d) _______ _______

Start date (e) ___________ this year **End date** Present

Description
In my position at this niche (f) _________________ law firm I take pride in being the first face-to-face contact for clients before they see one of our lawyers specialising in the fields of IT, e-commerce, and data protection law. My duties involve:

- (g) ___________ client meetings
- (h) ___________ solicitors' calendars
- (i) ___________ a high-volume of client calls

Skills

(j) _________________, time-management, customer service

2.11 LinkedIn™ also has a Volunteer experience section to highlight skills developed in unpaid positions.

Discuss an example of either your work experience or your volunteer experience that could be included in your LinkedIn™ profile. Remember to include:

- position title
- company name
- description of responsibilities
- transferable skills you developed

Education section

2.12 A strong academic background is important for any legal professional and can be highlighted in your LinkedIn™ Education section.

Read the following example from Ethan's Education section and choose the correct preposition to complete each gap. You may use each preposition more than once. Some gaps do not need a preposition.

on	of	for	in	to	at

Education

University of London
Bachelor's degree (LLB) Law, First Class Hons 2018–2021

Activities and societies
Throughout my law degree, I was actively involved (a)_________ the university's Mooting Society. In my first year I participated (b)_________ the International Mooting Competition where I developed my advocacy skills and in my second year I was elected treasurer (c)_________ the Mooting Society which helped me develop commercial awareness. I first discovered IT law when I was preparing (d)_________ a moot and I immediately became interested (e)_________ this topic.

Description
I studied law (f)_________ the University of London, taking compulsory core modules and choosing electives tailored to a career (g)_________ commercial law. At university I developed a range of skills, including research, legal analysis, and attention (h)_________ detail. I attended (i)_________ lunch-time lectures given by external experts to strengthen my knowledge in IT law. In my final year, I was awarded (j)_________ a prize for my dissertation 'Compliance with Data Protection Law'. It focused (k)_________ IT law because in the future I hope to specialise (l)_________ this area.

2.13 Complete the following table with your own education example. If you have already completed the Education section of your LinkedIn™ profile, try to improve it. Remember to include the following information:

- academic institution where you studied
- course title
- course start and end date
- grade you achieved
- extracurricular activities you participated in
- course description
- transferable skills

School	
Degree	
Start Year	**End Year**
Grade	
Activities and societies	
Description	

Skills & endorsements section

2.14 The Skills & endorsements section of your LinkedIn™ profile allows you to write keywords to highlight your abilities. Adding five or more skills can lead to 17 times more profile views and 27 times more profile features in search results.[2] Your connections can endorse you for each skill that you add, which establishes credibility and builds trust.

What five skills could you add to your profile? Some ideas are given in the following boxes:

Contract negotiation	Arbitration	Legal English

Recommendations section

2.15 Your LinkedIn™ Recommendations section comes after the Skills & endorsements section. In this section, you can ask for a recommendation from a connection by sending them a message. They can then respond by posting a recommendation on your profile.

Which of the following recommendation examples are more credible and why?

Example 1

I am the world's best lawyer.

Tim Hubble

Example 2

I truly believe Tim is one of the best lawyers I've ever had the pleasure of working with. Our company highly appreciates his pragmatic approach and commercially astute advice.

Jonathan Hargraves, Founder, InterEX

2.16 Audio 6.3

Listen to Ethan and Sofia discussing Ethan's recommendation request message to Sarah Draper, his supervisor at Fish and Friar LLP. Rewrite Ethan's recommendation request message so that it is more polite.

Recommendation request message Hey Sarah Thanks for being my supervisor at Fish and Friar LLP. I've learnt a lot during my time working for you!! (a)
I want you to write me a recommendation highlighting my knowledge of commercial law and interest in IT law. (b)

I need to get a training contract so I need your recommendation to build my credibility. (c)
Cheers Ethan (d)

Sending a connection request

2.17 After completing your profile, you should add relevant connections to build your LinkedIn™ network. For example, you may want to connect with someone you:

- work/worked with to ask about a job opportunity
- study/studied with to ask for their expertise
- met at an event to suggest collaborating

Who would you want to connect with and why?

2.18 When you send a connection request on LinkedIn™, you have the option to send a request with no message or with a customised message. Discuss what type of request you would prefer to receive from a person you:

- know well
- met once at a conference
- have never met and do not know

2.19 Ethan wants to connect with Tim Hubble. As they have never met before, Ethan writes a customised message. Read Ethan's connection request and use it to help you to write a personalised message to someone you want to connect with.

Salutation:	*Dear Tim*
Connecting reason:	*I saw your recent post about speeding up contracting with automated privacy policy drafting software. As a master's student I'm currently studying data protection law and I'm fascinated by legal tech. This topic really interests me and I'm curious to learn more. I'd love to connect to stay updated on your posts and know more about your work.*
Closing:	*All the best* *Ethan Mowry*

Other social media profiles

Developing your brand

2.20 Tim Hubble was impressed with Ethan's proactive approach in sending a connection request. He invited Ethan for an interview and offered him a training contract. In his first week at Express Law, Ethan receives the following email from Tim. Read the email and discuss what Ethan needs to do.

From: Tim Hubble tim.hubble@express-law.ai
To: Ethan Mowry ethan.mowry@express-law.ai
Subject: Social media profile and engagement

Hi Ethan

How's it going? It'd be great if you could set yourself up another profile on social media this week. Some of our clients (and potential clients) hang out on Twitter™ and Instagram™ – so we should too! 😎

You can easily set up a profile with the following info:

- profile name, e.g. *Ethan Mowry*
- username, e.g. @Ethan_Mowry
- short description, e.g. *I advise businesses on legal matters related to IT law and data protection ...*

Just make sure your profile reflects the firm's brand! People see us as modern, professional, personal, simple, efficient, and business-focused. 😉

Once you're all set up, find some hashtags to follow, e.g. #bigdata #cloudcomputing #techlawyers so you can start engaging. And use relevant hashtags in your profile and posts so that people can find you ...

Cheers

Tim

Express Law ⚡ ***Modern lawyers for innovators***

2.21 Tim's email in Exercise 2.20 mentions *brand*. A *brand* is a set of beliefs we have about the identity of a person or company. A brand is developed through the products and services of a company and maintained through communications which reflect the company's identity.

Ethan has created two bios for his social media profile, but he is not sure which one reflects Express Law's brand of being *modern, professional, personal, simple, efficient, and business-focused*. Read the examples and discuss these questions:

a. Which one do you prefer and why?
b. Which one best reflects Express Law's brand and why?

Example 1

Ethan Mowry

👩‍⚖️♂ #commercialtraineelawyer

📱 #ITlaw & #dataprotection

💬 I give straight-forward legal advice to help your business succeed

🌐 www.express-law.ai

Example 2

Ethan Mowry

Ethan is a trainee commercial lawyer at Express Law, a markedly unique law firm, with a sophisticated and sincere team of adept lawyers who advise businesses on complex technology law and data protection matters.

2.22 Think about your own personal brand and discuss these questions:

a. What adjectives do you want people to associate with you as a legal professional? Some ideas are given in the following boxes:

Traditional	Honest	Reliable	Accurate	International
Creative	Cutting-edge	Winners	Ambitious	Caring

b. How can your social media profile reflect your personal brand?

Discovering people and content

2.23 In his email, Tim mentioned that Ethan should follow some hashtags. The hashtag '#' symbol can be used to find people and companies to follow which are in line with your interests. Using relevant hashtags in your profile also helps other people discover you.

Discuss what hashtags you would use:

- to find people and content aligned with your interests
- in your own profile to help other people discover you

Some ideas are given in the following boxes:

#contractdrafting	#commerciallaw	#englishforlawyers	#lawupdates	
#lawyer	#lawfirm	#litigator	#legalservices	#lawstudent

3. Engaging with your connections

This section is about engaging with your connections by staying active on social media.

Legal issues

3.1 Audio 6.4

When engaging on social media, lawyers, like anyone else, must comply with the law. Additionally, in many jurisdictions lawyers belong to a regulated profession, and must behave in accordance with their code of conduct.

Listen to some lawyers talking about issues which can arise on social media. Match the lawyer to the issue. The first answer is given as an example.

Lawyer	Issue
a. *Christina* →	1. Witness tampering
b. Helena	2. *Unintentionally creating a lawyer–client relationship*
c. Giovanni	3. Infringing intellectual property rights
d. Patrizia	4. Breaching the duty to act with integrity
e. Edmund	5. Breaching client confidentiality

3.2 Listen to Audio 6.4 again. How could the lawyers avoid these issues in the future?

3.3 Review the expressions for giving an opinion and talking about social media issues in Phrase bank 6.1:

Phrase bank 6.1	
Giving an opinion	**Social media issues**
In my opinion, lawyers can/cannot post whatever they want on social media because ...	*If a lawyer posts something incorrect on social media, they could be held liable because ...*
If you ask me, posting on social media is/is not different for legal professionals compared to other professionals because ...	*A lawyer has a duty to act with integrity and must be professional on social media, for example ...*
My view is that lawyers should be careful when posting on social media because ...	*A lawyer has a duty to maintain client confidentiality therefore ...*
My position on this is that I highly doubt a lawyer would face any issues for posting on social media because ...	*If a lawyer connects with witnesses in a court case, this could be a problem because ...*

3.4 Give your opinion on the following statements about posting on social media. Use the expressions in Phrase bank 6.1.

- Legal professionals cannot post whatever they want on social media.
- Posting on social media is different for legal professionals compared to other professionals.

Posting on social media
Commenting and sharing

3.5 Some people avoid engaging on social media because they think it requires too much time and effort. Two ways to engage with minimal effort are:

- sharing other people's content; and
- commenting on other people's posts.

When you share other people's content, simply add one sentence saying what the content is about, for example: *Here is an interesting article about preventing cyberattacks.*

Simple ways to comment on other people's posts include:

- asking a question about the post
- answering a question about the post
- tagging someone who should read the post
- congratulating the author

What other ways can you comment on a post?

3.6 Review the expressions for commenting on a social media post in Phrase bank 6.2:

Phrase bank 6.2

Asking a question

Thank you for this post. Could you tell me where I can find more information about [topic]?

I read your post and found it very helpful. I'm not sure I understood the part about [specific topic] correctly. Could you please clarify what you meant by [quote from post]?

Answering a question

In your post, you asked the question [quote question from post]. From what I understand, a possible answer could be ...

Tagging someone

[tag person], I think this could be an interesting post for you.

[tag person], you could be interested in this.

Congratulating the author

That's great news! I wish you all the best.

Well done [name of author]! What a great achievement.

Congratulations! Good luck with this new role.

3.7 Read the following posts and respond to each one using the technique stated under each post. Use Exercises 3.5 and 3.6 as a guide.

Mari Osborne @mari.s.oborne

It's not every week that ends with such fantastic news. I am truly honoured to be a finalist for the top ten arbitration lawyers in Asia for the International Lawyer Association for Alternative Dispute Resolution Awards. The online award ceremony will take place on 25th November at 5:30 UK time. Register (no fee) at: https://lnk/7725narb

#arbitration #adr #internationallawyer

Comment on this post:

Salim Ahmed Founding Director of Clear Legal Language Ltd

The top skill for international lawyers nowadays is the ability to use plain English. Business clients do not want to see legal jargon. Here's a picture of a force majeure clause I rewrote as part of the 'Clear Legal Writing and Drafting Course' I'm currently studying. Do you prefer legalese or plain English?

#plainenglish #legalese #contractdrafting

Share this content adding one sentence:

Writing posts

3.8 On many social media platforms, you can post your own content or share content from other authors. Some platforms allow you to write long posts and others limit the word count. You can share posts on the following topics:

- work opportunities
- client feedback
- company, industry, or professional news
- helpful tips and resources

Read the following example posts and discuss these questions:

a. What is each post about?
b. Are social media posts more informal than other types of legal writing? Why?
c. Who could each post be helpful for and why?
d. What impact could each post have on the author's reputation?

EXAMPLE 1

I'd like to share with you a video I made on top data protection issues businesses are facing and how to deal with them. Data protection is one of the hottest topics right now for legal compliance, so don't get left behind. Click the link to watch the video. I'd love your feedback on the video, so please comment below. Was this relevant for you? How are you dealing with these issues? www.vidi.tv/data-protection

#dataprotection #datacompliance #GDPR

EXAMPLE 2

At #JNPMediaLLP, our media lawyers @jnp_llp_media_lawyers @jnp_media_llp can't wait for the judgment in the important #JimmyDay libel case ⏱👀. Judgment's about to be given live & could have major implications for our media clients! ⚖ #medialaw #libel #defamation

EXAMPLE 3

HOW CAN ROBOTS BE JUDGES!!!!???? ...... THIS ARTICLE SAYS THAT BY 2050 ROBOT JUDGES WILL BE THE NORM IN COURTS! ...... RUBBISH!!!!!!!! I AIN'T GONNA HAVE NO ROBOT JUDGE DECIDE MY CASES!!!

EXAMPLE 4

Welcome Wilko van Willers, who joins our law firm's expanding global antitrust team in Paris. Find out more about our team and career opportunities with us here: http://lnk/a553f

3.9 Review the expressions for writing a social media post in Phrase bank 6.3:

Phrase bank 6.3

Work opportunities

Our firm is recruiting. Find out more about our career opportunities here: [website link].

Client feedback

Here is what our clients are saying about our services [positive feedback quote]. Thank you for your feedback, it makes our work worthwhile!

What a fantastic testimonial [client testimonial]. It was a pleasure to assist you with your [matter description].

Company or industry news

[news story title] is relevant for [industry name] for three reasons: [reasons].

At [law firm name], we are eagerly awaiting the [judgment/enactment of new law]. This is important for the [industry name] because [reasons]. What are your thoughts on this topic?

Today we welcome [employee name] to our firm, who is joining our [department name].

Professional news

I am honoured to share with you that I am a finalist in [award name]/have been awarded [award name].

I am happy to make this announcement. Today is my first day at [law firm name], where I'm starting my new job as [job title].

Next week I will be starting the [course name] course at [institution name]. It's the start of a new journey for me, and I'm looking forward to this new challenge.

Helpful resources

Recently I've been watching the legal series [TV series name]. I love it because [reasons].

Today I read the article [article name] about [description]. I'm sharing it because [reasons].

I'd like to share with you a video I made on/about [description]. I'd love your feedback, so please comment below.

3.10 Use the language from Phrase bank 6.3 to write a post on a topic of your choice. You can refer to Exercise 3.8 for topic ideas.

Posting pictures

3.11 On most social media platforms, you can post images, including photos or graphics containing text.

Read the following examples of images you could post. Which of these images could be appropriate for a lawyer or a law firm to share on social media? Why?

a. A photo of a legal expert speaking at a conference you attended.
b. An image with a motivational quote.
c. A photo of a law textbook you are reading.
d. A photo of you on holiday at the beach in swimwear.
e. A plain background image containing your top contract drafting tips.
f. A screenshot from the video conference of your law firm's staff meeting.
g. A selfie of you with a client at a networking event.

3.12 When you publish a picture post, you should write a caption. A well-written caption includes:

- important information describing the picture, for example: *Here are my top tips for drafting contracts in English.*
- a call to action asking your connections to do something, for example: *Do you have any other tips to share?*

- hashtags helping others to discover your content, for example: *#contractdrafting #legalenglish #contractlawyer*

Look at Ethan's picture post and discuss the following questions:

a. Does this image cause any legal issues which Ethan should avoid?
b. What is the post about?
c. Who do you think is Ethan's target audience for this post? Is it relevant for them?
d. Does this post reflect Express Law's brand?
e. Has Ethan written his caption well? Why?

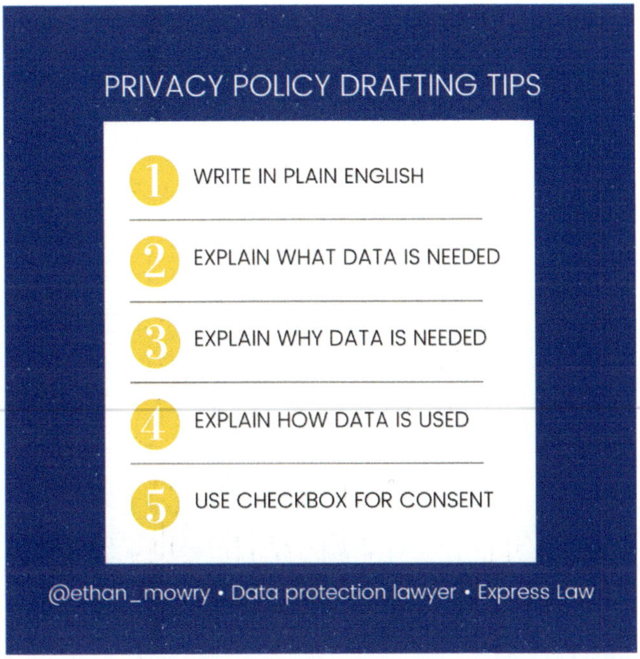

@ethan_mowry

📃Here are my top tips for drafting a privacy policy to help your business succeed.

🙋‍♂️Does your business need help drafting your privacy policy? At Express Law we are happy to help.

🌐 Visit: www.express-law.ai

📧 Email me: ethan.mowry@express-law.ai

#privacypolicy #gdpr #commerciallawyer #dataprotection

3.13 Create a picture post with a caption. Use Ethan's example in Exercise 3.12 as a guide. Make sure your post:

- uses an image appropriate for a lawyer to post
- is relevant to your target audience
- reflects your personal brand
- includes a well-written caption

Creating your own content
Producing a podcast

3.14 Another way to engage with your audience on social media is to create your own podcast. Discuss the following questions:

a. Do you listen to podcasts? If so, what do you like about them?
b. Do you think a podcast is a good way for you to market yourself or your law firm? Why?

3.15 Read Text 6.3 and answer the following questions:

a. What is the difference between a podcast and an episode?
b. What are some common podcast formats?

Text 6.3 Podcasting for lawyers

What is a podcast?

A podcast is like a radio show which is published online. Some common podcast formats are:

- solo show: the podcast host speaks by themselves
- co-host show: two podcast hosts have a conversation
- guest interview show: the podcast host interviews a guest
- panel show: the podcast host interviews many guests

What is a podcast episode?

A podcast is made up of a series of episodes focused on a specific topic. For example, *The cybersecurity and data protection podcast* could have episodes such as *Digital law tips for your business* or *How to deal with a data breach.*

Where can I publish my law podcast?

Many podcasters publish their episodes directly on social media platforms such as YouTube™. When an episode is published, listeners can stream it via a website on their computer or an app on their mobile phone. The podcast host can share the podcast episode on social media to engage their connections.

3.16 Audio 6.5

Listen to the introduction and conclusion to Express Law's podcast episode, where Ethan is being interviewed by his colleague. Tick the parts from the following list which are included in the audio.

Podcast introduction and conclusion checklist

a. podcast name	○
b. description of the podcast	○
c. episode name	○
d. episode number	○
e. description of episode	○
f. disclaimer	○
g. website links	○
h. social media links	○
i. call to action	○
j. thank you to listeners	○
k. information about the next episode	○

3.17 Review the expressions for introducing and concluding a podcast episode in Phrase bank 6.4:

Phrase bank 6.4	
Phrases to introduce your podcast	**Phrases to conclude your podcast**
Hi everybody, this is [host name] from [website name] and you're listening to the [podcast name] podcast.	*That's the end of this episode. Thank you for listening to the [podcast name].*
This is the show about [podcast description].	*You have just listened to the [podcast name] with your host [host name].*
Today you are listening to episode [episode number] entitled [episode name] about [episode description].	***Call to action phrases***
You can find out more about this podcast episode by visiting [website link] and by joining me on social media. My social media accounts are [social media profile name].	*If you enjoyed this episode, please subscribe and share it with your friends and colleagues.*
As always, I must mention that nothing I say in this podcast episode constitutes legal advice.	*Connect with us on [social media platform name], search for [social media profile name].*
	Catch our next episode about [episode information].
	Check us out at [website link].

3.18 Produce a short podcast episode to market yourself as a lawyer or your law firm. Use a topic of your choice, or an episode title from the following boxes:

The new law your company needs to comply with …	Meet our legal team: an interview with …	Talking about legal tech with …

Use the expressions in Phrase bank 6.4 to introduce and conclude your podcast. In your main content, include:

- a definition of the topic
- a reason why the topic is important
- three details about the topic

Writing a blog post

3.19 Writing a blog post is another way to engage with your audience on social media. Discuss the following questions:

a. Do you read a blog? What is your favourite blog and why?
b. Have you ever published a blog post? What was it about?

3.20 Read Text 6.4 and summarise the steps involved in writing a blog post. For example, you could say:

- *To summarise, this text is about ...*
- *In a nutshell, the text says ...*
- *The main points of this text are ...*

Text 6.4 How to write a blog post: a step-by-step guide for you and your law firm

A blog is a popular way to raise awareness about the services you or your law firm provides. Follow these five simple steps to get started with your first post.

Step 1: know your target audience and purpose

Ask yourself the following questions in order to establish your target audience and purpose:

- Who do I want to read this blog post?
- Why do I want them to read this?

Step 2: choose your post type

Select your post type from the following list:

- How-to-guide: tells readers the step-by-step process to achieve a goal
- List: gives essential information on a topic in a list structure
- Checklist: contains a list of actions needed to complete a task
- News: details current affairs and comments on events
- Personal story: recounts a personal experience

Step 3: write your blog post

Research your topic and put pen to paper. Your blog should have:

- a title
- a clear structure
- headings
- short paragraphs
- keywords
- images

Step 4: proofread your post

Proofread your content to avoid grammatical errors and spelling mistakes. An even better option is to ask someone else to proofread it as they may be able to spot inaccuracies which you have missed.

Step 5: publish your post

Publish your post on your website and then share it on social media. Some social media platforms even allow you to publish a blog post article directly on the platform.

3.21 The following blog post types were all mentioned in Text 6.4. Match the blog post type with their titles. The first answer is given as an example.

Blog post type	Blog post title
a. *How-to-guide* →	1. The recent case of *Johnson v Peach* and why it matters
b. List	2. *How to write a plain English client care letter*
c. Checklist	3. Top 5 legal research databases
d. News	4. My experience passing the bar exam
e. Personal story	5. Your construction contract essentials checklist

3.22 Write your own short blog post on a topic of your choice. Use Text 6.4 as a guide.

Planning your social media activity

3.23 Often people do not stay active on social media because they find it difficult to think of something to post on the spot or they simply forget to do it. Planning social media posts in advance is a way to avoid these problems and there are many online platforms which allow you to schedule posts.

Ethan has started planning his social media activity using a social media planner. Look at Ethan's example[3] and then complete the social media planner with your own posts for Tuesday and Wednesday. Use Ethan's example in Exercise 3.12 and Phrase bank 6.3 as a guide.

Remember to plan content that:

- does not cause any legal issues
- is relevant to your target audience
- reflects your personal brand
- includes a well-written post or caption

	Social media planner	
Monday		📅Here I am checking this week's agenda. On Thursday I'm co-presenting at our weekly data compliance evening event. 😟If you're confused about what your company needs to do to comply with data protection laws, come to our event and see my presentation on 28th July 2022 at Express Law, 115 Aldgate, London. Register for free here: www.express-law.ai/events #contractdrafting #traineelawyer #privacypolicy
Tuesday	**A written post (no picture):**	
Wednesday	**A picture post (picture and caption):**	

Test yourself

1. Name three keywords you could include in your LinkedIn™ profile and explain how these could boost SEO.
2. Describe how you can reflect a modern brand in your social media profile.
3. Give three hashtags you could you use in your social media profile and explain why you would use them.
4. What legal issues can arise when engaging on social media?
5. Explain three ways of posting on social media to engage with your connections.

Notes

1 American Bar Association, '2019 Websites & Marketing' (*ABA*, 23 October 2019) <https://www.americanbar.org/groups/law_practice/publications/techreport/abatechreport2019/websitesmarketing2019> accessed 30 April 2022
2 LinkedIn™, 'Rock Your LinkedIn Profile' <https://www.linkedin.com/learning/rock-your-linkedin-profile/got-skills-adding-skills-and-getting-endorsed> accessed 30 April 2022
3 Photo by Fa Barboza on Unsplash <https://unsplash.com/photos/Lf3S2zRXKXk> accessed 30 April 2022

7 Job applications and interviews

About this chapter

Overview

This chapter is about job applications and interviews in the legal sector. The first part introduces the topic. It includes employment language and common acronyms and abbreviations used in job adverts. The second part looks at the recruitment process. It focuses on the skills that recruiters look for and the stages in the recruitment process. The third part is about applying for a job in the legal sector and includes sections on writing a covering letter and CV. The final part looks at how to prepare for a job interview and answer interview questions.

Learning objectives

By the end of this chapter, you should be able to:

- understand the language of job adverts
- identify the key skills that a legal professional needs
- write a covering letter for a legal position
- write your own CV
- prepare for job interview questions

Test yourself at the end of the chapter to check that you have achieved the learning objectives.

1. Introduction

1.1 How would you look for a job or work experience in the legal sector? Discuss how you could use the methods in the following boxes. If you are a practising lawyer, explain how you found your current position.

Recruitment agency	LinkedIn™
University careers service	Job board website
Word of mouth	Law careers fair
Law firm's website	Speculative application

1.2 This section looks at four different job adverts in the legal sector. Read each advert and choose an appropriate synonym from the boxes for each underlined word in the advert. The first answer for Advert 1 is given as an example.

DOI: 10.4324/9781003140207-7

Advert 1 synonyms	work placement *(a) vacation scheme*	transactional	litigation

Advert 1

Our (a) vacation scheme provides an insight into life at Marsh & Rayling, giving you the opportunity to actively experience the work of a modern commercial law firm.

The vacation scheme lasts four weeks. You can experience both (b) contentious and (c) non-contentious work by choosing two of the following practice areas: banking, commercial, dispute resolution, employment, M&A, real estate. You will work with our current trainee solicitors and carry out tasks such as research, drafting memoranda, and attending client meetings and conference calls.

We are looking for candidates who are excellent communicators and team players and who can demonstrate commercial awareness, good analytical skills, and the ambition to pursue a career in commercial law.

We are an equal opportunities employer and we welcome applications from diverse backgrounds.

Apply now

Advert 2 synonyms	past achievements	available job	additional advantages

Advert 2

Our client is a leading full-service international law firm in Dubai, with a number of established offices in the MENA region. They currently have a (d) vacancy for a junior Associate (0–3 PQE) in their TMT department.

The team in Dubai deals with a full range of commercial TMT matters, advising local and international clients on major technology contracts, large-scale outsourcing transactions, data privacy, and IT security.

The ideal applicant will be a team player and a creative thinker with excellent interpersonal skills and an excellent (e) track record in a leading commercial law firm.

Salary range £90,000–120,000 p.a. (tax free) plus (f) benefits.

For an initial discussion about this exciting opportunity, please contact Hayden Price on 0207 235 6759.

Advert 3 synonyms	things happen quickly	thorough	working from home

Advert 3

Legal Counsel, Frankfurt or Paris

MüllerBank, Frankfurt or Paris

About us

MüllerBank is a market leader in the Fintech industry. Our platform allows businesses to integrate a wide range of solutions, including digital banking, payments, and lending services.

About the job

We are looking to expand within the EU and have an opening for an experienced Legal Counsel, reporting to the GC. (g) Remote working is possible in this role.

You will be responsible for providing legal support to all business units; assisting with corporate and governance matters; giving legal advice in the areas of banking and capital markets, financial regulation, data protection; and drafting and negotiating commercial contracts.

About you

You are a qualified lawyer in France or Germany and you can speak and write fluently in English. You have (h) sound regulatory experience from a leading commercial law firm or Fintech business. You are passionate about Fintech, have good organisational skills, and are ready to work in a (i) fast-paced environment.

Prospective applicants should send a covering letter and curriculum vitae, in English, to Anna Fischer, HR Manager – Europe, at annafischer@muellerbank.de, with the subject line Legal Counsel position.

Advert 4 synonyms	lead	lawyers moving from one firm to another	people in a law firm whose work is charged to clients

Advert 4

LawMove specialises in (j) lateral hires. We have extensive experience of placing equity and salaried partners in national and international commercial law firms.

Our client is a leading commercial law firm, looking for a senior R&I lawyer to (k) head up its insolvency team.

You will ideally be an existing partner with a sizeable following and able to hit the ground running. You will be required to develop client relationships and win new work but also take the time to mentor junior (l) fee earners within the team.

Competitive salary c. £450,000.

Discuss this opportunity in confidence with LawMove on 020 973 2875.

1.3 Read the adverts in Exercise 1.2 again and answer these questions:

a. How is Advert 1 different from the other adverts?
b. Which advert is about an in-house legal position?
c. Which advert would be appropriate for a newly qualified lawyer?
d. Which adverts were placed by recruitment agencies?

1.4 The adverts in Exercise 1.2 use the following abbreviations and acronyms. Complete the table with what the abbreviations and acronyms stand for. Then discuss what they mean. The first answer is given as an example.

Acronym	Meaning
a. M&A	*Mergers and acquisitions*
b. MENA	
c. PQE	
d. TMT	
e. IT	
f. EU	
g. GC	
h. R&I	
Abbreviation	**Meaning**
i. p.a.	
j. c.	

Vocabulary and pronunciation note

Advert is an abbreviation of *advertisement*. It is sometimes shortened to *ad*. Advertisement can be pronounced in different ways. In BrE, it is usual to put emphasis on the *ver* part of the word: *advertisement* (əd'vɜtɪsmənt). In AmE, it is usual to put emphasis on the *tise* part of the word: *advertisement* (ædvɜ'tazsmənt).

2. The recruitment process

The skills that recruiters are looking for

2.1 Discuss the following questions:

a. What skills does a commercial lawyer need?
b. Are the skills required of a senior lawyer different from those of a junior lawyer?
c. Which skills are mentioned in the job adverts in Exercise 1.2?

2.2 Audio 7.1

a. Listen to a student's podcast interview with Johnny Parker, recruitment partner at Marsh & Rayling. Complete the Skills column in the following table with the five skills Johnny thinks every commercial lawyer needs. The first skill is given as an example.

Skills	Examples
1. *Interpersonal skills*	*Ability to communicate with people.* *Understanding people and having empathy.* *Being able to explain complex legal issues in a way that the client can understand.*
2.	
3.	
4.	
5.	

b. Listen to Audio 7.1 again and complete the Examples column in the table with examples of each skill that Johnny gives. Some examples for the first skill are given.

2.3 Discuss specific examples from your own experience for each of the five skills mentioned in Exercise 2.2:

Here is an example of interpersonal skills:

- *I had to explain the effect of Brexit on enforcement of judgments to the client's Head of Global Operations.*

Here is another example of interpersonal skills, from a student who does not have any experience working in a law firm:

- *I did some work experience in a retail environment where I had to communicate with customers on a daily basis.*

2.4 In Audio 7.1, Johnny mentions the hot topic of ESG, which is an acronym for environmental, social, and governance. Discuss a hot topic that you have seen recently in the legal or business news. You can use one of the following topic ideas or suggest your own:

- The future of the workplace
- The regulation of Big Tech
- What ESG means for businesses
- Artificial intelligence and the legal sector
- Dispute resolution after Brexit
- The legal status of digital assets

The different stages in the recruitment process

2.5 Audio 7.2

Listen to the next part of the podcast interview with Johnny. Decide if the following statements are true or false and correct any false statements.

	True	False
a. The recruitment process starts by students sending their covering letter and CV to the law firm.	○	○
b. There are a lot of resources to help with the psychometric test.	○	○
c. During the video interview, you can pause your recording to check your answers.	○	○
d. The final stage of the process is a one-hour interview with the firm's Managing Partner.	○	○

2.6 Listen to Audio 7.2 again and complete the following diagram with the different stages in Marsh & Rayling's recruitment process. Each space represents one word.

a. Complete the ______ ______ ______

↓

b. A ______ test

↓

c. A ______ ______

↓

d. The ______ ______

2.7 If you already have some experience working in a law firm, explain how you were recruited. Was the process similar to or different from the process described in Audio 7.2?

If you do not have any experience working in a law firm, talk about the recruitment process for another job or work experience, or for the application and enrolment process for a university place.

3. Applying for a job in the legal sector

This section looks at how to write a covering letter and a CV.

Vocabulary note

A *covering letter* is also called a *cover letter*. *CV* is an abbreviation of *curriculum vitae*. It is more common to use the abbreviation *CV*. Another word for a CV is a *resume* (ˈrezəmeɪ), also less commonly spelt *résumé*.

3.1 Here is Advert 3 from Exercise 1.2. Read the advert again and answer the following questions:

a. What job is being advertised?
b. What information about MüllerBank is given in the advert?
c. What skills are required for this job?
d. What is the first stage in the recruitment process?
e. Which person should potential applicants write to and what subject line should they use?

Advert 3

Legal Counsel, Frankfurt or Paris

MüllerBank, Frankfurt or Paris

About us

MüllerBank is a market leader in the Fintech industry. Our platform allows businesses to integrate a wide range of solutions, including digital banking, payments, and lending services.

About the job

We are looking to expand within the EU and have an opening for an experienced Legal Counsel, reporting to the GC. Remote working is possible in this role.

You will be responsible for providing legal support to all business units; assisting with corporate and governance matters; giving legal advice in the areas of banking and capital markets, financial regulation, data protection; and drafting and negotiating commercial contracts.

About you

You are a qualified lawyer in France or Germany and you can speak and write fluently in English. You have sound regulatory experience from a leading commercial law firm or Fintech business. You are passionate about Fintech, have good organisational skills, and are ready to work in a fast-paced environment.

Prospective applicants should send a covering letter and curriculum vitae (in English) to Anna Fischer, HR Manager – Europe, at annafischer@muellerbank.de, with the subject line Legal Counsel position.

3.2 What other information would you like to have about MüllerBank if you were applying for this job?

Writing a covering letter

A letter usually describes a written document which is physically sent in the post, but a covering letter can also be written in the body of an email, or written in a separate document which is attached to an email.

3.3 Angela Werner would like to apply for the position at MüllerBank and needs to write a covering letter. Read Text 7.1 about how to write a good covering letter and answer these questions:

a. What is the purpose of a covering letter?
b. What information should you include in a covering letter?
c. How can you make a covering letter more personal?
d. What should you do before sending your covering letter?

Text 7.1 How to write a good covering letter

The purpose of a covering letter is to explain why you are the best person for the advertised job. Many people write a standard covering letter, but it is important to make each application personal.

Remember that you are not writing an essay. Keep your letter short and to the point.

Follow our quick guide to writing a good covering letter for a legal position:

Salutation

Think about how you will address the person that you are writing to and start your letter with an appropriate salutation.

☞ Make it personal: Find the name of the person dealing with the applications for the position and address your letter to that person, rather than writing '*to whom it may concern*'.

Opening paragraph

Explain why you are writing and how you heard about the position. Write in full sentences, using the first person singular.

☞ Make it personal: Use the law firm or company's name and refer to the specific legal position that you are applying for.

Second paragraph

Give brief details of your background and your current job. Explain your motivation for applying for the position based on your research into the law firm or company.

☞ Make it personal: Be enthusiastic about why you really want this particular role at this particular law firm or company.

Third paragraph

Show why you are suitable for this position. This is your chance to highlight the legal experience and relevant skills that you have. Give specific examples from your work to support what you say.

☞ Make it personal: Relate your examples to the particular skills required for the position. Don't copy and paste from other applications.

Closing paragraph

Attach your CV and look forward to the next stage of the recruitment process.

☞ Make it personal: thank the employer for taking the time to consider your application.

Finally, don't forget to proofread your covering letter before you send it off!

Vocabulary note: *enclose* or *attach*

Use the verb *enclose* if you are physically sending a hard copy of a document in the post and use *attach* if you are sending an electronic copy of a document by email.

3.4 Angela has read Text 7.1 about how to write a good covering letter. Read the following notes that she has made:

Salutation: Check job advert for contact details
Opening paragraph: Remember that I found the advert on LinkedIn™
Second paragraph:

- Dual-qualified lawyer (English and German)
- Five years' experience as a senior associate in the Fintech team at Alston LLP's Frankfurt office, three years as a junior associate in their London office
- Passionate about Fintech: founding member of the Women in Technology Network
- Interested in MüllerBank because of their focus on innovative financial services solutions and want to move in-house so can work more closely with their internal business teams

Third paragraph:

- At Alston LLP I have developed a wide range of experience in financial regulatory matters. Example 1: I advised a major bank on a restructuring deal, which included the sale of its payment processing subsidiary. Example 2: I presented a client webinar earlier this year explaining the impact of the government's latest review of Fintech
- Good organisational skills: I handle a large workload and have to manage my time effectively to meet tight deadlines. I feel well prepared for their fast-paced environment

Closing paragraph: Don't forget to thank the employer for considering my application

3.5 Angela has found the following covering letter template. She has inserted her contact details, the employer's contact details, and the subject line. Read the template and answer these questions:

Which of the following would be the most suitable opening paragraph for Angela's covering letter?

a. *I'm writing about the legal job on LinkedIn™.*
b. *I am truly honoured to apply for the position of Legal Counsel, which was advertised on LinkedIn™.*
c. *I am writing to apply for the position of Legal Counsel at MüllerBank, which was advertised on LinkedIn™.*

Covering letter template

Angela Werner
Kaiserstraße 12
40257 Frankfurt am Main
[Date]

Anna Fischer
HR Manager – Europe
MüllerBank
Sent by email to annafischer@muellerbank.de

Dear Anna Fischer,
Legal Counsel position

[Opening paragraph]

[Second paragraph]

[Third paragraph]

[Closing paragraph]

[Ending]
[Signature]

3.6 Review the expressions for writing a covering letter in Phrase bank 7.1 (which continues on the next page). Then write Angela's covering letter for the legal position at MüllerBank. Use Angela's notes in Exercise 3.4, and the template and your answer from Exercise 3.5.

Phrase bank 7.1

Opening paragraph

I am writing to apply for the position of [job title] at [law firm/company], which was advertised on [name of website or social media platform].

Following your advertisement on [name of website or social media], I am writing to apply for the position of [job title].

Second paragraph

I am currently working as [position] at [law firm/company] in [town, country].

I have been working at [law firm/company] for [length of time].

Third paragraph

In my current position, I have acquired expertise in [e.g. cross-border mergers and acquisitions]. For example, I advised a client on ...

During my time at [law firm/company] I have gained experience in a wide range of [e.g. commercial real estate] matters. For example, I have dealt with ...

I have enhanced my knowledge of [e.g. data protection law] by [e.g. contributing to the firm's monthly privacy updates].

My experience in [e.g. M&A] developed my ability to work in a team as I had to liaise with lawyers across different departments.

I developed good organisational skills when working in the [e.g. litigation] department as I had to [e.g. work to strict time limits].

I spent [length of time] working at ... *I am very interested in the role of [position] because ...* *This position is particularly appealing to me because ...* *I am keen to work for [law firm/ company] because...* *I am passionate about [area of law] because ...*	**Closing paragraph** *Thank you for considering my application.* *I enclose/I attach my CV.* *I would welcome the opportunity to discuss how I can make a positive contribution to [law firm/company].* *I would welcome the chance to discuss my application in more detail with you.* *I look forward to learning more about this position.* *I look forward to discussing how my experience would be beneficial for [law firm/company.]*

3.7 Write a covering letter for a job in the legal sector. You can write a covering letter for one of the job adverts in Exercise 1.2 or for another legal position that you would like to apply for. Make sure you include:

- your name and contact details
- the name and address of the person you are writing to
- why you are writing and how you heard about the position
- brief details of your background, current job, and your motivation for applying
- why you are suitable for this position, highlighting your experience and skills
- your CV as an attachment

Writing a CV

3.8 A CV in England usually includes the following sections. Read the sections and discuss these questions:

a. Which of these sections would you include in a CV in your culture?
b. What other sections would you include in a CV in your culture?
c. How is a CV different from a LinkedIn™ profile?

a. Full name | b. Contact details | c. A short personal profile

d. Voluntary work experience | e. Professional work experience

f. Education | g. Interests | h. Skills

3.9 Most recruiters prefer you to keep your CV to a maximum length of two pages. It is a matter of style how you present the information in your CV. However, recruiters are increasingly using artificial intelligence to screen CVs in an automated preliminary selection phase. Complex designs may prevent the computer from reading your CV and lead to it being rejected.

Discuss what length and style of CV is usual in your culture.

3.10 Angela Werner has started writing her CV for the Legal Counsel position at MüllerBank. She has found a useful CV checklist on a legal recruitment agency's website.

Read Text 7.2 Getting it right: a CV checklist and then read Angela's CV. Tick the sections on the checklist that Angela has completed.

Text 7.2 Getting it right: a CV checklist	
○	**Header** • Include your name and contact details, including your email address and telephone number.
○	**Profile** • Summarise your main skills and career aims in a few lines. • Write in the first person singular and use full sentences. • Make it relevant to the position that you are applying for. • Reduce your word count by eliminating compound adjectives: *self-motivated, detail-oriented, highly organised.*
○	**Professional work experience or voluntary work experience** • Include the job title, name of employer, and dates for each role. • List positions in reverse chronological order, starting with your current job. • Summarise your key achievements with bullet points. • Write in note form excluding the subject of the verb: *Managed a cross-disciplinary team in a complex tax litigation case.* • Use figures to add value to your achievements: *Managed a team of 15 fee earners in a $10 million tax litigation case.* • Keep this section brief by including less detail for older roles.
○	**Education** • Include dates, name of the qualification, and where you studied. • List qualifications in reverse chronological order, starting with your most recent qualification. • Include module or thesis titles if these are relevant to the position you are applying for. • If you are currently a student, put this section before your work experience. • If you have a lot of work experience, you can limit this section to qualifications relevant to the position.
○	**Skills and interests** • Include skills and interests which are relevant to the position you are applying for.

Angela Werner	Kaiserstraße 12 40257 Frankfurt am Main +49 33452 98760 awerner@hmail.com
Education	**London Law School**, 2011–2012 Legal Practice Course, passed with Distinction **University of London**, 2008–2011 Law with German Law, 2:1 LLB (Hons.) • Spent one year studying German law at Freiburg University • Awarded R.H. Thurlow prize for thesis on Artificial Intelligence and the Law • Treasurer of the University Law Society **International School of Berlin**, 2006–2008 International Baccalaureate, total 40/45 points
Skills and interests	**Women in Technology Network**, 2018–present Founding member. Organised networking event in Frankfurt in 2019 attended by over 100 professionals. **Languages** English and German native speaker French C1 level **IT skills** Proficient in C++ and Java

3.11 The profile section of your CV allows you to tailor your CV to the position that you are applying for by highlighting your relevant skills and career aims.

Review the profile section in Text 7.2. and compare the following profile sections for Angela. Which of these profile sections follow the CV checklist? Which do you prefer?

Profile a.	Self-motivated senior Fintech lawyer with highly developed organisational skills looking to contribute legal and regulatory expertise to a well-regarded company.

Profile b.	I am an experienced lawyer looking for an opportunity to work for a company where I can use my legal and regulatory expertise.

Profile c.	I am an English and German-qualified Fintech lawyer with more than 8 years' experience. I am looking to join a company where I can use my legal and regulatory expertise and contribute to business strategy.

3.12 Angela has started writing the work experience section of her CV. Review the work experience section in Text 7.2 and then read the following description of Angela's current position. How could this description be improved?

Professional experience	**Alston LLP, Frankfurt**, September 2017–present Senior Associate, FinTech team In my current position I have developed expertise in a wide range of regulatory matters for clients in the Fintech industry, including companies, start-ups, banks and private equity investors. I led a team of 5 fee earners in a client bank's €10 million sale of its payment subsidiary. Other notable transactions included advising a private equity firm on its investment in a software start-up and providing data privacy compliance advice to a leading financial technology company. In addition, I have been involved in presenting a number of client webinars on topical Fintech issues. The latest webinar was in January 2022 and was entitled *'Fintech: all you need to know about the Government's latest review'*. I have also supervised junior lawyers in our team.

3.13 Rewrite Angela's key achievements using bullet points. Remember that you do not have to include the subject of the verb. The first bullet point has been completed as an example.

Professional experience	**Alston LLP, Frankfurt**, September 2017–present Senior Associate, FinTech team • *Developed expertise in a wide range of regulatory matters for clients in the Fintech industry, including companies, start-ups, banks and private equity investors.* • • • • •

3.14 Read the following examples of verbs that you can use in the work experience section of your CV. Which of these verbs did you use in Exercise 3.13?

advise	draft	lead	manage
negotiate	provide	present	research
develop	assist	supervise	represent

Grammar note

When using bullet points in the work experience section of your CV, use the present simple tense if you are talking about something that you regularly do in your current position. For example:

- Advise clients on compliance issues.

Use the past simple tense if you are talking about an action in the past or an achievement. For example:

- Advised a multinational on a £400 million carve-out transaction.

3.15 Read the next part of the work experience section in Angela's CV and complete each space with one of the verbs from Exercise 3.14. This section refers to Angela's past work experience and so you should conjugate the verbs accordingly.

Professional experience	**Alston LLP, London,** September 2014–September 2017 Junior Associate, Corporate and risk team (a) ______________ client companies on compliance issues. (b) ______________ and (c) ______________ multi-million pound commercial contracts. (d) ______________ other fee earners with large-scale regulatory due diligence. **Dawson Hoyle LLP, London,** September 2012–September 2014 Trainee Solicitor. Seats in Commercial, Litigation, Banking, and M&A departments. (e) ______________ EU legislation on data protection law for an article in our client newsletter.

3.16 Write your own CV or if you already have a CV in English, try to improve it. Remember to follow the checklist in Text 7.2 and proofread your CV when you have finished writing it.

4. Preparing for a job interview with a law firm

4.1 Here is Advert 1 from Exercise 1.2. Read the advert again and answer the following questions:

a. What information about the vacation scheme is given in the advert?
b. What skills do Marsh & Rayling require?
c. How do you apply for the vacation scheme?

Advert 1

Our vacation scheme provides an insight into life at Marsh & Rayling, giving you the opportunity to actively experience the work of a modern commercial law firm.

The vacation scheme lasts four weeks. You can experience both contentious and non-contentious work by choosing two of the following practice areas: banking, commercial, dispute resolution, employment, M&A, real estate. You will work with our current trainee solicitors and carry out tasks such as research, drafting memoranda, and attending client meetings and conference calls.

We are looking for candidates who are excellent communicators and team players and who can demonstrate commercial awareness, good analytical skills, and the ambition to pursue a career in commercial law.

We are an equal opportunities employer and we welcome applications from diverse backgrounds.

Apply now

Video interviews

4.2 Audio 7.3

Listen to two students, Annabelle and Victor, talking about Advert 1 and answer the following questions:

a. At what stage is Victor in the recruitment process?
b. What does Annabelle suggest that Victor should do before he starts the interview?
c. How much time will Victor have to answer the interview questions?
d. How does Annabelle suggest that Victor can practise for the interview?

4.3 Refer to your answers in Exercise 4.2. Have you ever had a video interview? What other advice would you give Victor about preparing for this interview?

4.4 Audio 7.4

a. Listen to the second part of Annabelle and Victor's conversation. What is the STAR method for answering interview questions and what do the letters STAR stand for?
b. Read the transcript for Audio 7.4 and complete the table with Victor's STAR examples for the skill of ambition. The first example is completed.

Skill	S	T	A	R
Ambition	*I wanted to organise a mooting competition in my law faculty*			

4.5 The following table includes some of the other skills mentioned in Advert 1. Use the STAR method to complete the table with examples of these skills from your own experience.

Skill	S	T	A	R
Team player				
Excellent communicator				
Good analytical skills				

4.6 Audio 7.5

Practise answering video interview questions using your examples in Exercise 4.5.

Instructions
In Audio 7.5, you will hear three interview questions. After each question you will have one minute to prepare your answer. At the end of this time you will have three minutes to say your answer. Once you start the audio you cannot pause or end it until you have answered all of the questions.

4.7 Reflect on your video interview in Exercise 4.6, using the self-assessment questions in Appendix A.

Face-to-face interviews

4.8 Audio 7.6

After the video interview, the next stage in Marsh & Rayling's recruitment process is an assessment centre. The assessment centre includes a face-to-face interview with some of Marsh & Rayling's partners.

Listen to extracts of two face-to-face interviews by Marsh & Rayling partners Johnny Parker and Alice Mason. The first interview is with a candidate called Geraldine and the second interview is with a candidate called Sarah. Answer the following questions:

a. What is your impression of each candidate from these interview extracts?
b. Which candidate uses the STAR method to answer one of the interview questions?
c. Which candidate ends their answers confidently and how do they do this?

Interview questions

4.9 Read Text 7.3 about law firm interview questions. Discuss other questions that you could add to the three categories. If you have had a job interview for a legal position before, discuss which questions you were asked.

Text 7.3 Law firm interview questions

It can be difficult to predict the precise questions that you will be asked in a law firm interview. One way to prepare for an interview is to divide the types of questions you may be asked into three main categories and practise answering these.

The three main categories are: questions about you and your skills; questions about the law firm; and more general questions about the legal sector as a whole. Here is a list of example questions that you might be asked in each category:

1. **You and your skills**

Tell me about yourself.
Why do you want to be a lawyer?
Why would you make a good lawyer?
What are your strengths and weaknesses?

What motivates you?
Where do you see yourself in five years' time?
Tell me about a time when you had to work under pressure.
Explain a situation when you had to resolve a conflict.

2. **The law firm**

Why do you want to work for this law firm?
Why do you want to work in corporate law?
Why don't you want to work in real estate law?
What makes us different from other law firms?
What challenges does this law firm face?
What will you do to develop business at this firm?

3. **The legal sector**

What are the key issues facing the legal industry today?
What will be the impact of legal tech on lawyers and their clients?
How do you think [topical subject] will affect law firms?
Describe the law firm of the future.
Explain a recent court decision in commercial law.

4.10 Review the expressions in Phrase bank 7.2:

Phrase bank 7.2	
Giving yourself time to formulate an answer	**Questions you can ask the interviewer**
So, can I just check that I've understood the question correctly. What you'd like to know is ...?	*Could you tell me more about the day-to-day responsibilities in this role?*
Could I just have a moment to think about that please?	*Could you explain more about the organisation of the department?*
That's an interesting question. I'm just thinking about the best way to answer that.	*Will there be opportunities to travel in this role?*
Ending questions confidently	*What type of in-house training do you offer?*
And so that is an example of when I had to [repeat question, e.g. work in a team]	
And that is what convinced me that [e.g. I wanted to become a lawyer]	
So that is why ...	
So, to conclude, my answer is ...	

4.11 Practise answering interview questions with a partner. Choose whether you are going to play the role of the candidate or the interviewer. Then read your instructions and role-play the interview. After you have finished, switch roles.

Candidate instructions

You are applying for a job in the legal sector. You can apply for one of the positions in the job adverts in Exercise 1.2 or for another legal position of your choice. Tell the interviewer which job you are applying for so that they can prepare some interview questions.

The interviewer will ask you four questions and then you can ask the interviewer a question. Refer to Phrase bank 7.2 for expressions that you can use in the interview and remember to use the STAR method to respond to questions about your skills and experience.

Interviewer instructions

You are going to interview the candidate for a job in the legal sector. First, speak to the candidate to find out which job they are applying for so that you can prepare some interview questions.

Refer to Text 7.3 and your discussion in Exercise 4.9. Choose four questions to ask the candidate. Choose at least one question about the candidate and their skills, one question about the law firm, and one question about the legal sector. At the end of the interview, invite the candidate to ask you a question.

4.12 Reflect on your interview role-play in Exercise 4.11. If you played the role of the candidate, use the self-assessment questions in Appendix A. If you played the role of the interviewer, use the peer-assessment questions in Appendix A.

Test yourself

1. Identify two acronyms used in job adverts and explain what they mean.
2. What is commercial awareness and how can you obtain this?
3. Give two points that you would include in a covering letter.
4. How can you write a good profile section in your CV?
5. What is the STAR method of answering interview questions?

8 Contract drafting and review

About this chapter

Overview

This chapter is about drafting and reviewing commercial contracts. The first part introduces the topic and discusses common types of commercial contracts. The second part looks at the typical structure of a commercial contract. The third part focuses on understanding contract language and drafting more clearly. It includes sections on legalese, modal verbs, expressions of time, and sentence structure. The fourth part looks at points to consider when reviewing a commercial contract.

At the end of the chapter, there is a section on the future of contracts, looking at the potential impact of legal technology and legal design on contract drafting and review.

Learning objectives

By the end of this chapter, you should be able to:

- explain different types of commercial contracts
- identify the different parts of a contract
- understand commercial contract language
- recognise how to draft more clearly
- appreciate how legal tech and legal design can be used in contract drafting and review

Test yourself at the end of the chapter to check that you have achieved the learning objectives.

1. Introduction

1.1 What are the aims of a lawyer in drafting or reviewing a contract? Do you agree or disagree with the following suggestions? Would you add any other aims?

To protect the client's interests	To negotiate the business deal
To reflect the parties' agreed terms	To identify risks in the parties' deal
To produce a document that is weighted in favour of their client	To produce a document that their client can understand

DOI: 10.4324/9781003140207-8

Common types of commercial contracts

1.2 The focus of this chapter is on commercial contracts. A commercial contract means a contract made between parties who are businesses. These are sometimes called B2B contracts (business to business). In contrast, B2C contracts (business to consumer) are contracts where one party is a business but the other party is a consumer, buying goods or services for their personal use.

The following box contains a list of common types of commercial contracts. Discuss the following questions:

a. Have you heard of these contracts before?
b. What parties are involved in each contract?
c. What is the purpose of each contract?

Check the Glossary for definitions of these contracts.

Common commercial contracts

1. Sale of goods contract	2. Services agreement
3. Distribution agreement	4. Franchise agreement
5. Share purchase agreement	6. Joint venture agreement
7. Commercial lease	8. Licence agreement
9. Employment contract	10. Settlement agreement
11. Non-disclosure agreement	12. Loan agreement

Vocabulary note: *agreement* or *contract*

In contract titles, *agreement* and *contract* are often used as synonyms. For example, we could refer to a *sale of goods contract* or a *sale of goods agreement*. In some commercial contracts, it is more common to use *agreement* rather than *contract* in the title. For example, a *share purchase agreement*.

1.3 Read the following extracts of lawyers talking about their work. What types of commercial contracts would these lawyers draft and review? Use the list of common commercial contracts in Exercise 1.2 and you can also add your own examples. There can be more than one type of contract for each lawyer.

Lawyer	Types of contracts
I am a corporate lawyer working in M&A.	a.________________
I specialise in commercial real estate, representing landlords and tenants in a wide range of property matters.	b.________________
I am an employment lawyer. I act mainly for employers. I spend a lot of my time dealing with disputes and trying to keep cases from going to court.	c.________________
I am an in-house lawyer for a national chain of restaurants. Most of my work involves granting rights to companies to use our corporate logo and business model, to help expand our brand.	d.________________
I work with start-ups, advising on all aspects of starting and developing a business, including securing funding, dealing with suppliers and customers, and promoting products in new markets.	e.________________

1.4 Use the language from Exercise 1.3 and the examples in Exercise 1.2 to explain your area of work and the types of contracts that you draft or review. If you are a student, choose an area of work that you would like to specialise in and explain the types of contracts that a lawyer in this area would draft or review.

If you cannot find a precise English translation of the contracts you work with, explain who the parties to the contract are and the purpose of the contract. For example:

I draft and review what we call [construction contracts]. This type of contract is made between the [owner of land] and [a contractor] in which [the contractor agrees to carry out works on the owner's land].

1.5 Audio 8.1

David Lin is a work experience student, and Amelia Newman is a senior associate at the London office of international law firm Bracker and Price LLP. Listen to David speaking to Amelia Newman about contract drafting and answer the following questions:

a. What types of contracts does Amelia draft?
b. Who is responsible for drafting a contract?
c. What synonym for *precedent* does Amelia use?
d. Where can you find precedents?
e. What are some of the advantages and disadvantages of using precedents?

1.6 Refer to Exercise 1.5 and discuss these questions:

a. What is another meaning of the word *precedent* in legal English?
b. Can you think of any other sources of precedents, other than the ones that Amelia mentions?

Vocabulary note

The word *draft* can be used as both a noun and a verb. In Audio 8.1, Amelia says:

- *the buyer's lawyer drafts the contract* (verb)
- *but in other types of contracts ... it is usually the seller's lawyer who produces the first draft* (noun)

2. Contract structure

2.1 Audio 8.2

English-language commercial contracts usually follow a similar structure. When you are familiar with this structure, it makes it easier to find your way around a contract.

Listen to Amelia explaining the structure of a contract. Complete the following diagram with the parts of a contract in the order in which Amelia mentions them. The first answer is given as an example.

The parts of a contract

- ~~*introductory paragraph*~~
- signature blocks
- recitals
- definitions
- other core provisions
- boilerplate
- main provisions
- words of agreement

Contract structure diagram

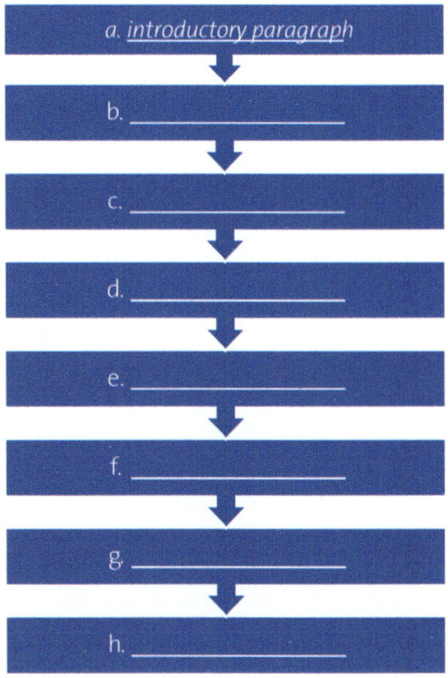

Vocabulary and pronunciation note

Commercial contracts can also include *schedules*. Schedules are found at the end of a contract, either before or after the signature blocks. Other similar words to *schedule* are *exhibit*, *appendix*, or *annex*. The main purpose of a schedule is to remove information from the main body of the contract to make the contract easier to read. For example, in a share purchase agreement, schedules could include more information about the shareholders of the company and its subsidiary companies.

Schedule can be pronounced with a *sch* sound like *school* (ˈskedʒuːl) or a *sh* sound like *shoe* (ˈʃedʒuːl).

2.2 Practise identifying the parts of a contract. First, check your answer to Exercise 2.1 in the Answer key. Then read the Example contract at the end of this chapter and label the different parts of the contract. For example:

This is the introductory paragraph:

THIS SHARE PURCHASE AGREEMENT is made on [ ]

BETWEEN:

(1) [ ] LIMITED, a company incorporated and registered in England and Wales (company number [ ]), whose registered office is at [ ] (the **'Seller'**); and
(2) [ ] LIMITED, a company incorporated and registered in England and Wales (company number [ ]), whose registered office is at [ ] (the 'Buyer').

2.3 Listen to Audio 8.2 again. Decide if these statements are true or false and correct any false statements.

	True	False
a. You do not have to include recitals in a contract.	O	O
b. Condition precedent means a template document.	O	O
c. If you want to know which law governs the contract, you will usually find this in the boilerplate clauses.	O	O
d. It is not necessary to review the boilerplate clauses because these are the same in every contract.	O	O
e. It is good practice to draft the introductory paragraph and the signature blocks at the same time.	O	O

2.4 There are different words in legal English for referring to the contents of a contract: lawyers talk about the *terms* or the *provisions* of a contract. When they want to refer to a specific provision in the contract, they use one of the following words:

- *clause*
- *article*
- *section*
- *paragraph*

Which word did Amelia use in Audio 8.2?

3. Contract language

When drafting and reviewing contracts, a lawyer needs to use language which reflects the parties' agreed terms and which is understandable to those who read the contract.
This section looks at particular aspects of English language in commercial contracts. It focuses on how to draft clearly and avoid ambiguities.

Legalese

3.1 Read the following extract of the first page of a contract. What are your first impressions when you read this? You can choose from the following or add your own thoughts:

- This contract must have been drafted in the last century!
- This language is too complicated for me to understand.
- I think I understand the general meaning of this extract, but I do not understand some of the words.
- All modern contracts are drafted like this. I am used to seeing this language and I do not have a problem with it.

THIS SALE OF GOODS AGREEMENT is made on [ ] by and between Turbulent Dryers Limited (Company no. 1234567) whose registered office is at Roundtree Business Park, Roundtree Lane, Leeds, LS14 6HY (hereinafter referred to as the 'Vendor') and Top Salons Limited (Company no. 9101112) whose registered office is at 74 Wentworth Road, Manchester, M14 6RS (hereinafter referred to as the 'Purchaser').

WITNESSETH

WHEREAS, the Vendor is in the business of selling professional hairdryers to hairdressers.

WHEREAS, the Purchaser is in the business of owning and operating a chain of hairdressing salons.

WHEREAS, the Vendor has agreed to sell the Goods to the Purchaser and the Purchaser has agreed to purchase said Goods from the Vendor subject to the terms and conditions hereinafter set forth.

NOW, THEREFORE, in consideration of the premises and the mutual covenants and agreements herein and for other good and valuable consideration the receipt and sufficiency of which are hereby acknowledged the parties hereto agree as follows:

3.2 The extract in Exercise 3.1 contains a lot of legalese. Legalese is a particular style of writing that some lawyers use, which includes old-fashioned language and long sentences.

a. Compare the extract in Exercise 3.1 with the first page of the example contract at the end of the chapter. What differences do you notice?

b. Rewrite the extract in Exercise 3.1 in a modern style using the example contract as a guide. For example, you could replace '(*hereinafter referred to as the 'Vendor'*)' with (*the 'Seller'*).

3.3 One aspect of legalese which is commonly found in contracts is words with a *here-* or *there-* prefix followed by one or more prepositions. The prefix *here-* means *this* and the prefix *there-* means *that*. For example:

- *hereinbefore* means *before in this document*
- *therein* means *in that document*

Pronunciation note

Pronounce the prefix and the prepositions separately:

hereinbefore is pronounced: *here – in – before*
therein is pronounced: *there – in*

Practise pronouncing the legalese in the following table and then complete the table with the meanings of these words in the extract in Exercise 3.1. The first answer is given.

Legalese	Meaning
a. hereinafter	*afterwards in this Agreement*
b. herein	
c. hereby	
d. hereto	

3.4 The *here-* and *there-* prefix formulations can be useful. For example, in the extract in Exercise 3.1 the drafter has used the *here-* prefix to avoid repeating *this Agreement*. However, the problems with using this type of language are that:

- it can be difficult to understand
- it can create ambiguities

Read the following section 29 from a real contract[1] and answer these questions:

a. What does *herein* mean? What does the prefix *here-* refer to?
b. The word *herein* creates an ambiguity in this clause because there are at least two possible meanings. How could you avoid this ambiguity?

29. This Agreement is made solely for the benefit of the Issuers and the Portfolio Manager, their successors and assigns, and no other person shall have any right, benefit or interest under or because of this Agreement, except as otherwise specifically provided herein. The Swap Counterparty shall be an intended third-party beneficiary of this Agreement.

For more examples, see the Legalese to Plain English Quick Reference in Appendix B.

Modal verbs

3.5 Modal verbs are auxiliary verbs which affect the meaning of other verbs in a sentence. Read the following modal verbs and discuss these questions:

a. What do each of these verbs mean in general English?
b. What do each of these verbs mean in legal English?

shall	must	may	will	should

3.6 In legal English, particularly in contract drafting, some modal verbs are used in different ways from general English.

Read the following clauses in the example contract at the end of this chapter and answer the questions:

a. In clause 2.1, what does *shall* mean?
b. In clause 8.1, what does *shall not* mean?
c. In clause 4.4, what does *may* mean?

3.7 Read Text 8.1 about the word *shall* and answer these questions:

a. What is a reason for not using *shall* in legal writing?
b. Which modal verb could you use instead of *shall* to impose an obligation?
c. Why do lawyers use *shall* in commercial contracts?
d. What approach does Ken Adams suggest?

Text 8.1 The *shall* debate

'*Delete every shall. Shall isn't plain English,*' says Bryan Garner.[2]
'*Banish shall; use must instead*' says Joseph Kimble.[3]

While modern legislation in the UK and the USA uses the word *must* for imposing obligations, the word *shall* is still commonly found in commercial contracts. In their book, *Clarity for Lawyers*, Mark Adler and Daphne Perry suggest that '*Lawyers like to use shall because it is traditional*'.[4] Perhaps lawyers are afraid to change language which has already been tried and tested and so this perpetuates the use of the word *shall*?

But is there anything wrong in using *shall* in commercial contracts? One problem is that there is no consistency in the use of the word *shall*. *Shall* is sometimes used in sentences where there is no obligation on a party to the contract. Take this example:

- *'Business Day' shall mean any day (other than a Saturday, Sunday, or public holiday) during which banks in London are open for business.*

There is no obligation in this provision. A definition is a statement of fact and should be written in the present simple tense:

- *'Business Day' means any day (other than a Saturday, Sunday, or public holiday) during which banks in London are open for business.*

Ken Adams puts it like this:

> *A symptom of verb-structure chaos in traditional contract drafting is overuse of 'shall'. By contrast, in my framework 'shall' serves only to impose a duty on a party that is the subject of the sentence, as in 'Acme shall purchase the Shares'. To make it easier to spot instances of 'shall' being used in other contexts, I encourage people to see if a sentence makes sense if in your mind you replace 'shall' with 'has (or have) a duty to'.*[5]

Applying Ken's *has a duty* test to the previous example, we can see that *shall* does not make sense in this context:

- 'Business Day' *has a duty to* mean any day (other than a Saturday, Sunday, or public holiday) during which banks in London are open for business.

So, should you delete *shall* and use *must* instead? It is simply a matter of choice. But whatever word you choose, make sure you use it consistently and only for the purpose of imposing obligations. This will make your commercial contracts easier to read.

3.8 In each of the following contract clauses, decide whether the word *shall* is imposing an obligation on a party to the contract. If *shall* is not being used to impose an obligation, rewrite the clause. Use clauses 4 and 14 in the example contract at the end of the chapter as a guide.

a. The Completion Date shall mean 25 June 2022.
b. This Agreement shall be conditional on the satisfaction of the Condition Precedent on or before the Completion Date.
c. The Buyer shall be entitled to waive the Condition Precedent at any time.
d. In the event that the Condition Precedent is not satisfied or waived on or before the Completion Date, this Agreement shall terminate with immediate effect.
e. On completion the Buyer shall pay the Purchase Price to the Seller in the manner set out in clause [ ].
f. This Agreement shall be governed by English law.

Expressions of time

3.9 Contracts contain many different expressions of time. One important expression is the duration or length of the contract. Read the following clause from a commercial lease and answer these questions:

a. What does the word *term* mean in this clause?
b. What is another meaning of *term* in legal English?
c. Is it clear when the term of this lease starts and ends?

> 2.1 The Landlord leases the Property to the Tenant for a term of five years from 01/05/2022.

3.10 Prepositions can cause ambiguities in expressions of time because it is not always clear whether the dates they refer to are included in the time period or not.

The language in the following boxes can help make time periods clearer:

starting on	ending on	from and including
up to and including	on or before	no later than

In each of the following clauses, identify the potential ambiguity in the expression of time and then rewrite the clause to make it clearer, using the expressions from the boxes. The first answer is given as an example.

a.	Clause	The term of this Agreement is for a period from 1 May 2022 to 1 May 2025.
	Ambiguity	*It is not clear if the dates of 1 May 2022 and 1 May 2025 are included in the time period.*
	Rewrite	*The term of this Agreement is for a period starting on 1 May 2022 and ending on 1 May 2025.* Or: *The term of this Agreement is for a period from and including 1 May 2022 up to and including 1 May 2025.*

b.	Clause	The Contractor shall commence the Works by 23 July 2022.
	Ambiguity	
	Rewrite	

c.	Clause	The interest rate for the period commencing on the Closing Date until 24 September 2022 is [ ].
	Ambiguity	
	Rewrite	

d.	Clause	The Company shall employ the Executive for a term of two years between 1 June 2022 and 1 June 2024.
	Ambiguity	
	Rewrite	

3.11 Other expressions of time in a contract relate to how quickly a party must perform an obligation.

Read the following clauses from a services agreement and answer these questions:

a. Are the expressions of time in each clause precise or vague?
b. What is the effect of using vague language in these types of clauses?

1. The Service Provider shall provide the Services to the Customer in accordance with the Specifications. The dates for delivery of the Services are set out in the Specifications and time is of the essence for these dates.
2. The Customer shall make all payments under this Agreement promptly. If the Customer fails to make payments on time, the Service Provider may stop work on the site pending payment and the Service Provider shall not be liable for any delays caused as a result.
3. The Customer shall provide in a timely manner any equipment that the Service Provider may reasonably require for the Services.
4. The Customer shall report to the Service Provider any defects in the Services as soon as reasonably practicable after any such defect comes to the attention of the Customer.
5. On termination of this Agreement all sums payable to the Service Provider become due immediately.

Sentence structure

3.12 In her book, *How to Write Simple and Effective Small Works Contracts in 500 Words,*[6] Sarah Fox says:

> *'Your small works contract will be easy to read if it has clear headings, short sentences and simple words.'*

Read the following contract clause and answer these questions:

a. Does this clause have a clear heading, short sentences and simple words?
b. How many times did you have to read this clause to understand its meaning?
c. What do you notice about the structure of the first sentence?
d. List the three ways in which the parties can terminate this contract.

> 10. This Agreement may be terminated by either party at any time prior to the expiration of the Term upon six months' notice in writing to the other party. Either party shall have the right to terminate this Agreement forthwith upon notice in writing to the other party in the event that after the date hereof there is a material breach of any term of this Agreement provided that where such breach is capable of being remedied a party shall only be entitled to terminate where the breaching party has not remedied such breach within thirty (30) days of written notification thereof. Either party shall have the right to terminate this Agreement with immediate effect upon notice in writing to the other party should the other party become insolvent or have an administrator, administrative receiver, receiver, or liquidator appointed over its assets.

3.13 Compare the contract clause in Exercise 3.12 with the following alternative version of the same clause and answer these questions:

a. Is the alternative version easier to understand? Why?
b. Which modal verb has replaced the expressions *shall have the right to* and *shall be entitled to*?
c. Which word has replaced the word *forthwith?*
d. Which word has replaced the words *in the event that*, *provided that*, and *should?*

> **10. Termination**
>
> 10.1 Either party may terminate this Agreement at any time by giving six months' written notice to the other party.
>
> 10.2 Either party may terminate this Agreement immediately, by giving written notice to the other party, if:
>
> 10.2.1 the other party commits a material breach of this Agreement and, if the breach is capable of remedy, fails to remedy the breach within 30 days of being notified in writing to do so; or
>
> 10.2.2 the other party becomes insolvent or an administrator, administrative receiver, receiver, or liquidator is appointed over its assets.

3.14 Clause 10.2 in Exercise 3.13 uses tabulation. Tabulation can make a contract clause clearer and easier to read. It is a useful way of dividing a long sentence or paragraph into subsections where the sentences or parts of the sentence contain common introductory language.

Read Clause 10.2 in Exercise 3.13 again and answer these questions:

a. What is the common introductory language in this clause?
b. What punctuation is used in this clause?

3.15 The following clause contains restrictive covenants. It is a clause from an employment contract. A *covenant* is a legal English word for a promise. A *restrictive covenant* is a promise not to do something, in other words, a prohibition.

a. Underline the language for expressing prohibitions in the clause.
b. What do you notice about the language for expressing prohibitions in this clause?
c. Which modal verb could you use to express these prohibitions?
d. Using your modal verb from (c), identify the common introductory language in this clause. Then rewrite the clause using tabulation.

For a period of one year immediately following termination of the Employee's employment, the Employee shall refrain from soliciting or enticing any Company employee to leave the Company and the Employee agrees not to accept into employment or use the services of any person who is a Company employee on the Termination Date. The Employee undertakes not to directly or indirectly engage or be interested in any business carried on in competition with any of the business of the Company and commits not to use any of the Company's trading names.

4. Contract review

4.1 When a lawyer receives a draft contract from the other side, they need to review it. This means that they need to read the draft contract to check that it reflects the terms that the client has agreed and that it protects the client's interests.

Discuss your experience reviewing draft contracts. If you are a student, discuss what you think you would find difficult if you had to review a contract.

4.2 Audio 8.3

Listen to Amelia explaining to David how she reviews a contract and compare the points she mentions with your discussion in Exercise 4.1. The clauses David and Amelia refer to are the clauses in the example contract at the end of this chapter.

4.3 Listen to Audio 8.3 again and complete the following clauses. Each space represents one word.

a. *The Buyer ______________ pay the Purchase Price at Completion by telegraphic transfer to the Seller's solicitors.*
b. *The Seller and the Buyer __________ __________ their __________ __________ to procure the satisfaction of the Conditions Precedent as soon as possible...*

Absolute and qualified obligations

4.4 In Audio 8.3, Amelia talks about *absolute* and *qualified* obligations.

a. What is the difference between an absolute and a qualified obligation?
b. Which of the clauses in Exercise 4.3 is an absolute obligation and which is a qualified obligation?

4.5 *To use efforts* (AmE), or *endeavours* (BrE), to do something means to try to do something. But how much time, money, and energy needs to be spent in trying could vary. The following boxes show examples of adjectives that are used with the word *efforts* to qualify obligations in commercial contracts. These expressions have not been consistently interpreted by the courts, and there is no agreement among academics about what they mean.

best efforts	*reasonable efforts*	*commercial efforts*	*business efforts*

a. In Audio 8.3, what problem does David identify in using these types of expressions in commercial contracts?
b. What reason does Amelia give for using this type of language?

Explaining contract clauses to a client

4.6 Audio 8.4

Listen to the final part of David's conversation with Amelia, in which Amelia explains three contract clauses to David. The clauses she refers to are the clauses in the example contract at the end of this chapter.

Match the following clauses on the left to the correct definitions on the right.

Clause	Definition
a. warranty	1. a clause which restricts the amount of compensation that is recoverable under the contract
b. indemnity	2. a statement in the contract promising that something is true
c. limitation of liability	3. a promise to reimburse specified losses

Vocabulary note: *warranty* or *guarantee*

Warranty and *guarantee* have multiple meanings in legal English. In B2C contracts it is common for *warranty* or *guarantee* to mean a promise to repair or replace defective goods. For example, a washing machine might have a *two-year warranty* or *a two-year guarantee.*

A *guarantee* can also mean a promise to answer for the debt of another person. For example, a loan agreement could include a *guarantee* by a third party to repay the loan if the borrower does not pay.

4.7 When lawyers are reviewing contracts, they often need to explain to a client what particular contract clauses mean.

Read the transcript for Audio 8.4 and identify all the expressions that Amelia uses to explain contract clauses to David.

4.8 Review the expressions for explaining contract clauses to a client in Phrase bank 8.1:

Phrase bank 8.1
Explaining contract clauses to a client
This clause says that ...
[clause] means that ...
See [clause]: it says here that ...
This clause explains the situation if ...
According to this clause ...
You can see an example in [clause] ...
This clause contains ...

4.9 With a partner, take it in turns to explain clauses 13 and 14 in the example contract at the end of the chapter as if you were speaking to a client. Use the expressions from Phrase bank 8.1.

For example, for clause 14.1, you could say:
This clause says that English law applies to the contract.

5. The future of contracts

This section looks at developments in legal technology and legal design which are impacting contracts.

Legal tech

5.1 What is *legal tech*, also known as *law tech*? Discuss how you would define it and then check the Glossary.

5.2 All lawyers use technology to some extent when drafting and reviewing contracts. For example, in Audio 8.1 Amelia talks about a database of precedents that she can use to draft a contract.

The following boxes contain some other examples of legal tech. Which of these are you familiar with?

artificial intelligence	e-signatures	smart contracts
contract management system	document automation	playbook

5.3 Use the examples from Exercise 5.2 to complete Text 8.2 about legal tech.

Text 8.2 Are you familiar with legal tech?

(a) ________________, sometimes called digital contracts or self-executing contracts, are contracts written in computer code on a blockchain. They contain agreed conditions for performance and once these conditions are met, obligations are performed automatically. This type of contract was used by insurance company AXA in their 'fizzy' product: if the customer paid for insurance and a flight was two hours or more late, then a compensation payment was made automatically to that customer.[7]

While these types of contracts are still quite rare, it is likely that your business has digitalised other aspects of the contracting process. Most companies have some type of (b) ________________.This could simply be a method of digitally storing your signed contracts or it could cover the whole contract lifecycle so that you can keep track of the creation, revision and performance of contracts. (c) ________________ could be useful here too: this allows a computer to perform a task which would typically be performed by humans. For example, it could quickly identify which of your contracts contain a force majeure clause or a non-competition clause.

Do you use templates to create draft contracts? You could speed up this process by using (d) ________________ which will generate a draft contract based on your answers to set questions. And don't forget your (e) ________________. This document or spreadsheet will give guidance on what changes to the draft contract can be accepted by your team during negotiations.

Finally, forget about physically signing a contract. Wet ink signatures are a thing of the past! Most contracts are now executed with (f) ________________

5.4 Read Text 8.2 again and discuss these questions:
- a. Which types of legal tech could be used in contract drafting and contract review?
- b. What is the advantage of document automation?
- c. Can you think of any disadvantages of using legal tech in contract drafting and review?

Legal design

5.5 Have you heard of *legal design*? What do you think it is?

5.6 Read Text 8.3 about legal design and answer these questions:
- a. What is the difference between legal tech and legal design?
- b. What does *information architecture* mean?
- c. How can you create white space in your contract?
- d. What techniques can you use to make key terms more visible?

Text 8.3 Legal design

Legal tech is about using technology in the contract drafting and review process, whereas legal design is about the way in which the information in a contract is presented.

Legal design is not simply about making a contract look nice by adding different colours and fonts, it is about organising information in the contract so that readers can more easily read and understand a contract and find the key information they need. Legal designers use the expression *information architecture* to refer to the organisation of the information in a contract.[8]

Here are some elements of good design that you can use in your contracts:

Plain English

Start by improving the contract language. Remove surplus words and legalese. Write in plain English.

Layout

Avoid blocks of dense text. Create white space with paragraphs, headings, and lists. You could use a question-and-answer format to display your text, and you could also use tables or columns.

Contents page

Use a table of contents, particularly if it is a long contract. This will help your reader navigate the document.

Key terms at the beginning of the contract

The main provisions of a commercial contract are usually found towards the beginning of a contract. Consider making these even more prominent by including a summary or table of key terms on the first page.

Highlight important terms

Some contracts highlight important terms using CAPITAL LETTERS, but this can still be difficult to read.

⚠ Instead, use icons or boxes to highlight text.

Diagrams

Use diagrams, flowcharts and timelines to help your reader visualise information.

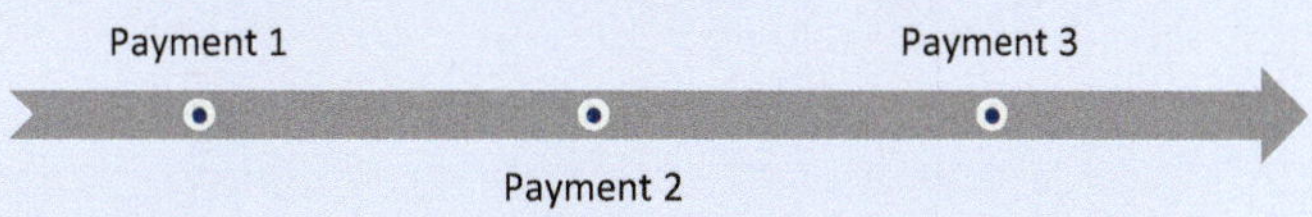

In the modern business world, clients want to be able to easily understand their contracts. The association *World Commerce & Contracting* highlights how large companies like Shell have used legal design to improve their commercial contracts.[9]

How will you use legal design?

5.7 Practise using legal design. Read the following liquidated damages clause. How could you improve the design of this clause? Identify what information it includes and then, using the elements of good design from Text 8.3, present it in a more accessible way.

Check the Glossary for a definition of liquidated damages.

LIQUIDATED DAMAGES

ALL TIME LIMITS FOR COMPLETION OF THE WORKS ARE OF THE ESSENCE OF THIS AGREEMENT. THE CONTRACTOR AGREES THAT THE WORKS WILL BE COMPLETED ON OR BEFORE THE COMPLETION DATE. THE CONTRACTOR AND THE OWNER AGREE THAT FOR EACH WEEK THAT THE WORKS REMAIN INCOMPLETE AFTER THE COMPLETION DATE, THE OWNER WILL BE PAID THE SUM OF ONE THOUSAND FIVE HUNDRED DOLLARS ($1,500) AND THE PARTIES ACKNOWLEDGE AND AGREE THAT THE SUM REFERRED TO IN THIS CLAUSE IS A REASONABLE AND PROPER ESTIMATE OF THE OWNER'S ANTICIPATED LOSSES AS A RESULT OF THE COMPLETION OF THE WORKS NOT HAVING BEEN COMPLETED ON OR BEFORE THE COMPLETION DATE.

Test yourself

1. Explain the purpose of and the parties involved in two different types of commercial contracts mentioned in this chapter.
2. Where would you find the boilerplate provisions in a commercial contract?
3. Which modal verb is commonly used to impose an obligation in a commercial contract?
4. What is the difference between absolute and qualified obligations?
5. Describe one way in which legal design can be used to improve a commercial contract.

Example contract

Note: This document has been prepared as an illustration of contract structure and language. It is not an example of perfect drafting. It is an incomplete document and should not be used in legal practice.

THIS SHARE PURCHASE AGREEMENT is made on [ ]

BETWEEN:

(1) [ ] LIMITED, a company incorporated and registered in England and Wales (company number [ ]), whose registered office is at [ ] (the 'Seller'); and
(2) [ ] LIMITED, a company incorporated and registered in England and Wales (company number [ ]), whose registered office is at [ ] (the 'Buyer').

BACKGROUND

The Seller has agreed to sell and the Buyer has agreed to buy the Shares subject to the terms and conditions of this Agreement.

IT IS AGREED:

1. DEFINED TERMS

1.1 'Business Day' means any day (other than a Saturday, Sunday, or public holiday) when banks in the City of London are open for business.

1.2 'Claim' means any claim made by the Buyer for breach of the Warranties.

1.3 'Company' means [ ] LIMITED, further details of which are set out in part 1 of schedule 1.

1.4 'Completion' means the completion of the sale and purchase of the Shares in accordance with this Agreement.

1.5 'Completion Date' means [ ].

1.6 'Conditions' means the conditions set out in schedule 2.

1.7 'Disclosure Letter' means the letter from the Seller to the Buyer, with the same date as this Agreement, relating to the Warranties.

1.8 'Encumbrance' means any interest of any person (including any right to acquire, option or right of pre-emption) or any mortgage, charge, pledge, lien, assignment, hypothecation, security interest, title retention or any other security agreement or arrangement.

1.9 'Group Company' means a subsidiary company listed in part 2 of schedule 1.

1.10 'Purchase Price' means the price that the Buyer shall pay to the Seller for the Shares in accordance with clause 3.1.

1.11 'Shares' means [ ] [ordinary] shares of £[ ] each in the Company.

1.12 'Warranties' means the warranties in clause 6 and schedule 4.

2. Sale and purchase

2.1 The Seller shall sell and the Buyer shall buy the Shares, with full title guarantee and free from all Encumbrances.

2.2 Title to the Shares shall pass to the Buyer on Completion and the Shares shall be sold and purchased together with all rights and benefits attached to or accruing to them at, or at any time after, Completion.

3. Purchase price

3.1 The Purchase Price is [ ]

3.2 The Buyer shall pay the Purchase Price at Completion by telegraphic transfer to the Seller's solicitors. The receipt of the Seller's solicitors will give a full and valid discharge of the Buyer's obligation under this clause.

4. Conditions

4.1 Completion of the sale and purchase of the Shares under this Agreement is conditional on the Conditions being satisfied or waived by the parties on or before the Completion Date.

4.2 The Seller and the Buyer shall use their reasonable efforts to procure the satisfaction of the Conditions as soon as possible but in any event before the Completion Date.

4.3 If at any time the Seller or the Buyer becomes aware of a fact or circumstance that might prevent any of the Conditions being satisfied, it shall immediately notify the other parties.

4.4 At any time the Buyer or the Seller may waive the Conditions on such terms as the Buyer may decide.

4.5 If any of the Conditions are not satisfied or waived on or before the Completion Date, this Agreement immediately ceases to have effect except for any rights or liabilities that have accrued under this Agreement.

5. Completion

5.1 Completion shall take place at the office of the Buyer's solicitors on the Completion Date.

5.2 On completion, the Buyer shall pay the Purchase Price in the manner specified in clause 3.2 and the Seller shall deliver the documents set out in schedule 3.

6. Warranties and indemnities

6.1 The Buyer is entering into this Agreement on the basis of, and in reliance on, the Warranties.

6.2 The Seller warrants and represents to the Buyer that each Warranty is true on the date of this Agreement and on Completion except as disclosed in the Disclosure Letter.

6.3 Where any Warranty refers to the knowledge, information, belief or awareness of the Seller (or any similar expression), the Seller shall be deemed to have such knowledge, information, belief and awareness as the Seller would have obtained had they made careful enquiries into the subject matter of that Warranty.

6.4 Without prejudice to any other right or remedies available to the Buyer, the Seller shall indemnify the Buyer against all losses which the Buyer incurs, directly or indirectly, as a result of any breach of the Warranties.

7. Limitation of liability

7.1 The liability of the Seller for all Claims shall not exceed £[ ].

7.2 The Seller shall not be liable for a Claim unless the amount of that Claim, or a series of connected Claims of which that Claim is one, exceeds £[ ].

7.3 The Seller shall not be liable for a Claim unless the Buyer has given the Seller notice in writing of the Claim within the period of 24 months beginning with the Completion Date.

8. Confidential Information and announcements

8.1 The Seller shall not disclose to any person this Agreement or any trade secret or other confidential information it has or acquires in relation to the Company.

8.2 The Seller shall not make any announcement concerning the terms of this Agreement without the prior written consent of the Buyer except as required by law or by any regulatory or governmental body (in which case the Seller shall consult with the Buyer in order to agree the content of any such announcement).

9. Notices

9.1 Any notice given under this Agreement shall be in writing, and shall be delivered by hand, or by prepaid recorded delivery first class post, or by registered airmail (in the case of an address for service outside the United Kingdom).

9.2 The addresses for service of notices on the Buyer or the Seller are its registered office address or such other address for service in the United Kingdom as a party may from time to time notify the other.

9.3 A notice served in accordance with this clause 9 shall be deemed to have been received:

9.3.1 if delivered by hand, at the time of actual delivery to the correct address

9.3.2 if delivered by prepaid recorded delivery first class post, two Business Days from the date of posting

9.3.3 if delivered by registered airmail, five Business Days from the date of posting

9.4 If receipt under this clause 9 occurs on a day which is not a Business Day or after 5.00 p.m. on a Business Day, the relevant notice shall be deemed to have been received at 9.00 a.m. on the next Business Day.

10. Assignment

10.1 No party shall assign, transfer, charge, or deal in any other way with this Agreement or any of its rights under this Agreement without the prior written consent of the other party except that the Buyer may assign its rights under this Agreement to a Group Company.

11. Severance

11.1 If any provision of this Agreement (or part of any provision) is or becomes illegal, invalid or unenforceable, the legality, validity and enforceability of any other provision of this Agreement shall not be affected.

12. Entire agreement

12.1 This Agreement constitutes the entire agreement between the parties with respect to all matters referred to in this Agreement. This Agreement supersedes any previous agreements between the parties relating to such matters.

13. Variation

13.1 No variation to this agreement shall be effective unless made in writing and signed by or on behalf of all the parties to this Agreement.

14. Governing law and jurisdiction

14.1 This Agreement and any disputes or claims arising out of or in connection with its subject matter are governed by English law.

14.2 The parties agree that the courts of England have exclusive jurisdiction to settle any dispute or claim that arises out of or in connection with this Agreement.

This Agreement has been executed by the parties on the date first above written

Schedule 1
The Company
Part 1: Details of the Company
Part 2: Subsidiary companies

Schedule 2
Conditions

Schedule 3
Completion

Schedule 4
Warranties

1. Litigation
   1.1 No civil, criminal, arbitration, administrative or other proceeding in any jurisdiction is pending or threatened by or against the Company

SIGNED BY [*director or authorised signatory name*] ....
Duly authorised for and on behalf of [*company name*]

SIGNED BY [*director or authorised signatory name*] ....
Duly authorised for and on behalf of [*company name*]

Notes

1 *Bayerische Landesbank v Aladdin Capital Mgmt. LLC* 692 F 3d 42 (2d Cir 2012)
2 Bryan A Garner, *Legal Writing in Plain English* (2nd edn, The University of Chicago Press 2013) 125
3 Joseph Kimble, *Writing for Dollars, Writing to Please: The Case for Plain Language in Business, Government, and Law* (Kindle edn, Carolina Academic Press 2014) 281
4 Mark Adler and Daphne Perry, *Clarity for Lawyers* (The Law Society 2017) 141
5 Ken Adams, 'Here's How the "Has a Duty" Test Works' (*Adams on Contract Drafting*, 20 August 2020) <https://www.adamsdrafting.com/heres-how-the-has-a-duty-test-works/> accessed 19 March 2022
6 Sarah Fox, *How to Write Simple and Effective Small Works Contracts in 500 Words* (Kindle edn, 500 Words Ltd. 2020) 249
7 AXA, 'AXA goes Blockchain with Fizzy' (*AXA*, 13 September 2017) <https://www.axa.com/en/magazine/axa-goes-blockchain-with-fizzy> accessed 23 April 2022
8 World Commerce & Contracting, 'Contract Design and Simplification' (*World Commerce & Contracting*) <https://www.worldcc.com/Research-Analytics/Contract-Design-Simplification> accessed 23 April 2022
9 Ibid.

9 Contract negotiations

About this chapter

Overview

This chapter is about negotiating commercial contracts. The first part introduces the topic and defines what negotiating means for lawyers. The second part focuses on preparing for contract negotiations, looking at researching the other side, understanding what the client wants, and prioritising terms to negotiate. The third part looks at understanding and using language effectively during negotiations. It includes ways to make proposals and counterproposals, to accept and reject proposals, and to close negotiations.

Throughout the chapter, there are exercises related to common business phrasal verbs and idioms which may feature in commercial negotiations. The chapter ends with a role-play commercial contract negotiation scenario.

Learning objectives

By the end of this chapter, you should be able to:

- prepare effectively for contract negotiations
- identify different stages in contract negotiations
- use appropriate language during negotiations
- determine effective strategies to reach solutions
- understand common idioms and phrases used in negotiations

Test yourself at the end of the chapter to check that you have achieved the learning objectives.

1. Introduction

1.1 Read the following quote about negotiation from *Getting to Yes: Negotiating an Agreement Without Giving In*[1] and discuss these questions:

   a. Do you agree with this definition?
   b. How would you define negotiation?
   c. When do lawyers negotiate?
   d. How is negotiating as a lawyer different from negotiating in your personal life?

> *'Negotiation is a basic means of getting what you want from others. It is back-and-forth communication designed to reach an agreement when you and the other side have some interests that are shared and others that are opposed.'*

DOI: 10.4324/9781003140207-9

1.2 Read Text 9.1 about the negotiating experience of Bea Bento, a Brazilian in-house commercial lawyer. Decide if these statements are true or false and correct any false statements.

Bea:	True	False
a. writes about negotiating settlement agreements	○	○
b. often drafts completely new terms without a template	○	○
c. thinks patience is the most important thing in negotiations	○	○
d. thinks that understanding other people's emotions helps in negotiations	○	○

Text 9.1 An in-house lawyer's experience negotiating contracts

What negotiating experience do you have?

I have negotiating experience as an in-house lawyer and previously as an associate at a law firm. As an in-house lawyer, most of the time, the negotiations start with the commercial team, who focus on the commercial aspects of the deal, but once we start to draft the contract it is in my hands to negotiate specific clauses with the other party, balancing legal risks with business objectives.

What types of contracts have you had to negotiate?

Most of them are business partnerships regarding some value-added services for our marketplace customers. These are strategic contracts that don't follow a standard contracting process, so often some clauses must be drafted from scratch.

What do you find challenging about negotiations?

I would say that the most important and challenging thing for negotiations are communication skills. Sometimes you know how you should approach the situation, but you don't have the communication skills – the right words, the tone of voice, body language – to do so. Communication skills are also different from culture to culture, language to language. Learning how to express yourself is the most valuable thing in a negotiation.

What are your strengths in negotiations?

My strengths are that I'm pretty open to learning and practising soft skills. Being humble and empathetic have also been a good companion to me in my negotiations.

1.3 Review the expressions for talking about your negotiating experience in Phrase bank 9.1:

Phrase bank 9.1	
Negotiating experience *As a [area of law] lawyer, I often negotiate [type of contracts]. With these contracts, it is important to negotiate clauses such as [list types of clauses].* *While I don't have any experience negotiating as a lawyer, in my personal life I have used negotiation skills before. For example [give an example].*	**Challenges** *The things I find challenging about negotiations are [list challenges].* **Strengths** *The things I do well when I negotiate are [list strengths], which make me a good negotiator.*

1.4 Discuss the following questions about your negotiating experience as a lawyer. If you have not negotiated as a lawyer before, talk about negotiating experience from your personal life. You may use the expressions in Phrase bank 9.1.

a. What negotiating experience do you have?
b. What types of contracts or conflicts have you negotiated?
c. What do you find challenging about negotiations?
d. What are your strengths in negotiations?

2. Preparing for contract negotiations

Understand the context

2.1 Audio 9.1

Negotiation is just one stage in the contracting process. The exact stages may differ depending on the type of contract and the parties involved.

Fabian Nilsson is a trainee lawyer and Jakob Lindberg is his supervising partner. They work at an international law firm based in Sweden called Aaberg and Adelsköld LLP. Fabian and Jakob are discussing an upcoming negotiation and how this fits into the contracting process.

Listen to Audio 9.1 and complete the diagram on the right with the stages of the contracting process provided on the left. The first answer is given as an example.

Stages of the contracting process

- ~~*The parties agree on some of the commercial aspects*~~
- The other side's lawyer drafts the first version of the contract
- The final version of the contract is sent to the parties and signed
- The other side's lawyer reviews the contract amendments
- The lawyers meet to negotiate the contract terms
- The lawyer who receives the first version marks up the contract
- The other side's lawyer drafts the final version of the contract

Diagram of contracting process

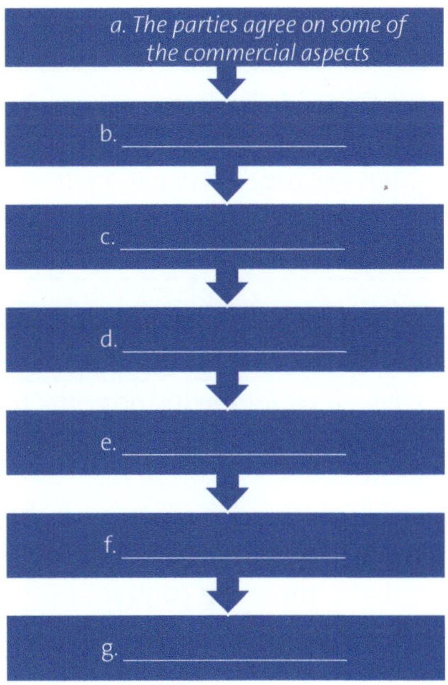

Vocabulary note

Ways to refer to the party with whom your client is negotiating a commercial contract are: *other side*, *other party*, or *counterparty*. You can also use these terms if your client is negotiating a settlement agreement as well as: *opposition* or *opposing party*.

2.2 Here are some common business phrasal verbs and idioms used in Audio 9.1 and their definitions. Match the phrasal verbs and idioms on the left to the correct definitions on the right. The first answer is given as an example.

Phrasal verb and idioms	Definitions
a. *have a word with someone (idiom)*	1. to update someone
b. take up (phrasal verb)	2. *to speak with someone*
c. bring someone up to speed (idiom)	3. to amend, to edit
d. draw up (phrasal verb)	4. to prepare something official in writing
e. mean business (idiom)	5. to respond
f. mark up (phrasal verb)	6. to work as fast as possible
g. to work against the clock (idiom)	7. to be serious
h. to come back (phrasal verb)	8. to accept

Vocabulary note: *to mark up* or *to red line*

In BrE, *to mark up* (verb) means to make changes to a document so that both the original and the new version can be seen. In AmE, this can be called *to red line* because the first set of changes are usually shown in red ink. These words can also be used as nouns: *the mark-up*; *the red-line*, and adjectives: *the marked-up copy*; *the red-lined copy*.

2.3 Fabian receives an email from Jakob about the upcoming negotiations. Read Jakob's email and answer the following questions:

a. Why are Fabian and Jakob going to meet?
b. What will they discuss in the meeting?
c. What does Fabian have to do before the meeting?

From: Jakob Lindberg j.Lindberg@ aaberg-adelskold.llp
To: Fabian Nilsson f.nilsson@aaberg-adelskold.llp
Subject: Preparing for the forthcoming negotiations

Dear Fabian

Following our discussion, I would like to schedule a meeting with you so that we can prepare for the forthcoming contract negotiations. There are quite a few things we need to discuss in the meeting, for example: researching the other side and understanding their perspective; understanding what our client wants, needs, and why; and prioritising what we will negotiate. Hanna, my secretary, will send through a meeting invitation shortly.

I attach some background information about the deal. Please read it before the meeting. This will help you understand the context of the negotiations, including who the parties are and what the negotiations are about.

Please also carry out some research into Autologica and its lawyer before our meeting.

Very best

Jakob
Jakob Lindberg
Partner | Commercial

2.4 Read the attachment to Jakob's email and answer the following questions:
a. Which law firm and which lawyer represents each party?
b. What do we know about each party?
c. What contract is being negotiated?

Aaberg and Adelsköld LLP

Case Reference: RBM012089000
Date: 11 January 2022
Lawyer: Jakob Lindberg

Background to negotiations of supply of goods agreement

- Our client, RB Motors, is one of the top ten car manufacturers in the world, founded in 1905 in Sweden. RB Motors wants to create the world's most sustainable vehicles. It is committing $20 billion over the next five years to develop electric vehicles.
- Autologica is a manufacturer of electric batteries.
- RB Motors and Autologica expressed a desire to enter into an agreement: RB Motors (customer) and Autologica (supplier).
- Autologica sent RB Motors their first draft of the supply of goods agreement.
- RB Motors instructed Aaberg and Adelsköld LLP to review the contract and a marked-up version was sent to Autologica's lawyers.
- The parties and lawyers will meet to negotiate the contract on 18 January 2022. Clarissa Porterfield, J&J LLP acts for Autologica. She will be joined by her new associate, Brent Riley.

Research the other side

2.5 Fabian carries out some research into Autologica and its lawyer. Read the following notes that Fabian has made and discuss why it is helpful to have this information before the negotiations.

Fabian's research notes

Autologica

- *Silicon Valley up-and-coming start-up (USA) founded in 2018 by Rodrigo Django (CEO)*
- *Has a growing client base including 'Auto-drive' (competitor of RBM)*
- *There was a case against Autologica related to late delivery during the Covid-19 pandemic, it settled out of court and it is unclear what happened*
- *Autologica has publicly declared an ambitious five-year growth strategy, so it is probably eager to get big clients to attract investors*
- *Rodrigo Django was recognised by SV Business Leader Awards as Most Visionary and Innovative Leader in Sustainability*

Clarissa Porterfield

- *Partner at J&J LLP, 'BigLaw' firm based in the USA, rumours she is currently being considered to become an equity partner in the firm*
- *10 years' experience negotiating commercial contracts*
- *Strong reputation for closing tough deals*
- *American, graduated from Harvard Law School*
- *Represents many top companies in the automobile sector*

Vocabulary note: *upcoming* or *up-and-coming*

Upcoming (adjective) means *will be happening soon. Up-and-coming* (adjective) means *making good progress and likely to achieve great success soon.*

Understand what your client wants, needs, and why

2.6 It is important to find out from your client what they want to change in the contract and why, as well as to use your own legal knowledge and experience to propose contract amendments which best protect your client from legal risks. You should also predict what the other side wants and why, and think of a range of suitable options which you can propose in negotiations in order to reach an agreement.

The following boxes contain headings of clauses contained in the supply of goods agreement between Autologica and RB Motors. What could Autologica, the supplier, and RB Motors, the customer, want in relation to each clause and why?

Payment terms | Force majeure | Warranty

2.7 Read the following marked-up delivery clause from the supply of goods agreement involving RB Motors and Autologica. The parts in red and the deleted parts show the changes that Jakob made to the original version. Jakob's internal comments are on the right.

Discuss these questions:

a. What amendments has Jakob made?
b. Why does RB Motors, the customer, want or need these amendments?
c. What do you think Autologica wants or needs in relation to this clause?

7. Delivery 7.1 The Goods shall be delivered on the date and at the address specified on the Order. 7.2 The Customer shall have 4 Business Days following delivery to inspect the Goods. ~~The Customer may not reject any delivery of Goods due to an incorrect volume of Goods being supplied.~~ If the Goods exceed the tolerance levels stated in the Order the Customer may reject all or part of the Goods and the Supplier shall promptly and at its own cost arrange for redelivery of the Goods in compliance with the Order. 7.3 ~~Time of delivery is not of the essence. The Supplier shall use its reasonable endeavours to meet delivery dates but such dates are approximate only.~~ Time of delivery is of the essence. If the Supplier fails to deliver the Goods on time, the Customer may: a. reject and return any delivery of Goods at the Supplier's expense; b. terminate this Agreement immediately by serving notice in writing on the Supplier; c. procure similar goods from an alternative supplier; and d. recover from the Supplier all losses, damages, costs and expenses incurred by the Customer arising from the Supplier's late delivery.	*We know of a contractual dispute between Autologica and another company regarding late delivery during the COVID-19 pandemic. Eymen Demir (CEO of RBM) told me that RBM also had late delivery problems in 2020-2021 with another supplier. Late delivery is an issue for RBM because it means delays in RBM's production line, financial losses, potential liability in relation to other contracts. Incorrect volumes are also a problem as they can cause losses and logistical problems, e.g. storage of extra Goods.*

Vocabulary note

In negotiation terminology, what a party *wants or needs* is referred to as a *position* (noun) and the *reason why* a party wants it is referred to as an *interest* (noun).

Prioritise which terms to negotiate

2.8 When negotiating a commercial contract, you cannot change everything. Instead, you must decide which clauses are the most important and focus negotiation efforts on them.

Fabian reads an article to help him understand which terms to prioritise in the supply of goods agreement. Read Text 9.2 and decide if the following statements are true or false. Correct any false statements.

	True	False
a. Terms which help the company do business include price and delivery.	○	○
b. Terms which protect the company from legal risks include limitation of liability and indemnification.	○	○
c. In contracts involving long-term business relationships, it is important to have many non-negotiables.	○	○
d. Having a range of reasonable options can speed up negotiations.	○	○

Text 9.2 Prioritise terms to negotiate in commercial contracts

When preparing for negotiations it is important to prioritise the terms you will negotiate. But according to World Commerce & Contracting, '*The terms we most often negotiate are not the same as those that negotiators say are most important. A consequence of this is that contracts and negotiations are designed to deal with failure, not to facilitate success*'.[2] So what terms should you prioritise? Here are three aspects which must all be taken into account when deciding.

1. Consider which terms are important from the business perspective

See things from your client's perspective. Ask your client what is important for them. You will probably discover that they want to negotiate terms that help them do business. They need to know what to do, how to do it, when to do it, and how much they will pay or receive. Important terms for achieving business objectives include the scope and goals of a project, responsibilities of the parties, price, and delivery. These terms also cause the most disputes, so focusing on getting these right could help prevent disputes from arising.

2. Consider which terms are important from the legal perspective

As a lawyer, you need to protect your client from legal risks. If a dispute arises, you need to ensure that your client is compensated for loss or limited in their liability towards the other party. Important terms for protecting your client from legal risks include limitation of liability, indemnification, termination, warranties, and liquidated damages.

3. Consider your client's big picture

You may know which clauses to focus on, but what about your approach? Prioritising is also about determining which terms are non-negotiable and which ones you can be flexible on. To help you decide this, you should understand the main goals of your client. In many cases, the client's main goals are to develop long-term business relationships and negotiate contracts quickly and cost-effectively. In these situations, non-negotiables should be kept to a minimum. Wherever possible, try to have a range of reasonable options and alternative solutions so that you can reach an agreement quickly.

2.9 After reading the article, Fabian asks Jakob what the main goals are for RB Motors. Read the following statement from Jakob and discuss these questions:

a. What are the two main goals of RB Motors?

b. How could these goals affect Jakob's approach to the negotiations?
c. Refer to Exercise 2.5. What do you predict the big-picture goals are for Autologica?

RB Motors' first main goal regarding this contract is to get the deal done quickly. The sooner it can start manufacturing and selling its new sustainable cars, the sooner it can start making a profit. Its second main goal is to establish a long-term business relationship with Autologica. A lasting relationship brings many benefits, for example, stability.

3. During a negotiation

Structure of negotiations

3.1 During negotiations, there are a number of things which happen. Put these options in the correct negotiation stage to complete the following diagram. There is no strict order and some options may appear in more than one stage. Each stage has been completed with one option as an example.

a. make compromises	~~b. introductions~~	c. reject proposals
d. make concessions	e. ask questions	f. accept proposals
~~g. review agreed points~~	h. make small talk	i. make counterproposals
j. discuss next steps	k. clarify positions	~~l. make proposals~~
m. introduce agenda	n. strengthen proposals	

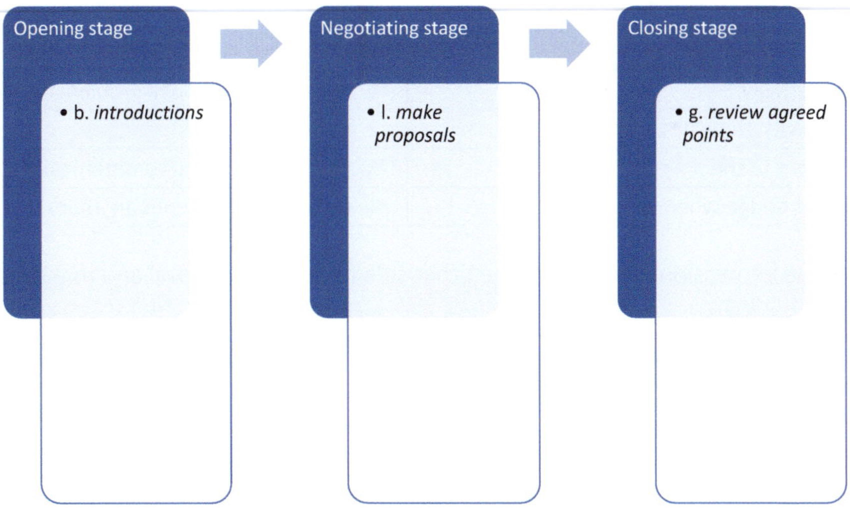

Opening and making proposals

3.2 Audio 9.2

In the opening stage of negotiations the parties and the lawyers introduce themselves and refer to organisational matters such as the agenda for the meeting. They may also engage in small talk to break the ice. After this, they start to negotiate when one side makes a proposal.

Listen to Audio 9.2. Jakob and Fabian are meeting Clarrisa and Brent to negotiate the supply of goods agreement. Decide if the following statements are true or false and correct any false statements.

	True	False
a. The lawyers will call each other by their full names.	○	○
b. Clarissa hopes to reach a reasonable solution.	○	○
c. The lawyers are not under time pressure.	○	○
d. The lawyers will consider each clause in turn.	○	○

3.3 Listen to Audio 9.2 again and complete the following sentences. These sentences are all phrases for opening negotiations. Each space represents one word.

a. *We're* _________ _________ *to working together to reach a satisfying and reasonable solution for both parties.*
b. *Likewise, we're happy to be working with you and hope this will be the beginning of a* _________-_________ _________.
c. *I'm sure you understand the importance of agreeing to our terms quickly, given the* _________ _________.
d. *My suggestion is that we work through the contract* _________ _________ _________.

3.4 Here are some common business idioms used in Audio 9.2 and their definitions. Match the idioms on the left to the correct definitions on the right.

Idioms	Definitions
a. make headway	1. to not worry about a problem until it happens
b. crack on with things	2. to make progress
c. get straight to the point	3. to continue doing something quickly
d. cross that bridge when we come to it	4. to talk directly about an important subject

3.5 Review the expressions for inviting the other side to make a proposal and making a proposal in Phrase bank 9.2:

Phrase bank 9.2	
Inviting the other side to make a proposal	**Making a proposal**
Let's look at the [clause title] clause. *Could you begin by explaining your amendments to clause [clause number]?*	*We suggest amending this clause from stating [original clause wording] to [amended clause wording]. This is important to my client because [reasons].*
Could you tell us about your proposed changes to the [clause title] clause?	*We propose changing the clause so that it reads as follows [read amended wording]. The key reasons for this are [reasons].*
We received your amendments and invite you to start with your first point.	*We would like to insert the wording [new wording] into this clause. This is because [reasons].*

3.6 Jakob wants to make the following amendment to the supply of goods agreement:

1.1 Defined Terms
Force majeure means any event beyond the control of the parties which could not have been reasonably anticipated or avoided by a party. Mechanical difficulties, shortage or increase of price of raw materials are not force majeure.

Read Jakob's notes about this clause and then write a dialogue where Clarissa invites Jakob to make a proposal and Jakob makes and explains the proposal. Use the phrases in Phrase bank 9.2.

Jakob's notes

- *RB Motors wants to limit the scope of the Force Majeure definition to reduce the likelihood that Autologica could claim force majeure and not perform its contractual obligations*
- *The company had a problem in the past with this and it doesn't want it to happen again*

Clarifying, explaining, and summarising

3.7 Audio 9. 3

It is important to listen carefully to the other side when they make proposals. You need to make sure that you have understood what the other party means before deciding how to react. Ask questions to clarify matters and summarise your understanding. If you are the one making the proposal, you must be prepared to explain your point further.

Listen to Audio 9.3. The following phrases are all appropriate for clarifying, explaining, and summarising in negotiations. Tick the phrases which Clarissa and Jakob use.

Asking for clarification and explanation	
○	a. *I didn't understand what you said. Could you please explain it again?*
○	b. *Thank you for explaining those points, but I'm afraid we don't understand. Could you elaborate?*
○	c. *Could you clarify your point please? What did you mean by ...?*
Giving explanations and clarifications	
○	d. *No problem. I'll try to explain this further.*
○	e. *Let me reword this. In other words, we mean ...*
○	f. *Returning to my point, what I was trying to say was ...*
Summarising your understanding	
○	g. *Thank you for clarifying that point. So we understand that ... is that correct?*
○	h. *If I understood correctly, you mean ... Is that right?*
○	i. *Let me summarise our understanding of your point. You would like ... because ... Did I miss out anything?*

Making counterproposals and accepting

3.8 In negotiations, you may accept the initial proposal, but if you do not fully agree with it you may make a counterproposal. A counterproposal is an alternative proposal which is made by the party who rejects the initial proposal.

Review the expressions for making counterproposals and accepting in Phrase bank 9.3:

Phrase bank 9.3

Making counterproposals	**Accepting**
We can't accept that, but we'd like to make a counterproposal. As an alternative to your proposal, we suggest ...	*We understand where you're coming from, and we accept this change.*
We accept the first part of this clause in principle, but we would like to suggest an alternative for the second part, it is ...	*Yes. I think we can agree to that.*
We have a different proposal. Would you consider the following ...?	*You've convinced us! Yes, we accept.*
	Yes, we're on the same page.
	Agreed.

3.9 Practise making counterproposals and accepting with a partner. Choose a role as either Clarissa or Jakob. Read clause 7.2 and the thoughts of your character. In your role-play, make counterproposals which reflect what your character is thinking to reach an agreement. Use the expressions in Phrase bank 9.3. There is no right or wrong solution.

7.2 The Customer shall have 4 Business Days following delivery to inspect the Goods. ~~The Customer may not reject any delivery of Goods due to an incorrect volume of Goods being supplied.~~ If the Goods exceed the tolerance level stated in the Order, the Customer may reject all or part of the Goods and the Supplier shall promptly and at its own cost arrange for redelivery of the Goods in compliance with the Order.

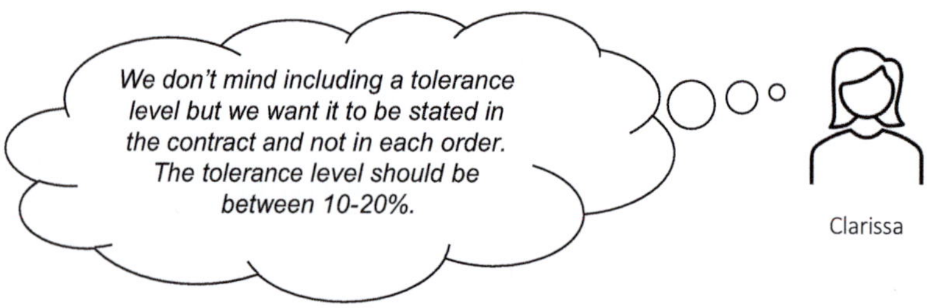

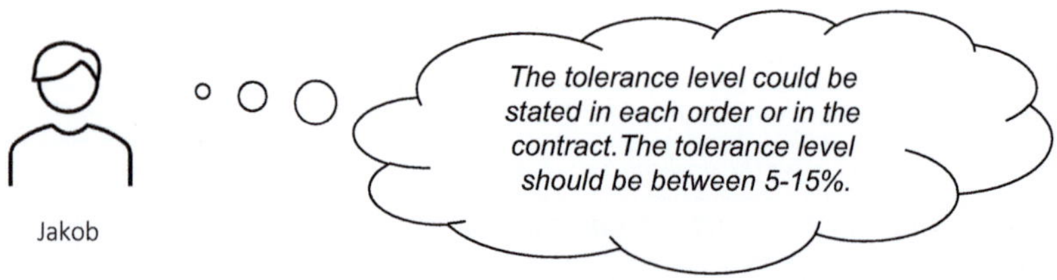

Rejecting proposals

3.10 Audio 9.4

If a proposal or counterproposal is not acceptable, then you will reject it. Listen to Audio 9.4 and decide if the following statements are true or false. Correct any false statements.

	True	False
a. Jakob consults with Fabian on this clause.	○	○
b. The parties cannot reach an agreement on this clause.	○	○
c. This point is only important for Clarissa.	○	○
d. The lawyers break for lunch.	○	○

3.11 Listen to Audio 9.4 again and complete the following sentences. These sentences are all phrases for expressing disagreement. Each space represents one word.

a. *This amendment is* ________ *impossible for us.*
b. *Well, Clarissa, I'm afraid that actually this is* ________ *an important point for our client.*
c. *Yes, we can understand that, but including time is of the essence is a* ________ *problem for us.*
d. *It's something we are* ________ *not willing to change.*
e. *I hear what you're saying, but it seems like we have a* ________ ________ *of a disagreement.*
f. *I'm sorry, delivery is* ________ *significant for us. Perhaps you could reconsider your position?*

3.12 Read Text 9.3 about how disagreement is expressed in different cultures and discuss these questions:

a. How do Clarissa and Jakob express disagreement differently?
b. How do you express disagreement in your culture?

Text 9.3 Disagreement across cultures

Erin Meyer states in her book *The Culture Map*[3] that in some cultures it is common and appropriate to express absolute disagreement to a proposal using *upgraders*. Upgraders are words which exaggerate the disagreement, such as *totally, completely, absolutely*. In other cultures, however, direct confrontation may be considered impolite and is avoided by using *downgraders*. Downgraders are words which downplay the disagreement, such as *partially, a little bit, maybe*.

Therefore, in international negotiations when one party says, '*I totally disagree with this clause*' and another says, '*Maybe we disagree slightly with this clause*', they could potentially mean the same thing: that you need to negotiate this clause because there is a disagreement.

If you are from a culture that uses upgraders and you notice that the other side is using downgraders, you can adapt your style by introducing downgraders to sound more polite.

On the other hand, if you are from a culture that uses downgraders and you notice the other side using upgraders, be careful. It is easy to sound rude if you do not understand the nuances of this disagreement style. Stick with your disagreement style and remind yourself to not get offended or react negatively to the other side's direct disagreement. Remember, they are not being rude; it is only a matter of culture.

3.13 The following words can be categorised as either upgraders or downgraders and classed as adjectives or adverbs. Adjectives are usually used to describe a noun. Adverbs are used to modify or qualify a verb, adjective, or another adverb.

Complete the following diagram by putting the words in the correct category and word class. The first example for each category and word class is given.

~~*a. pretty*~~	~~*b. huge*~~	c. minor	d. quite
e. small	f. just	g. big	h. major
i. probably	~~*j. a little bit*~~	k. really	l. incredibly
m. strongly	n. totally	~~*o. absolutely*~~	p. perhaps

	Upgraders	Downgraders
Adjectives	*b. huge*	*j. a little bit*
Adverbs	o. absolutely	*a. pretty*

3.14 Practise expressing disagreement with upgraders and downgraders. Read the transcript of Audio 9.4 with a partner. Replace Clarissa's upgraders with downgraders. Replace Jakob's downgraders with upgraders.

Dealing with deadlock

3.15 In Audio 9.4, the lawyers reach a deadlock. This means that they are unable to reach an agreement. Discuss the following questions:

a. How do the lawyers deal with the deadlock?
b. What would you do in this situation?

3.16 Read Text 9.4 on dealing with deadlock and decide if the following statements are true or false. Correct any false statements.

	True	False
a. Using a competing strategy is good for relationships.	O	O
b. If the clause is not important to your client, you should concede your proposal.	O	O
c. Taking a break can help parties rethink their strategies.	O	O
d. In a compromise, both parties get exactly what they want.	O	O
e. Reaching a win–win solution requires parties to collaborate.	O	O

Text 9.4 Dealing with deadlock

When you hit a deadlock in contract negotiations, use these strategies to move things forward.

1. Keep competing

If this clause amendment is so important to you, you may decide to keep negotiating using the competing strategy to get exactly what you want. You will need to convince the other side to agree to your point by strengthening your proposal. You may show the other side that you are willing to walk away from negotiations if they do not accept your terms, or offer to trade terms by saying, '*If you accept our change here, then we could accept your change to clause 5*'. The danger with a competing strategy is that you may end up damaging the relationship and in a worst-case scenario the other party may walk away.

2. Accommodate the other side

The opposite way to deal with deadlock is to simply give up and accommodate the other side's needs. If the clause is not a priority for your client this would be a good strategy. Giving the other side what they want will make them happy without having much of a negative impact for you. On the other hand, if you are dealing with an important clause amendment for your client, prioritising the other side's needs above your own is a bad choice. Your client will be frustrated and disappointed when they find out you conceded this proposal.

3. Avoid the disagreement

You may want to say to the other side, '*Let's take a break and deal with this clause later*'. Of course, if you react to every disagreement in this way, the other side could get frustrated, and negotiations could break down. However, sometimes taking a break can be a wise move. Some time out can help both parties calm down after a stressful disagreement and allow them to rethink their strategies on a particular clause.

4. Suggest a compromise

When both sides are at loggerheads, some flexibility may be needed to reach an agreement. In this situation you may want to propose a compromise. A compromise is where parties meet somewhere in the middle between their two opposite proposals. Although neither party gets exactly what they want, the solution will be considered fair.

5. Try to reach a win–win solution

There may be a solution which could satisfy both parties 100%. To reach a win–win solution, parties need to stop thinking of the negotiations as a battle and start working together. They need to listen to each other in order to fully understand what they want and why and then to create innovative solutions which are mutually beneficial. If you opt for this strategy, it will take time, energy, and creativity, but if successful it will certainly strengthen the business relationship.

Vocabulary note

In negotiation terminology, *BATNA* means *Best Alternative to a Negotiated Agreement*. This is the option your client has if they do not reach an agreement with the other side. If your client has a good alternative, they are in a strong position and can use this as leverage to persuade the other side to agree to their terms.

Reaching a compromise

3.17 Compromising is a powerful strategy to reach a fast and fair agreement. But before you are able to meet the other side in the middle, you must understand how much your client is willing to compromise.

Before the negotiations, Jakob and Fabian discussed the payment clause in the supply of goods agreement with the CEO of RB Motors. This clause sets out how much time RB Motors has to pay the invoices:

4. Payment
4.1 The Supplier shall invoice the Customer for the Goods on delivery of the Goods.
4.2 The Customer shall pay the Supplier's invoice within 30 days of receipt.

RB Motors would like to have more than 30 days to pay the invoices. Jakob and Fabian considered what would be the best, reasonable, and worst time range for RB Motors. They also predicted what Autologica might consider to be an acceptable time range.

Read Jakob's notes and answer the following questions:

What is the time range which Jakob:

a. knows will be acceptable to RB Motors?
b. predicts will be acceptable to Autologica?
c. predicts will be acceptable for both parties?

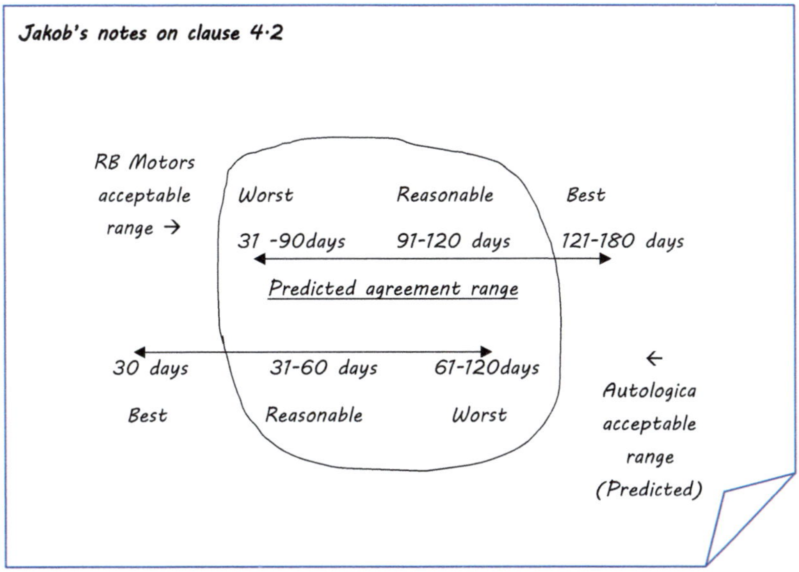

Vocabulary note

In negotiation terminology, the area where parties can potentially agree is referred to with the acronym *ZOPA* (noun), which stands for the *Zone of Possible Agreement* (noun).

3.18 When you know what is acceptable for your client and you have predicted this for the other side you can make proposals to reach a compromise in negotiations.

Read this quote from Alex Hamilton's book *Sign Here: The enterprise guide to closing contracts quickly*.[4] What is Alex saying? Do you agree with what he says?

'Companies often adopt a maximalist approach in their contracts, trying to win as much as possible on every point rather than being reasonable and heading straight to the middle ground. This might be appropriate for the most critical points in the deal ... but I consider this a fundamental mistake when applied generally across the contract:

- *Speed to close: Unreasonable terms create negotiations that slow down signing the agreement, reducing its value.*
- *Losing deal: Unreasonable terms can even kill deals. The other side may engage to see if you are serious, but if you continue to insist on your positions, they might walk away.'*

3.19 Review the expressions for compromising in Phrase bank 9.4:

Phrase bank 9.4	
Finding out information	**Suggesting a compromise**
Let's try to reach a reasonable solution for both parties. What would be reasonable for you?	*Perhaps we can compromise on this amendment. Can you meet us in the middle? We propose [state your new proposal].*
Your position is [state their position]. Our position is [state your position]. How could we reach a compromise?	*Although our ideal outcome would be [state ideal position] to be fair for both parties, we propose that we split the difference and [state proposal].*

3.20 Practise reaching a compromise with a partner on the payment term. Read clause 4 and then choose a role as either Clarissa or Jakob. Use the expressions in Phrase bank 9.4 and Jakob's notes in Exercise 3.17 to role-play a dialogue.

4. Payment
4.1 The Supplier shall invoice the Customer for the Goods on delivery of the Goods.
4.2 The Customer shall pay the Supplier's invoice within 30 days of receipt.

Finding a win–win solution

3.21 Audio 9.5

In many cases, compromising can be an effective strategy to reach a solution. However, when it is not an option, you have to find another way. If the parties to the contract are looking to create a long-term business relationship you may want to find a win–win solution. To do this, it is important to see things from the other side's perspective and work together to reach a solution.

Listen to Audio 9.5. The following questions are all appropriate for exploring options. Tick the phrases which Clarissa and Jakob use.

Questions for exploring options	
O	a. *Could you explain why [point] is so important for you?*
O	b. *Could we get your perspective on this?*
O	c. *What can we both do to resolve this issue?*
O	d. *What do you think? What's your view on this?*
O	e. *How can we solve this problem together?*
O	f. *How can we find a solution that will work for both parties?*
O	g. *Is there a way we can achieve both of our objectives?*
O	h. *Do you have any suggestions for a solution that suits both parties?*

3.22 Listen to Audio 9.5 again and complete the following sentences. These sentences are all phrases which encourage collaborating to reach a solution. Each space represents one word.

a. *We'd like to ________ ________ ________ on this and see things from your perspective.*
b. *Please put yourselves in our ________.*
c. *We'd like to try to reach a ________ solution.*
d. *This potentially works for ________ ________ ________.*
e. *We're on the ________ ________. That seems to achieve the objectives of both parties.*

3.23 Practise negotiating the following jurisdiction clause with a partner. First, read clause 12 and then choose a role as either Clarissa or Jakob. Next, read your character role. After, use the phrases from Exercise 3.21 and 3.22 to negotiate the clause and reach a win–win solution.

There is no right answer for this exercise. If each party is satisfied with the solution, you have reached a win–win outcome.

12. Jurisdiction. Any dispute arising out of or in relation to this Agreement shall be subject to the exclusive jurisdiction of ~~the New York Courts~~ the courts of Sweden, with the District Court of Stockholm as the court of first instance, to which the parties to this Agreement hereby submit.

Jakob representing RB Motors (customer)

You want to discourage litigation and would prefer to settle disputes via negotiations in good faith. However, if litigation must take place, then you want it to happen in Sweden. If there is a case against you, you definitely want it to be heard in Sweden as it is important to use a court system you trust. You also do not want to travel so far for proceedings.

Clarissa representing Autologica (supplier)

You want to discourage litigation and would prefer to settle disputes via negotiations in good faith. However, if litigation must take place, then you want it to happen in New York. If there is a case against you, you definitely want it to be heard in New York as it is important to use a court system you trust. You also do not want to travel so far for proceedings.

3.24 Refer to Exercise 3.23 and discuss the following questions:

a. What solution did you reach?
b. Are both parties satisfied with this solution?
c. What are some other possible solutions?

Closing negotiations

3.25 Audio 9.6

Listen to Audio 9.6 and decide if the following statements are true or false. Correct any false statements.

	True	False
a. Clarissa recaps what was agreed in the negotiations.	○	○
b. There are no outstanding clauses to be agreed on.	○	○
c. The lawyers will finish the negotiations via email.	○	○
d. Jakob will draft the final contract.	○	○
e. The aim is to sign the contract the week of 28th February.	○	○

3.26 Listen to Audio 9.6 again. Match the phrases on the left to the correct definitions on the right. The first answer is given as an example.

Phrases	Definitions
a. *This is where we currently stand.*	1. We have not finished the negotiations.
b. There are still a few outstanding clauses.	2. *I'm going to explain our current position.*
c. We've covered a lot of ground today.	3. Can you reasonably achieve it?
d. Is that doable for you?	4. Can we note this date, but it may be changed later?
e. I'll get the ball rolling.	5. If we achieve our tasks by the proposed deadlines ...
f. If everything goes to plan ...	6. I will start doing a task.
g. Can we all pencil that into our diaries?	7. We did a lot in this meeting.

4. A negotiation role-play

4.1 You are going to conduct a contract negotiation for a commercial property lease. A lease is a type of contract in which the owner of a property (the landlord) grants to the other party (the tenant) the right to use the property for an agreed period of time in return for a payment called rent.

Instructions

First, read the Common information for both parties and then choose the role of either Sazkar or Cedida-Comis. Next, read the Confidential information for your role only. Then read the Lease extract.

After preparing, role-play the negotiation making sure that you:

- open the negotiation
- make proposals and counterproposals
- clarify, explain, and summarise proposals
- accept and reject proposals
- deal with any deadlock
- reach a solution using a range of negotiation strategies
- close the negotiation

Common information for both parties

Sazkar is a multinational health care provider. It wants to open its first private hospital in Brazil, close to the city of São Paulo. It requires property for the hospital with good surrounding infrastructure.

Cedida-Comis is the owner of a large industrial unit in Atibaia, near São Paulo, which is suitable for the hospital. However, the property is in very poor condition.

One advantage of this property is that it only had one owner prior to Cedida-Comis. Cedida-Comis is the only legal owner of the property in accordance with the certificate of ownership issued by the competent Land Registry, which is not always the case with properties in Brazil.

Cedida-Comis is proposing to grant a lease of the property to Sazkar. Cedida-Comis has already sent a draft lease to Sazkar and Sazkar wants to make some changes to it.

The CEOs of the two companies, accompanied by their lawyers, are going to meet to negotiate the lease.

Confidential information for the landlord, Cedida-Comis

Cedida-Comis does not have other assets. Its financial position is weak. Its last tenant, Gangstarz, caused problems after changing ownership: Gangstarz failed to pay the final three months' rent and property taxes. Gangstarz also left the property in a very poor state of repair and is not contactable. Cedida-Comis wants to avoid having these issues again. Securing this deal is important as it has been difficult to find a new tenant for this property.

Cecida-Comis's position on the lease clauses:

Term

Cedida-Comis wants to secure a lease of 5–10 years.

Subletting

Cedida-Comis does not want the tenant to sublet because of the problems with the previous tenant. If subletting is really necessary, it wants the tenant to ask for permission beforehand and provide the subletting agreement with details of the subtenant. The subtenant must be prohibited from further subletting, and the tenant will remain responsible for the rent due and other terms and conditions under this lease.

Alterations to the property

The property is in need of major improvement and Cedida-Comis estimates repair costs of between R$4.5–6 million (R$ means Brazilian Reais). Cedida-Comis wants the property to be improved by the tenant. Cedida-Comis cannot afford to carry out the repairs itself or pay the tenant for the repairs. It could offer the tenant a rent-free period for a maximum of ten months for the repairs to be carried out.

Any structural repairs require Cedida-Comis's consent and relevant licences from public authorities.

Termination

Due to the problems with the previous tenant, Cedida-Comis wants to be able to terminate the lease if issues arise.

If the tenant wants to terminate early, before the Termination Date, it should pay a penalty. Under Brazilian law, a party has a right to early termination of the lease, subject to a penalty. It is important to fix this penalty in the contract to avoid wasting time and money later, because if the lease does not stipulate the penalty, the law provides that it will be determined by the court. The penalty for the tenant's early termination is often stated in terms of monthly rent proportional to the time left on the lease. For example, if the term of the lease is for ten years and the penalty is four months' rent, if a party terminates after five years they would pay 50% of four months' rent = two months' rent. If they cancel after 7.5 years, they pay a 25% penalty = one months' rent. Cedida-Comis would like to set a high penalty of eight months' rent.

Confidential information for the tenant, Sazkar

It has been very difficult for Sazkar to find property in this location that is suitable, according to the local zoning rules, for its needs and that has the correct documentation. It is important for Sazkar to secure this lease.

Sazkar's position on the lease clauses:

Term

Sazkar wants a lease with a 15-year term.

Subletting

It is very important that Sazkar is able to sublet the commercial property because it wants subcontractors operating in the same building: for example, a lab centre and catering companies. Sazkar does not want to get permission from the landlord for every sublease or to show the subletting agreements to the landlord. Sazkar is willing to make clear that it is responsible for all damage to the property and for all rent due by the subtenants.

Alterations to the property

The property needs a lot of work; Sazkar estimates costs of approximately R$7 million (R$ means Brazilian Reais) to ensure the property is fit for use. Such work would benefit the landlord because it would be improving the building and increasing its value. Under Brazilian law, if the tenant carries out necessary improvements, such as fixing the roof, they have the right to be compensated by the landlord for these expenses. Sazkar is willing to pay upfront for the work and improvements, but it does not want to keep requesting permission from the landlord. Sazkar wants to make sure that it can install hospital rooms and a laboratory, construct a car park, paint the walls, and fix the roof. Sazkar wants to be compensated for the amount spent on the works and improvements, either through a direct reimbursement or through a rent-free period.

Note: If a rent-free period is introduced, the date of the first rent payment in the contract must be changed. Here is some suggested wording for a rent-free period which could be added to Clause 4.1: *The Tenant shall be entitled to a rent-free period commencing on 1 September 2023 and ending on [ ].*

Termination

Sazkar wants to be able to terminate the lease early if it notifies the landlord in writing and pays a penalty. Under Brazilian law, the tenant has a right to early termination of the lease subject to a penalty that is reduced proportionately during the term of the lease. It is important to fix this in the lease to avoid wasting time and money later, because if the lease does not stipulate the penalty, the law provides that it will be determined by the court. The penalty for late termination is often stated in terms of monthly rent proportional to the time left on the lease. For example, if the term of the lease is for ten years and the penalty is three months' rent, if a party terminates after five years they would pay 50% of three months' rent = 1.5 months' rent. If they cancel after 7.5

years, they pay a 25% penalty = 0.75 months' rent. Sazkar would accept a maximum three months' rent penalty.

As a general rule, Brazilian law stipulates that the landlord must not terminate the lease without reason before the end of the term. In addition, Sazkar wants to limit the landlord's ability to terminate the agreement by specifying the meaning of 'material breach' and giving Sazkar the opportunity to remedy a breach before termination.

Lease extract, marked up in red by Sazkar

3. Term

3.1 The Landlord leases the Property to the Tenant for a term of ~~10~~ 15 years commencing on 1 September 2023. The term of this Lease ends on 31 August ~~2033~~ 2038 (the Termination Date)

4. Rent

4.1 The Tenant shall pay the Rent to the Landlord by equal monthly payments in advance on the first day of each month. The first payment of Rent is to be made on the grant of this Lease for the monthly period commencing on 1 September 2023.

5. Subletting

5.1 The Tenant shall not sublet any part or all of the Property, without the prior written consent of the Landlord which ~~is given at the sole discretion of the Landlord.~~ shall not be unreasonably withheld.

6. Alterations to the Property

6.1. The Tenant may make ~~minor non-structural~~ alterations to the Property without the Landlord's consent provided that such alterations:

6.1.1 are paid for in full by the Tenant
~~6.1.2 do not affect the structural integrity of the building~~
~~6.1.3 receive the consent of the Landlord~~

12. Termination

12.1. The Landlord may terminate this Lease at any time before the Termination Date by giving the Tenant 30 days' written notice ~~with immediate effect~~ if the Tenant materially breaches this Lease. The Tenant shall have 30 days upon receipt of such notice to remedy the breach. A material breach occurs on~~, which includes but is not limited to~~:

12.1.1. the Tenant assigning or subletting this Lease without the prior written permission of the Landlord

12.1.2. the Tenant making improvements to the Property which are unauthorised by ~~the Landlord or~~ government authorities

12.1.3. the Rent being unpaid for 30 days after becoming due

12.2. The Tenant may terminate this Lease at any time before the Termination Date by giving the Landlord 30 days' written notice. If the Tenant terminates this Lease it shall pay the Landlord a penalty corresponding to two months' Rent to be reduced proportionally in accordance with Schedule 2.

4.2 Reflect on your negotiation role-play in Exercise 4.1. Use the self-assessment questions in Appendix A.

Test yourself

1. How can you prepare for contract negotiations? Name three things you can do.
2. Describe what happens in the opening stage of contract negotiations.
3. What is the difference between an upgrader and downgrader?
4. Explain two strategies you can use when you reach a deadlock.
5. Give an idiom from this chapter and its definition.

Notes

1 Roger Fisher, William Ury, with editor Bruce Patton, *Getting to Yes: Negotiating an Agreement Without Giving In* (first published 1981, Houghton Mifflin Company, 1991) xviii.

2 World Commerce & Contracting 'The Most Negotiated Terms 2020' 4 <https://www.worldcc.com/Portals/IACCM/Resources/9934_0_Most%20Negotiated%20Terms%202020.pdf> accessed 30 April 2022.

3 Erin Meyer, *The Culture Map: Decoding How People Think, Lead, and Get Things Done Across Cultures* (International edn, Public Affairs, 2015) 195–218.

4 Alex Hamilton, *Sign Here: The Enterprise Guide to Closing Contracts Quickly* (Alex Hamilton, 2010) 28.

10 Alternative dispute resolution

About this chapter

Overview

This chapter is about alternative dispute resolution (ADR). The first part introduces different methods of ADR and compares ADR with litigation. The second part focuses on arbitration and the skills of drafting an international commercial arbitration agreement. The third part looks at mediation. It includes skills for lawyers representing their clients as well as skills and techniques used by mediators. The chapter ends with a role-play of a commercial mediation scenario.

Learning objectives

By the end of the chapter, you should be able to:

- distinguish between adjudicative and non-adjudicative methods of ADR
- recognise when ADR may be more appropriate than litigation
- understand how to draft an arbitration clause
- explain the mediation process to a client
- use a variety of mediator skills to facilitate mediation

Test yourself at the end of the chapter to check that you have achieved the learning objectives.

1. Introduction

1.1 The traditional method of resolving civil commercial legal disputes is through litigation. In litigation, one party brings a case against the other party in a court of law, and the case is decided by a judge. However, in many jurisdictions, litigation is now considered a last resort. This means that courts expect parties to try to settle their dispute using alternative dispute resolution methods before filing a claim or even during the litigation process. Alternative dispute resolution is often referred to using the acronym ADR. Read the following quote from The Jackson ADR Handbook[1] and discuss the following questions.

a. How would you define ADR?

b. What specific ADR methods can you think of?

> *'The term 'alternative dispute resolution' has no agreed definition. For the purpose of this Handbook the phrase is used to cover the full range of alternatives to litigation potentially available to resolve a civil dispute.'*

DOI: 10.4324/9781003140207-10

1.2 Read the following descriptions introducing various ADR methods and choose a heading for each one from the options given.

1. Mediation	2. Negotiation	3. Arbitration
4. Conciliation	5. Expert determination	6. Adjudication

a. ____________________

This method is almost always the first step parties use to try to resolve a dispute. Lawyers act on behalf of their clients to try to reach a settlement through discussion. Parties may leave the process at any time and if a solution is reached, it will only become binding if the parties sign a settlement agreement.

b. ____________________

A neutral third party called a mediator is appointed to facilitate negotiations and help the parties reach their own outcome. The process is flexible and if the parties reach a solution, it will only become binding if the parties sign a settlement agreement.

c. ____________________

This process is similar in some ways to litigation. An arbitral tribunal composed of an arbitrator, or a panel of arbitrators, hears each party present their case and issues a decision which is called an arbitral award. This award is final and binding on the parties.

d. ____________________

This method is similar to mediation and often these terms are used interchangeably. The exact usage depends on the jurisdiction. A conciliator will often give his or her opinion on the merits of the dispute and propose solutions.

e. ____________________

This method is similar to arbitration and is mostly used in specialised commercial fields such as the construction industry. A neutral third party called an adjudicator hears the parties and reaches a decision. This decision may or may not be binding on the parties depending on procedural rules set by the industry or the parties.

f. ____________________

An expert is appointed by the parties to determine a dispute involving a valuation or a highly technical issue. The parties have flexibility in setting out the process and usually agree that the decision will be binding.

1.3 ADR methods are categorised as *adjudicative*, also called *binding*, or *non-adjudicative*, also called *non-binding*. In adjudicative methods, at least one independent third party assumes a role similar to that of a judge. They decide the dispute and issue a decision which is usually binding on the parties. In most non-adjudicative methods, at least one independent third party facilitates the parties to resolve the dispute. The outcome is not usually binding on the parties until they have signed a settlement agreement.

Refer to Exercise 1.2 and answer the following questions:

a. Which of these ADR methods are adjudicative and which are non-adjudicative?
b. Are all of these ADR methods used in your jurisdiction?
c. Do you have experience of using these ADR methods to settle disputes?

1.4 Audio 10.1

Listen to Audio 10.1, a podcast interview with Anoush Parsons, a supervising partner in the dispute resolution team at Pringer and Goldment LLP. Complete the following sentences, which are all reasons why ADR may be more appropriate than litigation. Each space represents one word.

Reasons for ADR

a. *Often ADR is ____________________ than litigation, especially non-adjudicative types such as mediation.*
b. *It's commonly known that courts in most jurisdictions face backlogs of cases ... ADR can lead to a ____________________ resolution.*
c. *The third reason why ADR is so popular is because the ADR process is ____________________ unlike litigation which is generally public.*

1.5 Listen to Audio 10.1 again. Can you think of any other reasons why parties may prefer ADR to litigation?

1.6 Audio 10.2

Listen to Audio 10.2, the next part of the podcast interview. Complete the following sentences, which are all reasons why litigation may be more appropriate than ADR. Each space represents one word.

Reasons for litigation

a. *If parties want to set a ____________________, they should use litigation.*
b. *Litigation can satisfy a party's desire for ____________________.*
c. *If the case involves __________ - __________ or even ____________________ allegations, then the law may require, as a matter of public interest, that the case be decided in a court of law.*

1.7 Listen to Audio 10.2 again. Can you think of any other reasons why parties may prefer litigation to ADR?

1.8 Practise explaining what ADR is and reasons to use it with a partner. Read the scenario and then choose a role as either Finn Beck or Marlon Maier. Use the following information to role-play a lawyer–client meeting.

Scenario

AxxGazz, a German consultancy company specialising in providing engineering services to oil and gas projects, is in negotiations with PetroFirma, a Dutch company specialising in providing management services to oil and gas projects. The parties want to enter into a joint venture agreement.

Finn Beck, client

You are Finn Beck, the CEO of AxxGazz. Yesterday you attended a video conference meeting with PetroFirma. On the call PetroFirma mentioned that they would prefer to resolve disputes by ADR rather than by litigation. You do not understand what ADR means. Now you phone your lawyer, Marlon Maier, to ask for an explanation of ADR and reasons why you should use it instead of litigation.

Marlon Maier, lawyer

You are Marlon Maier, a junior lawyer at Pringer and Goldment LLP. Your client is Finn Beck, CEO of AxxGazz. You receive a call from Finn. He wants to understand ADR better. Explain to him what ADR means and the reasons for using ADR instead of litigation. Use Exercise 1.2 and the transcripts for Audio 10.1 and 10.2 as a guide.

2. Arbitration

This section focuses on the skills you need to draft an arbitration agreement and explain arbitration matters to clients.

An arbitration agreement

2.1 Audio 10.3

Marlon needs to understand arbitration better because Finn has now agreed with PetroFirma to include an arbitration clause in their joint venture agreement.

Listen to Marlon's meeting with Anoush, the supervising partner on this matter, and decide if these statements are true or false. Correct any false statements.

	True	False
a. An oral arbitration agreement is binding on the parties.	○	○
b. To relate a dispute to arbitration is a synonym for to submit a dispute to arbitration.	○	○
c. Parties may include an arbitration clause in their contract or draft a separate arbitration agreement.	○	○
d. Parties are not allowed to enter into an arbitration agreement once a dispute arises.	○	○
e. Party autonomy means that the parties must not have a relationship with any of the arbitrators.	○	○

2.2 Marlon reads the first part of his law firm's drafting notes, which set out some fundamental elements to consider when drafting an international commercial arbitration clause. Read Text 10.1 and answer these questions:

a. What is the difference between institutional and ad hoc arbitration?
b. What are the advantages and disadvantages of appointing one or three arbitrators?
c. What are some of the considerations to take into account when choosing the language of arbitration?

Text 10.1 Drafting notes, an international commercial arbitration clause, part 1

1. State the arbitration institution, if any, and procedural rules

Parties can choose between institutional and ad hoc arbitration. The main difference is that in institutional arbitration there is an institution which administers the arbitration and in ad hoc arbitration there is not.

In institutional arbitration, parties designate an arbitration institution to administer the arbitration, such as the Singapore International Arbitration Centre or the London Court of International Arbitration. Each arbitration institution has its own rules of procedure, called *arbitration rules*, which parties can choose to govern the procedural and administrative aspects of the arbitration. These rules can be automatically incorporated into the arbitration clause by reference and do not need to be written out in full.

In ad hoc arbitration, there is no arbitration institution involved and instead it is the arbitrators themselves who administer the process. The parties can set their own procedural rules, often adopting the United Nations Commission on International Trade Law[2] (UNCITRAL) rules.

In high-value cases, parties often prefer institutional arbitration, which can be time-effective and cost-efficient. If parties choose institutional arbitration, the arbitration clause should state the designated institution. In both institutional and ad hoc arbitration, the clause should state which procedural rules will govern the arbitration.

2. State the composition of the arbitral tribunal

Parties can choose the composition of the arbitral tribunal and how it will be appointed. This should be clearly stated in the arbitration clause. An arbitral tribunal is usually made up of one or three arbitrators and some jurisdictions prohibit the appointment of an even number of arbitrators.

A sole arbitrator will be faster and cheaper than three arbitrators, but high-value and complex disputes may require more varied expertise. Sometimes parties specify that one arbitrator will be appointed if the claim is under a certain value, and three arbitrators if the claim is over this threshold.

3. State the language of arbitration

Parties should choose the language for all arbitration communications, and this should be clearly stated in the arbitration clause. In international arbitration, English is commonly chosen, being the lingua franca of international business.

In any case, it is important to consider whether parties and arbitrators have sufficient knowledge of this language to conduct the arbitration. Without this, parties and arbitrators may take longer to understand and respond to communications and may have to rely on translators and interpreters. This will increase the time, cost, and potentially the accuracy of proceedings. Parties may decide to use the native language of one party. However, this automatically gives that party an advantage as they will not be reduced to communicating only what they *can*; they will be able to communicate exactly what they *want*. Parties may choose more than one language for arbitration, however, this is rarely done as it increases the costs and length of proceedings.

2.3 Read the following extracts from different arbitration clauses, which refer to elements mentioned in Text 10.1. Label each one from the options given.

1. Institutional arbitration	2. Ad hoc arbitration	3. One arbitrator
4. Three arbitrators	5. One or three arbitrators	6. Language

a. ____________________

The arbitration shall be conducted before a tribunal composed of three arbitrators. Each Party shall appoint an arbitrator within 30 days of the arbitration notice. If the appointed arbitrator accepts, the Party must notify the other Party within 7 days of acceptance. The two party-appointed arbitrators will jointly appoint the third arbitrator as president.*

b. ____________________

The language of the arbitration shall be English. Either party may submit documentary evidence in any other language if it provides a translation into English upon the request of the other party.

c. ____________________

Any dispute arising out of or in connection with this contract shall be submitted to and finally resolved by arbitration by the London Court of International Arbitration and governed by its Rules.

d. ____________________

The parties shall submit any dispute arising out of this contract to arbitration in accordance with the UNCITRAL Arbitration Rules.

e. ____________________

The arbitral tribunal shall comprise a sole arbitrator with expertise in the construction industry. If parties cannot agree on a sole arbitrator, the Institution shall appoint an arbitrator in accordance with the Rules.*

f. ____________________

If the claim value is $100,000 or less the arbitral tribunal shall consist of one arbitrator. If the claim value is more than $100,000 the arbitral tribunal shall consist of three arbitrators.

* These clauses set out a common practice for appointing arbitrators. If parties choose a one-person tribunal, they usually appoint an arbitrator they mutually agree on. If parties choose a three-person tribunal, each side usually appoints one arbitrator, and the parties or the party-appointed arbitrators agree on and appoint the president. If parties cannot agree on the arbitral tribunal:

- in institutional arbitration, the institution usually appoints the tribunal instead
- in ad hoc arbitration, the parties may need to seek assistance from the courts on this matter.

2.4 Marlon reads the second part of his law firm's notes on drafting an international commercial arbitration clause. Read Text 10.2 and answer these questions:
   a. What is the difference between the seat and the venue?
   b. What should parties consider when choosing the seat?
   c. What is the difference between the governing law of the contract and the governing law of the arbitration agreement?
   d. Is it necessary to always state the governing law of the arbitration agreement?

Text 10.2 Drafting notes, an international commercial arbitration clause, part 2

1. State the seat of arbitration

Parties should choose the *seat* of arbitration, also called the *place*, and state this in the arbitration agreement. The seat is the jurisdiction whose arbitration law governs the arbitration process. For example, if an arbitration clause states, '*The seat of arbitration shall be England*', the Arbitration Act 1996[3] will govern the arbitration process. The arbitral tribunal must act in accordance with this law throughout arbitration and if they do not, a party may bring a claim in a national court of the seat claiming that the arbitration award is invalid. The court will apply the arbitration law of the seat to determine whether or not to annul the award. If an award is considered to be valid and a party does not comply with it, the other party may bring proceedings in a national court of the seat to enforce the award.

The seat should not be confused with the physical or virtual location where proceedings are held, often referred to as the *venue*.

When selecting the seat, parties prefer jurisdictions with effective national arbitration laws, a high-quality judiciary, and those which are signatories to international arbitration agreements such as the New York Convention.[4] These aspects make it easier to challenge and enforce the award both nationally and internationally.

2. State the governing law of the contract

Parties should choose the governing law of the contract, also called the *substantive law*, *law of the contract*, or *applicable law*, which will be used to determine substantive matters of law. For example, if a claimant initiates arbitration claiming that the respondent has breached the contractual payment terms, the arbitral tribunal will apply the governing law of the contract to determine whether there has been a breach of contract. If the parties' contract states, '*This Sale of Goods Agreement is governed by the laws of England*', English contract law will be applied to the dispute.

3. If the governing law of the contract and seat are different, state the governing law of the arbitration agreement

Parties may choose a governing law of the arbitration clause. The governing law of the arbitration agreement will be applied to determine whether there is a valid arbitration agreement in existence and if so, how to interpret it. For example, if a claimant initiates arbitration, the respondent may bring proceedings in court, arguing that there was no valid arbitration agreement in place. To determine the validity of the arbitration agreement, the court will apply the governing law of the arbitration agreement. If the arbitration agreement states, '*The governing law of this Arbitration Agreement shall be the law of England*', the court will consider whether the elements to form a binding arbitration agreement were present in accordance with English law.

Where the governing law of the contract and seat are the same, the governing law of the arbitration agreement need not be stated. It only needs to be stated if the governing law of the contract and seat are different, to avoid ambiguity.

2.5 After reading the drafting notes, Marlon reads the law firm's template arbitration clauses.[5] Read the following clauses and label them as either ad hoc or institutional arbitration.

a. ____________________

Any dispute arising out of or in connection with this contract, including any question regarding its existence, validity or termination, shall be referred to and finally resolved by arbitration administered by the [*arbitration institution*] in accordance with the Arbitration Rules of the [*arbitration institution*], which are deemed to be incorporated by reference into this clause.

The Tribunal shall consist of [*one/three*] arbitrator(s).

The seat, or legal place, of arbitration shall be [*city, country*].

The language to be used in the arbitral proceedings shall be [*language*].

The governing law of the contract shall be the substantive law of [*jurisdiction*].

b. ____________________

Any dispute, controversy, difference, or claim arising out of or relating to this contract, including the existence, validity, interpretation, performance, breach, or termination thereof or any dispute regarding non-contractual obligations arising out of or relating to it shall be referred to and finally resolved by arbitration under the UNCITRAL Arbitration Rules in force when the Notice of Arbitration is submitted.

The law of this arbitration clause shall be [*jurisdiction law*].
The appointing authority shall be [*name of institution or person*].
The place of arbitration shall be [*city, country*].
The number of arbitrators shall be [*one/three*].
The arbitration proceedings shall be conducted in [*language*].

Vocabulary note

Many arbitration institutions provide model clauses and commonly use the modal verb *shall* to express an unambiguous obligation to arbitrate.

2.6 Here are some nouns, verbs, collocations and phrases used in the example arbitration clauses in Exercise 2.5. Match the words on the left to the correct definitions on the right. The first answer is given as an example.

Nouns	**Definitions**
a. *arbitration institution* →	1. a person or institution chosen by parties to a dispute or determined by arbitration rules to assign the arbitrator(s)
b. arbitral proceedings	2. *an organisation which provides administrative services for arbitration and which has its own set of arbitration rules to govern the arbitration procedure*
c. notice of arbitration	3. action taken in arbitration to settle a dispute
d. appointing authority	4. a document notifying the other side that a party is submitting a dispute to arbitration
Verbs	**Definitions**
a. deem	1. to find a solution which generally cannot be appealed
b. finally resolve	2. to happen
c. arise (arise, arose, arisen)	3. to consider
Collocations and phrases	**Definitions**
a. in force	1. in relation to
b. arising out of	2. including the writing of another document into this document
c. in connection with	3. valid, in effect
d. in accordance with	4. originating from
e. incorporated by reference	5. following, under

2.7 Marlon, acting on behalf of AxxGazz, sent a joint venture agreement to PetroFirma's lawyers. The original draft of the joint venture agreement stated that dispute resolution would be through litigation. PetroFirma's lawyer has responded with an email and a red-lined version of the dispute resolution clause.

Read the following email and highlight the wording in the amended dispute resolution clause which causes these problems:

a. It does not show an unambiguous commitment to arbitrate.
b. It states an incorrect name of arbitration institution.
c. The seat is ambiguous.
d. The governing law of the arbitration agreement is ambiguous.

From: Henrick Baker henrick.baker@zeelandlaw.nl
To: Marlon Maier marlon.maier@pringergoldment.llp
Subject: Amendments to joint venture agreement (PetroFirma and AxxGazz)

Dear Marlon

Thank you for the joint venture agreement. As you know, PetroFirma have agreed with AxxGazz to use arbitration instead of litigation. Here is our amendment to the dispute resolution clause to reflect this.

The main amendments are as follows:

- The governing law is Dutch law
- The seat is the LCA
- The venue is Rotterdam
- The language of arbitral proceedings should be Dutch
- The preferred arbitral tribunal composition is one arbitrator

Marked-up clause:

~~**Governing Law:** This contract is governed by the laws of Germany.~~

Dispute resolution: ~~In the event of a dispute arising under this Agreement between the Parties, the Parties irrevocably submit to the exclusive jurisdiction of the courts located in Berlin, Germany.~~ *This Joint Venture Agreement (JVA) shall be governed by and construed in accordance with Dutch law. If any dispute arises a Party may serve on the other a notice of arbitration to finally resolve disputes by arbitration administered by the London Court of Arbitrage in accordance with its rules. Within thirty (30) days of the notice of arbitration being issued by the initiating Party, the Parties may together appoint (1) one arbitrator. The venue of the arbitration is Rotterdam, the Netherlands or otherwise as agreed by the Parties. The arbitration proceedings shall be in the Dutch language.*

Looking forward to your response.

Many thanks
Henrick Baker
Associate Zeeland Law

Vocabulary note

Sometimes the dispute resolution clause, in particular the arbitration clause, is referred to as the *midnight clause*[6] because it is often one of the last clauses to be considered and drafted late at night. This can result in a *pathological clause*,[7] a clause which is badly drafted and ineffective.

2.8 Practise advising on a dispute resolution clause with a partner. Read the amended dispute resolution clause in Exercise 2.7 again. Then read the scenario and choose a role as either Finn or Marlon. Use the following information to role-play a lawyer–client meeting.

Scenario

After receiving the email from Henrick Baker, PetroFirma's lawyer, Marlon meets his client, Finn, to discuss the dispute resolution clause.

Finn Beck, client

After reading the amendments to the dispute resolution clause you are confused. You have the following concerns that you want to check.

- Is the governing law now Dutch law? You would prefer something more neutral, for example, using the laws of England and Wales.
- What's the London Court of Arbitrage? Will you need to travel to London? That's not a problem.
- Is one arbitrator enough? What if there is a complex dispute? Cost isn't an issue for AxxGazz.
- Will you have to travel to the Netherlands for arbitration hearings? You don't want to travel and would prefer to attend proceedings in London or online.
- You can't speak Dutch. How can you deal with proceedings if the language is Dutch? You would prefer to use English.
- Are there problems with this clause?

Ask Marlon questions to understand the clause better. Marlon will ask you questions to find out what you would like to change so that he can amend the clause.

Marlon Maier, lawyer

Finn is confused about the dispute resolution clause. He will ask you questions to understand it better. Make sure you explain these aspects to him: the arbitration institution, the seat, the number of arbitrators, the arbitration language, and the governing law of the contract.

Discuss with Finn what he would like to change. There is some guidance in the Answer key on things you may want to mention.

2.9 After the meeting, Marlon must redraft the dispute resolution clause to reflect Finn's wishes, which he will then send to the other side to review.

Redraft the clause using the templates provided in Exercise 2.5 as a guide and include the following elements:

- **Arbitration institution:** the London Court of International Arbitration
- **Arbitration tribunal:** three arbitrators, one to be appointed by each party, and each appointed arbitrator to appoint the third arbitrator as the president
- **Language:** English
- **Seat:** London, England
- **Governing law of the contract:** the law of England and Wales

Multi-tiered dispute resolution

2.10 Sometimes contracts include a multi-tiered dispute resolution clause. A multi-tiered dispute resolution clause sets out the order of different ADR methods which parties must use to resolve their disputes.

Read the following multi-tiered dispute resolution clause[8] and answer these questions:

a. What are the methods parties must use to attempt resolution of the dispute?
b. Can a party submit a dispute to arbitration without trying to resolve the dispute by mediation first?
c. In the second paragraph, the words '*the dispute shall be referred to and finally resolved by arbitration*' are used. What would be the consequences of changing *shall* to *may* or *should*?

Multi-tiered dispute resolution

In the event of a dispute arising out of or relating to this contract, including any question regarding its existence, validity or termination, the parties shall first seek settlement of that dispute by mediation in accordance with the LCIA Mediation Rules, which Rules are deemed to be incorporated by reference into this clause.

If the dispute is not settled by mediation within 6 days of the commencement of the mediation, or such further period as the parties shall agree in writing, the dispute shall be referred to and finally resolved by arbitration under the LCIA Rules, which Rules are deemed to be incorporated by reference into this clause.

The language to be used in the mediation and in the arbitration shall be English.

The governing law of the contract shall be the substantive law of England and Wales.

In any arbitration commenced pursuant to this clause,

(i) the number of arbitrators shall be one; and
(ii) the seat, or legal place, of arbitration shall be London, England.

Vocabulary note

A multi-tiered dispute resolution clause is sometimes named after the types of dispute resolution methods specified in it. For example, the clause in Exercise 2.10 can be called a *Med-Arb clause* as it specifies using mediation first and then arbitration.

Technology and AI in arbitration

This section looks at developments in legal technology and artificial intelligence (AI) which are impacting arbitration.

2.11 Read Text 10.3 and discuss the following questions:
  a. How is technology currently being used in arbitration?
  b. In what ways could AI be used in the future?
  c. How would you feel representing a client in an online arbitration proceeding?
  d. What are the advantages and disadvantages of a robot arbitrator?

Text 10.3 Technology and AI in arbitration

The 2021 International Arbitration Survey[9] conducted by the School of International Arbitration at Queen Mary University of London in partnership with White & Case LLP highlights current trends in arbitration. Many people within the international arbitration sphere completed the survey and were interviewed on their perspectives. Regarding the use of technology, the results were as follows:

- 90% use videoconferencing at least sometimes
- 88% use hearing room technologies (e.g. multimedia presentations, real-time electronic transcripts) at least sometimes
- 80% use cloud-based storage at least sometimes
- 72% use virtual hearing rooms at least sometimes

According to Freshfield Bruckhaus Deringer's Annual International Arbitration Top Trends Publication 2020,[10] AI is currently mostly being used by lawyers to identify relevant documents to support legal proceedings in the e-discovery process. However, the publication reports that in the future, AI could potentially assist arbitration proceedings in the following ways:

- to predict the outcome of arbitration
- to create a fully immersive realistic hearing experience where parties wear virtual reality headsets
- to create robot judges who could act as arbitrators

3. Mediation

Mediation may be one step in a larger process towards resolving a dispute, or it may be a successful means by itself to find a solution. As a lawyer, you may represent a client in mediation, or you may be asked to act as a mediator. The first part of this section deals with skills related to representing your client and the second part deals with skills you need as a mediator in facilitative mediation. The mediator skills are still relevant for lawyers to use in mediation.

Lawyer skills

Types of mediation

3.1 Luca Babić has just started a new job as a lawyer at Kovačić Associates, a boutique law firm with expertise in employment law matters. Luca has just written a blog post about different types of mediation for the law firm's website.

Read Text 10.4 and label each heading with the correct option.

1. Evaluative mediation
2. Transformative mediation
3. Facilitative mediation

Text 10.4 Choosing the right type of mediation

Many parties choose mediation to settle their disputes, as it offers a cost-effective and time-efficient alternative to litigation and arbitration. It is appropriate for a range of disputes and can lead to improved relationships between the parties and creative solutions such as an apology from a colleague or the securing of a good reference letter. But some parties are confused about which type of mediation to opt for. This article sets out the main types of mediation to help you understand which one is best for you.

a. ____________________

The mediator asks questions and listens to the parties to help them understand what each of them wants and why. The mediator does not evaluate the strengths and weaknesses of each party's case, make recommendations about settlements, give legal advice, or impose decisions. Instead, the mediator helps the parties to reach their own mutually satisfactory solution. The focus is on the interests of the parties rather than the legal merits of each party's case. This form of mediation is most common.

b. ____________________

Each party presents their case to the mediator in a session which may resemble a mini-trial. The mediator evaluates the strengths and weaknesses of each case and gives an opinion on whose case is stronger. The mediator may recommend a settlement. The focus is on the legal merits of each party's case rather than the interests of the parties.

c. ____________________

The mediator uses a range of techniques to empower the parties and to help them to recognise each other's needs, interests, and perspectives. The focus is on improving the relationship and communication between the parties rather than the legal merits of each case or even reaching a resolution of the dispute. The parties have a lot of control over the process and the outcome of the mediation.

Whichever mediation type you opt for, remember that any settlement will only become binding once it is agreed upon and signed by the parties.

3.2 Refer to Exercise 3.1 and discuss the following questions:

a. What are the differences between the three types of mediation?
b. Are these three types used in your jurisdiction?

Advising on mediation

3.3 Luca receives the following email from Sofia Horvat, a potential client.

Read the email and then discuss why mediation could be the most suitable option instead of litigation or arbitration.

From: Sofia Horvat sofia.horvat.1990@mail-online.net
To: Luca Babić luca.babic@kovacic-associates.law
Subject: Forced to leave work and need advice

Dear Mr Babić

I found your law firm's website when I searched for 'employment law help' on the internet. I'm not sure if you can help me, but I'm unsure of who I should contact. I'll outline my problem so that you can get an idea of what happened.

I used to work at the Kiplington Hotel as an Events Officer. I worked there for over three years. I really enjoyed my work and I had a good relationship with all of my colleagues. Last year I became unhappy, mainly because of my manager, Richard. Richard's behaviour towards me changed and our relationship broke down. Here are a few things he did:

- He made me work more hours and do more tasks which weren't in my work contract with no extra pay.
- He promised to hire support for me and pay me a bonus, but he never did this.
- He criticised my work constantly, which made me feel bullied and unhappy.

I tried to talk to Richard about these issues, but he ignored me. Last month I resigned as I felt I didn't have any other choice. I haven't been paid my final salary or holiday pay. Now I'm struggling to find another job and I'm worried that I won't get a positive reference from the hotel when I apply for other positions.

Can you give me some advice on what I can do?

Kind regards
Sofia Horvat

3.4 Luca agrees to represent Sofia on this matter and he advises her to mediate this dispute. Sofia and her ex-employer, the Kiplington Hotel, agree to mediation and a mediation session is arranged with a mediator. The mediator sends all the parties and their lawyers a mediation agreement. A mediation agreement is a contract which sets out the terms and conditions for conducting the mediation. After receiving the mediation agreement, Sofia calls Luca to ask him some questions.

Read the following extract from the mediation agreement and answer Sofia's questions, making reference to the correct clause in the mediation agreement.

Sofia's questions

a. *I'm worried that Richard is going to be dishonest in the mediation. How do we know that he'll be honest?*
b. *There are some things that happened at work that I don't want any of my ex-colleagues (who are not part of the mediation) to find out about. Is it possible they'll find out about things I say in the mediation?*
c. *What do I do if I have something I want to say privately to the mediator?*

d. *What if I'm not happy with the solution, do I have to sign the agreement?*
e. *I'm worried I might get upset in the session. If it's all too much, can we stop the process?*
f. *If Ivan refuses to resolve the dispute, can I use this as evidence against the Kiplington Hotel if I go to court?*

Mediation Agreement

This agreement is dated 21 November 2022 and is between:
Sofia Horvat ('Claimant'); and
Kiplington Hotel ('Defendant') (together the 'Parties').

Background

(A) Sofia Horvat was previously employed as Events Officer by the Kiplington Hotel.
(B) A dispute has arisen between the Parties whereby Sofia alleges that she was forced to resign and is owed one month's salary and holiday pay.
(C) Ivan Sever, the HR Manager at the Kiplington Hotel, is appointed as the representative of the Kiplington Hotel and is authorised to settle the dispute.
(D) The Parties wish to try to resolve this dispute by mediation and have nominated Gillian Stone, a mediator from Resolution Chambers ('Mediator'), to conduct the mediation.
(E) Richard Frank, manager at the Kiplington Hotel who was responsible for managing Sofia, will appear as a witness.

It is hereby agreed as follows:

1. Commitment to mediation

The Parties shall cooperate in good faith with the Mediator and with each other to try to resolve the dispute.

2. Confidential and without prejudice

Any information concerning the dispute disclosed during mediation is confidential and without prejudice. The Mediator and the Parties shall only keep copies of documents related to the mediation after termination of this agreement if it is reasonable to do so. The Mediator will only share information from a private session with the other party with the disclosing party's permission. Communications related to the mediation cannot be used as evidence in court.

3. Settlement agreement

If the Parties reach a settlement in mediation, their representatives may draft a written settlement agreement which the Parties may sign at their discretion. The Parties will only be bound to the terms of settlement once it is written and signed by both Parties.

4. Termination of the mediation

Mediation is a voluntary process and parties will not be forced to stay if they do not want to. This agreement will be terminated:

(a) if a Party does not wish to continue, after consultation with the mediator; or
(b) if a settlement is reached by the Parties; or
(c) at the discretion of the mediator, after consultation with the Parties.

Vocabulary note

In some jurisdictions, such as England and Wales, the *defendant* in employment cases is called the *respondent*.

The mediation process

3.5 Audio 10.4

It is the day of Sofia's mediation. At the beginning of the session, the mediator gives an opening statement to explain the mediation process.

Listen to the first part of the mediator's opening statement and decide if these statements are true or false. Correct any false statements.

	True	False
a. The parties will address each other in a formal way, using titles and surnames.	○	○
b. The parties will sign the mediation agreement at the end of the day.	○	○
c. Ivan has authority to settle on behalf of the Kiplington Hotel.	○	○
d. The parties must be respectful, listen to each other, and not interrupt each other.	○	○
e. After the mediator's opening statement, Ivan will begin.	○	○

3.6 The exact structure of a mediation depends on the type of mediation, the parties, and the jurisdiction. Listen to Audio 10.4 again and complete the following timeline of the general mediation process using the options. The first answer is given as an example.

The parts of a mediation

- ~~mediator's opening statement~~
- lawyers draft the settlement agreement
- parties may hit a deadlock
- parties' opening statements
- parties reach a solution
- mediator reviews achievements
- parties may sign the settlement agreement
- exploring solutions in plenary and caucuses

Mediation process diagram

a. Mediator's opening statement
↓
b. ____________________
↓
c. ____________________
↓
d. ____________________
↓
e. ____________________
↓
f. ____________________
↓
g. ____________________
↓
h. ____________________

3.7 Practise explaining the mediation process with a partner. Read the scenario and then choose a role as either lawyer or client. Use the following information to role-play a lawyer–client caucus session during the mediation.

Scenario

After the mediator's opening statement, Sofia asks to speak to Luca privately.

Sofia, client

You are very nervous. When the mediator was giving the opening statement, you didn't listen to anything. You want to understand what will happen in the mediation.

Luca, lawyer

You notice that Sofia is very nervous. You must summarise and explain the mediation process to Sofia in a way that she can understand. Use Exercise 3.6 and the transcript for Audio 10.4 as a guide.

Mediator skills

Effective listening

3.8 Listening effectively is an essential skill for a mediator. Read Text 10.5 and discuss these questions:

a. What level do you usually listen at throughout your day and with different people?
b. Which level should a facilitative mediator listen at?
c. How is listening as a facilitative mediator in a mediation different from a lawyer in a client meeting?

Text 10.5 Three levels of listening

Madelyn Burley-Allen in her book *Listening The Forgotten Skill: A Self-Teaching Guide,*[11] goes beyond defining listening as active or passive and instead categorises listening into the following three levels.

Level 1: emphatic listening

The listener:

- pays full attention to the verbal and non-verbal communication of the speaker
- tries to see things from the speaker's perspective and is non-judgemental
- shows they are listening through verbal and non-verbal communication
- is empathetic to the speaker's feelings and thoughts

Level 2: hearing not listening

The listener:

- pays attention to the words the speaker is saying and not why they are saying it
- focuses on the logical meaning of the words and not the speaker's feelings
- may give the speaker the impression that they are fully listening and understanding
- may actually misunderstand what is being said

Level 3: distracted listening

The listener:

- sometimes listens but is often distracted by their own thoughts and judgements
- is most interested in what they can say rather than listening
- does not show they are listening through verbal or non-verbal communication
- may misunderstand what is being said

3.9 Practise listening at different levels with a partner. Role-play the mediation with Sofia speaking to Gillian, the mediator, using all of the following three scenarios. Choose a role as either Sofia or Gillian. When you have finished role playing the first scenario, move on to the next one. You can take some time when you move to the next scenario to read the information for your role.

Scenario 1

Sofia speaks about her work situation before the dispute arose with her employer.

Gillian, mediator

Instructions

Ask Sofia to explain her work situation before the dispute arose with her employer. When she is talking, focus on other things. Avoid eye contact, look around the room, act distracted by fiddling with papers or clicking a pen. Interrupt Sofia with comments, or advice:

- *Let me tell you about my work ...*
- *I have a colleague ...*
- *I have a funny story ...*
- *In my opinion, you should ...*

Sofia, claimant

Instructions

The mediator will ask you to talk about your work situation before the dispute arose with your employer. When you tell your story, you must show the emotion of happiness and sadness through your voice and body language. You can include other emotions and you can add extra information.

Story

I used to work at the Kiplington Hotel as an Events Officer. I worked there for over three years. I really enjoyed my work and I had a good relationship with all of my colleagues. I worked very hard, I was good at my job, and everyone told me I was the best Events Manager the hotel had ever had. Last year I became unhappy. The whole work situation changed because of the pandemic. Everyone got really stressed and there were a lot of problems at work. I became unhappy mainly because of my manager, Richard. His behaviour towards me changed and our relationship broke down.

Scenario 2

Sofia speaks about the problems she faced at work.

Gillian, mediator

Instructions

Ask Sofia to explain the problems she faced at work. When she is talking pay attention to the words she says and the logical meaning of the words. Don't explore the deeper meaning of what she says and don't pay attention to her feelings. You can take notes about what she says. Use phrases to encourage her to continue:

- *Yes, I understand ...*
- *Yes, that's a difficult situation ...*
- *Mmm ... please continue with your explanation ...*

Sofia, claimant

Instructions

The mediator will ask you to talk about the problems you faced at work. When you tell your story, you must include the emotions of embarrassment and confusion through your voice and body language. You can include other emotions and you can add extra information.

Story

I think all the problems started when one of my colleagues, the Social Media Assistant, got Covid and was off work for a long time. Richard made me do her job as well as mine. These responsibilities were not in my contract, and I didn't get any extra pay for it. Richard made me work more hours to get everything done. He said if I didn't do it, he'd give me a bad employee performance appraisal. With so much more work than normal, I got stressed and sick. Richard promised to hire new support staff and pay me a bonus, but he never did this. Sometimes I made mistakes because I was overworked. Once I made a silly mistake and a customer complained about me. Richard shouted at me in front of my colleagues and the customer. I tried to talk to Richard about these problems, but he didn't listen.

Scenario 3

Sofia speaks about her response to her work problems.

Gillian, mediator

Instructions

Ask Sofia to explain what she did in response to her work problems. Pay full attention to what she says and the way she says it. Try to see things from her perspective. Ask questions to clarify what Sofia says. Summarise what she says to check you have understood correctly. Comment on what you notice about her body language and feelings. Show that you are listening through your body language.

- *It seems that you are feeling [emotion]. Is that right?*
- *You said [summarise a part of what she said]. Did I understand correctly?*
- *What do you mean by [repeat what she said]?*

Sofia, claimant

Instructions

The mediator will ask you to explain what you did in response to your work problems. When you tell your story, you must include the emotions of anger and worry, through your voice and body language. You can include other emotions and you can add extra information.

Story

Last month I resigned. I left work. I'd had enough. One day I came into the office and the computer wasn't working. Richard arrived late to work and started shouting at me. I couldn't cope anymore, so I walked out of the office. I felt I didn't have any other choice. I was so upset. I felt like all of those years I'd spent working for the company meant nothing. They didn't recognise all of my hard work. They didn't appreciate me!

After I left, I thought they'd pay me my final salary and holiday pay. I'm owed this, but they've never paid me. They need to pay me. I don't have a lot of savings, and I'm in financial difficulty. I need that money to pay my rent and bills.

I'm trying to find another job, but I'm really struggling. I've applied for a few positions, but I haven't got an interview yet. I'm worried the hotel won't give me a positive job reference, which I really need.

3.10 Refer to Exercise 3.9 and discuss the following questions:
  a. Which level was the mediator listening at in each part?
  b. As Sofia, did you feel listened to and understood in each part? Why?
  c. As Gillian, which part did you find easy, and which part did you find challenging? Why?

Reframing

3.11 Mediators sometimes use a technique called reframing to help parties communicate in a more productive way. The following Tweet™ by conflict-resolution expert Dr Tammy Lenski[12] contains two statements that could be said by a party to mediation.

Read the Tweet™ and answer these questions:
  a. What is the difference between the two statements?
  b. Which statement do you think is more helpful for resolving conflicts and why?

3.12 Read Text 10.6 about reframing and then answer these questions:
  a. What is the difference between framing and reframing?
  b. What are three examples of when reframing could be helpful?

Text 10.6 Reframing for better communication

Framing

Each party to a conflict has their own perspective on what the problem is, who is responsible, and how it can be resolved. The way each party views and describes the dispute is called framing.

The frame problem

A party's framing may prevent constructive communication and may lead to further conflict. If a party obsesses about the past, they may not be able to move forward in the present and the future. If a party concentrates on demanding one thing that they want and the other party disagrees, they may hit a deadlock. If a party focuses on blaming the other party, they won't be able to collaborate on reaching a mutual solution.

Reframing

Reframing is a technique where the mediator rewords what a party says in a more constructive way without losing the fundamental meaning. For example:

- A party talks about the past: the mediator rewords this to the present to help parties move beyond what cannot be changed to what is now in their control.
- A party states what they want: the mediator rewords this to show the reason why they want it, to help parties move beyond rigid demands and consider innovative alternatives to resolve the dispute.
- A party makes an accusation: the mediator rewords this to remove blame and acknowledge feelings, to help parties move towards a more productive dialogue.

Reframing can help parties to agree on the nature of the dispute and then to collaborate on solutions.

3.13 In Sofia's mediation, Gillian, the mediator, uses the technique of reframing. Read the following table, which shows the mediator's reframing. Choose the correct reframing reason to complete the table. The first answer is given as an example.

Reframing reason

1. ~~*Blaming the other party → acknowledging feelings*~~
2. Stating what a party wants → stating the reason why they want it
3. Focusing on the past → focusing on the present or the future

Sofia's statement	Mediator's reframing	Reframing reason
Richard is totally incompetent and a liar. He knew I couldn't cope. He promised to hire more staff and he didn't.	So, what you're saying is 'I felt upset and unsupported?'	a. *Blaming the other party → acknowledging feelings*
I should have received my last salary over a month ago. I remember this time last month, I checked my bank and again, it wasn't there! I was so angry!	So, the thing which is important to you right now is that you receive your salary?	b.
I want a good reference from the hotel! I don't understand why they haven't given me one already!	So, the reason behind this is that a good reference letter could help you find a new job?	c.

3.14 Refer to Exercise 3.13. Rewrite the following statements with an appropriate reframing the mediator could make. These statements are made by Ivan. The first answer is given as an example.

Reframing reason: blaming the other party → acknowledging feelings

Ivan		Mediator's reframing
Sofia knew Richard was under a lot of pressure during the pandemic, she ignored this and was impatient and rude.	→	a. *So you're saying that Richard felt under pressure and ignored?*
Sofia made lots of mistakes, her standard of work was low.	→	b.

Reframing reason: focusing on the past → focusing on the present or the future

Ivan		Mediator's reframing
We kept explaining to Sofia that we couldn't pay her salary because of ongoing financial difficulties.	→	c.

Reframing reason: stating what a party wants → stating the reason why they want it

Ivan		Mediator's reframing
We want to reach an agreement today … we've wasted enough time and money on this already!	→	d.

Reality testing

3.15 Sometimes parties to a mediation have unrealistic ideas about how to resolve the dispute. For example, they may be demanding an unrealistic amount of damages that the other party cannot agree to or threatening to sue the other party when neither party really wants this. These unrealistic ideas do not help to resolve the dispute. When this happens, the mediator can use the technique of reality testing.

Read the following examples showing how the mediator uses the technique of reality testing. Discuss what you think reality testing means and then compare your answers to the explanation given in Exercise 3.16.

Sofia

They must give me a positive reference stating that I was their best Events Manager.

Mediator's reality testing

You mentioned that your work declined in the last month, so how will that work in practice?

Sofia

I demand £100,000 to settle the dispute!

Mediator

How did you arrive at this figure?

Sofia

If the hotel doesn't agree to give me what I want, I can just sue them, and I'll win because employees always win.

Mediator

How sure are you that you would win? How much could a lawsuit cost? How long could it take? What would you do with the time and money you could save if we resolve this now?

3.16 Reality testing is where the mediator asks a party questions, usually in a private session, which helps them to reach a more realistic perspective. When using this technique, the mediator must be careful to ensure that they do not compromise their neutral position by judging a party as having right or wrong ideas. This is important to maintain the trust of each party.

Read the following demands from Ivan. How could you respond as a mediator using the reality testing technique?

Ivan

We'll pay half her final salary, but we won't pay any compensation or holiday pay.

Mediator

a.

Ivan

We're happy for it to go to the Employment Tribunal. It won't cost us anything in the end because she'll end up paying all our fees … when she loses!

Mediator

b.

Ivan

We'll give her a reference… a negative one though!

Mediator

c.

Mediation role-play

3.17 You are going to role-play a mediation between three parties and the mediator:

1. Speedy-Grill
2. CleanCo*
3. DrainEx
4. Mediator

*In reality, CleanCo would be represented by their insurance company because the company has gone into liquidation.

Instructions

Read the following common information for all parties and then choose a role. Your role can be a representative of one of the parties or the mediator. Next, read your party role and do not read the other party roles. Then role-play the mediation.

If you play the role of a party (not the mediator) make sure that you:

- effectively listen
- try to reach a solution
- follow any rules set by the mediator

If you play the role of the mediator, make sure that you use the mediator skills of:

- effective listening
- reframing
- reality testing

Common information for all parties and mediator

Speedy-Grill is a new fast-food drive-through restaurant at a motorway service station. It needed a solution to deal with the sewage from its toilets and kitchen. Speedy-Grill entered into a contract with DrainEx, a consulting company specialising in drainage.

DrainEx advised Speedy-Grill that there were three options to dispose of the sewage:

1. connect Speedy-Grill's pipes to the main sewer;
2. treat the sewage on site and discharge it to a drainage field; or
3. treat the sewage on site and discharge it to a soakaway.

DrainEx advised that the first option would be expensive, the second option required more space, and the third option was practical and the least expensive. Speedy-Grill chose option 3 and asked DrainEx to design and construct the soakaway.

Speedy-Grill then entered into a separate contract with CleanCo, a company specialising in sewage treatment, to design and construct the sewage treatment plant on the restaurant site.

Soon the project was operational. The sewage was being treated in the treatment plant and then discharged to the soakaway. Before long, the field next to the restaurant became flooded, giving off a bad smell, and after a few months the problem was still there.

Speedy-Grill discovered that the soakaway was not draining because the treated sewage from the treatment plant was not of appropriate quality for the soakaway and caused blocking.

After some enquiries, Speedy-Grill discovered that:

1. CleanCo designed the treatment plant following industry-standard guidance about treating sewage from restaurants. This guidance had not been updated to include drive-through restaurants.
2. Speedy-Grill's sewage is very different to a regular restaurant. There is much less water due to the water-saving toilets and a high concentration of milk and coffee grounds.
3. CleanCo assumed the treated waste would be discharged to a drainage field.
4. CleanCo has gone into liquidation.

Speedy-Grill has sent a letter before claim to DrainEx and CleanCo claiming £150,000 damages to remedy the problem. Speedy-Grill has suggested trying to resolve the dispute through mediation before going to court as the court case could cost more than the damages sought.

Speedy-Grill, CleanCo and DrainEx are going to meet for a mediation session to try to resolve the matter.

Each party is keen to resolve the dispute through mediation. None of the parties want to be held fully responsible and none of them want to go to court where they risk losing the case and paying the full costs of remediation.

Note: A sewer is an underground system of pipes which takes waste away from a site to be treated at a different location.

A drainage field is a specially designed grassy area. Here, waste that has been partially treated in an onsite treatment plant is disposed of through a network of underground pipes with holes in them. The soil bacteria further treat the waste.

A soakaway is a specifically designed hole in the ground which is filled with stones or similar material. Here, waste that has already been fully treated in an onsite treatment plant is disposed of and soaks into the soil.

Party roles

Speedy-Grill

You own a drive-through restaurant. You have no experience in sewage treatment or drainage. You contracted experts in these areas to do a job and they failed.

You followed the advice from DrainEx that the soakaway was the best option, but now it is not draining. You told CleanCo that the sewage was coming from your restaurant, and they did not treat it correctly.

CleanCo and DrainEx should recognise that they were both wrong and pay for their failures. However, you are not sure that CleanCo can pay as they have gone into liquidation.

You are willing to admit that you also made mistakes and think that all parties should contribute to fixing the problem as quickly and efficiently as possible.

CleanCo

You did your job and do not think you are responsible, at least not 100%. Speedy-Grill misinformed you by saying that it was a *restaurant*. Speedy-Grill should have told you specifically that it was a *drive-through*. Speedy-Grill gave you information about how much waste should be treated daily but not what type of waste it was or to what standard it should be treated.

You followed industry-standard guidance on sewage treatment from a restaurant. You believe you should have been informed by DrainEx that the treated sewage would be discharged to a soakaway. It was reasonable to assume that the treated sewage would be discharged to a drainage field.

You want Speedy-Grill and DrainEx to admit their mistakes. You cannot pay any money to resolve this issue yourself as you have gone into liquidation, but your insurance is still in place and your insurer could pay. However, the insurer wishes to minimise its potential exposure. Therefore, you want to limit your contribution to resolving this issue.

DrainEx

You are experts in drainage and not in sewage treatment. You designed and constructed the soakaway following industry-standard guidance. For the soakaway to work, the sewage needs to be treated properly first. The soakaway is not draining due to the failure of CleanCo to treat the sewage properly.

You believe CleanCo are 100% responsible and that a reasonable and responsible sewage treatment contractor would have:

- enquired to find out the exact type of restaurant that Speedy-Grill ran. They should have known that drive-through sewage is different to restaurant sewage and must be treated differently.
- asked Speedy-Grill or DrainEx about where the treated sewage would be discharged to and not assumed it was to a drainage field.

You believe Speedy-Grill wants to bring a claim against you because CleanCo has gone into liquidation. This isn't fair. You think CleanCo should pay for all the damages. They should admit they are to blame and pay for their mistakes. However, you are also worried that if the case goes to court you may end up paying 100% of the damages.

Mediator

You are the mediator for the case and you will be using facilitative mediation. Prepare an opening statement to explain what mediation is, what parties can expect in the process, and set some rules the parties must follow. Use the mediation agreement in Exercise 3.4 and the transcript of the mediator's opening statement in Audio 10.4 as a guide. At the end of your statement, explain that as the mediation was proposed by the claimant, Speedy-Grill, you invite them to start. Use mediator skills throughout the mediation. At the end of the mediation make sure you summarise what the parties achieved.

3.18 Reflect on your mediation role-play in Exercise 3.18. Use the self-assessment questions in Appendix A to evaluate your own performance as either a lawyer representing a client in mediation or a mediator.

Test yourself

1. Name two adjudicative and two non-adjudicative methods of ADR.
2. Give two reasons why a party may prefer ADR to litigation.
3. What does *arbitration institution* mean, and why would you state it in an arbitration clause?
4. Explain the structure of a mediation, starting with the mediator's opening statement.
5. What is the difference between the mediator skills of reframing and reality testing?

Notes

1 S Blake, J Browne, S Sime, *The Jackson ADR Handbook* (3rd edn, OUP 2021) 2, para 1.03.

2 Arbitration Rules (United Nations Commission on International Trade Law).<https://uncitral.un.org/en/texts/arbitration/contractualtexts/arbitration> accessed 29 April 2022.

3 Arbitration Act 1996 (England, Wales and Northern Ireland), c.23 <https://www.legislation.gov.uk/ukpga/1996/23> accessed 29 April 2022.

4 New York convention United Nations Convention on the Recognition and Enforcement of Foreign Arbitral Award (New York, 10 June 1958) <https://www.newyorkconvention.org/> accessed 29 April 2022.

5 These clauses have been adapted from the following model clauses: LCIA Arbitration and ADR Worldwide, 'Recommended Clauses' <https://www.lcia.org/dispute_resolution_services/lcia_recommended_clauses.aspx> accessed 9 December 2021.
Singapore International Arbitration Centre, 'SIAC Model Clause' <https://siac.org.sg/model-clauses/siac-model-clause> accessed 9 December 2021.
HKIAC, 'Model Clauses' <https://www.hkiac.org/arbitration/model-clauses> accessed 29 April 2022

6 A Redfern, M Hunter with N Blackaby, C Partasides, *Law and Practice of International Commercial Arbitration* (4th edn, Sweet & Maxwell 2004) 132.

7 Frederic Eisemann, 'La clause d'arbitrage pathologique' in Eugenio Minoli *Commercial Arbitration- Essays in Memoriam* (Unione Tipografico Rom 1974) 129.

8 DIFC LCIA Arbitration Centre, 'Recommended Clauses' <http://www.difc-lcia.org/recommended-clauses.aspx> accessed 12 January 2022.

9 White & Case and Queen Mary University '2021 International Arbitration Survey: Adapting Arbitration to a Changing World' (*Queen Mary University of London School of International Arbitration Research*, 2021) <https://arbitration.qmul.ac.uk/media/arbitration/docs/LON0320037-QMUL-International-Arbitration-Survey-2021_19_WEB.pdf> accessed 12 January 2022.

10 Freshfields Bruckhaus Deringer 'International Arbitration: Illuminating the Top Trends in 2020' <https://www.freshfields.com/495e22/contentassets/ef85f9eb59e945ef8d10e93b089e78bb/08100_pg_dr_international-arbitration-trends-2020-interactive_v4.pdf> accessed 12 January 2022.

11 Madelyn Burley-Allen, *Listening: The Forgotten Skill: A Self-Teaching Guide* (2nd edn, John Wiley & Sons, Inc. 1995) ebook location 220 of 1791.

12 Tammy Lenski, Twitter <https://twitter.com/tammylenski/status/901144704724733953?ref_src=twsrc%5Etfw%7Ctwcamp%5Etweetembed%7Ctwterm%5E901144704724733953%7Ctwgr%5E%7Ctwcon%5Es1_&ref_url=https%3A%2F%2Ftammylenski.com%2Fconflict-resolution-tools%2Freframes%2F> accessed 29 April 2022.

11 Advocacy

About this chapter

Overview

This chapter is about advocacy in first instance civil trials and in arbitration. The first part introduces what advocacy is and the skills it requires. The second part focuses on written advocacy. It compares court documents used in English litigation to those used in US litigation and arbitration, and gives an overview of persuasive legal writing techniques. The third part looks at oral advocacy. It presents language for describing people in a trial and the order of proceedings. It also considers how to present in court in a persuasive manner using language effectively. Throughout the chapter, there are exercises relating to legal terminology used in BrE, AmE, and arbitration, and expressions to make comparisons.

The chapter ends with a role-play cross-examination scenario. The scenarios used in this chapter focus on cases in the courts of England and Wales. However, the skills can be adapted to other English-speaking courts, such as those in the USA, and to arbitration hearings.

Learning objectives

By the end of the chapter, you should be able to:

- describe different documents used in legal proceedings
- make comparisons between documents across jurisdictions
- understand a range of persuasive techniques in written and oral advocacy
- identify the people involved in a trial and the structure of a trial
- use appropriate language to address people in court and ask questions

Test yourself at the end of the chapter to check that you have achieved the learning objectives.

1. Introduction

1.1 Read Text 11.1 and discuss these questions:

a. What is the difference between *advocacy* in general English and legal English?
b. What skills does a lawyer need for advocacy?
c. Is *advocate* a synonym for *lawyer*?
d. What types of lawyers who advocate are mentioned in the text?
e. Are written and oral advocacy both used in your jurisdiction?
f. Is there a type of lawyer who specialises in advocacy in your jurisdiction?

DOI: 10.4324/9781003140207-11

Text 11.1 Advocacy for lawyers

Advocacy is a word used in general and legal English with different meanings. The Cambridge Dictionary defines the general English noun *advocacy* as:

> '*Public support for an idea, plan, or way of doing something:*
>
> - *She is renowned for her advocacy of human rights.*
> - *a nonprofit advocacy group*'.[1]

Advocacy has a broad meaning in general English, but a specific meaning in legal English. Here is a legal English definition:

> '*... advocacy is the art of conducting cases in court*'.[2]

Advocacy involves many oral skills when presenting the client's version of the facts in a case, asking witnesses questions to further the client's case, and persuading the adjudicator to decide in the client's favour. However, advocacy also involves other skills, such as preparing cases for court by researching and analysing the law, interviewing clients and witnesses, and drafting legal documents.

In reality, few cases end up at trial and some cases are argued and won on paper through written advocacy. Therefore, a legal English definition of advocacy could be:

The work performed by a lawyer when they prepare for or represent a client in litigation or arbitration.

If there is a legal English meaning of *advocacy*, is there also a legal English meaning of *advocate*?

In general English, *advocate* is a broad term for a person, not necessarily a lawyer, who represents and speaks on behalf of someone else or for a cause. Although *advocate* is used in many jurisdictions to mean *lawyer*, in England, *advocate* is not a synonym for *lawyer*.

In England, there are two types of lawyers: *barristers*, sometimes referred to as *counsel*, and *solicitors*. Traditionally barristers specialised in advocacy and solicitors specialised in transactional work. However, solicitors can automatically represent clients in the lower courts and arbitration. If they take a qualification to become a *solicitor-advocate*, they gain the same rights of audience as barristers to represent clients in all courts.

In the USA, there is only one type of lawyer, called an *attorney*. They can do transactional work as well as represent clients in litigation and arbitration. A lawyer who focuses on litigation work may refer to themselves as a *litigator*, whereas a lawyer who focuses on non-court-based work may refer to themselves as a *transactional lawyer* or *deal lawyer*.

Vocabulary note

In England, barristers or solicitor-advocates who have been recognised for their excellency in advocacy are appointed as counsel by the monarch. They are called *QC* meaning *Queen's Counsel*, or *KC* meaning *King's Counsel*, depending on the reigning monarch of the time. The colloquial name for this type of advocate is a *Silk* because they wear a silk gown.

1.2 Write three questions that you could ask someone to learn about their advocacy experience. Use the suggestions in the following boxes to help you think of your own questions.

Have you ever represented a client in court or arbitration?	*What advocacy experience do you have?*	*Would you prefer to act for clients at first instance or on appeal?*

1.3 Practise asking and answering questions about advocacy with a partner using the questions you thought of in Exercise 1.2. Take it in turns to ask and answer questions. If your partner does not have court advocacy experience, encourage them to speak about court advocacy they have seen in a television series or film.

2. Written advocacy

Court documents

2.1 Asim Atef is an Egyptian qualified lawyer who specialises in intellectual property law. This chapter focuses on two cases he is working on with an English law firm. The first case is discussed in this written advocacy section, and the second case is presented in the oral advocacy section.

In the first case, Asim is assisting on a case involving EgyptLux Ltd, an international company headquartered in Egypt. An English company, Cheapomart Ltd, is infringing EgyptLux Ltd's trademarks in England. EgyptLux Ltd wants to bring a claim in England.

Asim thinks about what court documents are needed for litigation in England. Use your own knowledge to match the court document name on the left to the correct definition on the right. The first answer is given as an example. Then read Text 11.2 to complete your answers.

Document name	Definition
a. *witness statement*	1. gives a concise statement about the nature of the claim, the remedy sought, and value of the claim.
b. claim form	2. *sets out the written testimony of the witness.*
c. particulars of claim	3. sets out which allegations the defendant denies and why.
d. defence	4. the claim form, particulars of claim, defence, counterclaim, reply to defence, defence to counterclaim.
e. statement of case	5. sets out the allegations of fact which the claimant must prove in order to win the case.
f. application notice	6. sets out the points which a party will orally argue in court.
g. skeleton argument	7. sets out a request for the court to decide a subsidiary matter.

Text 11.2 What documents are required for civil litigation in England?

'When you draft a document for court, you are starting the process of persuasion'.[3] But what documents do you need to draft for English civil litigation? This article sets out the main ones.

Claim form and particulars of claim

To start a court case in England, the claimant or their lawyer completes a claim form and particulars of claim. The claim form sets out brief information about the claim, such as the parties' names and addresses, the nature of the claim, the remedy sought, and the value of the claim. The particulars of claim set out the allegations of fact, which the claimant must prove in court to win the case.

Defence and counterclaim

The defendant responds to the claim with a defence. The defence states which allegations the defendant denies and why. The defendant may also file a claim in response to the claimant's claim, to be dealt with in the same proceedings. This is called a counterclaim.

Statement of case

A statement of case refers to the set of documents in which the parties state the basis of their case. The claimant's statement of case consists of the claim form, particulars, and any reply to the defence and defence to a counterclaim. The defendant's statement of case comprises the defence and any counterclaim.

Witness statements

A party must disclose any evidence it will rely on in court to the other party. This includes witness statements. Witness statements are written testimonies of witnesses who a party intends to call at trial to present oral evidence.

Skeleton argument

Before the trial, parties exchange skeleton arguments, sometimes called case summaries, and send these to court. The skeleton argument briefly sets out the points on which a party will orally argue in court.

Application notice

At various stages before the trial, and even during a trial, a party may write to the court asking it to decide a subsidiary matter which is related to the main trial. For example, a party may ask the court to order an injunction.

To make such a request, a party must submit an application notice to the court briefly stating what court order the party is seeking and why. This should be supported by evidence and a skeleton argument. The party making the application is called the applicant and the other party is called the respondent. The judge's decision on this issue is written in a document called an order.

2.2 Audio 11.1

Asim goes for lunch with his colleagues Zhara, a lawyer who specialises in arbitration, and Mahmoud, a lawyer who often works on litigation cases with American law firms. Asim explains what documents he has to prepare for court and his colleagues compare these to the documents used in US litigation and in arbitration.

Listen to Audio 11.1 and complete the table with the equivalent documents used in American English and arbitration.

BrE	AmE	Arbitration
Claim form and particulars of claim	a.	b.
Defence	c.	d.
Statement of case	e.	f.
Witness statements	g.	h.
Skeleton argument	i.	j.
Application notice	k.	l.

Vocabulary note: *parties to a case*

In England, a civil trial is between a *claimant* and *defendant* whereas in the USA it is between a *plaintiff* and *defendant*. In arbitration, the parties are often called the *claimant* and *respondent*.

In England, an appeal is between the *appellant* and *respondent*. In the USA, the same terms are used, although *appellant* and *appellee* are more common. There is no mechanism for appeal within the arbitration process.

2.3 Listen to Audio 11.1 again and complete the following sentences. These sentences are all appropriate for comparing similarities or differences. Each space represents one word.

a. *The names are* _________ _________ *those in England.*
b. *I think,* _________ _________, *in the USA it's known as the complaint.*
c. *And* _________, *counterclaim is a term used in the USA.*
d. *If I'm not mistaken, this happens in arbitration* _________ _________.
e. *Yes,* _________, *we use the term counterclaim.*
f. *He said that* _________ *the official expression is statement of case in England, in practice the term pleadings is still used.*
g. *I know it's* _________ _________ *in arbitration.*
h. *The US process is* _________ _________ _________ *as in England.*
i. *The* _________ _________ _________ *a skeleton argument is probably a brief or memorandum of law.*

j. *Again, arbitration uses a mixture of terms which are _________ _________ those used in English and US litigation.*

2.4 Review the expressions for comparing in Phrase bank 11.1:

Phrase bank 11.1	
Expressing similarities	**Expressing differences**
Likewise ...	*While ...*
Similarly ...	*In contrast ...*
The closest thing to [something(s)] is/are [something(s)].	*[something(s)] is/are different from [something(s)].*
It's the same in [place or process].	*The [something(s)] is/are not the same as the [something(s)].*
This happens in [place or process] as well.	
[something(s)] is/are similar to [something(s)].	

2.5 Practise explaining court documents with a partner. Role-play a meeting taking it in turns to be the client and lawyer in the following scenarios. You may use the vocabulary in Exercise 2.2 and expressions for comparing in Phrase bank 11.1.

Scenario 1

A client from London will start a claim in the lawyer's jurisdiction.

Client

You want to know what documents are used in the legal process in the lawyer's jurisdiction and how they compare to English documents.

Lawyer

You must explain the documents required in the legal process in your jurisdiction and compare them to English documents.

Scenario 2

A client from London will start a claim in the USA.

Client

You want to know what documents are used in the US legal process and how this compares to arbitration.

Lawyer

You must explain the documents required in the US legal process and compare them to those required for arbitration.

2.6 Asim prepares and files the claim form for his client. Read the following extract from the claim form and discuss these questions:

a. Who are the parties to this case?
b. Which court will hear this case?
c. What are the *causes of action*, in other words, legal reasons, for bringing a claim?

Claim Form

In the
High Court of Justice, Business and Property Courts,
Intellectual Property List (CHD),
Intellectual Property Enterprise Court

Claimant(s) name(s) and address(es) including postcode	**Defendant(s) name and address(es) including postcode**
Egypt Lux Ltd 5000 Port Said Cairo Governorate Egypt	Cheapomart Ltd Derby Road UK W159 3PQZ

Brief details of claim

The Claimant claims that the Defendant is:

i. infringing its UK registered trade marks UK00555999781 and UK00555999782; and
ii. passing off goods in packaging identical or confusingly similar to the Claimant's goods.

Vocabulary note

A *trade mark* is a distinctive word, logo, colour, sound, or a combination of these things, which allows customers to recognise a brand and trust its quality.

Registered trade marks are protected from infringement under statute in England. *Trade mark infringement* happens when a trader, without the trade mark owner's permission, uses an identical or similar trade mark in connection with similar or identical goods or services as those protected by the trade mark registration. This leads to a likelihood of confusion on the part of the public.

Unregistered trade marks are protected under the common law of tort in England. *Passing off* happens when a competitor sells goods or services with a similar name, mark, or *get up* (appearance) of goods or services of another trader, which misleads the public. This misrepresentation must cause some damage to the goodwill, in other words, the reputation, of the trader.

2.7 Asim must include the type of remedy his client seeks in the claim form. Here are some common remedies and their definitions.

a. Match the remedy on the left to the correct effect on the right. The first answer is given as an example.

b. Which remedies could be appropriate in this case?

Remedy	Effect
1. *damages* →	a. the defendant is ordered to fulfil their contractual obligations
2. an account of profits	b. *the defendant is ordered to pay a sum of money to the claimant*
3. injunction	c. a legal document is corrected to reflect the parties' true intention
4. delivery up or destruction	d. a voidable contract is set aside as if it never existed
5. specific performance	e. the defendant is required to quantify and pay the amount of profit gained from an activity to the claimant
6. rescission	f. the defendant is prohibited from doing something (prohibitory) or obligated to do something (mandatory)
7. rectification	g. a party is ordered to pay the legal costs of the case
8. costs	h. the defendant is ordered to deliver infringing items to the claimant or destroy them

Vocabulary note: *relief* or *remedy*

Sometimes the word relief is used instead of remedy. According to Bryan A. Garner, '*Relief has historically been more commonly used in the context of the courts of equity, and remedy in the context of courts of law*'.[4] Therefore, it is more common to seek *relief* if applying for *an injunction, specific performance, account of profits, rescission*, or *rectification*, and to seek a *remedy* if applying for *damages*.

However, in practice these terms are used interchangeably.

2.8 Read the following extract from the next part of Asim's claim form and complete the sentences using the appropriate remedy from Exercise 2.7. Each space represents one word. The first answer is given as an example.

The Claimant prays for the following relief:

1. An *injunction* to enjoin the Defendant from infringing the Claimant's registered trade marks.

2. An (a) ________ to enjoin the Defendant from continuing to pass off the Claimant's goods by advertisement, sale, offer for sale, or stocking of goods in packaging identical or confusingly similar to the Claimant's goods.

3. An order for (b)________ ________ or ________ upon oath of all goods in the possession or control of the Defendant, the possession or control of which would constitute a breach of the injunctions set out in paragraph 1 and 2 or any of them.

4. An inquiry as to damages suffered by the Claimant (including damages under the Intellectual Property (Enforcement, etc.) Regulations 2006) or at the Claimant's election an (c) _________ of _________ for the infringement of the Claimant's trade mark.

5. An order for the payment from the Defendant to the Claimant in response to the inquiry set out in paragraph 4 of (d) _________ found due, together with interest charged thereon, assessed pursuant to section 35A of the Senior Courts Act 1981 or charged at such rate as the Court deems equitable.

6. An order granting an award of punitive damages for the Defendant's wilful violation of the law.

7. An order for the dissemination and publication of the judgment at the Defendant's expense.

8. (e) _________.

9. Further or other relief.

2.9 Read the following extract from the next part of Asim's claim form. Decide if these statements are true or false and correct any false statements.

	True	False
a. The claimant only expects to recover *nominal*, in other words, a small amount, of damages.	O	O
b. The amount of damages will be determined before establishing the defendant's liability.	O	O
c. In intellectual property claims, it is common to deal with liability and damages separately.	O	O

Value
The Claimant is currently unable to quantify the recoverable amount of damages or account of profits however it believes the amount is substantial. Following the normal procedure for intellectual property claims, there will be a bifurcated trial, dealing firstly with the Defendant's liability and, if the Claimant succeeds in establishing the Defendant's liability, secondly with quantum.

2.10 Audio 11.2

Listen to Audio 11.2, where Asim is in a video conference call with Liz Benetton, the lawyer from the British law firm he is assisting on this case. Complete the following sentences showing some differences between AmE and BrE. Each space represents one word.

a. AmE: The Claimant prays for the following relief
BrE: The Claimant _________

b. AmE: An injunction to enjoin the Defendant from
   BrE: An injunction to ________ the Defendant from
c. AmE: An order granting an award of punitive damages
   BrE: ________
d. AmE: there will be a bifurcated trial
   BrE: there will be a ________ ________

2.11 After drafting the claim form, Asim starts preparing the particulars of claim. The particulars of the claim, like the US *complaint* and the *request for arbitration*, tell the claimant's story. In your opinion, what are the elements of a good story?

2.12 Review the expressions for telling a story for the particulars of claim in Phrase bank 11.2:

Phrase bank 11.2	
Introduction *The Claimant alleges that the Defendant has [actions done, e.g. used a trade mark that is similar to the Claimant's], which constitutes [cause of action, e.g. an infringement of trade mark].* *This is a claim for [remedy, e.g. damages] arising out of [cause of action, e.g. trade mark infringement] under [law, e.g. the Trade Marks Act 1994].* **Characters** *The Claimant [name] is a registered company in [jurisdiction], with its registered office at [address]. The Claimant is a company which [describe business activities]. To the best of the Claimant's knowledge, the Defendant [name] is [describe Defendant's business].*	**Middle** *The Claimant is the proprietor of the UK trade mark no. [number], which comprises the following elements [describe trade mark].* *The Defendant has infringed the registered trade marks in that, prior to the filing of the claim form, and without licence of the Claimant it has performed the following acts [describe infringing acts].* **End** *By reason of these acts of [cause of action, e.g. trade mark infringement], the Defendant has caused the Claimant loss and damage. The claimant seeks [describe remedy].*

2.13 Read Asim's following notes about the case and then practise storytelling with a partner. Take it in turns to tell your own story of this case using the expressions in Phrase bank 11.2. Make sure you include these elements:

- **Introduction:** What is this case about? Summarise briefly what this case involves.
- **Characters:** Who are the parties? Explain who the parties are and what they do.
- **Middle:** What happened? State the facts and allegations against the defendant.
- **End:** What was the result? State the impact of the defendant's wrongdoing and the remedy the claimant seeks.

Parties

- Claimant "EgyptLux Ltd", a global producer of bath products, has been selling Puraque in the UK since 1990
- Defendant "Cheapomart Ltd", a UK discount supermarket, started selling Pureace in the UK in 2022

Claimant's reputation

- Bellissima Beauty Awards UK awarded Puraque the 'Best Bath Scrub' award in the years 2019, 2020, and 2021
- Quantax, an independent consumer researcher, carried out a survey in 2021, and found that Puraque was the best-known and most-trusted bath scrub

Claimant's trade mark registrations

Registered trade mark UK00555999781: word 'PURAQUE' in capital letters; colour #a6a6a6; TT Drugs font; lined triangle logo above wording. Registration date: 1 March 1990

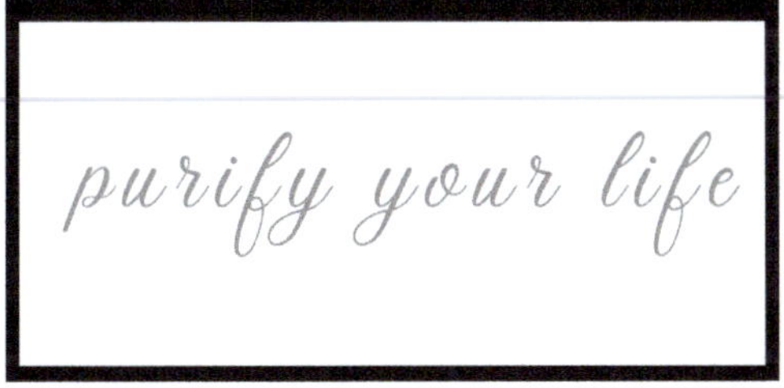

Registered trade mark UK00555999782: word 'Purify your life' in lower case letters; colour #a6a6a6; Stoic font. Registration date: 1 March 1990

Defendant's trade mark infringement and passing off (Claimant's product left, Defendant's product right).

Trade Marks Act 1994 section 10[5]

(2) A person infringes a registered trade mark if he uses in the course of trade a sign where because –

(b) the sign is similar to the trade mark and is used in relation to goods or services identical with or similar to those for which the trade mark is registered, there exists a likelihood of confusion on the part of the public, which includes the likelihood of association with the trade mark.

(3) A person infringes a registered trade mark if he uses in the course of trade in relation to goods or services, a sign which –

(a) is identical with or similar to the trade mark where the trade mark has a reputation in the United Kingdom and the use of the sign, being without due cause, takes unfair advantage of, or is detrimental to, the distinctive character or the repute of the trade mark.

Impression on the public

Londoner Express Newspaper Article 'Three tips for saving money':

'Tip #3. You can save a lot simply by switching from expensive brands to cheaper identical alternatives. For example, Cheapomart's selling a Puraque look-alike at half the price and it's exactly the same. We couldn't tell the difference'.

@Dannipanni social media influencer:
'Bought Cheapomart's Puraque copy! LOVE IT! Never buying Puraque again! 🤩'

Persuasive writing

2.14 The particulars of claim, like other court documents, must be persuasive. Asim and his colleagues discuss how he can make his writing persuasive. Read the following comments and discuss these questions:

a. Do you agree with what the lawyers say?
b. How would you make your writing persuasive?

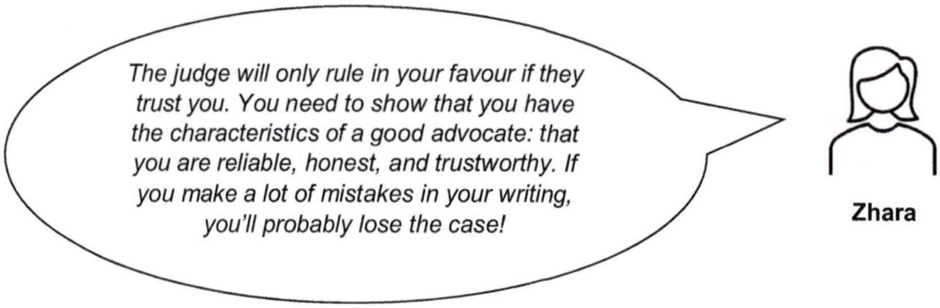

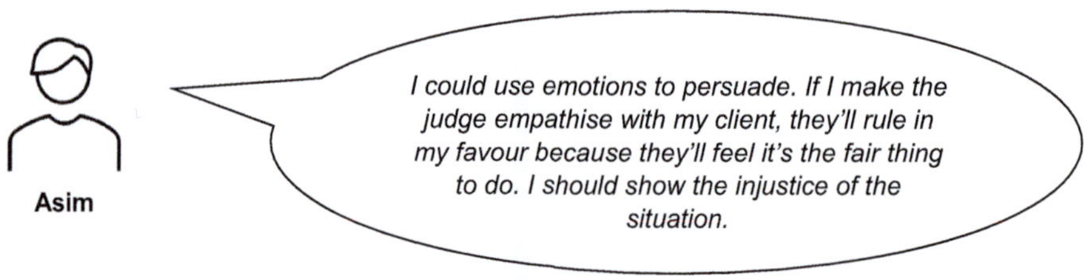

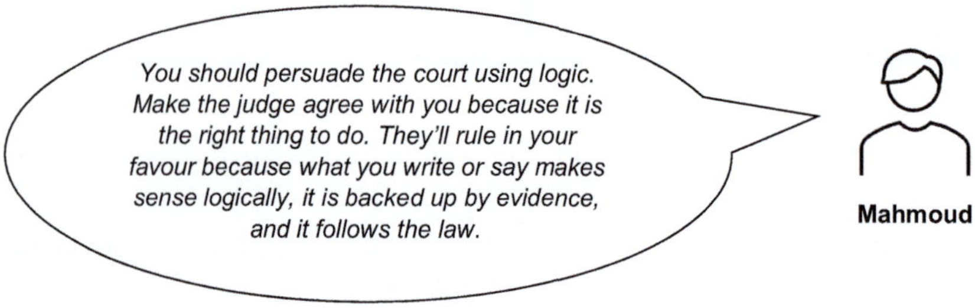

Vocabulary note

The three techniques referred to in Exercise 2.14 are ancient Greek rhetorical techniques: *ethos*, *pathos*, and *logos* meaning *character*, *emotion*, and *logic* respectively in English. Rhetoric is the art of persuasion, and these ancient techniques are still used by lawyers today when they need to persuade.

Persuading with character

2.15 As Zhara mentioned in Exercise 2.14, using your character is one persuasive technique. One characteristic of a good lawyer is that they are accurate. Accuracy comes in many forms, for example, accurate use of:

- legal vocabulary
- punctuation
- spelling
- grammar
- legal research
- typing

If a judge detects inaccuracies in your legal documents, they may start doubting your credibility. This could result in a judgment against your client. Therefore, making sure your legal writing is accurate is one element of making your writing persuasive.

This exercise focuses on a few aspects of accuracy: accurate spelling, grammar, and punctuation. Read the following extract from Asim's particulars of claim. Correct the spelling, grammar, and punctuation mistakes which are underlined.

The Parties

The Claimant ("EgyptLux Ltd") is and (a) have at all material times been a private limited company with registered company number 7791153. It was (b) incorporate in Egypt and its registered office address is 5000 Port Said, Cairo, Governate Egypt.

(c) egyptlux is a well-known global business engaged in the business of (d) designing manfactering and selling premium personal care products in countries across the world, including (e) especifically, in the United Kingdom.

The Defendant ("Cheapomart") is a company incorporated (f) with the laws of England and Wales (company number 00596789111), with its registered office address (g) on Derby Road, UK, W159 3PQZ.

Cheapomart (h) carry on business in the UK as a discount supermarket, and to the best of the (i) Claimants knowledge and belief, (j) she operates through over 800 stores in the UK as well as through its website www.cheapo.mart.

Persuading with emotion

2.16 As Asim mentioned in Exercise 2.14, emotions play an important role in persuasion. He has tried to use emotion in his writing by using a range of adjectives and adverbs. Adjectives and adverbs can be objective or subjective. When something is objective, we can prove it to be true. When something is subjective, it is based on a personal opinion and someone could disagree with it:

	Objective	Subjective
Adjective	Puraque is the *top-selling* bath scrub brand in the UK. (Could be proved with statistics)	Puraque is a *brilliant* product. (This is the opinion of one person and not of another)
Adverb	EgyptLux Ltd arrived first to the bath scrub market in the UK. Cheapomart Ltd started selling their product *later*. (Could be proved by showing that Puraque sold their products before Cheapomart)	Puraque was selling *wonderfully* in the UK until Cheapomart introduced Pureace. (This is the opinion of one person and not of another)

Using objective adjectives and adverbs help give accurate information and lead the reader or listener to form their own judgement. Subjective adjectives and adverbs can be persuasive, but if used too much they could make your writing appear unreasonable. In reality, each judge has their own preferences and the usage differs across cultures.

Read this extract from Asim's particulars and:

a. identify all the adjectives and adverbs
b. for each one, decide whether it is more objective or subjective
c. decide which adjectives and adverbs to delete or change to make this text more reasonable

One of EgyptLux Ltd's well-known products is Puraque. For many years, Puraque has been the leading sea salt scrub brand by sales and reputation in the UK.

The following elements have been used continually on the extremely recognisable packaging of Puraque since 2012:

(i) a luxurious gold colour scheme contrasting with a white box;
(ii) an effortlessly minimalist layout comprising central fonts and well-spaced text;
(iii) an impressive illustration of a beautiful woman's face in the centre and gorgeous frames on the four corners of the rectangular box; and
(iv) the powerful brand name with a triangular logo on the upper part of the front of the packaging.

These distinctive and recurrent elements indicate to the average consumer that the product is the marvellously magnificent Puraque.

Persuading with logic

2.17 As Mahmoud mentioned in Exercise 2.14, logic plays an important role in persuasion. Asim has written different parts of his particulars but is struggling with the logical order and headings. Read the following extracts and:

a. label each paragraph with a heading from the options
b. decide on a logical order for the paragraphs

a. Public impression	b. Damage, loss, and relief	c. Passing off
d. Trade mark infringement		e. The Defendant's acts of infringement

1. ______________________________

By reason of the acts of trade mark infringement complained of in this claim, the Defendant has caused the Claimant loss and damage, in respect of which the Claimant is entitled to and will seek an inquiry as to damages, or at the Claimant's election, an account of the Defendant's profits.

The Claimant is entitled to and seeks interest on all sums found due at such rate and for such period as the Court deems fit pursuant to section 35A of the Senior Courts Act 1981[6] or under the inherent jurisdiction of the Court.

2. ______________________________

The Defendant is using a get-up for Pureace which bears the following similarity to that of Puraque:

a. a gold colour scheme contrasting with a pure white box;
b. a minimalist layout comprising simple centralised fonts and well-spaced text;
c. an illustration of a woman's face in the centre and frames on the four corners of the rectangular box; and
d. the brand name with a triangular logo on the upper part of the front of the packaging.

The Defendant's Pureace packaging amounts to a misrepresentation likely to cause the public to believe that Pureace is actually Puraque, and such misrepresentation has damaged and continues to damage the Claimant's goodwill.

3. ______________________________

In support of the foregoing statements, Annex 2 shows examples, of which the Claimant is aware, of media coverage in the press and social media of the Defendant's Pureace. Such examples describe Pureace by reference to the marked similarity with the Puraque. Here are some extracts from Annex 2:

4. ______________________________

The Defendant is using, without the consent of the Claimant, a sign which is similar to the UK Registered Trade Marks in relation to goods which are identical to the UK Registered

Trade Mark goods. Due to this similarity, there is a likelihood of confusion on the part of the public, which includes the likelihood of association between Pureace and Puraque.

5. ____

At a time not precisely known to the Claimant, but prior to the date of filing this Claim Form and without licence of the Claimant, the Defendant has designed, manufactured, and sold a bath scrub product under the name 'Pureace' in the UK. Pureace is available to purchase in the Defendant's UK stores and online via the Defendant's UK website at www.cheapomart.co.uk.

On 1 January 2022, the Claimant's legal representatives wrote a letter before claim to the Directors of the Defendant setting out the Claimant's allegations of trade mark infringement. The Defendant's legal representatives responded on 10 January 2022, denying the allegations. Copies of this correspondence are attached to these Particulars of Claim as Annex 1.

Unless restrained by the Court, the Defendant threatens to continue the acts complained of below:

3. Oral Advocacy

Preparing for court

People at a trial

3.1 The second case that Asim has been working on with Liz Benetton involves a client called Parlo Ltd. Parlo Ltd is a small Egyptian tech company which created the app *Bespeak*. Bespeak posts automatic tailored comments on social media. Parlo Ltd owns a UK patent for the technical process used in the app. In 2021 a company called Incoms PLC started selling the app *Talkomate* which appears to use the same process as Bespeak. Parlo Ltd is bringing a case against Incoms PLC for infringing their patent and the trial has been listed for next month.

Asim will watch the trial and he wants to be prepared for it. He has made a list of people who usually attend a civil trial in England. Read Asim's list and discuss these questions:

a. What role does each person play in a civil trial? Check the Glossary for definitions.
b. Who else would you expect to attend the trial?
c. Who attends a civil trial in your jurisdiction?

Who will be at the trial?

- *Witnesses*
- *Expert witness*
- *The press*
- *The public*
- *Clerk*
- *Usher*
- *Court reporter*

Pronunciation note

There are two correct ways to pronounce *clerk*. The BrE pronunciation of *clerk* (klɑːk) rhymes with *bark, dark, park*. The AmE pronunciation of *clerk* (klɜːk) rhymes with *lurk, work, perk*.

Structure of a trial

3.2 Audio 11.3

Listen to Asim discussing the upcoming trial with his colleagues and complete the following steps to show the order of proceedings in an English civil trial. Each space represents one word. Some steps are given as examples.

a: Opening speech
The claimant's lyer introduces the claimant's case

↓

b: _______ - _______ -_______
The claimant's lawyer questions its own witness

↓

c: _______ - _______
The defendant's lawyer questions the claimant's witness

↓

d: _______ - _______
The claimant's lawyer questions its own witness again

↓

e: Repeat steps a-d switching parties

↓

f: _______ _______
The defendant's lawyer and then the claimant's lawyer conclude their case

↓

g: Delivery of judgment
The judge delivers the judgment immediately or at a later date

Pronunciation note

There are two ways to say the *v* in a civil court case citation, such as *Parlo Ltd v Incoms PLC*. In British English, *v* is read as *and*. For example, *Parlo Ltd v Incoms PLC* is read as *Parlo Ltd and Incoms PLC*. In American English, *v* is read as *versus* or *vee*. For example, *Parlo Ltd v Incoms PLC* is read as *Parlo Ltd versus Incoms PLC*.

3.3 Listen to Audio 11.3 again. In the Audio, Zhara and Mahmoud compare the order of proceedings in US litigation and arbitration to English litigation. Complete the following sentences, which are all appropriate for expressing either similarities or differences when comparing. Each space represents one word.

a. *OK. It's ________ the ________ as arbitration.*
b. *Yes, but in the USA there is often a jury, ________ in almost all English civil cases there's not.*
c. *So, in England, the lawyer delivers their opening speech to the judge ________ ________ to the jury.*
d. *So ________ this to arbitration, on the ________ ________, arbitration is like English litigation as there isn't a jury either, but on the ________ ________ it's slightly different, because the lawyer delivers the opening speech to the arbitrators.*
e. *It's ________ ________ in US litigation ________.*
f. *It sounds like the processes are ________ ________.*
g. *I imagine it's ________ or ________ the ________ in US litigation and arbitration, right?*
h. *Yes, the processes are ________. But in litigation you're trying to convince the judge, ________ ________ ________ in arbitration, where you must convince the arbitrators.*

3.4 Review the expressions for comparing in Phrase bank 11.3:

Phrase bank 11.3	
Expressing similarities	**Expressing differences**
[something(s)] is/are exactly the same as [something(s)]. *[Something(s)] is/are like this in [place or process] too.* *[something(s)] is/are the same in [place or process].* *The processes are [quite/very] similar.* *It's more or less the same in [place or process].*	*[statement] whereas [contrasting statement].* *[statement] rather than/instead of [contrasting statement].* *On the one hand, [statement expressing similarity], but on the other hand [statement expressing difference].* *[Something(s)] is/are quite similar in [place or process], though/although [contrasting statement].*

3.5 Practise explaining the structure of a civil trial with a partner. Role-play a meeting taking it in turns to be the client and lawyer in the following scenarios. You may use the vocabulary in Exercise 3.2 and expressions for comparing in Phrase bank 11.3.

Scenario 1

A client from London will start a claim in the lawyer's jurisdiction.

Client

You want to know what will happen in legal proceedings in the lawyer's jurisdiction and how this compares to legal proceedings in England.

Lawyer

You must explain the structure of legal proceedings in your jurisdiction and compare this to legal proceedings in England.

Scenario 2

A client from London will start a claim in the USA.

Client

You want to know what will happen in legal proceedings in the USA and how this compares to arbitration.

Lawyer

You must explain the structure of legal proceedings in the USA and compare this to the structure of arbitration.

Presenting in court

Following rules of etiquette

3.6 Whether presenting in court or arbitration, lawyers are expected to follow rules of etiquette. Read the following examples and discuss these questions:

a. Why is it important to follow etiquette?
b. What are some examples of court etiquette in your jurisdiction?
c. Should etiquette be the same in physical proceedings and online proceedings?

Stand up and bow when the judge enters and exits the court room	Address the judge and other participants using correct titles
Stand when addressing the court or being addressed	Do not interrupt the judge or your opponent when they are talking

Using your poise

3.7 Before you even open your mouth to speak in court, you have the opportunity to show that you are a credible lawyer through your poise. Poise means behaving or moving in a way that conveys self-confidence, self-control, and dignity.

Read the following statements related to poise. In your opinion, which lawyers are confident and persuasive and why?

a. The judge was talking and counsel for claimant sat there with his head down frantically rustling through his papers. It looked like he couldn't find a document.

b. The lawyer sat up straight, with her arms lightly folded in front of her on the desk, her chin was slightly raised and she was paying attention to the judge.

c. The lawyer arrived late to the hearing, his shirt wasn't ironed, and he wasn't wearing a tie. He didn't look smart. He was slouching and kept both hands in his pockets.

d. When the lawyer gave her opening speech she looked tense. She was holding a pen which she kept clicking and fiddling with … It was distracting.

e. When he stood up everything about his posture said 'confident!' His back was straight, his feet slightly apart, his shoulders relaxed.

3.8 Use the statements from Exercise 3.7 to complete the following checklist with points to do or not do to appear credible and confident in court. The first two points are given as examples.

Checklist: persuading with poise

Do	Don't
1. *When seated, sit up straight*	1. ______
2. *Keep control of your hands*	2. ______
3. ______	3. ______
4. ______	4. ______
5. ______	5. ______

Using your voice

3.9 Your voice is a powerful tool of persuasion. If used correctly, you can show that you are credible and confident. Read the following checklist of dos and don'ts for using your voice to persuade. Why is it important to do or not do these following points? What points would you add to the list?

Checklist: persuading with voice

Do	Don't
1. speak at a reasonable pace	1. speak too fast
2. use a calm and reassuring tone	2. use an angry or frustrated tone
3. speak at a reasonable volume	3. speak too quietly
4. end statements with a downward inflection	4. end statements with an upward inflection
5. articulate words clearly	5. mumble and slur words
6. use pauses to think	6. hesitate and use fillers

3.10 Audio 11.4

Listen to Audio 11.4, where lawyers are introducing themselves in court. Use the checklist in Exercise 3.9 to discuss how well the lawyers use their voices in their introductions. The lawyers in their speaking order are called:

- Mr Dixon
- Mr Lee
- Ms Wilson

Introducing and addressing people in court

3.11 Listen to Audio 11.4 again and complete the following sentences. These sentences highlight common language used in court introductions in the USA and in England. Each space represents one word:

a. *Mr Dixon: ________ ________ I am Mr Dixon and I appear with my ________ ________ Mr Smith on behalf of the claimant Parlo Ltd and with my ________ Ms Derby and Mr Reynolds from Baker and Sons LLP. My learned friends Ms West and Mr Morrison appear for the defendant Incoms PLC.*

b. *Mr Lee: Your Honor, I ________ ________ Mr. Stone and Ms Baynes for the plaintiff.*

c. *Ms Wilson: May it ________ ________ ________. Your Honor, my name is Ms Shaya Wilson. ________ ________ ________ at Sykes law firm. I ________ ________ ________ ________ an attorney from my firm, Mr Mitchell, we're from the New York office. ________ ________ ________ lawyer, Ms Nelson, who is local counsel in this case.*

Vocabulary note

In the USA, *May it please the court* is a traditional phrase which is used as an icebreaker at the beginning of oral argument.[7] It is also used in England but not in arbitration.

To appear (BrE, AmE) means to formally present oneself in court as a lawyer or witness.

3.12 Read the following table stating some common ways to address people in court and arbitration. Are there special ways to address people in court in your jurisdiction?

Addressing people in court		
	BrE	**AmE**
Judges	My Lord/My Lady (senior judiciary) Your Honour/Sir/Madam (lower judiciary)	Your Honor
Another lawyer on your team or opposing counsel	My friend (traditionally referring to a solicitor) My learned friend (traditionally referring to a barrister) or Mr/Miss/Ms/Mrs + [Surname]/[Full name]	Mr/Miss/Ms/Mrs + [Surname]/[Full name]
The party bringing the case	The claimant/Mr/Miss/Ms/Mrs + [Surname]/[Full name]/[Company name]	Plaintiff/Mr/Miss/Ms/Mrs + [Surname]/[Full name]/[Company name]

The party defending the case	The defendant/Mr/Miss/Ms/Mrs + [Surname]/[Full name]/[Company name]
Witness	Mr/Miss/Ms/Mrs + [Surname]/[Full name]

Pronunciation note

My Lord and *My Lady* are usually pronounced *M'Lord* (mə lɔːd) and *M'Lady (mə leɪdiː).*

Learned in *My learned friend* is not pronounced in the same way as the past tense of *learn* as in *learn'd* (lɜːnd), instead it is pronounced *learn id* (lɜːnid).

The same BrE and AmE language used in court can also be used in arbitration, with the following exceptions:

Addressing people in arbitration	
Arbitrator	Mr/Miss/Ms/Mrs + [Surname]/Arbitrator + [Surname]
A panel of arbitrators	Members of the tribunal
The party defending the case	The respondent/Mr/Miss/Ms/Mrs + [Surname]/[Full name]

3.13 Practise introducing yourself in court with a partner using the following scenario. Choose your role as judge or lawyer and use the vocabulary in Exercises 3.11 and 3.12 to role-play the beginning of a court case. When you introduce yourself as the lawyer make sure you:

- follow the rules of etiquette
- follow the persuasive poise and voice checklists
- address people correctly

After you have introduced yourself as the lawyer, switch roles.

Scenario

It is the first day of the civil trial in England between *Gonzo Ltd v Trewitz PLC*. Gonzo Ltd is suing Trewitz PLC for breach of contract.

Judge

It is the morning. Welcome the lawyers to court. You have read the written papers, including the contract and skeleton arguments. You would like the lawyer for the claimant to introduce themselves before hearing their opening statement.

Lawyer

You are representing the claimant Gonzo Ltd. Introduce yourself with your full name. You are assisted by Ms Frankel, a lawyer from your law firm, Artusi Associates. You should also introduce the opposition. The lawyer representing the defendant is called Elena Silvers, from Coopers LLP.

Questioning witnesses

3.14 Read Text 11.3 and discuss these questions:

a. What types of questions are allowed in examination-in-chief?
b. Why aren't leading questions allowed in examination-in-chief?
c. Why are leading questions encouraged in cross-examination?

Text 11.3 Questioning in court

Questioning is an important part of advocacy in litigation and arbitration. Lawyers must ask their own witnesses questions in examination-in-chief. They must also ask the opposing party's witnesses questions in cross-examination. In many jurisdictions, there are strict rules about the types of questions a lawyer can ask different types of witnesses.

In examination-in-chief, lawyers must ask questions that give the witness freedom to tell their own version of the facts. Lawyers can ask open questions which begin with inquiry words such as *when, where, what, who, why, how,* or invitations such as *could you explain, could you describe*. For example:

> *'When was the document published?'*

And in some jurisdictions lawyers may ask closed questions, providing they are not suggesting an answer on a disputed fact. A closed question limits the scope of an answer. For example:

> *'Was the document published before or after you left the company?'*

However, in many jurisdictions, including the USA and England, lawyers must not ask leading questions in examination-in-chief. A leading question leads the witness to give a specific answer the lawyer wants. This is because a leading question contains the desired answer as a statement. For example:

> *'This document was published about June 2020. That's correct, right?'*

While leading questions are not allowed in examination-in-chief, in cross-examination leading questions are not only allowed they are also key to conducting a successful cross-examination. This is because the lawyer can control the witness to get an anticipated answer which supports their case.

3.15 Read the following questions that could be asked of a witness and decide whether they are leading or non-leading.

a. *What happened next?*
b. *You arrived at the office at around 10:30, correct?*
c. *You saw the defendant process that transaction, right?*
d. *Why did you do that?*
e. *What time was it?*
f. *How tall was the person you saw?*

Examination-in-chief

3.16 The lawyer's aim in examination-in-chief is to elicit evidence from their witness in a clear, memorable, and persuasive way to prove their case.

Asim has prepared some examination-in-chief questions for a witness in the case. The problem is that they are all leading questions. Read his notes and use inquiry words such as *when, where, what, who, why, how,* or invitations such as *could you explain, could you describe* to transform these leading questions into non-leading ones.

Examination-in-chief of Mr Karim Hassan

a. Your name is Mr Karim Hassan?

b. You live in England?

c. Your highest level of education is a Master's degree?

d. You work at Parlo Ltd?

e. You first became interested in automated communications at university?

3.17 Audio 11.5

In civil trials in England, and in arbitration, it is common for the written witness statements to serve as the witness's testimony. This means that the oral examination-in-chief is very brief.

Listen to Audio 11.5 where a lawyer is conducting an examination-in-chief and complete the following sentences. These sentences are all appropriate for a lawyer conducting examination-in-chief. Each space represents one word.

a. *Please could you turn to page 25 of the _________ _________? I think it's _________ 2.*
b. *If you look through that _________ _________, what do you see at the bottom of the final page, page 28, after paragraph 30?*
c. *Whose _________ is it?*
d. *And are the contents of your witness statement _________ to the best of your knowledge and belief?*
e. *Please now turn to page 29. What _________ do you see?*

Vocabulary note

In England, a *bundle* is a ring binder file or an electronic file of all the relevant documents for a court case. It is used by the judge, claimant, defendant, and witnesses. A *trial bundle* normally includes an index, statements of case, witness statements, and exhibits. An *exhibit* is a document or physical object used as evidence in court.

The sections in a bundle are normally organised with dividers and *tabs*. A *tab* is a small piece of paper or label which sticks out from a file and is used to easily identify sections or documents in it.

The term *bundle* is used in arbitration. The closest thing in the USA to a *trial bundle* is a *trial binder* or *trial notebook*.

3.18 Practise conducting an examination-in-chief with a partner. First, read the example witness statement at the end of this chapter. Then choose a role as the lawyer or the witness and role-play an examination-in-chief using the following scenario.

Scenario

You are in court for the trial of *Parlo Ltd v Incoms Ltd*. It is time for the examination-in-chief of Karim Hassan, the joint director of Parlo Ltd.

Lawyer

You are the lawyer for the claimant and are conducting an examination-in-chief. The witness statement will serve as your witness's testimony, so you only need to confirm:

- your witness's name and address
- that the witness statement belongs to your witness
- that the contents of the witness statement are true

Witness

You are Karim Hassan. Your lawyer will ask you questions in examination-in-chief. You may need to look at your witness statement in order to answer their questions.

Cross-examination

3.19 The lawyer's aim in cross-examination is to elicit evidence from the opponent's witness in order to:

- strengthen their own case; and
- undermine the opponent's case.

The lawyer should try to control the witness through leading questions. To form a leading question, you state the desired answer, using a rising inclination to form a question as follows:

Desired answer	→	Leading question
He suggested a licensing price.	→	He suggested a licensing price?

In some instances, it is necessary to change the pronoun as follows:

Desired answer	→	Leading question
I saw Mr Richie at the office yesterday.	→	*You saw Mr Richie at the office yesterday?*

Complete the following table by transforming the desired witness answer into a leading question.

Desired witness answer	Leading question
a. This morning I showed some slides to explain how Bespeak works.	
b. I heard Jasper Johnson yesterday discuss the source code for Talkomate.	
c. Our patent application in Egypt was rejected.	
d. We first met Jasper Johnson in 2019.	

3.20 Another common technique used when asking leading questions is to add a phrase at the beginning or end of the leading question:

Phrases at the beginning	Phrases at the end
Do you agree with me that ...	That's correct, right?
Would you agree with me that ...	Right?
I'm right when I say that ...	Am I right?
Am I right when I say that ...	Correct?
You agree that ...	Yes?

For example:

Leading question
This report was published around June 2007?

→

Leading question with phrase
You agree that this report was published around June 2007?

Leading question
This email had an attached proposal?

→

Leading question with phrase
This email had an attached proposal, right?

Complete the following table by transforming the desired witness answer into a leading question.

Desired witness answer	Leading question
a. The videos we made contained information about the process used in Bespeak.	
b. The AI for Progress Group was a group of computer hackers.	
c. I did not invent android.	
d. At that point I didn't think he had infringed our patent.	

Cross-examination role-play

3.21 Practise conducting a cross-examination with a partner.

Instructions

First, read the Example witness statement and the Example exhibit extracts at the end of this chapter. Then choose a role as the lawyer or the witness and role-play an examination-in-chief using the following scenario.

Scenario

You are in court for the trial of *Parlo Ltd v Incoms Ltd*. It is time for the cross-examination of Karim Hassan, the joint director of Parlo Ltd.

Lawyer

You are the lawyer for the defendant, Incoms PLC, and are conducting a cross-examination. You should ask questions that show that:

- Parlo Ltd should not have been granted a UK patent because firstly, it uses a process it did not invent such as emails and social media, and secondly, some of the app ideas were shared at the London Tech Fair, which brought the idea into the public domain before the patent application was filed.
- Karim is not a credible witness. For example, his university thesis shows that he does not agree with patents, but then he filed a patent for Bespeak.
- Incoms PLC did not infringe the UK patent because Talkomate uses a different process.

Remember your aim is to try to advance your own case and to undermine the claimant's case. Ask leading questions to keep control of the witness.

Witness

You are Karim Hassan. The lawyer for the opposition will ask you questions in cross-examination. You may need to look at your Example witness statement and Example exhibit extracts in order to answer their questions. If the lawyer asks you a leading question, you can answer yes or no. If the lawyer asks you a non-leading question, you can talk more.

Example witness statement

IN THE HIGH COURT OF JUSTICE BUSINESS AND PROPERTY COURTS OF ENGLAND AND WALES INTELLECTUAL PROPERTY LIST (ChD) PATENTS COURT	Made on behalf of Claimant Witness: Mr K. Hassan 1st Statement of witness Dated: 14 January 2022 Exhibits: KH 1-3 Claim no. HP-2022-007HC7

BETWEEN:

PARLO LTD

Claimant

– AND –

INCOMS PLC

Defendant

WITNESS STATEMENT OF KARIM HASSAN

Personal Background

1. I live at 176 Giza Governorate, Egypt. As joint director of Parlo Ltd, I am authorised to make this Statement on behalf of the Claimant. The contents are based on my own knowledge and are true to the best of my knowledge, information and belief.
2. I received a bachelor's degree in Computer Science in 2016 from the University of Cairo. At university, I became interested in automated communications. My thesis was entitled *Using AI to Foster Human Connections*, attached at Exhibit KH1.

Development of Bespeak

3. In 2017 I co-founded Parlo Ltd, with my university peer Ur Nabil, to create AI products in communications. In my role as head software developer, I developed Bespeak from January–December 2017. Bespeak is an app which uses a novel computer programming process to connect to users' social media accounts and automatically respond to posts.
4. In June 2018, we filed for UK patent No. 257980 in England to protect this process, it was granted in December 2019, Exhibit KH2. Throughout 2019 and 2020 Parlo tried to secure funding to further develop the app as a commercial product. We secured funding in 2020 and were due to launch in June 2021.

Incoms PLC Patent Infringement

5. On 5th January 2019 I attended the London Tech Fair to showcase Bespeak. I met Jasper Johnson, a PhD student at London University, who was showcasing his research in the field of AI communications. At that time, he was interning at Incoms PLC, and he told me that Incoms could be interested in licensing our patent. Jasper visited Parlo's office several times from March–December 2019. During these visits, he saw technical and confidential app documentation.
6. In January 2020, Parlo offered Jasper a job. He rejected this offer and said that he had started a job at Incoms to develop a product similar to Bespeak. On 1st January 2021, I was shocked to learn that Incoms had launched a free app, Talkomate, with exactly the same process as Bespeak. I sent Jasper a WhatsApp raising my concerns, communications are at Exhibit KH3.

Page 21

...

20. I believe that unless ordered not to, the Defendant will continue to provide its service resulting in a loss of profit to the Claimant.

STATEMENT OF TRUTH

I believe the facts stated in this witness statement are true.

Signed: *Karim Hassan* Dated: 14 January 2022

Page 22

Example exhibit extracts

Exhibit KH1: Thesis of Karim Hassan: *Using AI to Foster Human Connections*

... Currently the law acts as a barrier to the development of AI. When companies patent ideas they block progress. I propose a new human right to global communication without barriers where people are free to connect across artificial geographical borders online. Information must stay within the public domain and not be privatised ... (page 25 of bundle, tab 5)

Exhibit KH2: the Claimant's UK Patent No. 257980

Abstract: A process for generating automatic reactions to social media communications. The app is composed of a post analyser system and a decision tree which connects to users' emails, social media accounts, and online dictionaries to gather information ... (page 27 of bundle, tab 6)

Exhibit KH3: WhatsApp transcript between Karim Hassan and Jasper Johnson

6 January 2019

Jasper: Guys your app is so cool, maybe Incoms PLC could license your patent ...

20 December 2019

Karim: Hey! We've been issued the UK patent, is Incoms still interested?

Jasper: Hey, I'm not interning there anymore ...

Karim: Really!? Ur and I want you to come here, there could be a position for you ...

Jasper: Cool. But I've got a lot on right now ... Let's speak later.

30 January 2020

Karim: Hey Jasper, hope you had a nice break. So, let's have a call to talk.

Jasper: So ... Incoms offered me a job! We're working on automated communications too, but you know, using my university research ... very different to your stuff.

Karim: Oh congrats! Your research was so ground-breaking. Looking forward to hearing about it! And it's free! #Informationfreedomrevolution!
14 January 2021

Karim: Hey Jasper! Congrats on your app. It's very cool. But we need to talk ... it seems similar to Bespeak ...

Jasper: No, trust me, we figured out a different way to do things. Don't worry.

Karim: Yes, I trust you. But could we speak about it?

(page 28 of bundle, tab 7)

3.22 Reflect on your cross-examination role-play in Exercise 3.5. If you played the role of the lawyer, use the self-assessment questions in Appendix A. If you played the role of the witness, use the peer-assessment questions in Appendix A.

Test yourself

1. What is a statement of case?
2. Compare a skeleton argument to the closest equivalent in US litigation.
3. Name three techniques you can use in your legal writing to persuade.
4. Explain the structure of a trial starting with the claimant's opening statement.
5. Describe when leading questions can be used in legal proceedings and give an example of this question type.

Notes

1 Advocacy <https://dictionary.cambridge.org/dictionary/english/advocacy> accessed 28 April 2022.
2 A. Elkington, J. Holtam, G. M. Shield, T. Simmonds, *Skills for Lawyers 2020/2021* (CLP 2011) 13.1.
3 Peter Lyons, *Advocacy A Practical Guide* (Wildly, Simmonds & Hill Publishing 2019) 73.
4 Bryan A. Garner *Garner's Dictionary of Legal Usage* (3rd edn, Oxford University Press 2011) 767.
5 Trade Marks Act 1994, s 10.
6 Senior Courts Act 1981, s 35A.
7 Bryan A. Garner, 'What Judges Really Think About the Phrase "May It Please the Court?"' (ABA Journal, 1 April 2013)<https://www.abajournal.com/magazine/article/what_judges_really_think_about_the_phrase_may_it_please_the_court> accessed 29 April 2022.

Appendices

Appendix A

Self-assessment questions

Use the following questions to assess your performance in the activities in this book:

1. How did you feel during this activity?
2. Did you follow the instructions?
3. What did you do well?
4. What did you find challenging?
5. What could you do better next time?
6. Did you use phrases and vocabulary from the chapter?
7. Could you now use this skill confidently in real life?

Peer-assessment questions

Use the following questions to assess your partner's performance in the activities in this book:

1. How did you feel during this activity?
2. Did your partner follow the instructions?
3. What did your partner do well?
4. What could your partner do better next time?
5. Did your partner use phrases and vocabulary from the chapter?

Appendix B

Legalese to Plain English Quick Reference

This quick reference guide gives some plain English alternatives to legalese. It is not a complete list of all legalese but it includes common words and expressions.

Legalese	Plain English alternative
aforementioned; aforesaid; above-mentioned	Specify what you are referring to. For example, *in the aforementioned clause* → in clause 5.2
at the present time	now
ex parte	without notice to the other party
forthwith	immediately; now

further particulars	more details
hereby	by this [document/agreement]
herein	in this [document/agreement]
hereinafter	afterwards in this [document/agreement]. In definitions, it can be removed: (~~*hereinafter referred to as*~~ *the 'Company'*)
hereinbefore	before in this [document/agreement]
hereto	to this [document/agreement]
in case of	if
in order to	to
in the event that	if
in the instant case; in the case at hand; in the present case	in this case
in relation to; in respect of; with respect to	about
in view of the fact that	as; because
notwithstanding	despite
notwithstanding the fact that	even if; although
provided that	if; on condition that (for a condition) but; except that (for an exception) and (for adding more information)
pursuant to	under; by
render	give
said	the; this; that
same	it; them
set forth in	stated in
such	the; this; that
thereby	by that; as a result of that
therein	in that [document/agreement]
thus	therefore
whereas	In contract recitals, it can be removed: ~~*Whereas*~~ *the Seller has agreed to sell ...*
whereby	by which
wherein	in which
whereof	of which
witnesseth	This word can be removed

Transcripts

Chapter 1: Networking

Audio 1.1

Anton: I graduated from the University of London last year with an undergraduate law degree. I'm searching for a job. I really want to get a training contract with a law firm, but I don't have much work experience. I want to attend networking events so that I can meet other trainee lawyers and recruiters who can give me tips on applications.

Leya: I'm an in-house lawyer at Comtech, a telecommunications company based in the Netherlands. I work in the Amsterdam office. A lot of my work involves negotiating, drafting, and reviewing contracts in English. I'm interested in attending events where I can improve my contract drafting skills in English and where I can meet other contract lawyers. I'd love to build a support network so that we can share information with each other. Oh, and my boss is also interested in me meeting contacts in Asia as we are expanding in that region.

Feven: I'm a senior associate at Cane Canner, a multinational full-service law firm headquartered in London. I work in mergers and acquisitions, and work on high-value international deals, especially in the tech sector. I'm interested in attending events where I can develop my knowledge and my reputation as an M&A lawyer. I have ten years' experience in this field and was recently recognised as a rising star in this area. I want to connect with other M&A lawyers and business people in general. I want to make partner in the firm and that means I need to gain new clients.

Audio 1.2

Anton: When I enter a room, I look for someone who's on their own. We're all in the same boat at a networking event; we're all a bit nervous. And it can be uncomfortable when it seems like everyone is in a conversation except you. Most people on their own are just waiting for someone to introduce themselves. Yes, it can be a bit daunting to do this because you have to do a lot of speaking, but it's a great way to practise! And I always find I have better conversations and make better connections one-to-one.

Oh, but if they're glued to their phone, maybe they're busy. I don't want to disturb them. Then again, sometimes I check my social media on my phone. So, I'd probably just politely say, '*Hi, are you busy? Do you mind if I join you?*' to check it's OK.

Leya: At a networking event I always avoid couples. I mean two people who are standing together and chatting. They probably know each other. Maybe they're colleagues or friends. They might be having a private conversation or discussing a confidential client matter; it would be really awkward to interrupt that. I'd be the third wheel. Look, it's not a hard and fast rule. If the only option is to join a couple, then obviously I'd join them. But given a choice, I'd go with a small group. I like small groups because, to be honest with you, I'm a bit nervous about speaking English and in a small group I can listen to others and then when I feel more confident, I can speak if I want to.

Feven: Often during networking I'll try to join a large group, at least to start with. Yes ... OK! ... Some people might say that it can be difficult to actually make strong connections with people in large groups, and I'd probably agree with that. But I find large groups are really great for finding out information. It's true that big groups often end up with just a few people talking and everyone else listening, so it can be hard if you want to practise speaking, but normally the people doing all the talking have something interesting to say. If that's not the case and the conversation is boring, well, you can quietly sneak away. That's not exactly something you can do when you're having an intimate conversation with one other person!

Audio 1.3

Anton: So, Ingrid, what brings you to this event?

Ingrid: Oh, I'm interested in becoming a solicitor after university, so I came to this event to find out more information. What about you, why are you here?

Anton: Well, I finished my law degree last summer. I graduated from the University of London and I really like this law firm. They've got a strong sports law practice and that's an area I want to specialise in.

Ingrid: Did you say the University of London?

Anton: Yes, that's right.

Ingrid: Ah! That's where I'm studying! I'm really enjoying it but there's so much work. I have to write my dissertation next year. I'm trying to think of a topic for it ... What did you choose?

Anton: I looked at new legal challenges developing in esports. It's a fascinating area.

Ingrid: I must admit, that's not an area I know much about. How did you become interested in it?

Anton: Well, I love sports; I play a lot of football, and well, this will sound really geeky, but I also really like computer games! So esports is a great fit for me. Do you like sports?

Leya: So Zul, where are you from?

Zul: I'm from Singapore. I live in a neighbourhood called River Valley. Do you know it?

Leya: Unfortunately, I've never been. The closest I've got to Singapore is Thailand. I went backpacking when I was a student and loved it. But I suppose Singapore is quite different, right?

Zul: Yes, there are differences. Singapore is much smaller than Thailand. But Singapore is very multicultural and very much geared towards international business. And perhaps as you know, English is the official language of Singapore, so it's spoken a lot.

Leya: And, what's the food like? I don't think I've ever eaten Singaporean cuisine before.

Zul: Well, our traditional food is influenced by many different cuisines. Interestingly, food is very important to us! In fact, many people greet each other by saying, '*Have you eaten?*' It's like saying, '*How are you?*'

Leya: Oh! So Zul, have you eaten?

Zul: I'm going to. Thank you!

Leya: Shall we go over to the food table then?

Zul: Yes, good idea!

Feven: Hi, I'm Feven Tadesse. Do you mind if I sit here?

Sudhvir: Hello Feven, please do; my name is Sudhvir Singh.

Feven: Nice to meet you and thank you for organising such a wonderful event.

Sudhvir: Thank you, Feven. I must say I have an excellent team behind me.

Feven: That's very important ... Oh, look, it's started to rain!

Sudhvir: Yes, typical British weather! You know, we were thinking of arranging the gala dinner outside on the roof terrace, but everybody said, you know, you can't trust the weather here. So instead, we decided to do it inside. What do you think of the view?

Feven: It's spectacular! I can see all the major sights from here. There's Tower Bridge, oh and St Paul's Cathedral!

Sudhvir: Yes, I recommend to all participants that they try and do some sightseeing after the conference tomorrow. Are you attending tomorrow?

Feven: Yes, of course. And you mentioned in your conference introduction that next year the conference will be held in Milan, how did you decide on the location?

Sudhvir: Well, we shortlisted a few venues and then took a vote as a board. We all felt that the Milan venue stood out in terms of accessibility and venue facilities. But I must say, I'm looking forward to it. Cycling is quite a hobby of mine and the conference will be at the same time as the Giro d'Italia, it's a famous bike race. Hopefully I'll be able to see some of it live! Have you heard of this race before?

Audio 1.4

Anton: So Ingrid. What do you do at university?

Ingrid: I'm a second-year law student at the University of London. I'm currently studying all the core modules: Land Law, Law of Torts, The Law of the EU, and Equity and Trusts. I've chosen one elective; it's Music and Entertainment Law. I chose this elective because I'm really interested in music and film. I play the piano and enjoy listening to film soundtracks. In the future I'd like to represent artists and record labels to help them protect their IP rights. It's my dream to represent celebrities in this area!

Leya: Zul, you mentioned that you work in Singapore as a lawyer. What exactly does your work entail?

Zul: So, I'm a senior associate in the real estate team in Allens and Forsyth LLP, a law firm in Singapore. I help both national and foreign clients with contentious and non-contentious commercial real estate matters. For example, I work a lot on commercial lettings, and sales and purchases. I don't know if this happens in your jurisdiction, but here a lot of my cases are being heard online now. A few weeks ago, I won a case where I represented a commercial tenant in a dispute relating to rent reduction and damage caused to the property. The hearing was on Zoom. My colleagues have nicknamed me Robolawyer due to my tech skills!

Feven: So Sudhvir, I know you are the President of the International Society for M&A Lawyers, but I saw in the conference programme that you're a lawyer as well. Is that correct?

Sudhvir: Yes, Feven. I'm a senior tax lawyer in the London office of Mine Parsons, an international law firm. I advise companies on a wide range of UK and cross-border corporate tax issues, and I often advise on tax issues in mergers. Some people think of tax as a ... how can I say ... a somewhat boring area, but I don't. I find it very satisfying helping clients in such an important area for their businesses. And the best thing about my job is that I get to use my language skills. For example, in January I advised a leading European real estate investment trust on the tax aspects of a major transaction involving a joint venture with a Chinese sovereign investment fund. I enjoyed travelling to Beijing and Brussels for this deal and I got to speak some French and Mandarin.

Audio 1.5

Anton: I met Ingrid at the Bengal Jackman Open day. Ingrid is a second-year law student at the same university I attended, the University of London. Ingrid and I exchanged our Instagram™ usernames at the event and followed each other. I said I'd send her an Instagram™ direct message with a link to a helpful website for law exam revision. It's a site that I found really helpful for studying.

Leya: I met Zul Chang on the Drafting International Contracts Five-Day Course. Zul is a real estate lawyer in Singapore and when I mentioned that the company I work for wants to open an office in Singapore he said he might be able to help. We connected on LinkedIn™ and I'd like to send a follow-up message to say that my boss will get in touch with him about a commercial lease.

Feven: I met Sudhvir at the 12th Annual Conference on Mergers and Acquisitions in the Technology Sector. We sat next to each other during dinner and we discovered we both had a passion for cycling! Sudhvir is the President of the International Society for M&A Lawyers and he suggested that I become a member of the board. It's something I'm really interested in. We exchanged WhatsApp™ contact details. I'm going to send him a message to say that I've decided to put myself forward for the position.

Chapter 2: Telephoning and conference calls

Audio 2.1

Angela: Hi, Claire, is everything OK?

Claire: Well actually, Angela, I'm a bit nervous about this telephone conversation with Sophie Driscoll tomorrow.

Angela: On the Agile Design file?

Claire: Yeah.

Angela: I thought your supervising partner, Marc, was leading that call?

Claire: He was supposed to, but he's just told me that he's got another meeting at the same time. I don't feel ready for this, and it will be completely in English.

Angela: Oh, I see. But you speak English well. It shouldn't be a problem for you.

Claire: That's kind but I find it so difficult to speak on the telephone. Do you have any friendly words of advice?

Audio 2.2

Angela: Claire, the best tip I can give you is to be prepared. Do you have an agenda for the call?

Claire: Uh, no, not really, Angela. Sophie said in her email that she will fill me in tomorrow, but I can ask Marc if he has any more details.

Angela: Yes, Marc is always happy to help his associates, so that would be good. And then you can check that you have all the English vocabulary that you need before the call.

Claire: Yes, good idea.

Angela: And another suggestion is to try to put yourself in an English mindset before the call.

Claire: English mindset? What do you mean?

Angela: For example, you could read or listen to the news in English, or have a chat with a colleague in English and practise your pronunciation, so that you're ready to speak in English when the call starts.

Claire: OK, thanks Angela, I'll try ...

Audio 2.3

Claire: Hello, Claire Monet speaking.

Sophie: Hi Claire, it's Sophie Driscoll from Agile Design. How are you?

Claire: Good, thanks. And you?

Sophie: Not too bad, thanks. Very busy as always! I'll have to keep it brief, I'm afraid.

Claire: Of course. I understand that you wanted to talk about a design right infringement.

Sophie: Yes, that's right. One of our products is a type of lap desk: a portable desk that you can use anywhere in your home: in a chair, on the sofa, even in bed if you like! We rolled it out last year.

Claire: Sorry Sophie, I'm not familiar with the expression *'rolled it out'*. What do you mean by that?

Sophie: Oh, it's just an informal way of saying that we started selling the product to the public. We launched the product on the market 12 months ago.

Claire: And I imagine it's become very popular with people working from home?

Sophie: Exactly! And the best feature of this desk is that ...

Claire: Hello? Sophie, are you still there? *[they start to lose connection]*

Sophie: You're breaking up ...

Claire: Hello? Hello? I've lost you Sophie ...

Sophie: Hello? Hello? I think we got cut off.

Claire: Yes, sorry, I didn't hear what you said. You were talking about the best feature of the desk. Could you just repeat that, please?

Sophie: Yes, so the best feature of this desk is that it has a semi-circular design which makes it attractive and really comfortable to use.

Claire: I see. And so is it this semi-circular shape that you have protected by registering your design?

Sophie: That's right, I just want to point out that Agile Design is the proprietor of a registered design and we haven't granted any licences or assigned any of our intellectual property rights in this product, but now we've discovered that another company called Ideal Home is importing and marketing a similar-shaped desk under a different name and of course at a cheaper price. We're really concerned as not only are they offering a cheaper alternative but people are going to confuse our desk with this other product of an inferior quality. So we need to do something immediately.

Claire: Sorry Sophie, that was a bit fast for me. Can I just check I've understood correctly? So, you believe that a company called Ideal Home is infringing your registered design as they are selling a similar product to your semi-circular lap desk. Is that right?

Sophie: Yes, that's right.

Claire: As you know, there must be a high level of similarity between the products for an infringement claim to succeed.

Sophie: Yes, I believe we have a strong case. Claire. I can send you more information and pictures of the products.

Claire: OK, thanks. I think that the best course of action would be to send a letter before claim to Ideal Home. I can draft this for you once I've had a look at the additional information.

Sophie: Great, thanks. Send me the draft and let's speak again before the end of the week.

Claire: No problem. Thanks for your call, Sophie. Bye.

Sophie: Bye.

Audio 2.4

Claire: Hello, I'm Claire Monet.

Anya: Hi Claire, I'm Anya Marshall; I represent Ideal Home. Can you see me and hear me OK?

Claire: Yes, no problem. Pleased to meet you, Anya. You're the first to join the call. I am just waiting for everyone else to arrive. You're an hour behind us in London, is that right?

Anya: Yes, that's right. My partner, Paul Turner, will be a bit late as he is stuck in another meeting.

Sophie: Hello everyone, Sophie Driscoll here ...

Claire: And I see that Philip Prescott has just joined us too. Hello Mr Prescott ... Mr Prescott, I think you're on mute.

Philip: Oh yes, sorry. Hello, and please – call me Philip.

Marc: Good morning everyone. I'm Marc Leblanc.

Claire: Hi Marc. It's Claire. We can hear you, but we can't see you.

Marc: Oh yes, sorry, I forgot to turn my camera on. There ... is that better?

Claire: Yes, but there's a lot of traffic noise coming from somewhere. Perhaps everyone can mute their microphones unless they're speaking ...

OK, thanks everyone. Right, I think everyone is here except Paul, who might be a bit late, so let's make a start. Perhaps it would be useful if everyone could quickly introduce themselves? So, I'm Claire Monet, associate here at Garniers, representing Agile Design. And perhaps Marc, you can introduce yourself next?

Marc: Yes, I'm Marc Leblanc, a partner at Garniers, working with Claire.

Claire: And Sophie next?

Sophie: Hi, I'm Sophie Driscoll, in-house legal counsel for Agile Design.

Claire: And Philip, could we hear from you?

Philip: Yes, I'm Philip Prescott, head of products at Ideal Home.

Claire: Anya's just written in the chat box that she has a problem with her microphone.

Anya: It's OK now! Hi everyone, I'm Anya Marshall, partner at Hatton Marshall, acting on behalf of Ideal Home.

Claire: Thanks Anya, and it looks like Paul is joining. Paul, are you there?

Paul: Yes, hello, Paul Turner here. Sorry for being late. My previous meeting ran over. I'm also a partner at Hatton Marshall and I'm assisting Anya in this matter.

Claire: Hello Paul and thanks everyone for attending this meeting. So, as you know, the reason for this meeting is to discuss my client's letter before claim, hopefully with a view to reaching an amicable solution so that we can avoid court proceedings. I'd like to hand over to Sophie now so that she can start by explaining Agile Design's position.

Sophie: Thanks Claire. Just bear with me while I share my screen. Can everyone see my slides? ...

Audio 2.5

Sophie: So here you can see a photo of Agile Design's lap desk, and on the next slide is a photo of Ideal Home's product and ...

Paul: Sorry to interrupt, but ...

Claire: Sorry, who's speaking?

Paul: It's Paul. Can I just say something?

Claire: Could you just let Sophie finish her point?

Paul: Yes, sorry, please go ahead Sophie.

Sophie: Thanks. So here is my third slide showing our registered design and I think the similarities between the products are very clear.

Claire: Paul, do you want to add something now?

Paul: Yes, thanks. I was just going to say that we know from case law and legislation that the legal issue here is whether my client's product produces on the informed user a different overall impression from that produced by the registered design. If it does, then there is no infringement.

Philip: Philip here. Look, I didn't follow that. Can you say that again?

Paul: Well ...[and Anya at the same time: What ...]

Paul: After you, Anya.

Anya: Thanks. So basically Philip, what Paul is trying to say is that if a consumer who wanted to buy a lap desk compared your version with Agile Design's, would it give the overall impression of being different? And ...

Philip: Let me just stop you right there! Of course it's different. Our desk has straight corners whereas yours has rounded ones and anyway, our desk is half an inch shorter than yours. I was ...

Claire: Philip has frozen. Oh dear, he's dropped out of the call. Hopefully he'll be able to reconnect ...

Marc: It's Marc. Can I just come in here? In my view, the differences that Philip was talking about are only minor, and a consumer would be unlikely to notice these.

Anya: I'm afraid we can't agree with you there.

Sophie: Sophie here. Look, this is causing my company a lot of reputational harm. The Directors want me to act quickly on this. If we can't reach an agreement, then I will have to instruct Garniers to start proceedings.

Anya: OK. Let me speak to Philip and get back to you. Can you give us another few days?

Sophie: Yes, we can agree to that.

Marc: Marc here. Shall we wrap it up there?

Claire: OK, yes. So just to recap what we said: Anya will speak to Philip and get back to us in a few days. Shall I schedule another call for this Friday?

Anya: Yes, that's fine for me.

Paul, Marc and Sophie: Me too.

Claire: Thanks everyone. Bye.

Chapter 3: Client meetings

Audio 3.1

Katie: Hello. Mr Jones? I'm Katie Thomas, a solicitor in our litigation department. Pleased to meet you.

Mike: Mike Jones. Nice to meet you too.

Katie: You can just leave your umbrella by the door. It's awful weather today, isn't it?

Mike: Yes, not what we expect in the summer!

Katie: Would you like a coffee before we start?

Mike: That would be great, thank you.

Katie: [*speaking to her assistant*] Hi Sandra, would you bring in some coffee please?

So, Mr Jones, I understand from our brief phone conversation that you'd like some advice about a contract?

Mike: Yes, that's right.

Katie: OK, well the purpose of this meeting is for me to find out more about the matter and explain what action you might be able to take. Perhaps you could start. What's happened?

Mike: Well, as you know, my company, MPJ Limited, makes packaging for the food industry.

Katie: Uh-huh.

Mike: And we had a big order from a company called Organibars. Organibars wanted us to supply a machine to provide eco-friendly wrappers for a new range of organic chocolate bars. Organibars are part of a global group and we were hoping that this could lead to a lot more business for us.

Katie: Right ... What happened next?

Mike: Well, we started work on the machine and did a test run, but now they are refusing to pay us. They want to change the specifications of the machine because they've changed the dimensions of their chocolate bars. We can do this, but we've told them that it'll increase the price of the machine. And they say that they're not prepared to pay an increased price. Surely they can't just refuse to pay us and demand changes to the machine? That's not fair.

Katie: Mmm, I can see why you feel angry about this. Can I just check that I've understood correctly? Your main objective is to be paid for the work you have done, and you will agree to change the specifications of the machine if Organibars pays an increased price?

Mike: Yes, and I really want to keep a good relationship with Organibars.

Katie: I understand. Do you have a copy of your contract?

Mike: We didn't actually sign a contract as such. We agreed some heads of terms and then we started work. Organibars were really keen for us to start making the packaging machine as they wanted to launch their new range of organic chocolate bars as soon as possible.

Katie: So what you're saying is that you don't have a signed contract but you had agreed some heads of terms?

Mike: Yes.

Katie: And what did the heads of terms include?

Mike: I can send you a copy of them. We agreed on the specifications of the machine, the delivery date, and the price.

Katie: And did they mention the possibility for Organibars to make changes to the specifications of the machine?

Mike: No.

Audio 3.2

Katie: Before being able to fully advise you, Mr Jones, I'll need to see the heads of terms, but from what you have told me so far, I'm not sure that you have a legally binding contract with Organibars.

Mike: Sorry, I don't follow you.

Katie: To put it simply, a heads of terms document is a document which usually just sets out the main terms of your deal before negotiation of a full contract.

Mike: In other words, this document is not a contract?

Katie: Well, it's an uncertain area of the law which is decided on a case-by-case basis. In my view, there are three possible outcomes in your case: the first is that you do not have a contract with Organibars. However, even without a formal contract, I recommend that you request a reasonable payment for the work you have already done.

Mike: Yes, exactly!

Katie: The second possibility is that a court may decide that there *is* a contract, on the basis of the heads of terms. This means that you would have to supply the machine specified in the heads of terms and Organibars would have to pay for this. A third scenario is that Organibars claim that even though it was not mentioned in the heads of terms, it was agreed that they could make changes to the specifications of the machine without having to pay an increased price, although in my opinion it would be difficult for Organibars to prove this.

Mike: Oh dear, it all sounds very complicated. I don't want to go to court over this. I'd really like to sort this out amicably with Organibars.

Katie: I agree. I think that going to court should be a last resort. On the one hand, going to court would allow you to demand payment for the work you have done. On the other hand, this would put you in a confrontational situation. The advantage of resolving this dispute amicably is that it could help maintain your commercial relationship with Organibars. And I must warn you that if you do go to court and you lose your case you might have to pay Organibars' legal costs, in addition to your own costs.

Mike: Yes, yes, that's too risky and I really want to resolve this as soon as possible.

Katie: OK, I suggest trying to reach an agreement with Organibars. There are a number of options: you can organise a meeting with Organibars yourself, or I can arrange a meeting with you, Organibars, and both parties' lawyers present.

Mike: Right. I'll have a think about it. Shall I send you the heads of terms in the meantime?

Katie: Yes, thank you. I'll send you a summary of today's meeting and I'll wait to receive your instructions before taking any further steps. I already explained my fees when we spoke on the phone, but I will also send you my firm's engagement letter, which explains more about our billing arrangements, client care and other terms of business. Please let me know if anything is not clear.

Mike: It's fine for now. Thank you very much.

Katie: It was nice meeting you, Mr Jones. Let me show you out ...

Audio 3.3

Paul Fairley: If you want to start proceedings against someone, the first thing you need to consider is whether the defendant is worth suing: do they have any money? Ah, yes, and we would also need to check the limitation period. This would be six years for a contract claim. Next, a letter before claim would be sent and we would want to think about ADR at this point. If we can't settle the case then we'll start proceedings: a claim form will be issued and served on the defendant. Then the claim will be allocated to a track and directions will be given. Oh, of course, that's only if a defence is filed. And then at some point there will be a trial.

Audio 3.4

Paul Fairley: There are three main steps in this procedure, as you can see in this diagram. Just to explain: the claimant is the person making a claim, that's you, and the defendant is the other party to the case.

Step one explains what we would do before starting proceedings. First, we, as lawyers, would check the limitation period. This is the period of time, defined by law, within which you can make a claim. In your case, you must bring your claim within six years of the date of the breach of contract. Secondly, you, as the claimant, should think about the costs of litigation and check whether the defendant is worth suing. Then, before starting proceedings, you will send a letter before claim to the defendant. This is a summary of the basis of your claim and what you want from the defendant. At this point, you and the defendant should try to reach an agreement, in other words, settle your claim. People sometimes use the expression *ADR*. This stands for *Alternative Dispute Resolution*, which means using alternative methods of resolving a dispute, rather than going to court. I can give you more information about this.

If you can't reach an agreement then we move on to step two, which relates to starting proceedings. As the claimant, you start proceedings by sending a claim form to the court. After that, you will serve the claim form and the particulars of claim on the defendant. If the defendant contests the claim, they will file a defence. There are time limits to respect for serving the claim form and the particulars of claim and for filing the defence.

The next step is for the court to allocate the claim to one of three tracks depending on the type and value of the case.

Step three explains how the case will proceed to trial. The court gives directions and sets a timetable for how the case will proceed. The parties have to disclose documents and exchange witness statements and expert reports. The court will also set a date for the trial. In your case it will probably take at least a year before it will get to trial. Finally, the trial will take place. But even if you obtain a judgment in your favour at trial, you might still have to take action to enforce the judgment if the defendant does not comply with its terms.

Chapter 4: Legal writing

Audio 4.1

Judith: Well, I mainly communicate with my clients and other lawyers by email. I spend most of my days writing emails. Usually these are just short emails asking for documents, setting up meetings, getting updates, and so on. If I need to write a longer email, for example, if I need to give some legal advice to a client, then I need to spend a bit more time on this.

I know we're all busy but I do think it's important to stop and think before writing. By that, I mean that we need to think about the purpose of our writing: so, why am I writing this email or drafting this document and who is going to read it? This is important because I might use a more formal style when writing to another lawyer, but with some of my regular clients I would probably be more informal.

But the other thing is that I need to get my message across as accurately and efficiently as I can. You know, my clients are busy business people with decisions to make and deadlines to meet. They don't have time to read long emails or documents: they want me to get straight to the point. I've even heard of judges telling off lawyers for making their written submissions too long!

So I have to be concise and think about how I am going to organise all the information I want to include, and this isn't easy. Also, I have to keep my language clear and unambiguous. I think some people call this plain English but for me it is just about writing in language that the client can understand.

Audio 4.2

Judith: Hi Theo, I have a client who would like some advice about redundancy. I wondered if you could help me with this. Do you know what redundancy means?

Theo: I think so, Judith. Isn't redundancy where an employer dismisses an employee because their job no longer exists, or no longer needs to be done?

Judith: Yes, good. Often it's due to the employer facing financial problems.

Theo: Is there a specific area of redundancy law that you would like me to research?

Judith: No, I think that the client needs an overview of the law. We need to make it clear that just because the client is restructuring its business, it doesn't automatically mean that it can make employees redundant.

Theo: Yes, I understand. Because a redundancy situation is clearly defined in legislation.

Judith: That's right, it's set out in the Employment Rights Act 1996[1], so we need to explain that definition, and also explain the procedure that an employer must follow.

Theo: Does the Act define that too?

Judith: No, but the employer has to use a fair procedure. Essentially, this involves a consultation period and fair selection criteria.

Theo: Consultation? Is that when the employer has to meet with the employees to explain the redundancy proposals?

Judith: Yes, and the timescale for this depends on how many employees are being made redundant.

Theo: OK, no problem. So I will mention consultation.

Judith: Good. And don't forget to include the amount of redundancy payment that an employee can claim.

Theo: Right. Shall I put this together in a memorandum for you? What's the deadline?

Judith: Yes, that would be good. By the end of the week, please. I'll be around on Thursday if you have anything you want to discuss.

Theo: OK, thanks.

Audio 4.3

Janice: Hi Sanjit, I'm just calling you with reference to the Bryson case.

Sanjit: Hi Janice, how can I help?

Janice: Well, in the aforementioned case, the claimant's lawyers have requested that we provide witness statements pertaining to the same. In the event that said witness statements are not available, can they be provided forthwith in order to comply with the court's directions pursuant to the Civil Procedure Rules? Notwithstanding this, can we also provide further particulars of the matters still at issue in the instant case?

Sanjit: I'm not really sure what you mean, Janice ...

Chapter 5: Presentations

Audio 5.1

Angus: Hi Matt. Is now a good time to talk about the webinar? I just had a few questions I wanted to ask you.

Matt: Absolutely! Fire away!

Angus: OK, thanks. So firstly, I just wanted to check who will be hosting the webinar. Will it just be me or ...

Matt: Well, I thought we could bring in Marcin Wójcik, you know, the guy who is on secondment from the Warsaw office. You could co-present.

Angus: Oh yeah. Marcin. No problem, I'll speak to him. OK, next, I wanted to ask who will be attending this webinar.

Matt: So, we'll send out a general invitation to existing clients of the firm, but we also want to attract new clients. I suggest we put something on social media and I've got a contact at the local entrepreneurs' association, so we're going to advertise it to their members too.

Angus: Right, so any idea about the number of people we can expect at the webinar?

Matt: It's hard to say because it's the first one we've done. Probably around 30 people. I'm hoping that we'll build interest as we go through the series.

Angus: I'm just thinking about the content and activities that I might include ...

Matt: Well, just remember Angus that the people attending the webinar are likely to be very business-centric. They'll want you to get to the point quickly. So just concentrate on the main business structures relevant to start-ups.

Angus: Yes, you're right, so I'm thinking of sole traders, partnerships, and limited companies.

Matt: Good, but they won't be lawyers so go easy on the legal language!

Angus: OK, got it! And so, my next question is how long should the webinar be?

Matt: Let's say 45 minutes max; 30 minutes for the presentation and 15 mins for the Q&A.

Angus: Right, so just to be clear Matt, we'll be doing the webinar live? We're not pre-recording it?

Matt: Yes, we'll do it live. That way it can be interactive. I think these participants will want to ask questions. We can record it and post it on the firm's website afterwards.

Angus: OK, and one final question, what's our main aim for this webinar?

Matt: Well, what we'd like the participants to take away is some knowledge about the common business structures chosen by start-ups. But our main aim is to attract new clients. We want people starting a new business to see that we have a team of experts dedicated to their needs, so that they think of us first when they need legal advice. And we also want them to sign up for the next webinar!

Angus: OK, so let's make sure we follow up with them after this webinar.

Matt: Good point, Angus.

Audio 5.2

Angus: Hi Marcin. Thanks so much for agreeing to present this webinar with me.

Marcin: No problem, Angus. I'm looking forward to it. I'm a bit nervous about presenting in English, though.

Angus: OK, don't worry. We need to talk about the structure of the presentation anyway. So, if you're feeling nervous, I could do the introduction.

Marcin: OK, thanks Angus.

Angus: So I'll start by welcoming the audience and introducing both of us. Then I'll introduce the topic.

Marcin: Great. And do we have a title for the webinar?

Angus: Not yet. Basically, it's about the legal aspects of business organisations for start-ups.

Marcin: We need something that sounds a bit more dynamic, so that people want to attend.

Angus: How about *Start-ups: choosing a business structure*.

Marcin: Yes, not bad. Or we could turn it into a question, to make it sound more personal. Something like: *Which business structure is right for my start-up?*

Angus: Yes, I like that. OK, and then I can explain the organisation of the presentation ...

Marcin: Sorry to interrupt, Angus, but maybe before that it would be good to have something to capture the audience's attention. Presenters often start with an interesting question or fact.

Angus: OK ... I need to have a think about that ...

Marcin: Yeah, let's brainstorm some ideas later.

Angus: OK, then next I'll explain how the presentation will be organised. I thought we could have three main parts: firstly, we will explain sole traders; secondly, partnerships; and finally, companies. For each type of structure, we can explain the advantages and disadvantages for start-ups.

Marcin: OK. I don't mind presenting the parts on sole traders and partnerships and then you can cover companies.

Angus: OK, thanks Marcin. I'm happy with that. And then, in the final part of the introduction, a bit of housekeeping.

Marcin: Housekeeping?

Angus: Yes, you know, general points about the organisation, so for example I will explain that if anyone has any questions, they should write them in the chat box and we will deal with them at the end.

Audio 5.3

Angus: Why have we chosen this topic to start our webinar series? Well, we've noticed that start-ups have usually put together a good business plan to obtain funding for their idea but haven't thought so much about the appropriate legal structure for their business. We want to help you understand more about the common types of business structures so that you can decide which one is right for you.

Angus: Did you know that small businesses account for 99.2% of the total private sector businesses in the UK?[2] Yes, more than 99% of all businesses are small businesses, just like yours. So, what business structure do people choose and why? That's what we are going to look at today.

Angus: Steve Jobs once said, 'Woz and I started Apple in my parents' garage when I was 20'.[3] Within ten years, Apple was a $2 billion company. I wonder what business structure Steve Jobs and Steve Wozniak chose when they started out? Our aim today is to help you understand more about the common types of structures chosen by start-ups in the UK and their advantages and disadvantages.

Angus: Do you know what types of business structures are available? I'm going to launch a poll so that you can type your answers ... OK, let's have a look at the results ... Interesting! You've mentioned a few different options. Today we are going to focus on which of those are commonly chosen by start-ups.

Audio 5.4

Marcin: Hi Angus. Did you have chance to look at my slides?

Angus: Yes, I did Marcin. Would now be a good time to talk about them?

Marcin: Sure.

Angus: OK, well the title slide is good. I like the way you've used the firm's standard slide template, which includes the firm's logo. Have you thought about using this template for all the slides to ensure consistency?

Marcin: Yes, I could do that. And what did you think about my other slide?

Angus: Actually Marcin, I found it quite difficult to read the text because of the font.

Marcin: Oh yes, I see. But don't worry, if I use the firm's template, that will be better.

Angus: Good. And what about the amount of information on the slide, Marcin? It might be a good idea to create bullet points with summaries of your points. You can expand on these when you speak.

Marcin: Right.

Angus: Would you like to have a look at this together?

Marcin: That would be helpful, thanks.

Angus: OK, let's see ... Matt said not to use too much legal language so perhaps it would be better to use the expression *sole trader* as this is more understandable than sole proprietorship. Similarly, the audience might not understand the expression *unincorporated* and *separate legal entity*. So how about ... *owns and runs a business alone*. That can be your first bullet point.

Marcin: But that's not a complete sentence, Angus!

Angus: I know, but it's OK not to write in full sentences on slides, Marcin. We just include key words and sometimes leave out the subject and the verb. So you could list the advantages of being a sole trader under separate bullet points like this... full control of the business ... keep all profits after tax ... easy to set up.

Marcin: I see, so then I could list the disadvantages in plainer language under separate bullet points too ... personally responsible for business debts ... home and other personal assets at risk.

Angus: Exactly.

Marcin: Thanks for your feedback, Angus.

Audio 5.5

Marcin: Actually Angus, the part that I'm most concerned about is the question and answer session at the end of the presentation.

Angus: The Q&A? Yes, I know what you mean Marcin. It's difficult to prepare for that. But we could try to anticipate some questions people might ask and think about how we would answer them.

Marcin: Good idea! Let's practise now. We have a question here which says, '*If I start my business as a sole trader, can I change my structure later*'?

Angus: So if this question came up in the Q&A I'd probably start by saying, '*That's a good question*'. See how this gives me time to think about it, Marcin?

Marcin: Yes, clever.

Angus: And then, once I've thought about it, I'd say, *'And the answer is yes, you can change your structure and in fact I have an example of that. We acted for the successful pharmacy delivery app, Pharmaroo. The owner and creator of the app started as a sole trader, but has now incorporated, in other words, has formed a company'.*

Marcin: I love the example. It shows our expertise in this area.

Angus: Exactly! Now let me ask you a question. Marcin, you talked about partnerships. It seems to me that one of the main disadvantages of this structure is that the partners have personal responsibility for all of the business debts. Is there a way to limit the partners' financial exposure?

Marcin: Can I just check that I've understood you correctly?

Angus: Oh Marcin, that's a good way to give yourself time to think too. Good.

Marcin: So, you want to know if there is a way to limit the partners' personal responsibility? Actually, there is another structure, called a limited liability partnership. This involves more set-up costs but can limit a partner's financial exposure to the amount that they have invested in the business. Does that answer your question?

Angus: Yes, thank you. Good to check that they are happy with your answer. And perhaps you could suggest that you contact them after the webinar with more details about this. You could say, *'I'd be happy to talk to you separately about that. Could I contact you after the webinar?'.*

Marcin: OK. But what if I really don't know the answer to a question?

Angus: Well, instead of just saying that you don't know, you could say, *'I will have to check the answer to that question and get back to you'.*

Marcin: OK. Thanks Angus.

Audio 5.6

Marcin: Thanks for helping me practise the presentation, Angus.

Angus: No problem, Marcin. Go ahead.

Marcin: So, hello everyone. The first topic I'm going to talk about is sole traders. As you can see from this slide, we can define a sole trader as one person who owns and runs a business ...

Angus: Sorry to interrupt, Marcin. That's a nice confident start, but I can't see your slides.

Marcin: Oh. I seem to have a problem sharing my screen. Hang on, I'll try again ... let me see ... I'll just click here ... Can you see them now?

Angus: Yes, that's fine now. But it would be a good idea before the real webinar to check that all your equipment is working properly.

Marcin: I agree. OK, so what this slide shows is that a sole trader means someone who owns one hundred percent of their business.

Angus: I like the way you're using language that the audience will be able to understand, Marcin. This will help you to connect with them.

Marcin: Thanks Angus. OK, to continue: The advantage of this is that a sole trader keeps full control of their business and keeps all profits after tax and another advantage is that it is easy to set up.

Angus: Maybe you could add some pauses, Marcin? Like this: The advantage of this [pause] is that a sole trader keeps full control of their business [pause] and will be able to keep all profits that the business makes after tax [pause]. Another advantage is that it is easy to set up as a sole trader.

Marcin: I see Angus. Using pauses emphasises the points much better.

Angus: Yes, and it gives your audience time to consider what you have said.

Chapter 6: Social media marketing

Audio 6.1

Ethan: Wow! I didn't realise LinkedIn™ was the world's largest professional network. I set up a profile ages ago, but it just says, '*Ethan. Law student*'. That's it! I'm definitely going to update it now.

Sofia: Yeah. Actually, I need to set up a profile; I don't have one yet. I always thought there was no point. It's not like I've got loads of work experience ...

Ethan: Yes, but I think Linda said that even voluntary positions are important, right?

Sofia: Yeah, I made a note of what she said ... *'40% of all hiring managers view volunteer experience as equivalent to regular employment'.*[4]

Ethan: Great!

Sofia: Yeah, so I'm definitely going to add in the voluntary vacation scheme I did at Smith Jones LLP last year.

Ethan: That's a really good law firm and their vacation scheme is so competitive. That will look great on your profile.

Sofia: I hope so ... but unfortunately I don't have any paid legal work experience.

Ethan: Don't worry. Linda said that if we don't have any specific legal experience we can add other work positions to highlight our transferable skills.

Sofia: Transferable skills. Oh yes! She meant soft skills which could apply to many different jobs.

Ethan: Exactly. You should add your summer job as a sales assistant. It's not related to law, but it's a good way to show transferable skills like time management, attention to detail, and teamwork.

Sofia: That's a great idea! And ... didn't Linda mention you get more profile views if you have an up-to-date current position?

Ethan: Yeah, she did. I'm working as a receptionist at a law firm at the moment; I'll add that.

Sofia: Good for you! I don't have a job yet. But there are a lot of other sections I could fill in.

Ethan: Hmm, we've got a lot to do! Hey, shall we meet up at lunch in the café and update our profiles together? We can share ideas about what to write and help each other with proofreading. What do you think?

Sofia: Yes! Linda stressed the need of proofreading your profile. Great idea.

Audio 6.2

Sofia: Hey Ethan! Sorry, I'm late.

Ethan: Hi Sofia! No worries, it gave me a chance to check what I'd already got in my profile. I've just updated my Headline and current position.

Sofia: Oh, well done.

Ethan: Would you mind checking it?

Sofia: Sure, let's take a look. OK. So your current positions says you are a receptionist at a law firm.

Ethan: Yes. Well, it's just part-time; I work once a week on a Friday afternoon, covering maternity leave.

Sofia: Well, it's great to have law firm experience ... So, the firm is called Fish and Friar? Is that the correct spelling? F I S H and then Friar F R I A R?

Ethan: Yes, that's right.

Sofia: OK and it's in East London. And ... let me carry on reading ... OK so ... this is listed as your current position. It says, '*start date: December this year*' and '*end date: present*', which means you're still working in this position. Is that right?

Ethan: Yes, the maternity leave will end sometime next year.

Sofia: OK, so let's look at your description ... '*In my position at this niche commercial law firm, I take pride in being the first face-to-face contact for clients before they see one of our lawyers specialising in the fields of IT, e-commerce, and data protection law. My duties involve organising client meetings, updating solicitors' calendars, and handling a high-volume of calls*'. Good. Then it says... '*Skills: communication, time management, customer service*'.

Ethan: What do you think?

Sofia: Nice! I really like how you've explained exactly what you do, included keywords related to legal practice, and some transferable skills.

Audio 6.3

Ethan: Sofia, do you think I should change anything before sending this recommendation request?

Sofia: Let me see. So, it says, '*Hey Sarah, Thanks for being my supervisor at Fish and Friar LLP, I've learnt a lot during my time working for you*', with two exclamation marks ... Um, Ethan, perhaps you should say '*Dear Sarah ... thank you for ...*' instead of '*hey Sarah thanks for ...*' and you should get rid of the contraction '*I've*' and put '*I have*'. Also, put a full stop instead of exclamation marks.

Ethan: OK, so it should say '*Dear Sarah ... Thank you for being my supervisor at Fish and Friar LLP, full stop, I have learnt a lot during my time working for you, full stop*'.

Sofia: Yes. OK, so then it says, '*I want you to write me a recommendation highlighting my knowledge of commercial law and interest in IT law*' ...

Ethan: What's wrong?

Sofia: You could make this part more polite. I think you should start with, '*I'm writing to ask if you could provide me with a recommendation*' and then continue with what you've written there.

Ethan: Good, idea, that sounds more professional and polite.

Sofia: OK, so, the next part says, '*I need to get a training contract, so I need your recommendation to build my credibility*'.

Ethan: This part doesn't sound quite right either.

Sofia: Yes, it would be better to say, '*As you know, comma, I am hoping to get a training contract, comma, and your recommendation would help to build my credibility*'.

Ethan: Yes, that's better.

Sofia: Oh, and here at the end you say, '*Cheers, Ethan*'. That's probably too informal. I would say, '*Kind regards or best wishes, Ethan*'.

Ethan: OK, yes, you're right. Thanks Sofia!

Audio 6.4

Christina: Last week I posted a '*Top Data Protection Compliance Tips*' video on social media. Someone commented on this video saying they had followed this advice, and it was incorrect. Now they want to sue me for negligence. Next time, including a disclaimer making it clear that my videos do not constitute legal advice, would help.

Helena: Last year I went to Barcelona for an M&A conference. At the end of the event, I took a photo with some new friends I'd made. It's a nice picture with some street art in the background and I posted it on social media. This morning I saw a comment on the post saying, '*I am the street artist who created that design! You don't have a licence to use this work! That's my copyright!*' I'm a lawyer – how could I have made this mistake! It's so important to gain permission for posting copyrighted work.

Giovanni: I've been representing clients in complex commercial litigation for years. I've never had a problem with social media before. But now the opposition in a case is accusing me of tampering with witnesses because I'm connected with one on social media. I didn't even realise we were connected ... I've never even spoken to him!

As a litigator I need to be very careful who I connect with and not accept every random connection request I get.

Patrizia: I post a photo every morning on social media. My followers love seeing what I'm wearing to work! But yesterday, I had to delete a photo of me posing in the office because I realised if you zoomed in you could see some client files in the background. I should always double-check my photos don't contain any confidential information in them before posting.

Edmund: A lawyer in my law firm was involved in a heated debate on social media. His posts were really rude. Someone complained and commented on the thread, '*I've reported you to the authorities. Your comments are offensive*'. Instead of removing the post, my colleague responded in all caps, '*DON'T READ THEM IF YOU'RE OFFENDED!!!*'. Some people act in an inappropriate way on social media even though they wouldn't do this in real life. When I'm about to post on social media, I ask myself, '*Is it acceptable for me to post this as a lawyer? Would I say this in real life?*'

Audio 6.5

Katia: And we're back for another episode of the Express Law podcast, the podcast that keeps you updated on legal issues related to IT, cyber security, and privacy and data protection law.
I'm your host Katia Kowalska and this episode is entitled 'Compliance with GDPR: an interview with Ethan Mowry'. As the title of this episode suggests, today I'm interviewing Ethan Mowry, trainee lawyer at Express Law. We'll be talking about what big and small businesses need to do in order to comply with the General Data Protection Regulation. So ... now let's *express*! Ethan, are you there?

Ethan: Hi Katia, yes, I'm here. Thanks for having me on the show today.

Katia: Thanks Ethan. Let's dive straight in. Ethan, what is GDPR?

Ethan: Well, Katia, GDPR stands for the General Data Protection Regulation; it's a European regulation that regulates what companies can and can't do with people's data

...

and of course if your business or company doesn't comply with this regulation, you could be fined up to €10 million or up to 2% of the company's entire global turnover from the previous fiscal year.

Katia: Ouch!

Ethan: Ouch indeed!

Katia: So, that's a wrap! Thanks Ethan.

Ethan: Thanks Katia.

Katia: And thank you for listening to the Express Law podcast with me Katia Kowalska. Visit our website www.express-law.ai/gdpr-compliance to find a PDF download of Ethan's overview we mentioned during the episode. And you can also contact Ethan with questions you have about this episode; his email address is ethan.mowry@express-law.ai.

Finally, if you enjoyed this episode, please subscribe to the podcast and share it on social media. Thank you and goodbye.

Chapter 7: Job applications and interviews

Audio 7.1

Sam: A big warm welcome to Johnny Parker, recruitment partner at Marsh & Rayling! Thanks for coming on our student podcast today.

Johnny: No problem Sam. Happy to be here.

Sam: So perhaps you could start by explaining to our listeners what qualities you are looking for in applicants to your law firm?

Johnny: There are many qualities that we're looking for but I'm going to focus on five skills that I think every commercial lawyer needs. The first is good interpersonal skills.

Sam: You mean the ability to communicate with people?

Johnny: Yes, but it's more than that. It's about understanding people and having empathy. Sometimes you have to explain very complex legal issues in a way the client can understand.

Sam: I see. Yes, that's important. And your second point, Johnny?

Johnny: OK, the second skill is the ability to work in a team. In other words, to be a team player. In a commercial law firm, you will often have lawyers from a number of different disciplines working on a deal. This means that you need to build good relationships with your colleagues, show them respect, and be able to deal with conflict.

Sam: And that can't always be easy if you are working to tight deadlines?

Johnny: No, so my third point is that you need to have good organisational skills. For example, you need to be able to set priorities and manage your time effectively.

Sam: OK, Johnny, and what is point number four?

Johnny: Of course, a lawyer needs to have good analytical skills, so that's my fourth point. You need to be able to analyse a client's problem and find a solution. This involves identifying the legal issues and researching the relevant law. You're trained to do this in your legal studies, but sometimes you need to have the initiative to think of other solutions, what we might call thinking outside the box, or what some people call creative problem-solving.

Sam: But isn't that a bit difficult when we don't have much prior commercial experience?

Johnny: Well, Sam, perhaps that brings me on to my last point. We are also looking for commercial awareness.

Sam: Commercial awareness? Can you explain to our listeners what this means?

Johnny: Commercial awareness is about being aware of what's going on in the business world, so that you can understand the context in which your clients, and law firms, are operating.

Sam: OK, so how can we become more commercially aware?

Johnny: Well, you need to keep up to date with current legal and business issues: for example, you can read the legal, financial, and business news, or listen to podcasts, and you can follow trends on social media. Another good idea is to attend law firm webinars on current hot topics. One big topic at the moment is ESG.

Sam: ESG?

Johnny: Environmental, Social, and Governance issues ...

Audio 7.2

Sam: So, Johnny, we know what skills you're looking for, but can you tell us a little bit more about your recruitment process?

Johnny: Sure Sam. There are four parts to our recruitment process: first of all, students need to complete the online application form. This includes information about your education, grades, work experience etc.

Sam: So, similar to your CV?

Johnny: Yes, and similar to your covering letter too, since there is space for you to explain why you want to work at our firm. We also include some longer questions to ascertain your ambition and commitment to a career in law.

Sam: OK, and what comes next?

Johnny: Next, we ask you to complete a psychometric test ...

Sam: That sounds a bit scary! What's that? And how can students prepare for it?

Johnny: It's a test with MCQs to assess critical thinking skills. The best advice I can give to students is to do some of the practice tests which are widely available online.

Sam: And if students get through that stage, is there an interview?

Johnny: Yes, the next stage is a video interview. However, this is not a live interview. Once you launch the online interview, you can't stop it. You will have a set time in which to answer a series of questions, during which you will be recorded.

Sam: That sounds daunting too!

Johnny: It can be, but I would suggest that you train for this by recording yourself answering typical interview questions within a time limit.

Sam: So, do students ever get to meet someone in person?

Johnny: Oh yes! In fact the final stage is what we call the assessment centre. This involves a whole day at the office, when you get to meet the firm's lawyers, participate in some group exercises and have a face-to-face interview with some of our partners.

Sam: And any final words of advice for our listeners?

Johnny: I would say: be prepared and be yourself!

Audio 7.3

Annabelle: Hi Victor. How's it going? Did you apply for the vacation scheme at Marsh & Rayling? Any news?

Victor: Hi Annabelle. Yes, I did, and I've got some great news. I've just found out that I've made it through to the video interview stage.

Annabelle: Wow! Well done Victor.

Victor: Yes but apparently it's not a live interview. As far as I understand it, once I launch the interview application, I'll have a set time in which to answer some questions. You've had a video interview before, right? Any tips on how to prepare?

Annabelle: OK, yes, well obviously the main thing is to check that all your equipment is working correctly before you launch your interview.

Victor: You mean camera, microphone, internet connection?

Annabelle: Yes, and don't forget to check your lighting and your background! Oh, and turn off any notification sounds on your computer or your phone.

Victor: OK, good tips. And then when I launch the application, what happens?

Annabelle: Well, there should be a short introduction and then you'll be asked a series of questions. Usually, you have about a minute to think about your answer and then a few minutes to say your answer to the camera.

Victor: But there's nobody watching me live? Isn't that a bit strange?

Annabelle: Yes, I found it very uncomfortable seeing myself on camera, with no interaction from the other side. I think it would be a good idea to practise this, by recording yourself answering some example questions.

Audio 7.4

Victor: So what type of questions does a law firm usually ask in a video interview?

Annabelle: In my experience, the firm is looking to see if you have the skills that they require. I notice that in their advert they refer to ambition, so they might want to see evidence of this.

Victor: Oh, OK, and how should I show that?

Annabelle: Have you heard of the STAR method for answering interview questions, Victor?

Victor: The STAR method: S ... T ... A ... R. What's that?

Annabelle: It stands for Situation, Task, Action, Result. It helps you give evidence of your skills. Let's take an example. In the interview you could be asked this question: '*Give me an example of when you set yourself an ambitious goal*'.

Victor: OK, I've got a good example. It's when I wanted to set up a mooting competition in our law faculty.

Annabelle: Great example. OK, so using the STAR method we can say: *Situation:* I wanted to organise a mooting competition in my law faculty *Task:* I had to get permission from the faculty and organise the competition before the summer break. *Action:* What action did you take, Victor?

Victor: Well, I contacted the head of the law faculty, who gave their permission, and then I asked other students to help me and we organised the competition.

Annabelle: Try to focus on what you did Victor: use I, not we.

Victor: OK, so, I contacted the head of the law faculty, who gave their permission. Then I asked some other students to research a mooting question. I contacted some local barristers to see if they could judge the competition and then I advertised the competition through the campus platform.

Annabelle: Great! and the result was that – let's put some figures in here to make it sound better – *'over 50 students competed in the competition and it was such a success that I was asked to repeat it again this year'*.

Victor: Got it!

Annabelle: OK Victor, so let me ask you that question again: *'Give me an example of when you set yourself an ambitious goal'*.

Victor: My goal was to organise a mooting competition in my law faculty. I had to get permission from the faculty and organise the competition before the summer break. I contacted the head of the law faculty, who gave their permission. Then I asked some other students to research a mooting question. I contacted some local barristers to see if they could judge the competition and then I advertised the competition through the campus platform. The competition was a great success: over 50 students competed. And I've been asked to repeat it again this year.

Annabelle: Well done!

Victor: I think I will prepare some other example answers using the STAR method. Thanks Annabelle.

Audio 7.5

Narrator: Hello. This is the introduction to your interview. I am going to ask you three questions. After each question you will have one minute to prepare. The end of this time will be signalled by a beep. You will then have three minutes to say your answer to the question. The end of this time will also be signalled by a beep. I will then ask you the second question in the same manner and then the third question. You must not pause or end your recording until you have answered all of the questions.

Here is your first question: Give me an example of when you had to use good communication skills. You have one minute to prepare your answer, starting from now. You must say your answer now. That is the end of your time.

Here is your second question: Tell me about a time when you had to solve a difficult problem. You have one minute to prepare your answer, starting from now. You must say your answer now. That is the end of your time.

Here is your third question: Explain a situation where you had to work with other people on a project. You have one minute to prepare your answer, starting from now. You must say your answer now. That is the end of your time and the end of your interview. Thank you.

Audio 7.6

Johnny: Hello Geraldine. Pleased to meet you. I'm Johnny Parker, recruitment partner here at Marsh & Rayling and this is one of my partners, Alice Mason.

Alice: Hello Geraldine.

Geraldine: Hello.

Johnny: OK, Geraldine, we'll start by asking you a few questions and then at the end of the interview you'll have chance to ask us some questions too.

Alice: So, perhaps first of all, could you tell us about yourself? Why do you want to be a lawyer?

Geraldine: Yes, well, as you can see from my CV, I'm currently studying law at the University of London, and I play on the university hockey team.

Alice: OK, but why did you apply specifically to our firm, Marsh & Rayling, Geraldine?

Geraldine: Well, I know that it's best to do a vacation scheme at the end of the second year of your degree, and you cover a lot of different interesting areas ... erm ... I suppose...

Johnny: ... OK, next Geraldine I'd like you to tell me about a time when you had to work under pressure.

Geraldine: Oh I work best under pressure. I always leave it until the last minute to hand in my essays and ... erm... well... I always seem to get good grades.

Johnny: Right. And finally Geraldine, what's one of the key issues facing the legal industry today?

Geraldine: Well, I suppose it would be technology. I mean, who'll need lawyers if clients can do everything by themselves online, right?

Johnny: OK, thank you, Geraldine. Now, do you have any questions you'd like to ask us?

Geraldine: No, I think that's fine for me, thanks ...

Johnny: Hello Sarah. Pleased to meet you. I'm Johnny Parker, recruitment partner here at Marsh & Rayling and this is one of my partners, Alice Mason.

Alice: Hello Sarah.

Sarah: Hello Mr Parker, Ms Mason, pleased to meet you too.

Johnny: OK, Sarah, we'll start by asking you a few questions and then at the end of the interview you'll have chance to ask us some questions too.

Alice: So, perhaps first of all, could you tell us about yourself? Why do you want to be a lawyer?

Sarah: Yes, well, I'm currently a second-year law student at the University of London, and I also volunteer at the university's legal advice centre. I've found it really rewarding to help people solve their legal problems, and this is what has convinced me that I would like to practise as a lawyer.

Alice: OK, but why did you apply specifically to our firm, Marsh & Rayling, Sarah?

Sarah: Well, this year I chose options in commercial law and employment law. I know, Ms Mason, that you head up the firm's employment law practice, and I was attracted to the wide range of employment law issues that you deal with, acting for both businesses and individuals. So that is why I wanted to apply to your firm ...

Johnny: ... OK, next Sarah I'd like you to tell me about a time when you had to work under pressure.

Sarah: Could I have a moment to think about that please?

Johnny: Of course, take your time.

Sarah: Right, well, once when I was advising someone at the legal advice centre, I realised that the limitation period was about to expire. We needed to file a claim form immediately. I told my supervisor and then I acted quickly to complete the claim form, and I even ran to the court to file it by hand. Luckily I was just in time but now I never forget to check this point on a first interview with a client! So that's definitely a time when I had to work under pressure.

Johnny: OK, and finally Sarah, what's one of the key issues facing the legal industry today?

Sarah: In my opinion ESG, Environment, Social, and Governance, since it's something that not only law firms have to advise their clients about but that law firms also need to apply to their own operations. I noticed, for example, that Marsh & Rayling have already committed to making the firm net zero within the next five years. So I would say that ESG is one of the major issues today.

Johnny: OK, thank you Sarah. Now, do you have any questions you'd like to ask us?

Sarah: Yes, I just wondered whether there'd be the possibility of working with any of your overseas offices during the vacation scheme? ...

Chapter 8: Contract drafting and review

Audio 8.1

David: Hello Ms Newman. I wondered if I could ask you some questions about contract drafting. Do you have time now?

Amelia: No problem David. And please call me Amelia.

David: Thanks Amelia. So, you're a lawyer in the corporate department? Is that right?

Amelia: Yes, I work mainly in M&A: that's mergers and acquisitions.

David: So what types of contracts do you deal with?

Amelia: I mainly deal with SPAs.

David: SPAs? What are those?

Amelia: Sorry, David, that stands for share purchase agreements. It's where my client is buying or selling shares in a company.

David: OK, so how do you decide which party drafts the contract?

Amelia: Well, there's usually a convention in SPAs that the buyer's lawyer drafts the contract, but in other types of contracts, like sale of goods contracts, it's usually the seller's lawyer who produces the first draft.

David: I see, so there's no set rule, but lawyers usually know which party will be responsible for drafting the contract.

Amelia: Exactly.

David: And *how* do you draft a contract? Is it like writing an essay? Do you start from a blank page?

Amelia: It is funny you should ask that. I remember the first time I was asked to draft a contract. I was newly qualified and I didn't know where to start. My colleague told me to look in the firm's precedent bank.

David: Precedent bank?

Amelia: Yes, a precedent is a template document. My firm has a database of precedents for different types of transactions: sale of goods contracts, leases, licensing agreements, employment contracts, and so on. So if I want to draft an SPA, I don't have to start from scratch. I can simply use a precedent and adapt it to my client's transaction.

David: I see, so that must save a lot of time.

Amelia: Yes, but I have to make sure that it reflects my client's deal. No two transactions are exactly the same and it's important to check that all the clauses in the contract are appropriate for my client.

David: Is there anything else that you have to be careful about when using precedents?

Amelia: I would say two main things, David: firstly, be careful about copying and pasting clauses from various different precedents as you might end up with something that is inconsistent and ambiguous. Secondly, be careful when searching for precedents on the internet. They might be badly drafted and, more importantly, instead of being templates, they may be signed copies of contracts which incorporate all the negotiated amendments. This wouldn't be a good starting point for your first draft.

David: OK, I see ...

Audio 8.2

David: You talked about drafting a share purchase agreement, Amelia. Could you explain more about the structure of this type of contract?

Amelia: Well, David, not all contracts are the same, but most commercial contracts follow a similar structure. First of all, you have the introductory paragraph, which is sometimes called the preamble. The introductory paragraph includes the title of the contract, the names of the parties and the date of the contract. It's important to check that the names of the parties are correct, particularly when dealing with companies. Then we have the recitals: this is an old-fashioned word for background. The recitals are like a story, explaining why the parties wish to enter into the contract. Recitals aren't strictly necessary but can be useful for clarifying the intention of the parties if there is a dispute later on.

David: Is that the part that often begins with the word *whereas*?

Amelia: Yes, but in modern contracts, instead of *whereas* we use paragraphs with numbers or letters. After the recitals are the words of agreement, something like, '*the parties agree as follows* or *it is agreed*'. These words are a link between the beginning of the contract and the operative provisions.

David: Operative provisions? What does that mean?

Amelia: In other words, the parties' expressly agreed terms. Often the first clause after the words of agreement contains the definitions. Then we find the main provisions of the agreement. By this I mean the main or most important obligations of the parties.

David: So presumably, this would include the seller's obligation to sell the shares and the buyer's obligation to pay the agreed price.

Amelia: Yes, that's right, and in an SPA we would also find details about the completion date and any conditions precedent.

David: Conditions precedent? I'm confused. I thought that a precedent was another word for a template.

Amelia: Yes, but here it refers to conditions that have to be satisfied before the agreement comes into effect. For example, a share purchase agreement could include a condition that the buyer's shareholders have passed a resolution to approve the purchase of the shares.

David: OK, and so what would come after the main provisions?

Amelia: After the main provisions, we have the other core provisions of the contract. These would include warranties, indemnities, and confidentiality obligations. And then last but not least are the boilerplate clauses.

David: Oh yes, I've heard people talk about boilerplate, but I don't really understand what this means.

Amelia: Lawyers use this expression to refer to the general terms that you find at the end of most commercial contracts. For example, clauses dealing with how and where to send notices, and the governing law and jurisdiction. There is no real consensus on which clauses form part of the boilerplate but it's important to review these clauses, and not just assume that they are the same in every contract.

David: I understand. And so finally we have the signatures of the parties?

Amelia: Yes and it's important to check that the signature blocks match the names of the parties in the introductory paragraph.

David: Yes, that makes sense. Thanks for that explanation Amelia.

Audio 8.3

David: Amelia, could I just ask you what happens if you receive a draft contract from the buyer's lawyers. How do you review their draft? Where do you start?

Amelia: Well, I have to make sure that the terms of the contract reflect my client's deal. So I'll need to refer to my client's instructions and any heads of terms. I might also need input from other partners in my firm who specialise in tax or real estate law. Also, it's important to check what is missing from the contract as well as what is written.

David: So, for example, you need to check that the contract states the correct price?

Amelia: Yes, but I also need to check other obligations on the Buyer relating to the price; for example, when does the Buyer have to pay and how will the Buyer make the payment? In fact, it's important to check all obligations in the contract to see if they are absolute or qualified.

David: What do you mean?

Amelia: An absolute obligation means that you *have* to do something. If you don't do it, then you will be in breach of contract.

David: OK, that makes sense. So, for example, the Buyer's obligation to pay the purchase price would be an absolute obligation?

Amelia: Exactly. You can see here in clause 3.2 that it says: *The Buyer shall pay the Purchase Price at Completion by telegraphic transfer to the Seller's solicitors*. This is an absolute obligation. You are agreeing absolutely to do this.

David: So if the Buyer doesn't pay the price at completion by telegraphic transfer, then it will be in breach of contract.

Amelia: Right. But clause 4.2 is an example of a qualified obligation.

David: What do you mean by a qualified obligation?

Amelia: If you qualify a party's obligation, you reduce the obligation.

David: Let me see ... it says that *The Seller and the Buyer shall use their reasonable efforts to procure the satisfaction of the Conditions Precedent as soon as possible*. Reasonable efforts? That sounds a bit vague.

Amelia: Yes, using the words *reasonable efforts* reduces a party's obligation. Instead of *having to* achieve an obligation, it means that the party just has to *try to fulfil* the obligation. The problem is that we don't really know how hard the party needs to try and so it will be more difficult to prove a breach of contract.

David: So, won't this vague language lead to disputes?

Amelia: Maybe, and we could try to define more precisely in the contract what *reasonable efforts* means. But, to be honest David, there are usually more important aspects of the deal to discuss and this type of language at least allows some flexibility in defining obligations. Sometimes parties actually prefer flexibility and vague terms.

Audio 8.4

David: I know that using plain English in contracts makes them clearer. Do you spend a lot of time removing legalese?

Amelia: To be honest, no. Not unless there are any major ambiguities. I need to focus on the main commercial issues and risks for my clients.

David: So which parts of the contract do you spend the most time reviewing?

Amelia: I'd say mainly warranties, indemnities, and limitation of liability clauses.

David: Sorry, Amelia, I don't understand. What are warranties and indemnities? And what does limitation of liability mean?

Amelia: Let's have a look at some examples in this contract. A warranty is a statement in the contract promising that something is true. See paragraph 1 in Schedule 4, it says here that there are no proceedings pending or threatened by or against the company being sold. If I'm acting for the seller I need to check with my client that this is true. If it's not true then the buyer could sue the seller for breach of contract.

David: And I see that clause 6.4 uses the verb indemnify. Is this an indemnity clause?

Amelia: Yes. This clause explains the situation if there's a breach of the warranties. According to this clause, the seller would have to reimburse the losses suffered by the buyer, without the need for the buyer to claim damages in court.

David: That sounds like a big risk for our client.

Amelia: Yes, so I'll try to delete indemnities and I will also try to cap my client's liability.

David: Cap? What do you mean by that?

Amelia: Cap means that the seller's liability is limited to a maximum amount of money. You can see an example in clause 7.1. And clause 7.2 contains a minimum threshold which must be exceeded before any claims can be brought by the buyer.

David: OK. Thanks Amelia. I can see that I still have a lot to learn!

Chapter 9: Contract negotiations

Audio 9.1

Jakob: Hi Fabian, could I have a word with you?

Fabian: Yes of course.

Jakob: I was thinking, it might be interesting for you to get involved in a contract negotiation on one of my files. Are you ready to take up the challenge?

Fabian: Oh, yes, thanks Jakob! I'd like that.

Jakob: Great. So let me bring you up to speed on it. We're acting for RB Motors in negotiations with Autologica. The parties really mean business and have already negotiated and agreed on some of the commercial aspects of the business deal. After this, Autologica's lawyer sent us their first draft of the supply of goods agreement.

Fabian: OK, so the other side's lawyer drafted the first version of the contract and sent it to us?

Jakob: Yes, then I had a meeting with Eymen Demir, the CEO of RB Motors, as there were a few things he wanted to change in the contract. I also recommended a few changes to reduce any legal risks.

Fabian: So, did you mark up the contract?

Jakob: Yes, exactly. After receiving the first version from the other side's lawyer, we marked up the contract and sent back the red-lined copy to the other side. They reviewed our amendments and came back to us asking for a meeting to negotiate.

Fabian: OK. So what will happen next?

Jakob: Well, we're working against the clock here. First, we need to prepare for the negotiations. The lawyers, I mean us and the other side's lawyers, will meet to negotiate the contract terms. If we can reach an agreement, the other side's lawyer will draw up the final version of the contract. This will then be circulated to the parties for signing.

Audio 9.2

Clarissa: Welcome to our office. I'm Clarissa Porterfield; please call me Clarissa. This is my associate Brent Riley, and we're joined by Rodrigo Django, CEO of Autologica.

Jakob: Nice to meet you all. I'm Jakob Winter, this is Fabian Nilsson, a trainee at our firm, and this is Eymen Demir, CEO of RB Motors. Please, a first-name basis is also fine with us.

Clarissa: Thank you Jakob. And I'd like to thank you all for coming to this meeting today. We're looking forward to working together to reach a satisfying and reasonable solution for both parties.

Jakob: Thank you Clarissa. Likewise, we're happy to be working with you and hope this will be the beginning of a long-lasting relationship.

Clarissa: Excellent. I'm sure you understand the importance of making headway and agreeing to our terms quickly, given the time constraints. My suggestion is that we work through the contract point by point. Is that OK with you?

Jakob: Yes, good idea. There may be some instances where we have to cross-reference other clauses, but let's cross that bridge when we come to it.

Clarissa: Great. Let's crack on with things. First of all, in the delivery clause 7.1 is fine, but could you explain your amendments to 7.2?

Jakob: Certainly. We'll get straight to the point. We'd like to change this clause so that RB Motors has the right to inspect goods on delivery and reject all or part of them, if they don't comply with tolerance levels set out in each order.

Audio 9.3

Clarissa: Thank you for explaining those points, but I'm afraid we don't understand. Could you elaborate?

Jakob: No problem. I'll try to explain this further. Getting the correct volume of batteries is important for our client. Too many batteries mean we could incur costs for storage and too few means our production line may stop. Our client lost a lot of money in the past due to this exact problem with another supplier. We don't want that to happen again. And what's more, if we lose money due to this issue, it could cause problems with payments to Autologica. So, in our opinion, this clause amendment is fair and in the interests of both parties.

Clarissa: OK. Thank you for clarifying that point. So, we understand that you'd like to ensure that volumes are precise, give or take a certain tolerance level, and that if Autologica gets this wrong, this entitles RB Motors to potentially reject the order, is that correct?

Jakob: Yes.

Audio 9.4

Clarissa: So, let's move on to clause 7.3. Jakob, I'll be clear with you. This amendment is absolutely impossible for us.

Jakob: Ok. Let's see. Well, Clarissa, I'm afraid that actually this is quite an important point for our client.

Clarissa: Yes, we can understand that, but including *time is of the essence* is a huge problem for us. It's something we are totally not willing to change.

Jakob: I hear what you're saying, but it seems like we have a little bit of a disagreement. Let me just have a word with my client ... Eymen, let's have a quick chat about this ...

OK, so I understand ... I'm sorry, delivery is pretty significant for us. Perhaps you could reconsider your position?

Clarissa: Listen, I can see that we've reached a sticking point here. Let's take five, grab a coffee and move on to another clause. We can come back to this later.

Jakob: Right. OK.

Audio 9.5

Clarissa: We'd like to hear you out on this and see things from your perspective. Could you explain why including time is of the essence is so important for you?

Jakob: Yes, we can see this is an important issue for both of us. Let me explain. You know that the production line is relying on the batteries. If there is late delivery, then it can result in significant costs for our client. The reason why this clause is so important to us is because our client has had some problems in the past with this, and we don't want this to happen again. Can you understand our point of view?

Clarissa: Yes. But from our point of view you are essentially saying that if we are one hour late you can terminate the contract. You expect us to ensure on-time delivery every time. Please put yourselves in our shoes. How can we do this?

Jakob: OK. I see your point. We'd like to try to reach a mutual solution. How can we solve this problem together?

Clarissa: Right. I can assure you that Autologica uses a carrier which is a leader in the field. In fact, since changing carriers we've had a lot of positive feedback from our other customers on delivery.

Jakob: Could you perhaps provide us with something concrete on this?

Clarissa: Well, you've probably heard that Autologica is going through an IPO and our investor's report on our website has many comments about the speed and reliability of delivery. Brent, could you get that report up on your laptop so we can show them?

Brent: Sure, I'm on it ...

Jakob: Thanks, that would be quite helpful.

Brent: Got it ... Jakob, Fabian, Eymen, let me show you the report ... here ... look at these comments.

Jakob: I see. Yes, that does provide some reassurance. From our standpoint, we need to be sure that delivery is on time, and if my client incurs losses due to late delivery, they should be entitled to recover damages for any loss. From your side, we understand you need a little give or take on this. Do you have any suggestions for a solution that suits both parties?

Clarissa: I'm just brainstorming some ideas ... What about this?
The Supplier shall use best efforts to ensure that delivery is on time
...
within 15 Business Days of the scheduled delivery date.
This potentially works for both of us.

Jakob: Yes. Thank you, Clarissa. We're on the same page. That seems to achieve the objectives of both parties.

Audio 9.6

Clarissa: So, Jakob, Fabian, Eymen, let's review what we have agreed. This is where we currently stand.
Clause 1.1 Defined Terms, we decided to keep the original definition of force majeure. Clause 4.2 Payment, 30 days will change to 90 days. Clause 7, there are quite a few amendments. In 7.2, we will change the tolerance level ... and that change I mentioned to the liability clause brings us to the end of everything we've agreed on today.

Jakob: Thank you Clarissa. Yes, that's all clear and correct.

Clarissa: Excellent. We've made great progress today. But there are still a few outstanding clauses which we didn't have time to discuss.

Jakob: Right, we've covered a lot of ground today. Perhaps the last few amendments can be agreed via email?

Clarissa: That was also my thinking. Let's aim to finalise those outstanding points by the end of next week. Is that doable for you?

Jakob: It's a tight deadline, but we can work with it.

Clarissa: Thank you. After that, I'll get the ball rolling. I'll draw up the final agreement integrating all of our agreed amendments, and that will then be circulated to the parties. I think we can say that if everything goes to plan, I can get that done by the end of February. So, can we all pencil that into our diaries, that the signing could take place the week beginning February 28?

Jakob: Yes, certainly. Thanks, Clarissa. We believe we've reached a fair agreement on the terms. We look forward to finalising everything and then receiving your email with the revised contract.

Chapter 10: Alternative dispute resolution

Audio 10.1

Daryl: Today we've got Anoush Parsons on the show. Anoush is a supervising partner at Pringer and Goldment LLP and she specialises in ADR. Hi Anoush!

Anoush: Hi Daryl, great to be here.

Daryl: So Anoush, tell me, why do some clients opt for ADR instead of litigation?

Anoush: Well, Daryl, that's a great question and I'm going to give you three reasons why a lot of companies prefer ADR to litigation. First of all, cost. Often ADR is cheaper than litigation, especially non-adjudicative types such as mediation. However, it is difficult to generalise here as cost depends on a number of factors. Arbitration can end up being very expensive. Sometimes, if parties use ADR and there is some problem which means that the case goes to court anyway, obviously the whole process is going to be more expensive than if they had just gone straight to court in the first place.

Daryl: Wow. Double the cost!

Anoush: It could be. But as I said, generally ADR is cheaper than litigation.

Daryl: OK. What next?

Anoush: So, the second point is speed. It's commonly known that courts in most jurisdictions face backlogs of cases, there are court delays, complex rules to follow, and it can take years to get a final judgment due to the appeal process. ADR can lead to a faster resolution.

Daryl: OK. And what's the third reason?

Anoush: The third reason why ADR is so popular is because the ADR process is private unlike litigation which is generally public. This means that by using ADR instead of litigation parties can protect their reputations.

Daryl: OK. So some parties prefer ADR to litigation due to it generally being cheaper, faster, and confidential. Thanks, Anoush.

Anoush: Thanks Daryl.

Audio 10.2

Daryl: But Anoush, it's not always the case that parties prefer ADR. In fact, sometimes parties prefer to use litigation. Why is that?

Anoush: Yes, Daryl, you're quite right. Again, I'll give you three typical reasons why litigation may be a better option.

Daryl: Excellent, go ahead.

Anoush: Firstly, sometimes a dispute arises between parties because the law is not clear. They need to get a court judgment to clarify what the law is. A court precedent can give parties the certainty they need to carry on business in the future. This can only be done through litigation because decisions made or issued through ADR are private and of course are not case law.

Daryl: Right OK. If parties want to set a precedent, they should use litigation.

Anoush: Exactly. My second point is this. Litigation can satisfy a party's desire for vindication.

Daryl: Vindication? You mean when a party wants to prove they are right?

Anoush: Yes. Sometimes in a dispute where one party feels wrongly accused, wrongly blamed, they want to go to court to show to the public, to the media, '*look I was right. I didn't do it. Here is the proof*'. Litigation gives parties their day in court and the opportunity to publicly set the record straight. There's no way to get around the fact that litigation is the only option for this.

Daryl: OK, and what's the final reason?

Anoush: Last but not least is this. If the case involves quasi-criminal or even criminal allegations, then the law may require, as a matter of public interest, that the case be decided in a court of law.

Daryl: Quasi-criminal? What do you mean?

Anoush: I mean where part of the case could involve criminal allegations such as fraud. So, litigation may be required if criminal or quasi-criminal allegations are involved.

Daryl: Great! Thanks Anoush.

Audio 10.3

Anoush: Hi Marlon, I haven't got much time ... I'm afraid something came up last minute. But I'm going to send you our template arbitration clause and drafting notes which will give you all the information you need. So, let's be quick. Firstly, parties can only submit disputes to arbitration if they've agreed to do so in writing.

Marlon: OK. Anoush, what do you mean by *'submit disputes to arbitration'*?

Anoush: I mean, to use arbitration as the method to resolve a dispute, sometimes we say, *'refer disputes to arbitration'*. Both phrases are commonly used in arbitration agreements. The important thing is that they must be in writing.

Marlon: So, let me make a note of this, OK ... must ... be ... in ... writing. So Finn at AxxGazz told me that he'd agreed with PetroFirma on the phone to use arbitration. Are you saying that's not enough?

Anoush: An oral agreement is really not enough. You need to get the parties to agree to an arbitration clause in the contract or draft a separate arbitration agreement. Technically, parties can even sign an arbitration agreement once a dispute arises, but honestly Marlon, it's hard to get parties to agree on things when a dispute has arisen. So, it's simply much better to get it out of the way at the contracting stage.

Marlon: OK. Anoush, I know it sounds like a stupid question, but what are the main elements which I need to include in the arbitration agreement?

Anoush: It depends on what the parties choose. A key principle of arbitration is party autonomy, which means that parties have a lot of choice over how their arbitration will be conducted.

Marlon: OK. What kind of choices?

Anoush: I really don't have time to list them all but check the drafting notes for a guide. Once you know what the parties want, you can just go ahead and edit the template provision and include it in the joint venture agreement. If you've got any questions, drop me an email, OK?

Marlon: OK. Thanks Anoush.

Audio 10.4

Gillian: Welcome everyone. Thank you all for coming today to try to resolve this dispute. I'm Gillian Stone, and I'll be your mediator. Please call me Gillian. You all know each other of course. Just before this session I met briefly with each party and you signed the mediation agreement. You said that you're happy to use your first names. Is everyone OK with that?

Participants: Yes/OK

Gillian: Thank you. Before we begin, I'd just like go over a few things.
Firstly, I want to make a few points about mediation.
Mediation is a voluntary process. This means that

...

Now, I just want to check something. Sofia you're here as an individual and therefore you are able to make decisions about any solution yourself. But Ivan, can I confirm that you do have authority to settle as a representative of the Kiplington Hotel?

Ivan: Yes, yes, I do.

Gillian: Thank you. Now I want to talk about the structure of the mediation. As soon as I've finished giving my opening statement, I'll ask each of you to give your opening statement setting out your position on the dispute.

Once we have a clear understanding of the issues, we'll move on to the part of exploring solutions. Sometimes we'll meet all together in plenary sessions, and sometimes we'll meet in private sessions, called caucuses.

During this stage, you will propose solutions. At times, you may want to speak with the other side and me, without your lawyer. At other times, you may want to discuss solutions with your lawyer, and without me. There may be times when your lawyers want to meet together without you or me. Remember the process is flexible and you are in control.

When you have some ideas for a solution, there may be some negotiating. Another part of the process is that you may hit a deadlock. I can help you to try to move forward. Throughout the day, I'll suggest breaks, but any time you feel you need some time out, please just ask.

Hopefully the next part will be you reaching a solution. If this happens, your lawyers will draft a settlement agreement that works for both of you. You will only be bound by this, if you sign it. You can sign the settlement agreement in the mediation, or at a later date.

We'll finish at 5pm, and to close the session, in the final part of the mediation, I'll review what we have achieved.

Finally, I've just got a few rules. Please be respectful. Listen to each other. And don't interrupt each other. Is that OK with you all?

Participants: Yes/OK

Gillian: Sofia, Luca, as the claimant, you can go ahead and begin.

Chapter 11: Advocacy

Audio 11.1

Zhara: How's your litigation file going Asim?

Asim: Oh, thanks for asking Zhara; it's going OK. I'm preparing the claim form and particulars of claim at the moment. What do you call those in arbitration?

Zhara: The names are different from those in England. We call those the *request to arbitrate* or the *notice to arbitrate*. I think, in contrast, in the USA it's known as the *complaint*. Is that right, Mahmoud?

Mahmoud: Yes, in US litigation, it's called a *complaint*.

Asim: Interesting. So, we'll have to wait for the defendant to respond with the *defence* and maybe a *counterclaim*. I think in arbitration the defence can be called an *answer, or answer to the request*. Is that right Zhara?

Zhara: Yes, exactly. We also call them *defence* or *statement of defence*. Mahmoud, what's the *defence* called in the USA?

Mahmoud: It's called an *answer*. And likewise, *counterclaim* is a term used in the USA. If I'm not mistaken, this happens in arbitration as well. Right, Zhara?

Zhara: Yes, similarly, we use the term *counterclaim*.

Asim: Mahmoud, in the USA they still use the term *pleadings*, right?

Mahmoud: Yes! I remember speaking to an English lawyer about this word. He said that while the official expression is *statement of case* in England, in practice the term *pleadings* is still used.

Zhara: That's funny! In arbitration *statement of case* and *pleadings* are used!

Asim: Fascinating! So, next we'll need to prepare *witness statements*. I know it's the same in arbitration. But is the term *witness statements* used in the USA as well?

Mahmoud: I'd say *witness statements* are unusual in the USA, because witnesses are dealt with differently. The US process is not the same as in England. So, no, there's not really an equivalent word.

Asim: Oh, I didn't know that. Anyway, we'll instruct an English barrister to represent the client at trial and he'll draft the *skeleton argument*. *Skeleton arguments* are sometimes used in arbitration. It's a document that briefly sets out the main points to be argued at trial ... there isn't an exact equivalent in the USA, right?

Mahmoud: No, they don't have this. The closest thing to a skeleton argument is probably a *brief* or *memorandum of law*. In the USA you submit a *brief* in support of a *motion*. A *brief* sets out the arguments in favour of the motion. In England, I believe a *motion* is called an *application notice*.

Zhara: Again, arbitration uses a mixture of terms which are similar to those used in English and US litigation. We use both *motion* and *application notice*.

Audio 11.2

Liz: Hi Asim, good work on the claim form. I just wanted to flag up a few points to edit before filing. You've used a few American legal English words which aren't common in England. Can I ask, did you by chance use an American precedent?

Asim: Oh! Yes, I looked at a few claim forms and also US complaints to help me write it.

Liz: OK. Can you share your screen and edit as I explain?

Asim: Sure. Can you see?

Liz: Yes. Thanks. So firstly, you've written '*The Claimant prays for the following relief*'. This is common in US complaints, though of course they would say '*Plaintiff*', but in England we tend to say, '*The Claimant seeks*' with a colon after.

Asim: OK ... *The ... Claimant ... seeks* ... then a colon.

Liz: Then, in the part where you write about the injunctions, you use the verb *'enjoin'*. For example, you've written *'An injunction to enjoin the Defendant from ...'* and so on. In England, we would use the verb *restrain*, which means to prevent or limit. Restrain is sometimes used in the USA too. So please update those two instances of enjoin.

Asim: OK. *Restrain* instead of *enjoin* ... Done.

Liz: OK. Then, scroll down just a little to point 6, which starts with *'An order granting an award of punitive damages ...'* Right. In England, punitive damages, in other words, damages which are aimed to punish the defendant, are extremely rare. So please delete the whole of point 6.

Asim: OK ... deleting point 6.

Liz: Thanks. OK, can you scroll down ... fine, fine. Right. Here. The value section. You've said, *'there will be a bifurcated trial'*. So, in the USA and arbitration, it's common to use *bifurcated trial* or *two-stage trial* for a trial split into two parts, and even *trifurcated trial* for a trial split into three parts. However, in England, in this case, it's more common to use the term *split trial*. In fact, in England split trial specifically means a High Court trial where liability and amount of damages are tried separately. Which is exactly what we want.

Asim: OK. Understood ... *split ... trial*. Great. Done. Anything else?

Liz: No. That's all. Thank you Asim.

Audio 11.3

Zhara: Hi Asim, I heard you're going to watch the *Parlo Ltd v Incoms PLC* case in England. Can you explain to me and Mahmoud more about the order of proceedings in a civil trial in England?

Asim: Yes of course. So, the trial will begin with an opening statement by Mr Dixon. He's the barrister representing our client, Parlo Ltd, the claimant. The *opening speech*, which is also called an *opening statement*, or *opening submissions*, is the first opportunity we'll have to introduce our case.

Zhara: OK. It's exactly the same as arbitration and US litigation, right Mahmoud?

Mahmoud: Right.

Asim: Yes, but in the USA there is often a jury, whereas in almost all English civil cases there's not. So, in England, the lawyer delivers their opening speech to the judge rather than to the jury.

Zhara: Of course. So, comparing this to arbitration, on the one hand, arbitration is like English litigation as there isn't a jury either, but on the other hand it's slightly different, because the lawyer delivers the opening speech to the arbitrators.

Asim: Yes, exactly. So, the next part of the trial is the *examination-in-chief*, which can also be called *direct examination*. This is where we'll call a witness and Mr Dixon will ask them questions to elicit evidence.

Zhara: Yes, it's more common to say *direct examination* than *examination-in-chief* in arbitration.

Mahmoud: Yes. It's like this in US litigation too.

Asim: That's interesting. So, then the other side will *cross-examine* our witness, asking them questions to try to cast doubt on our case. And after cross-examination, we may have the opportunity to ask our witness questions to clarify any matters arising from the cross-examination. This latter part is called *re-examination*. Then we'll repeat the examination-in-chief, cross-examination, and re-examination with our other witnesses.

Mahmoud: Right, yes. It's like that in the USA too and it's often called the *re-direct*.

Zhara: Yes, it's similar in arbitration.

Asim: Right. It sounds like the processes are quite similar. After this, it's the same process for the defendant. They may give an opening speech, call witnesses for examination-in-chief; of course, this time we, I mean the lawyer for the claimant, will have the opportunity to cross-examine the defendant's witnesses. Then there will be their re-examination. I imagine it's more or less the same in US litigation and arbitration, right?

Zhara: Yes.

Mahmoud: Yes.

Asim: And then there are the *closing speeches*, also called *closing statements* or *closing submissions*. Firstly, the closing speech of the defendant and then, secondly, of the claimant. Here the parties remind the court of important aspects of the case and sum up why the judge should rule in their favour.

Zhara: Yes, the processes are alike. But in litigation you're trying to convince the judge, as opposed to arbitration, where you must convince the arbitrators.

Mahmoud: Yes, it's quite similar in the USA, though again, of course most of the time you're addressing the jury rather than the judge.

Asim: Right. And then finally the judge will issue the judgment, possibly immediately, but often the judge adjourns the trial for a short period to consider the judgment. I expect in our case, because it's quite complex, the judgment will be reserved to a later date.

Mahmoud: Yes, like in US litigation.

Zhara: Yes, it's like arbitration too, although arbitrators render an award not a judgment.

Audio 11.4

Clerk: On the matter of *Parlo Ltd v Incoms PLC*.

Judge:	Good morning. Please be seated. Thank you. You can take it that we have had a chance to read the papers submitted, including the patent registrations, the skeleton arguments, and we have an appreciation of the dispute. However, we would appreciate a summary of the facts for each party.
Mr Dixon:	My Lord, I am Mr Dixon and I appear with my learned friend Mr Smith on behalf of the claimant Parlo Ltd and with my friends Ms Derby and Mr Reynolds from Baker and Sons LLP. My learned friends Ms West and Mr Morrison appear for the defendant Incoms PLC. I appreciate that you have read the documents mentioned. I will proceed with my opening speech.
Judge:	Thank you.
Clerk:	Matter for hearing, *DataQX v Bitcoin Exchange*
Judge:	Good afternoon. Mr Lee?
Mr Lee:	Your Honor, I appear, ... erm ... with ...
Judge:	Please could you speak up?
Mr Lee:	Yes, Your Honor, I appear ... with Mr ... Stone and Ms ... Baynes for the plaintiff
Judge:	Right. Thank you. And Ms Wilson?
Ms Wilson:	May it please the court. Your Honor, my name is Ms Shaya Wilson. I'm an attorney at Sykes law firm. I have here with me an attorney from my firm, Mr Mitchell, we're from the New York office. We're joined by lawyer, Ms Nelson, who is local counsel in this case. I would like to introduce my client, the defendant Mr Cameron CEO of Bitcoin Exchange.
Judge:	Thank you.

Audio 11.5

Lawyer:	Ms Davies, open in front of you on the table is the trial bundle. Please could you turn to page 25 of the trial bundle? I think it's tab 2.
Ms Davies:	Yes, I've got it.
Lawyer:	Could you tell the court what document you see?
Ms Davies:	Yes. This is my witness statement.
Lawyer:	If you look through that witness statement, what do you see at the bottom of the final page, page 28, after paragraph 30?
Ms Davies:	There's a signature.
Lawyer:	Whose signature is it?
Ms Davies:	It's my signature.
Lawyer:	And are the contents of your witness statement true to the best of your knowledge and belief?
Ms Davies:	Yes.

Lawyer: Thank you. And now please could you turn to page 29. What exhibit do you see?

Ms Davies: It's an email referred to as JD1.

Lawyer: Did you write this email?

Ms Davies: Yes, I did.

Lawyer: Thank you Ms Davies. Please wait here; there will be some questions from the other side.

Notes

1 Employment Rights Act 1996, s139
2 Department for Business, Energy & Industrial Strategy, 'Business Population Estimates for the UK and the Regions 2021' (October 2021) <https://www.gov.uk/government/statistics/business-population-estimates-2021> accessed 27 April 2022
3 '"You've Got to Find What You Love", Jobs says', (*Harvard News* 14 June 2005) <https://news.stanford.edu/2005/06/14/jobs-061505/ > accessed 10 April 2022
4 LinkedIn™, 'Rock Your LinkedIn Profile' <https://www.linkedin.com/learning/rock-your-linkedin-profile/got-skills-adding-skills-and-getting-endorsed> accessed 30 April 2022

Answer key

Chapter 1: Networking

1.1 a. with; b. on; c. at; d. for; e. to; f. on; g. in

1.2 Suggested answers:

a. Networking is the activity of meeting new people and developing professional relationships.
b. Lawyers can network online on social media platforms and face-to-face at events.
c. Networking can lead to new clients, open up new opportunities, and even help you land your dream job.
d. Networking online can be cheaper and less time-consuming than networking in real life. However, networking in real life may help lawyers to start new relationships, build trust, and strengthen connections.

2.1 Suggested answers:

b. Plan travel, check the day, time, and location to ensure you are organised; prepare an outfit to ensure you look professional; research local culture to avoid saying or doing something inappropriate; research areas which could be used for small talk such as the event location, top news stories, and local cuisine.

2.2 a. 7; 8; b. 2; 3; 7; c. 2; 4; d. 5; e. 6

2.3 Anton

a. False, he graduated last year.
b. True.
c. False, he wants to get a training contract.
d. False, he does not have much work experience.
e. True.

Leya

a. False, she is an in-house lawyer.
b. True.
c. False, she works in Amsterdam.
d. True.
e. True.

Feven

a. False, she is a senior associate.
b. False, she works for a law firm.

c. True.
d. True.
e. True.

2.4 Suggested answers:
Text 1.3: This event is suitable for Feven because she is an M&A lawyer and it may lead to opportunities to develop her reputation and network.
Text 1.4: This event is suitable for Anton because he is looking for a training contract and this will give him the opportunity to meet trainee lawyers and recruiters.
Text 1.5: This event is suitable for Leya because the event is in Hong Kong and she is looking for contacts in Asia. She also wants to develop contract drafting skills and network.

3.2 a. an individual b. a small group c. a large group

3.3 b. an individual; a small group c. an individual d. two people e. a small group; a large group f. a large group g. a large group

3.7 Suggested answers:
a. Small talk is conversation to help break the ice, build trust, and build relationships.
c. Some common small talk topics mentioned in the text are: weather, food, travel, news, interests, work, studies, origins, the event. The text mentions that talking about personal topics and professional achievements are viewed differently across cultures.

3.8 Anton and Ingrid: e.; f.; g.; i.
Leya and Zul: b.; c.; h.
Feven and Sudhvir: a.; e.; i.; they also refer to sightseeing, which could be considered as c. travel.

3.9 a. Anton and Ingrid:
Open:
- What brings you to this event?
- What about you, why are you here?
- What did you choose?
- How did you become interested in it?

Closed:
- Did you say the University of London?
- Do you like sports?

Leya and Zul:
Open:
- Where are you from?
- What's the food like?

Closed:
- Do you know it?
- I suppose Singapore is quite different, right?
- Have you eaten?
- Shall we go over to the food table then?

Feven and Sudhvir:
Open:
- What do you think of the view?
- How did you decide on the location?

Closed:
- Do you mind if I sit here?
- Are you attending tomorrow?
- Have you heard of this race before?

b. Suggested answers:
Leya could ask Zul:
Open: What's your favourite food?
Closed: Have you tried this dish before?
Feven could ask Sudhvir:
Open: How did you become interested in cycling?
Closed: Have you been to Italy before?

3.14
a. An elevator pitch is a short persuasive speech that makes someone interested in an idea, person, or service.

3.15 Ingrid:
a. False, IP Law is not a core module.
b. False, she studies one elective.
c. True.
d. False, she is interested in films and enjoys listening to film soundtracks.
e. True.

Zul:
a. False, he is a real estate lawyer.
b. True.
c. False, he does contentious and non-contentious work.
d. True.
e. False, his nickname is Robolawyer.

Sudhvir:
a. True.
b. False, he works at an international law firm.
c. True.
d. False, he finds his work satisfying.
e. True.

3.16 Suggested answers:
Anton could ask Ingrid:
Open: Why did you choose the University of London? Where do you want to work in the future?
Closed: Do you enjoy studying law? Have you studied any IP law yet?
Leya could ask Zul:
Open: What's it like working in Singapore? What's a typical day like in your firm?

Closed: Do you enjoy your work? Do you prefer contentious or non-contentious work? Is it difficult representing clients in online hearings?
Feven could ask Sudhvir:
Open: How did you become interested in tax law? What's it like working at an international law firm?
Closed: Do you often use foreign languages in your work? Do you do any litigation?

3.18

a. direct
b. indirect
c. direct
d. direct
e. indirect
f. indirect

3.19

a. Step one introduces the person you are bringing into the conversation, whereas step two introduces the new contact that you are already talking to.
b. If the other two parties do not have something in common, skip step three.
c. If you want to change the topic, you could do this in step four.

3.20 Suggested answers:

a. Sudhvir, I'd like you to meet Jane, she is a former colleague of mine. Jane this is Sudhvir, the President of the International Society for M&A Lawyers. You both live in London, and you both work in the area of finance law. Jane, Sudhvir and I were just talking about his work as a tax lawyer ...
b. Oh hi! Sudhvir, let me introduce you to ... I want to say John, is that correct? ... John and I studied together at law school, but we haven't seen each other in a long time. Great to see you again. John please meet Sudhvir, the President of the International Society for M&A Lawyers. We were just talking about his work as a tax lawyer ...
c. Sudhvir, let me introduce you to my colleague, she works in our tax department. This is Sudhvir, the President of the International Society for M&A Lawyers; we were just talking about his work as a tax lawyer.
d. Hi Olaf, please come and join us. We both saw your presentation just now and found it very interesting. My name is [*name + position*] and this is [*Sudhvir + position*]. Would you mind if we ask you some questions? ...

3.21

a. polite
b. impolite
c. impolite
d. polite
e. impolite
f. polite
g. impolite
h. polite
i. polite

3.22 Exchanging contact details is important as this allows you to stay in touch with your new contact, which could bring opportunities.

4.1 Following up is important because it helps continue to build the relationship with your new contact, which may lead to opportunities.

4.2 a. 3; b. 1; c. 2

4.3 a. 2; b. 3; c.1

4.4 Suggested answers:

b. Email is generally more formal than social media and WhatsApp™ messages. However, the level of formality you use will depend on a range of factors, including culture and style. When you first contact your new acquaintance, you should remain professional, polite, and formal. After they have responded, you can match their level of formality.

c. The use of emojis differs across cultures. If you are unsure about using them, follow the lead of the person you are writing to. If they use them in their follow-up message, then you can also.

d. Keep your follow-up messages concise. An email may be slightly longer than a social media message or WhatsApp™ message.

4.6 Suggested answers:

Ingrid's message

> Hi Anton
>
> It was nice to meet you at the Bengal Jackman Open Day. I'm looking forward to you sending me that link as I really need to study.
>
> Thank you
> Ingrid

Anton's message

> Hi Ingrid
>
> It was nice to meet you too. I enjoyed sharing stories with you about studying at university. Here is the link to the website I was talking about. I hope you find it useful.
> www.ree-law-uk.com
> Let's stay in touch.
>
> Thanks
> Anton

Test yourself

1. See answer to 1.2 c.
2. See Text 1.2 Networking event preparation checklist
3. Ask open and closed questions
4. Some important things to include are:
   - what your position is or what you are studying
   - where you work or study
   - who you help or who you would like to help
5. Some parts to include in a follow-up message are:
   - a salutation
   - previous contact
   - reason for writing
   - future contact
   - a closing

Chapter 2: Telephoning and conference calls

2.2 a. 1; 3; 4; 6; 9
b. 1; 4; 7; 8
c. 10
d. 2; 5

2.4 Contractions: who's, I'm, I'll, he's.

Phrasal verbs: hold on, put you through, call me back.

To hold on means to wait for a short time; to put someone through means to connect or to transfer the call to someone else; to call someone back means to telephone someone who has previously called you.

3.1

a. to have a brief conversation with someone.
b. to act for someone; to fill someone in on something.

3.2

a. She is nervous because she does not feel ready for the telephone call and finds it difficult to speak in English on the telephone.

3.3 Angela gives the following tips: be prepared; check if there is an agenda for the call; check that you have all the vocabulary you need; put yourself in an English mindset.

3.5

Problem 1: Sophie uses an expression that Claire does not understand.
Problem 2: Sophie and Claire lose connection.
Problem 3: Sophie speaks too quickly, and Claire is not sure that she has understood.

3.6

Problem 2: Explaining the problem: Sorry, I didn't hear what you said. Asking for clarification: Could you just repeat that, please?

Problem 3: Explaining the problem: Sorry Sophie, that was a bit fast for me. Asking for clarification: Can I just check I've understood correctly?

3.7 b. to break up
c. to get cut off
d. to point out

4.2 Suggested answers:

a. Advantages include being able to: see the other participants' body language, share your computer screen, share documents, and write messages using the chat box function.

4.3

a. True
b. True
c. False, lawyers have video meetings on a daily basis and they have back-to-back video meetings, which means that they have lots of meetings without breaks in between.
d. False, the text does not say this. It says that while there are advantages to video conferences, they are challenging in other ways.
e. True.

4.5

a. to arrange something.
b. Marc is asking Claire to check everyone's availability and arrange the video conference.

4.6 Conference call invitation

From: Claire Monet cmonet@garniers.com
To: Anya Marshall amarshall@hattonmarshall.llp
Subject: Agile Design and Ideal Home conference call

Dear Ms Marshall

I am writing to invite you to a meeting to discuss Agile Design's letter before claim to Ideal Home.

The meeting will take place on WebConf on Tuesday 26th October 2022, starting at 11:00 CET and finishing at 11:30 CET. Click on this link to join the meeting: http://web.conf./485723

Please do not hesitate to contact me if you have any questions.

Kind regards
Claire Monet

4.7

a. Can you see me and hear me OK?; I forgot to turn my camera on; chat box; share my screen; can everyone see my slides?

b. Claire seems to be leading the meeting.
c. Paul, because he was in another meeting that lasted longer than scheduled.

4.8 b. Partner at Garniers, acting for Agile Design.
c. In-house Legal Counsel for Agile Design.
d. Head of Products at Ideal Home.
e. Partner at Hatton Marshall, acting on behalf of Ideal Home.
f. Partner at Hatton Marshall, acting on behalf of Ideal Home.

4.9

a. From an English person's point of view, everyone is polite except Philip, who interrupts impolitely.
b. No.
c. Claire will schedule another call.

4.10 b. 10; c. 8; d. 1; e. 6; f. 4; g. 9; h. 5; i. 3; j. 7; k. 6

4.11 b. 7; c. 4; d. 6; e. 8; f. 3; g. 5; h. 1

4.12 b. to get back
c. to wrap up
d. to drop out
e. to come in
f. to hand over
g. to go ahead
h. to bear with (someone)

Test yourself

1. In an English law firm or company, it is usual to give your name or your department. For example, Hello, Janice Brooks speaking.
2. You can check if there is an agenda for the call, check that you have all the vocabulary you need, and put yourself in an English mindset.
3. See Phrase bank 2.2 for expressions for explaining the problem and asking for clarification.
4. A phrasal verb is a verb followed by a particle which changes the verb's original meaning. Examples include: to hold on, to point out, to wrap up.
5. See Text 2.3 How to improve your video conference experience.

Chapter 3: Client meetings

1.1

a. Lawyers have meetings with clients to take instructions and give advice; with the other side's lawyers to negotiate contracts or try to settle disputes; with colleagues to discuss cases or deal with management of the law firm; with potential clients to pitch their services.
b. face-to-face or by telephone or video conference.
c. different attitudes to punctuality.

1.3
a. to participate in; to take part in; to have; to invite someone to; to hold; to arrange; to organise.
b. to participate in; to take part in; to invite someone to.
c. Suggested answers:
to set up; to schedule; to cancel; to postpone.

2.1
a. MPJ Limited and Organibars Limited.
b. MPJ Limited makes packaging for the food industry. The CEO, Mike Jones, wants advice about a contract.
c. Build a relationship with the client; obtain more information about the issue from the client; understand the client's objectives; advise the client and discuss options; explain the next steps.

2.2
a. A conflict of interest is where there is a conflict between your personal interests and the interests of a client or a where there is a conflict between the interests of two clients. For example, if both parties to a legal dispute are current or new clients.
b. Katie can use the client contact details and other party contact details to check if there is a conflict of interest.

2.3
a. True.
b. True.
c. False, his main objective is to be paid for the work done.
d. False, she asks for a copy of the contract.

2.4 Suggested answers:
Someone who shows interest by nodding their head; someone who doesn't talk when others are speaking; someone who uses positive body language, for example, by maintaining eye contact.

2.7
b. uh-huh; right.
c. I can see why you feel angry about this.
d. Can I just check that I've understood correctly?; So what you're saying is that you don't have a signed contract, but you had agreed some heads of terms?

2.11 Suggested answers:
a. The speaker may have felt that Student A was not listening very well because they lost eye contact while taking notes.
b. While taking notes, it may have been difficult for the listener to follow everything that Student B was saying. It might be better to wait until Student B has finished speaking before writing your notes.

2.12
a. Open questions:

- What's happened?
- What happened next?
- What did the heads of terms include?

Closed questions:

- It's awful weather today, isn't it?
- Would you like a coffee before we start?
- I understand that you'd like some advice about a contract?
- Can I just check that I've understood correctly? Your main objective is ...?
- Do you have a copy of your contract?
- You don't have a signed contract but you had agreed some heads of terms?
- Did they mention the possibility for Organibars to make changes to the specifications of the machine?

b. The open questions start with the word what. The closed questions use different formulations, including the words do and did.

c. Suggested answer: the open questions are useful for getting an overview of the situation. She uses closed questions to clarify points and obtain precise details of the case.

2.13

a. did you?
b. have I?
c. isn't it?

2.15

a. False, she is not sure that he has a legally binding contract with Organibars.
b. True.
c. False, she says that going to court should be a last resort.
d. True.
e. False, she suggests trying to reach an agreement with Organibars and she will wait to receive Mike's instructions before taking any further steps.

2.16

a. I propose filing a claim against Organibars or I propose that you file a claim against Organibars.
b. I advise entering into a new contract with Organibars or I advise that you enter into a new contract with Organibars or I advise you to enter into a new contract with Organibars.
c. I suggest stopping work on the packaging machine or I suggest that you stop work on the packaging machine.

2.17

a. In my view
b. I recommend that you
c. in my opinion
d. I think that
e. I must warn you that
f. I suggest trying

2.18 Suggested answers:

Advantages: the pros and cons are ..., the benefit of this is ..., one good thing about this is ...
Disadvantages: the problem with this is ...

2.20 b. 5; c. 1; d. 3; e. 4

2.23

a. An attendance note is a lawyer's record of what was discussed at the meeting with the client. It is also sometimes called a file note.
b. Suggested answers:
Attendance notes are useful in case the client later disputes what was said at the meeting. They can also be used to justify the amount of time spent on a file and they can help anyone else who looks at the file, for example, if a lawyer is on holiday.
c. It includes the background/facts of the case; the legal issues; the preliminary advice given by Katie, taking into account the client's objectives; and the next steps that Katie and Mike will take.
d. Katie needs to write to Mike with a summary of their meeting and send the firm's engagement letter. She then needs to wait until she receives Mike's instructions and arrange a meeting with Organibars if necessary.

3.1

a. litigation procedure
b. It is not very effective. Paul is hesitant and speaks with a monotonous voice. The different steps in the process are not very clear. Paul uses an acronym and legal terminology without explaining them.

3.2 He tries to organise the information into a chronological order and uses some linking words: the first thing; next; then, but in Audio 3.3 he does not use the other tips.

3.3 In Audio 3.4, Paul has organised the information into a chronological order and uses linking words to move from one part of the procedure to another. For example, *first*, *secondly*. He has also prepared a diagram for the client. Paul explains legal terms and acronyms. For example, limitation period and ADR. He also explains who has responsibility for each step of the procedure. He mentions time limits but is not very clear about the length of time. For example, he says that it will probably take at least a year before it will get to trial.

3.4

a. limitation period
b. costs
c. letter before claim
d. reach an agreement
e. claim form
f. serves
g. defence
h. tracks
i. directions

j. disclose; witness statements
k. trial
l. enforce

Test yourself

1. Active listening.
2. Open questions are useful for getting an overview of the situation. Closed questions can be used to clarify points and obtain precise details of the case.
3. Some expressions are: I recommend that you ...; In my opinion ...
4. Examples include: the attraction of this is that ... but the downside of this is ...
5. See Text 3.2 Explaining a procedure to a client.

Chapter 4: Legal writing

1.1 Suggested answers:
   a. She means that she is thinking about who is going to read what she is writing.
   b. Other types of writing include emails, letters, memoranda, reports, contracts; readers include clients, other lawyers, other professionals, judges.
   c. Make a note of your answer here and then see the five key skills for legal writing later in this chapter.

2.2 Subject line b. is the most appropriate. It makes it clear that you need information from the client. Answer a. is too vague. Answer c. is too long and does not make it clear that you need some more information.

2.4 Suggested answers:
e. or g. are appropriate for a lawyer to use in an email to a new client.
a. is informal and impersonal as it does not include a name and it would not be appropriate to use this in an email to a client.
b. and c. are too informal for an email to a new client. But these salutations would be appropriate in an email to someone you know well.
d. is too informal for an email to a new client but would be appropriate for a client you already know. American and English lawyers and clients often move quickly to using first names.
f. is not a correct formulation as the title *Mr* should be followed by a person's surname.
h. and i. are too formal for an email to a client, and i. is very impersonal.

2.5 a. Dear Ms Marsh or Dear Bryony Marsh
   b. Dear Alice or Hi Alice
   c. Dear Sir or Madam or Dear Human Resources Manager
   d. Dear Sir or Madam or Dear Pickfords or Dear Litigation Department

2.6 Suggested answers:
Appropriate endings in your email to Jeff Walters would be a. Yours sincerely, c. Best regards, or d. Kind regards.
a. is a formal ending. Use when your salutation includes the name of the person you are writing to, such as Dear Mr Harrison or Dear Peter Harrison. It is used more in letters than emails but would be appropriate in an email where you are writing to someone for the first time.

b. e. and f. are very formal endings. Use when your salutation does not include the name of the person you are writing to, such as Dear Sir or Madam or Dear Goldings. These endings would be appropriate in formal letters but are rarely used in emails.

c. and d. can be used with any salutation. They are more informal than Yours sincerely and are often used in professional emails.

g. can also be used with any salutation. It is a shortened version of Best regards. It is a friendly, informal ending and is appropriate in a professional email with someone you know well.

h. can be used with any salutation but it is a very informal ending, used with someone you know very well. In a professional context, you might use it with your colleagues, but not with clients or other lawyers.

2.7 a. Email 1 is appropriate because it is polite and uses the right level of formality.
c. and d. Suggested answers:

Email 1 is just right as it uses full sentences, polite language and plain English.

Email 2 is too informal as it omits pronouns: *Happy to meet* instead of *I will be happy to meet you*; uses contractions: *I'd* instead of *I would*; uses abbreviations: *Tues.* instead of *Tuesday*; and uses colloquial language and expressions, for example: *stuff* instead of *clause, ping over* instead of *send me.* You would only use this language if you were writing to someone that you knew very well, such as a colleague.

Email 3 is too formal as it uses a formal salutation and closing; impersonal language: *We, the writer;* old-fashioned expressions: *please be advised, forthcoming, remains at your disposal;* and the subjunctive mood: *we request ... be sent.* Some lawyers may write like this but you should not copy this style because it is old-fashioned and unclear. Lawyers sometimes use the pronoun *we* when writing to other lawyers, but in emails to other lawyers in non-contentious matters, lawyers would usually use the pronoun *I*.

Email 4 is between just right and too formal as some of the language is formal and unnecessary, such as *the matter of ... duly ... perusal.* Email 1 is better.

2.8

a. Tues. is an abbreviation of Tuesday; ASAP is an acronym, standing for as soon as possible; to reach out is a buzzword, meaning to contact; and ping over is a buzzword, meaning to send by text message or email.
b. 2. close of business, at the end of the business day; 3. for your information; 4. voice message; 5. carbon copy, when you include a person in copy to your email; 6. for example, from the Latin *exempli gratia*; 7. in other words, from the Latin *id est*.
c.
   a. 2. *A ballpark figure* is a noun phrase.
   b. 4. *The big picture* is a noun phrase.
   c. 5. *A game changer* is a noun.
   d. 8. *Someone's hands are tied* is an idiom.
   e. 10. *To kick off* is a verb. *A kick-off* is a noun, and can also be used as an adjective: a kick-off meeting.
   f. 1. *Leverage* is a noun. In financial English, leverage is an investment strategy.
   g. 3. *A long shot* is a noun.
   h. 9. *To be on the same page as someone else* is an idiom.
   i. 7. *To rock the boat* is a verb.
   j. 6. *A takeaway* is a noun. *To take away* is a verb.

d.

a. kick off
b. ballpark figure
c. long shot
d. big picture
e. rock the boat.

2.9 b.

Opening: Following our telephone conversation yesterday, I am writing to confirm our meeting next Tuesday, 19th October, at 10:00 at my office.

Middle: Please could you send me a copy of your employment contract before the meeting so that I can have a look at the non-competition clause?

Closing remarks: If you have any other questions, please do not hesitate to contact me.

2.10 Suggested answers:

a. is too direct, and would be considered impolite.
b. is between too direct and polite request. It is a demand, but sounds more polite than answer a. It would be appropriate for a lawyer to use this.
c. and f. are between a polite request and too indirect. These expressions may be interpreted as suggestions rather than requests.
d. is a polite request and it would be appropriate for a lawyer to use this.
e. is too indirect. It is not clear if this is a request or a suggestion.

2.12

b. I am writing to obtain some information.
c. Please see the attached document.
d. Here is the website link: www.harrisonmiller.com
e. I look forward to hearing from you.
f. Please do not hesitate to contact me if you have any questions.

2.13 Suggested answers:

a. Email to lawyer

From: *[Your email address]*
To: mm@murphycotton.co
Subject: Sale of Ramsford House from Singh Properties to Maxim Estates

Dear Ms Murphy,

I am acting for Singh Properties in connection with their sale of Ramsford House. I understand that you are instructed by the buyer, Maxim Estates.

I attach the draft contract for sale and look forward to receiving your comments as soon as possible.

Kind regards
[Your name]

b. Email to client

From: *[Your email address]*
To: ss@singhproperties.co
Subject: Sale of Ramsford House

Dear Sandip,

Following our meeting last week, I have now sent the draft sale contract to the buyer's solicitors. I will get back to you as soon as I have their comments.

Please let me know if you have any other questions in the meantime.

Kind regards
[Your name]

c. Email to colleague

From: *[Your email address]*
To: helen@lawfirm.co
Subject: Singh Properties: Sale of Ramsford House

Hi Helen

As discussed, I've just received instructions from Singh Properties to sell Ramsford House. The client needs some advice on tax law issues regarding this sale and I was wondering if you could help out on this?

I attach a copy of my attendance note from my recent meeting with the client. Perhaps we could talk about this later this week?

Many thanks
[Your name]

3.1

a. False, she spends most of her time writing emails.
b. True.
c. False, she might use a more formal style when writing to another lawyer, but would be more informal with some of her regular clients.
d. True
e. False, she refers to plain English and writing in language that the client can understand.

3.2 b.

Points 3, 6, 7, and 10 relate to the facts of the case and the types of restriction in Jeff's contract
Points 1, 5, and 8 relate to the legal issue and how the courts apply the law
Points 2 and 12 are your opinion on how the law applies to the facts of this case
Points 4 and 11 explain the risks of breaching the restrictions
Points 9 and 13 explain alternative options for the client to consider

3.3 A usual sequence would be d–b–e–a–c

An alternative answer would be for the lawyer's advice to come first, and the factual and legal background to the case after: a–c–d–b–e

3.5 Suggested answer:

From: Anthony Long along@long.co
To: Jeff Walters j.walters@home.com
Subject: Employment contract advice

Dear Jeff,

Following our meeting on Tuesday, I am writing to summarise my advice about the restrictions in your employment contract.

You explained that you would like to leave Fernview to start your own business, and we discussed different types of restrictions that an employer can include in an employee's contract. In your contract there are 2 relevant clauses: (1) a 'non-competition' clause, which prevents you from being involved in any business or activity which competes with Fernview's business, and (2) a 'non-solicitation' clause which means that you cannot approach any of Fernview's customers. Both of these clauses apply for the period of six months from the date of the end of your employment with Fernview.

The question is whether Fernview can enforce these clauses. To be enforceable, the clauses must be reasonable. Each case will depend on its own facts, but factors that the court will look at to determine reasonableness include the length and scope of the restrictions and the seniority of the employee. In a case earlier this year, the court decided that a six-month restriction period was reasonable.

In my opinion, Fernview might be able to argue that the clauses in your contract are reasonable. The restrictions are limited to a six-month period. In addition, in your position as a senior manager, you have had access to confidential company information and client data.

The risk of setting up your new business sooner than six months after you leave Fernview is that Fernview could go to court to try to obtain an injunction to stop you from working. Also, they could try to claim compensation if they can prove that you have taken some of their customers.

If you do not want to wait six months before starting your business, you could try negotiating with Fairview to release you from these restrictions. You were going to think about how you would like to proceed and get back to me.

I look forward to hearing from you. Please do not hesitate to contact me if you have any other questions.

Kind regards,
Anthony

3.6 Make a note of your answer here and then see the different methods mentioned in this part of the chapter.

3.7

a. Redundancy is where the employer dismisses an employee because their job no longer exists, or no longer needs to be done.
b. Judith wants an overview of redundancy law to give to a client.
c. A definition of redundancy, the procedure that the employer must follow, consultation, and the amount of redundancy payment.

3.9

b. Definition of redundancy or What is redundancy?
c. Redundancy procedure or What procedure must I follow?
d. Consultation or How do I consult with the employees?

3.10 b. Suggested answer:

Both types of headings would help a reader to navigate the document. Using the question formats might help a client to understand more easily what each paragraph is about as they are in plainer English and contain personal pronouns.

3.12

a. Length of consultation period or How long does consultation last?
b. The length of the consultation period will depend on the number of employees being made redundant.

3.14 Suggested answer:

Redundancy payments or Will I have to make any redundancy payments?

There are two different types of redundancy payments that you may have to make to an employee:

1. Statutory redundancy payment
   This is payable to any employee that has at least two years' continuous service. It is based on the employee's:
   - age,
   - length of service, and
   - weekly salary.
2. Contractual redundancy payment
   There may be a provision for an additional redundancy payment in the employee's employment contract.

3.16

a. When it becomes longer than two lines or around 25 words.
b. Make two or more shorter sentences, remove surplus words, use a list format.
c. Making shorter sentences, using a list format.

3.17 Suggested answer:

A contract of employment can be made orally or in writing. Even if the contract is made orally, the law says that the employer must provide some information in writing to the employee. This information must be given to the employee no later than their first day of work and must include:

- names of the employer and employee
- job title
- amount of pay
- hours of work
- place of work
- any other benefits
- amount of notice to terminate the employment

3.18

Sentence pair 1: using the possessive form.
Sentence pair 2: turning noun phrases into verbs.

3.19 Suggested answer:

On 15th February 2022, the Court of Appeal dismissed the respondents' appeal.

The appellants were food delivery drivers and claimed that they were employees. The respondents argued that the drivers were independent contractors. The Employment Tribunal found in the drivers' favour and the Employment Appeal Tribunal upheld the lower court's decision.

The respondents argued in the Court of Appeal that the drivers were free to work as much or as little as they wanted. They could also work for other delivery companies.

However, the Court of Appeal found that the respondents expected the drivers to be available at all times and a driver who refused to make a delivery would be penalised.

The Court of Appeal concluded that the drivers were employees because the respondents had control over them.

3.20

a. The trainee drafted a memorandum.
b. A memorandum was drafted by the trainee.
c. 1. Active voice: The employer (subject) must make (verb) a redundancy payment (object) to the employee.
   2. Passive voice: A redundancy payment (object) must be made (verb) to the employee by the employer (subject).

3.21

a. It allows your reader to identify the subject of the sentence and understand the core meaning of the sentence more effectively. It is important when you are imposing obligations or explaining who has the responsibility for an action.
b. When the focus is on the object rather than the subject or when you want to avoid responsibility for an action.

3.22

a. passive: Thank you for your email, which I (or we) received this morning.
b. passive: The sales manager assaulted the director.
c. active: A claim has been filed at the court by the claimant.
d. passive: I attach a copy of the claim form.
e. active: The sales manager has been dismissed by the employer.
f. passive: The parties will negotiate the amount of compensation.

3.23

a. The employer (subject), must provide (verb), a written statement (object). There are 16 words between the subject and the verb.
b. It is usually better to put the extra information at the end, and the core part of the sentence (subject, verb, and object) at the beginning. If you put the extra information at the beginning, it takes longer for the reader to reach the core part of the sentence.
c. The employer must provide a written statement of the main employment terms to the employee, even if the contract is made orally. This must be provided no later than the first day of work.

3.24 Suggested answer:

I understand that on 31st March 2022 your manager told you that the business was relocating. He said that the offices would be closing and you would be made redundant but that you should not worry because your employer would give you a redundancy payment.

Your employer offered you some other positions to avoid redundancy. You explained to your employer that those positions were not suitable because:

- the hours were not convenient for childcare reasons
- you would have to travel too far from home
- you had a medical condition which prevented you from undertaking complex tasks

Note that the words *therefore, however* and *furthermore* have been removed in the suggested answer. These types of words can help to link ideas in legal writing, but if you use good sentence and paragraph structure you do not need to use so many of these.

3.28 a.

Well, in the aforementioned[1] case, the claimant's lawyers have requested that we provide witness statements pertaining to the same.[2] In the event that[3] said[4] witness statements are not available, can they be provided forthwith[5] in order to[6] comply with the court's directions pursuant to[7] the Civil Procedure Rules? Notwithstanding[8] this, can we also provide further particulars[9] of the matters still at issue[10] in the instant[11] case?

1. this case
2. relating to it. But it would be better to say, '*that we provide the witness statements*'
3. If
4. the
5. immediately (or now)
6. to
7. under
8. despite
9. more details
10. remaining issues (or outstanding issues)
11. this

3.29

a. This is useful if your colleague writes well but otherwise could perpetuate bad habits.
b. Native speakers are not necessarily good writers. But they may be able to spot inaccuracies which you have missed.
c. This can be useful, as in Audio 4.3.
d. This can be useful to some extent. The readability statistics in Microsoft Word will also tell you the average length of your sentences, the percentage of passive sentences, and your score on plain English scales.

3.30

a. Sentence 2 is correct
b. Sentence 2 is correct
c. Sentence 1 is correct
d. Sentence 2 is correct
e. Sentence 1 is correct

Test yourself

1. If you know the client well, you could use the salutation *Dear [first name]* or *Hi [first name]*. For a new client, you could use the salutation *Dear [Mr/Ms/Miss surname]* or *Dear [full name]*. You could use the closing *Kind regards* or *Best regards* or *Best* if you know the client well. For a new client, you could use the closing *Yours sincerely*.
2. Put related points together to make paragraphs and then organise those paragraphs in a logical sequence.

3. A topic sentence is a sentence which introduces a paragraph and gives the reader an idea of what the paragraph is going to be about.
4. Two techniques are to remove surplus words and to use a list format.
5. See answer to 3.28.

Chapter 5: Presentations

1.1 Suggested answers:

Other examples could include an elevator pitch at a networking event or a presentation at a job interview.

2.1

a. He mentions webinars on corporate law topics.
b. He wants Angus to present the first webinar and he wants to have a chat about this.
c. He can speak to the marketing department.

2.2 Suggested answers:

Angus could also ask about the duration of the webinar and the number of expected participants.

2.3

a. Me (Angus) and Marcin Wójcik. Existing clients of the firm, new clients, members of the local entrepreneurs' association.
b. The main business structures relevant to start-ups: sole traders, partnerships, and limited companies.
c. The aim is for the participants to gain some knowledge about common business structures chosen by start-ups. The main aim is to attract new clients. And we also want participants to sign up for the next webinar.

2.5

a. False. Angus is going to give the introduction because Marcin is feeling a bit nervous about presenting in English.
b. False. They do not have a title but Marcin suggests: *Which business structure is right for my start-up?*
c. True.
d. True.
e. False. Housekeeping means general points about the organisation of the presentation.

2.6 Suggested answers:

Introduction 1 would be appropriate for Angus and Marcin's introduction. It uses polite and friendly language appropriate for an online webinar or in-person seminar for clients.

Introduction 2 uses a formal address, '*Good morning, ladies and gentlemen*', and some formal expressions such as '*Thank you for attending our presentation*'; '*Furthermore*', and '*The subject of our presentation is ...*', and it does not include contractions. This would be more appropriate for a formal presentation, such as a presentation at a conference.

Introduction 3 uses informal language such as the contraction '*you're watching*', and the idiom '*stay tuned*'. This would be more appropriate for a podcast interview.

2.7

a. In idea 1, Angus uses a rhetorical question; in idea 2, he uses a fact; in idea 3, he refers to a quote and also uses a rhetorical question; in idea 4, he uses a poll. And in each case, Angus makes a link to the aim of his presentation.
These are all good ideas for capturing an audience's attention. The advantage of idea 4 is that Angus can check what his audience already knows about the subject.

2.8 b. 9; c. 7; d. 5; e. 6; f. 3; g. 1; h. 4; i. 8

2.9 So, without further ado, I'll hand over to Marcin to get started.

2.12 a. 2, 7; b. 4, 8; c. 3, 5; d. 1, 6

2.13

b. Suggested answers:
A paperboard (also known as a flip chart), posters, collaborative shared documents, graphs, diagrams, videos, physical objects.

2.14 Make a note of your answer here and then see the next Exercise.

2.15

a. Angus suggests using the firm's template for all slides; creating bullet points with summaries of his points; not using too much legal language. Other suggested answers: using pictures or icons to illustrate key points.
b. Suggested answer.

Sole trader

- Owns and runs a business alone
- Advantages
  - full control of the business
  - keep all profits after tax
  - easy to set up
- Disadvantages
  - personally responsible for business debts
  - home and other personal assets at risk

2.16 Angus uses b; c; e; f; h.

2.17 a. Suggested answer:

Angus's feedback is indirect. For example, instead of saying, '*Your slides are not consistent*', he says, '*Have you thought about using this template for all the slides to ensure consistency?*'.

2.18 Suggested answer:

Partnerships

- Two or more people who own and run a business together
- Advantages
  - share the costs and running of the business
  - easy to set up
- Disadvantages
  - each partner personally responsible for all business debts
  - home and other personal assets at risk
  - potential for partnership disagreements

2.19 Sole traders

2.22 Suggested answer: This is a good conclusion because:

- '*To conclude*' indicates that the presentation is coming to an end.
- The first paragraph refers to the objectives of the presentation.
- The second paragraph summarises the key points that have been made during the presentation and also asks the audience a question: '*So, which business structure will you choose?*', which makes a link to the introduction to the webinar.
- The third paragraph looks forward to the next webinar and explains how the audience can sign up for this.
- The last paragraph thanks the audience for attending and invites questions.

2.23

a. It is difficult to prepare for the question and answer session.
b. You can try to anticipate some questions people might ask and think about how to answer them.
c. '*That's a good question*' and '*Can I just check that I've understood you correctly?*'
d. Because it shows their expertise in this area of law.
e. You could say, '*I will have to check the answer to that question and get back to you*'.

3.3 Angus mentions checking that your equipment is working properly before the webinar, using language that the audience can understand, and using pauses.

Test yourself

1. Who, what, and why?
2. Suggested answers: a rhetorical question, a fact, a quote, a poll.
3. No because you can just use key words, without using a subject or a verb.
4. You could say, '*I will have to check the answer to that question and get back to you*'.
5. See Text 5.1 and the answer to Exercise 3.3.

Chapter 6: Social media marketing

1.1 Suggested answers:

a. Social media refers to platforms that allow people and companies to create a profile, share content, and participate in online networking.
c. Lawyers can use social media to build their network, establish their reputation, stay up to date, market their legal services, and find work opportunities.

1.3 a. of; b. on; c. with; d. to; e. on/with; f. in; g. of; h. in; i. as

2.1 Suggested answers:

a. Personal information: gives essential information such as a profile photo, your full name, a very short description about who you are and what you do, your location, your current work position.
b. About: summarises who you are as a professional.
c. Experience: details your work experience, including past and present positions.
d. Education: details your formal education, including past and present positions.
e. Licenses & certifications: shows any licences or certificates you have with an option to link to an online copy.
f. Volunteer experience: details your voluntary experience, including past and present positions.
g. Interests: displays what you are following on LinkedIn™, such as influencers, companies, schools, and groups.
h. Skills & endorsements: details your skills and displays endorsements of those skills from your connections.
i. Recommendations: displays any references that your connections have given you.
j. Accomplishments: shows achievements such as publications, projects, honours and awards, test scores, and languages.

2.2

a. False, Ethan has a profile which does not contain much information, and Sofia does not have one.
b. True.
c. False, including non-legal work experience can highlight transferable skills.
d. True.
e. True.

2.3 Transferable skills are soft skills which can be applied to many different jobs. Ethan mentions time management, attention to detail, and teamwork.

2.4

a. SEO stands for search engine optimisation.
b. A search engine uses many techniques to choose which results to show a user, including the presence of searched for keywords in the online content.
c. You can improve the search engine ranking of your profile by including keywords.

2.5 Suggested answers:

a. Your target audience comprises the people or companies who you want to find your profile and read the content you post. Your target audience depends on what you want to achieve with your social media account. For example, if you are a lawyer looking for a job in banking law in Dubai, your target audience could be Dubai law firms with a banking law department.
b. The search terms depend on who comprises your target audience and what they are searching for. For example, if you are targeting the HR managers of banking law firms in Dubai, they may search for keywords such as *banking lawyer, job seeker, Dubai law firm* when they are head hunting.

2.6 Suggested answers:

Ethan's original Headline is vague, incomplete, and lacks keywords.

Ethan's updated Headline includes accomplishments; keywords; bullet points to separate phrases. This headline could attract recruiters.

2.8 Suggested answers:

Example 1 does not include much information; is written in the third person, which makes it less personal.

Example 2 includes lots of information; is written in the first person, which is common and acceptable on social media and which makes it more personal; includes keywords; uses paragraphs, headings, and bullet points, making it easy to read.

2.10 b. part-time; c. Fish; Friar; d. East London; e. December; f. commercial; g. organising; h. updating; i. handling; j. communication

2.12 a. in; b. in; c. of; d. for; e. in; f. at; g. in; h. to; i. no preposition; j. no preposition; k. on; l. in

2.15 Suggested answer:

Example 2 is more credible than Example 1 because it is a recommendation from a client rather than a self-recommendation.

2.16

(a) Dear Sarah

Thank you for being my supervisor at Fish and Friar LLP. I have learnt a lot during my time working for you.

(b) I'm writing to ask if you could provide me with a recommendation highlighting my knowledge of commercial law and interest in IT law.

(c) As you know, I am hoping to get a training contract, and your recommendation would help to build my credibility.

(d) Kind regards/best wishes.

Ethan

2.20 Suggested answer:

Ethan must set up a social media profile on another platform such as Twitter™ or Instagram™. His profile must reflect Express Law's brand. He must also explore hashtags to find content to follow and use in his own profile to help people discover him.

2.21 Suggested answers:

b. Example1 is modern and professional, using appropriate emojis and hashtags; personal, using first and second person singular; business-focused, referring to the language of business, using plain English, and an easy-to-read list layout. Due to these reasons, it best reflects Express Law's brand.

   Example 2 is traditional and serious, using a conservative style of one paragraph, complicated language, and a long sentence; impersonal, using the third person singular.

3.1 b. 3; c. 1; d. 5; e. 4

3.2 Suggested answers:

Adding a disclaimer could avoid unintentionally creating a lawyer-client relationship.

Gaining permission to post work could avoid breaching copyright.

Checking who you are connecting with could avoid being accused of witness tampering.

Double-checking that photos do not contain confidential information could avoid breaching client confidentiality.

Asking oneself whether the post is acceptable or not could avoid breaching a lawyer's code of conduct, such as a lawyer's duty to act with integrity.

3.5 Suggested answers:

Giving feedback to the author; giving an opinion; agreeing or disagreeing with the author; adding hashtags to the post.

3.7 Suggested answers:

Comment on this post: That's great news! I wish you the best of luck in the final.

Share this content adding one sentence: Here is an interesting post showing a force majeure clause in plain English.

3.8 Suggested answers:

a. Example 1: the author is sharing a resource. It is a link to a helpful video for businesses about top data protection issues. The post includes a call to action, asking readers to watch the video, and give feedback.

   Example 2: the author is sharing media industry news. The lawyers are excited about a forthcoming judgment which could be important for their media law clients.

   Example 3: the author is sharing legal tech news. The post is about an article they read about the possibility of robot judges in the future.

   Example 4: the author is sharing company news about the newly recruited lawyer, Wilko van Willers. The post includes a call to action, encouraging people to visit the law firm's website for further information.

b. The level of formality of social media posts is your personal choice and should be in line with your brand. It is more acceptable to use informal language and style when posting on social media than in other types of legal writing.

   Examples 1 and 2 use a level of informality which could be considered appropriate for legal professionals: contractions; symbols; hashtags, tagging, and emojis.

   Example 3 could be considered too informal for legal professionals as it misuses capital letters, punctuation, and grammar.

   Example 4 is written using formal language, which could be considered appropriate for legal professionals.

c. Example 1 could be helpful for lawyers who need to stay up to date with data protection issues; law firms who are recruiting a data protection expert; businesses who need a data protection lawyer. It provides a helpful video.

   Example 2 could be helpful for lawyers who need to stay up to date with media law; media people or businesses who need a law firm with expertise. It alerts the reader that an important media law judgment will be issued.

   Example 3 could be helpful for people interested in legal tech developments as it refers to an article about robot judges. However, no link to the article is provided.

   Example 4 could be helpful for job-seeking lawyers and businesses who need antitrust advice. It raises awareness about the firm and its opportunities.

d. Examples 1, 2, and 4 are well-written and could improve the person or law firm's reputation. The posts raise awareness about them and help to establish them as experts.

   Example 3 could have a negative impact on the person's reputation. The use of capital letters could give the impression that this person is aggressive. The grammatical errors and the fact that they did not include the link to the article could give the impression that they lack attention to detail.

3.11 Suggested answers:

The appropriateness of these posts depends on the law in your jurisdiction, the culture of your country, and the brand of you and your law firm. Here are some general points:

a. This post could show that you stay up to date on legal issues. You may need the speaker's permission and could consider tagging them.
b. This post could show that you are motivated. Make sure you have permission to use the quote, cite the source, and consider tagging the quote's author.
c. This post could show that you stay up to date and work hard. Check that you are not breaching copyright, cite the book, and consider tagging the book's author.
d. This could show your personality. However, it may be inappropriate in some cultures. You should consider what the aim of posting this picture is and how this will help you to market yourself as a legal professional.
e. This post could help develop your reputation.
f. This post could show your law firm's culture. Make sure you have team members' permission, that there is no confidential information on screen, and consider tagging team members.
g. This could show your personality. However, some people may consider it unprofessional. Make sure you get your client's permission to share this photo as you may be breaching

client confidentiality if you do not. With the client's permission, consider tagging them in the post.

3.12 Suggested answers:

a. This post does not appear to create any legal issues.
b. This picture post gives five tips for drafting a privacy policy.
c. Ethan's target audience could be business people. This could be helpful for existing and potential clients who need to comply with data protection law.
d. Yes. It is modern, professional, personal, simple, efficient, and business-focused.
e. Yes. He has included information about the post, a call to action, and hashtags.

3.15

a. A podcast is like a radio show which is made up of a series of individual episodes focused on a specific topic.
b. Some common episode types are solo show, co-host show, guest interview show, and panel show.

3.16 a.; b.; c.; e.; g.; i.; j.

3.21 b. 3; c. 5; d. 1; e. 4

Test yourself

1. See answers to 2.4 a. and 2.5 d.
2. See the answer to 2.21 b and 2.21 Example 1.
3. You can use hashtags to find people and content to follow and to make your profile more discoverable.
4. See answer to 3.1.
5. Writing posts, posting pictures, sharing other people's content, commenting on other people's posts.

Chapter 7: Job applications and interviews

1.1 Suggested answers:

A recruitment agency works for employers, helping them to find suitable candidates for jobs. It is useful because it advertises job offers from different employers. It might also advertise jobs that you will not find elsewhere.

Employers may advertise job offers directly on LinkedIn™ or your connections may also advertise job opportunities.

If you are a student, your university careers service may have details of job or work experience opportunities. Your university may also have connections with local employers.

A job board website is an internet platform which can connect you to employers and job opportunities.

Word of mouth is when someone in your network tells you about a job opportunity, even if this is not advertised.

A law careers fair is an event usually organised by universities. Law firms have stands at the event, where you can find out more information about the firm and their recruitment process.

A law firm's website may give information about job opportunities and the recruitment process at that particular firm.

A speculative application is when you send a job application to a law firm, even though no job has been advertised.

1.2

b. litigation
c. transactional
d. available job
e. past achievements
f. additional advantages
g. working from home
h. thorough
i. things happen quickly
j. lawyers moving from one firm to another
k. lead
l. people in a law firm whose work is charged to clients

1.3 a. It is for work experience. The other adverts are for qualified lawyers.
b. Advert 3.
c. Advert 2 (0-3 PQE).
d. Adverts 2 and 4 because they say, *'our client'*.

1.4

a. Mergers and acquisitions is an area of corporate law which includes the buying and selling of and combining of companies.
b. Middle East and North Africa. This is a geographical region.
c. Post-Qualification Experience. This means the number of years that you have practised as a qualified lawyer.
d. Technology, Media and Telecommunications. This is an area of practice that deals with legal issues related to different types of technology and communications, such as the internet and the mobile telephone industry.
e. Information Technology.
f. European Union.
g. General Counsel. This is the chief legal officer in a company.
h. Restructuring and Insolvency. This is an area of legal practice which advises businesses in financial difficulties.
i. per annum. This means per year.
j. circa. This means around, or approximately.

2.1 b. Suggested answers:

A senior lawyer may need to advise clients on more complex legal issues. They can be expected to work more independently. They may also need to lead a team of junior lawyers, which will require leadership and mentoring skills.

c.

Advert 1: excellent communicator; team player; commercial awareness; good analytical skills; ambition.

Advert 2: team player; creative thinker; interpersonal skills

Advert 3: speak and write fluently in English; good organisational skills; ability to work in a fast-paced environment.

Advert 4: ability to: head up a team, hit the ground running, develop client relationships and win new work, mentor junior fee earners.

2.2 a. Interpersonal skills, ability to work in a team (be a team player), organisational skills, analytical skills, commercial awareness.

b.

Skills	Examples
1. Interpersonal skills	*Ability to communicate with people.* *Understanding people and having empathy.* *Being able to explain complex legal issues in a way that the client can understand.*
2. Ability to work in a team	Building good relationships with colleagues. Showing respect for others. Being able to deal with conflict.
3. Organisational skills	Setting priorities. Managing time effectively.
4. Analytical skills	Analysing a client's problem and finding a solution. Identifying legal issues. Researching the law Thinking outside the box.
5. Commercial awareness	Being aware of the business world. Understanding the business of your clients. Reading the legal, financial, and business news. Listening to podcasts. Following trends on social media. Attending law firm webinars on current hot topics.

2.5

a. False. The recruitment process starts with an online application form.
b. True.
c. False. You cannot stop the interview once you have launched it.
d. False. The final stage is an assessment centre which includes a face-to-face interview with some of the partners. Managing Partner is not mentioned in the audio.

2.6

a. online application form
b. psychometric
c. video interview
d. assessment centre

3.1

a. Legal Counsel, based in Frankfurt or Paris, reporting to the General Counsel.
b. It is a market leader in the Fintech industry. Its platform allows businesses to integrate a wide range of solutions, including digital banking, payments, and lending services. It has the following practice areas: banking and capital markets, financial regulation, data protection; and drafting and negotiating commercial contracts.
c. You must be an experienced lawyer, qualified in France or Germany, speak and write fluently in English, have sound regulatory experience from a leading commercial law firm or Fintech business, be passionate about Fintech, have good organisational skills, and be ready to work in a fast-paced environment.
d. The first step is to send a covering letter and curriculum vitae in English.
e. Anna Fischer, HR Manager – Europe at annafischer@muellerbank.de with the subject line Legal Counsel position.

3.2 Suggested answers:
More information about the company, such as the number of employees and the number of offices; more details about the legal team and who the General Counsel is; recent deals that the company has been involved in.

3.3

a. To explain why you are the best person for the advertised job.
b. The name and address of the person you are writing to; why you are writing and how you heard about the position; brief details of your background, your current job and your motivation for applying; why you are suitable for this position by highlighting your experience and skills using specific examples from your work; attach your CV.
c. Address your letter to the name of the person dealing with the applications; use the company's name and refer to the specific position that you are applying for; be enthusiastic about why you want this role; relate your experience to the particular skills required for this position; thank the employer for considering your application.
d. Proofread it.

3.5 Suggested answer:
Answer 3 would be the most suitable. Answer 1 is too informal as it uses the expressions *I'm* and *legal job*. In Answer 2, the expression *I am truly honoured* could sound insincere.

3.6 Suggested answer:

Angela Werner
Kaiserstraße 12
40257 Frankfurt am Main
22nd September 2022

Anna Fischer
HR Manager – Europe
MüllerBank
Sent by email to annafischer@muellerbank.de

Dear Anna Fischer,

Legal Counsel position

I am writing to apply for the position of Legal Counsel at MüllerBank, which was advertised on LinkedIn™.

I am a dual-qualified English and German lawyer. For the last five years, I have been working as a senior associate in the Fintech team at Alston LLP in Frankfurt after spending three years as a junior associate in their London office. I am passionate about Fintech and a founding member of the Women in Technology network. I am very interested in MüllerBank because of its focus on innovative financial services solutions. The financial sector is currently facing significant regulatory changes and I am keen to move to the role of in-house Legal Counsel where I can work more closely with your internal business teams.

During my time at Alston LLP, I have gained experience in a wide range of financial regulatory matters. For example, I advised a major bank on a restructuring deal, which included the sale of its payment processing subsidiary. In addition, earlier this year I presented a client webinar explaining the impact of the government's latest review of Fintech. In my current position I have learned good organisational skills. I handle a large workload and have to manage my time effectively to meet tight deadlines, so I feel well prepared for MüllerBank's dynamic working environment.

I attach my CV and would welcome the opportunity to discuss how I can make a positive contribution to MüllerBank. Thank you for considering my application.

Yours sincerely,
Angela Werner

3.8 Suggested answers:

b. To avoid discrimination, it is not usual to include sections such as date of birth, age, or a photo on a CV in England and the USA, but these sections may be used in other cultures. References could also be included in a CV, or an employer could ask for these later if you are successful in your application.

c. Although a CV contains similar information to a LinkedIn™ profile, a CV is different because it is adapted to a specific job; the purpose of a CV is to apply for a job, whereas the purpose of a LinkedIn™ profile is to build a professional network in addition to finding work opportunities.

3.10 Angela has completed the header, the education, and the skills and interests sections.

3.11 Suggested answer:

Profile c. follows the checklist as it summarises Angela's skills and career aims and relates to the position that she is applying for. Profile a. is not written in the first person and uses a lot of compound adjectives. Profile b. is written in the first person, but it is not clear how much experience Angela has, nor which legal sector she works in.

3.12 Angela could use bullet points to summarise her key achievements. There is no need to write in complete sentences.

3.13

- Led a team of 5 fee earners in a client bank's €10 million sale of its payment subsidiary.
- Advised a private equity firm on its investment in a software start-up.
- Provided data privacy compliance advice to a leading financial technology company.
- Presented a number of client webinars on topical Fintech issues. For example, '*Fintech: all you need to know about the Government's latest review*' in January 2022.
- Supervised junior lawyers in our team.

3.14 Verbs used: lead, advise, provide, present, supervise.

3.15 Suggested answers:

a. advised
b. drafted
c. negotiated
d. assisted
e. researched

4.1

a. The vacation scheme lasts four weeks and you can experience contentious and non-contentious work by choosing two practice areas from banking, commercial, dispute resolution, employment, M&A, and real estate. You will work with current trainee solicitors and carry out tasks such as research, drafting memoranda, and attending client meetings and conference calls.
b. excellent communicator; team player; commercial awareness; good analytical skills, ambition.
c. You click on the 'apply now' button to start the application process.

4.2

a. The video interview stage.
b. Check all his equipment is working correctly.
c. About a minute to prepare and a few minutes to say his answer.
d. By recording himself answering some example questions.

4.3 Suggested answers:
Dress appropriately for an interview; find a quiet space where you will not be disturbed by others; check the angle of your camera so that you can maintain good eye contact; avoid looking down at your notes when you speak.

4.4

a. The STAR method helps give evidence of your skills. The letters stand for Situation, Task, Action, Result.
b.

Skill	Situation	Task	Action	Result
Ambition	*I wanted to organise a mooting competition in my law faculty.*	*I had to get permission from the faculty and organise the competition before the summer break.*	*I contacted the head of the law faculty, who gave their permission. Then I asked some other students to research a mooting question. I contacted some local barristers to see if they could judge the competition and then I advertised the competition through the campus platform.*	*The competition was a great success: over 50 students competed. And I've been asked to repeat it again this year.*

4.8

a. Suggested answers:
Sarah makes a good impression because she uses the interviewer's names, she answers their questions with specific examples, she uses the STAR method to explain an example of working under pressure, she shows that she has researched the firm and that she is aware of current issues in the legal industry. On the other hand, Geraldine's answers are not specific to this law firm and she does not answer the second part of the first question, '*Why do you want to be a lawyer?*'
b. Sarah.
c. Sarah. She uses expressions to recap the question at the end of her answer.

Test yourself

1. See Exercise 1.4.
2. It is about being aware of what is going on in the business world so that you can understand the context in which your clients and law firms are operating. See Exercise 2.2 for examples of how you can obtain this.

3. See Text 7.1.
4. See Text 7.2.
5. The STAR method is a technique for answering interview questions about your skills. It stands for Situation, Task, Action, Result.

Chapter 8: Contract drafting and review

1.1 Suggested answers:

It is not usually the lawyer's role to negotiate the business deal, but to focus on the legal risks. While a lawyer will want to protect their client's interests, if the draft contract is weighted too heavily in favour of their client, it could take longer to negotiate. It is important that a contract is drafted in language that a client can understand as the client will have to work with the contract once it has been signed.

1.2 Check the Glossary for definitions of these contracts and the parties involved.

1.3 Suggested answers:

a. Share purchase agreements; joint venture agreements; non-disclosure agreements.
b. Commercial leases.
c. Employment contracts; settlement agreements.
d. Possible answers are franchise agreements or licence agreements, but it is most likely to be franchise agreements on these facts because it refers to rights to a business model rather than rights to specific assets.
e. This lawyer could deal with all of the common commercial contracts examples, but the most relevant to the facts are: sale of goods contracts and services agreements for dealing with suppliers and customers, distribution agreements for promoting products in new markets, and loan agreements for securing funding.

1.5

a. Share purchase agreements.
b. There is no set rule. There is a convention in share purchase agreements that the buyer's lawyer drafts the contract.
c. A template.
d. Amelia mentions her firm's precedent bank and the internet.
e. The main advantage is to save time. The disadvantages are that they may not be appropriate for your client's transaction; they could lead to inconsistencies; they might be badly drafted; they might be the negotiated form of the contract.

1.6

a. A court decision which can be used as authority in a subsequent case.
b. Suggested answers:
   legal textbooks; legal databases.

2.1

b. recitals
c. words of agreement

d. definitions
e. main provisions
f. other core provisions
g. boilerplate
h. signature blocks

2.2 Recitals: BACKGROUND
Words of agreement: IT IS AGREED:
Definitions: Clause 1
Main provisions: Clauses 2 to 5
Other core provisions: Clauses 6 to 8
Boilerplate: Clauses 9 to 14
Signature blocks: SIGNED BY ...

2.3

a. True.
b. False, a condition precedent is a condition which has to be satisfied before the contract comes into effect.
c. True.
d. False, it is important to review these clauses and not just assume that they are the same in every contract.
e. True.

2.4 clause

3.2 a. The example contract is written in a modern, plainer English style.

The introductory paragraph is written in separate paragraphs. The words *by and* are not necessary before the word *between*. The modern words *Seller* and *Buyer* are used instead of *Vendor* and *Purchaser* and they are defined more simply, without using the expression *hereinafter referred to as*. The example contract does not use the archaic words *witnesseth* and *whereas*. The words of agreement are written in plain English.

b. Suggested answer:

In a modern, simple sale of goods contract, recitals are not really necessary. They have been included here as a drafting example.

THIS SALE OF GOODS AGREEMENT is made on ____________________
BETWEEN:

1. Turbulent Dryers Limited (Company no. 1234567) whose registered office is at Roundtree Business Park, Roundtree Lane, Leeds, LS14 6HY (the '**Seller**') and
2. Top Salons Limited (Company no. 9101112) whose registered office is at 74 Wentworth Road, Manchester, M14 6RS (the '**Buyer**')

BACKGROUND

(A) The Seller sells professional hairdryers to hairdressers.
(B) The Buyer owns and operates a chain of hairdressing salons.
(C) The Seller has agreed to sell and the Buyer has agreed to buy the Goods subject to the terms and conditions of this Agreement.

IT IS AGREED:

3.3 b. in this Agreement
c. by this Agreement
d. to this Agreement

3.4

a. One party in the case argued that herein meant *in this section 29* and the other party argued that it meant *in this Agreement*. It could also mean *in this sentence*.
b. Be clear what you are referring to. Use the words *in this section 29* or *in this Agreement*, depending on your meaning.

3.5

a. Modal verbs can have several different meanings in general English but these are the most common meanings:

   shall for a suggestion: *Shall we have a break for lunch now?*

   must for something you have to do, an obligation: *You must register online for the webinar.*

   may for permission: *May I borrow your pen?* or for possibility: *I may (or might) be away from the office next week.*

   will for the future tense: *Before the video conference, I'll check I can log in to the platform.*

   should for advice or a recommendation: *You should change the password on your email account. I've just received a spam email from you.*

b. In commercial contracts, the most common meanings are:

   shall for an obligation: *The Tenant shall pay the Rent.*

   must can also be used for an obligation: *The Tenant must pay the Rent*, and is also sometimes used for a condition: *To change the Specifications, the Customer must notify the Service Provider in writing of its requirements.*

   will for something that happens (not an obligation) in the future. For example, in clause 3.2 of the example contract: *The receipt of the Seller's solicitors will give a full and valid discharge ...*

   should is sometimes used for a condition: *Should the delay continue for a period of 60 days, either party may terminate this Agreement.* This is archaic. In modern language *if* is used.

3.6 a. an obligation: the Seller must sell and the Buyer must buy the Shares.
b. a prohibition: the Seller is not allowed to disclose confidential information.
c. the Buyer or the Seller have a choice, a discretion, to waive the Conditions on terms that the Buyer chooses.

3.7

a. *Shall* is not plain English
b. must
c. Lawyers use *shall* because it is traditional or because they are afraid to change language which has already been used for a long time.
d. Ken Adams suggests seeing if a sentence makes sense if you replace *shall* with *has a duty to.*

3.8

a. The Completion date *means* 25 June 2022.
b. This Agreement *is* conditional on the satisfaction of the Condition Precedent on or before the Completion Date.
c. The Buyer *may* waive the Condition Precedent at any time.
d. In the event that the Condition Precedent is not satisfied or waived on or before the Completion Date, this Agreement *terminates* with immediate effect.
e. (no rewrite: this is an obligation)
f. This agreement *is* governed by English law. Or 'English law *governs* this agreement.'

3.9

a. The duration of the lease
b. 1) A provision of the contract. 2) a word, especially a technical word.
c. No, because the date is not clear: it could mean 1 May 2022 (BrE) or 5 January 2022 (AmE). And using the word *from* means that it is not clear if we start counting the five-year period on the specified date, for example, 1 May 2022 or on the next day, 2 May 2022.

3.10

b. Ambiguity: it is not clear if the date of 23 July 2022 is included in the time period.

Rewrite: *The Contractor shall commence the Works on or before 23 July 2022.* Or *The Contractor shall commence the Works no later than 23 July 2022.*

c. Ambiguity: it is not clear if the date of 24 September 2022 is included in the time period.

Rewrite: *The interest rate for the period commencing on the Closing Date and ending on 24 September 2022 is [ ].* Or *The interest rate for the period commencing on the Closing Date up to and including 24 September 2022 is [ ].*

d. Ambiguity: it is not clear if the dates of 1 June 2022 and 1 June 2024 are included in the time period.

Rewrite: *The Company shall employ the Executive for a term of two years starting on 1 June 2022 and ending on 31 May 2024.* Or *The Company shall employ the Executive for a term of two years from and including 1 June 2022 up to and including 31 May 2024.*

3.11

a. Clause 1: The delivery dates are precise as they are specified in the Specifications. *Time is of the essence* does not add preciseness. This expression indicates that the dates for delivery of the Services are important terms of the contract, which could allow the Customer to terminate the contract if the delivery dates are not met.

   Clauses 2 to 5: These are all vague. There is no clear meaning of the expressions *promptly, timely manner, as soon as reasonably practicable*, and *immediately* although some writers believe that *immediately* is the quickest.

b. The effect is that we do not know exactly how much time the parties have to perform their obligations.

3.12 a. No. There is no heading, and the clause contains long sentences and legalese.

c. It is written in the passive voice.

d. A party can terminate by:
   1. giving six months' written notice to the other party at any time before the end of the term.
   2. giving written notice to the other party if there is a material breach of the contract, but if the breach is capable of being remedied, the other party has a period of 30 days from receipt of written notice to remedy the breach.
   3. giving written notice to the other party if the other party becomes insolvent.

3.13 a. Suggested answer:

   The alternative clause is easier to understand because it has a heading and is divided into subsections. The three ways of terminating the contract are clearly identified. The clause uses more modern language.

b. may

c. immediately

d. if

3.14

a. *Either party may terminate this Agreement immediately by giving written notice to the other party, if:*

b. There is a colon after *if*, there is a semi-colon at the end of clause 10.2.1 before the word *or* and there is a full stop at the end of the clause.

3.15

a. *shall refrain from, agrees not to, undertakes not to, commits not to.*

b. Different expressions are used. They are not consistent.

c. Shall not or must not.

d.

For a period of one year immediately following termination of the Employee's employment, the Employee shall not:

(a) solicit or entice any Company employee to leave the Company;
(b) accept into employment or use the services of any person who is a Company employee on the Termination Date;
(c) directly or indirectly engage or be interested in any business carried on in competition with any of the business of the Company; or
(d) use any of the Company's trading names.

4.2 Amelia mentions checking her client's instructions and any heads of terms; checking if she needs input from other partners in her firm; checking what is missing from the contract; checking when and how the Buyer pays the price; and checking to see if obligations in the contract are absolute or qualified.

4.3

a. shall
b. shall; use; reasonable; efforts

4.4

a. An absolute obligation means that you have to do something. If you do not do it, you will be in breach of contract. A qualified obligation reduces a party's obligation. You just have to try to fulfil the obligation.
b. In Exercise 4.3, clause a. is an absolute obligation and clause b. is a qualified obligation.

4.5

a. The problem that David identifies is that this language is vague. It might not be clear what a party has to do to comply with its obligation.
b. Amelia explains that this type of language allows flexibility in defining obligations and that usually there are more important aspects of the deal to discuss.

4.6 a. 2; b. 3; c. 1

4.7 The expressions Amelia uses are:

See paragraph 1 in Schedule 4: it says here that ...
This clause explains the situation if ...
According to this clause ...
You can see an example in clause 7.1.
And clause 7.2 contains ...

4.9 Suggested answers:
Clause 13: *This clause says that any changes to the contract have to be written and signed by all the parties.*

Clause 14.2: *Clause 14.2 means that if you want to take court action regarding any dispute under the contract, you will have to use the English courts.*

5.3

a. smart contracts
b. contract management system
c. artificial intelligence
d. document automation
e. playbook
f. e-signatures

5.4 a. Suggested answers:
Contract drafting: document automation, which could be part of a contract management system. The draft contract is generated from questions and answers. Contract review: artificial intelligence to look for certain contract terms; a contract management system to track the negotiation progress; a playbook to guide amendments and negotiations.
b. The main advantage is speeding up the contracting process.
c. Suggested answers:
The time and cost of selecting the legal tech provider and implementing new processes. For document automation to be successful, templates will need to be adapted into more modern, plainer English and this could take time to achieve.

5.6

a. Legal tech is about using technology in the contract drafting and review process, whereas legal design is about the way in which the information in a contract is presented.
b. It refers to the organisation of information in a contract.
c. By thinking about the layout of your document and using paragraphs, headings, and lists.
d. Include a summary or table of key terms on the first page of the contract, use icons or boxes to highlight text, or use diagrams, flowcharts and timelines to help a reader visualise information.

5.7 Suggested answers:

Version 1

⚠ Compensation for delay

1. The Contractor must complete the Works on or before the Completion Date.
2. It is important that the Works are completed on time.
3. If the Works are not completed on or before the Completion Date the Contractor must pay the Owner $1,500 for each week of delay.

Version 2
Compensation for delay

When will the Works be completed?	The Contractor must complete the Works on or before the Completion Date.
What if the Works are not completed on time?	It is important that the Works are completed on time. If the Works are not completed on or before the Completion Date the Contractor must pay the Owner $1,500 for each week of delay.

Test yourself

1. See Exercise 1.2. For example, in Audio 8.1, David and Amelia discuss a share purchase agreement which is a contract where a seller sells shares in a company to a buyer.
2. The boilerplate clauses come after the other core provisions and before the signatures.
3. *Shall*, but the word *must* can also be used to impose an obligation.
4. An absolute obligation means that a party to a contract has to do something; otherwise they will be in breach of contract. A qualified obligation reduces a party's obligation. For example, to use reasonable efforts means that a party just has to try to fulfil their obligation.
5. One example is to create more white space. For more examples, see Text 8.3.

Chapter 9: Contract negotiations

1.1 Suggested answers:

c. Lawyers negotiate the terms of contracts when their client wants to enter into a business relationship with another company. Lawyers negotiate settlement agreements when parties are in dispute and want to reach a resolution outside of court.
d. When lawyers negotiate, they represent a client and not themselves. Lawyers must act professionally and follow certain professional conduct rules when negotiating.

1.2

a. False, Bea writes about negotiating commercial contracts.
b. True.
d. False, Bea thinks that communication skills are the most important.
e. True.

2.1

b. The other side's lawyer drafts the first version of the contract.
c. The lawyer who receives the first version marks up the contract.
d. The other side's lawyer reviews the contract amendments.
e. The lawyers meet to negotiate the contract terms.
f. The other side's lawyer drafts the final version of the contract.
g. The final version of the contract is sent to the parties and signed.

2.2

b. 8; c. 1; d. 4; e. 7; f. 3; g. 6; h. 5

2.3

a. Fabian and Jakob are meeting to discuss things to prepare for forthcoming contract negotiations.
b. Fabian and Jakob will speak about the following topics: researching the other side and understanding their perspective; understanding what our client wants, needs, and why; and prioritising what we will negotiate.
c. Before the meeting, Fabian must read the background information attached to the email and carry out research into the other side and its lawyer.

2.4

a. Aaberg and Adelsköld LLP is the law firm and Jakob Lindberg is the lawyer representing RB Motors. Jakob will be joined by trainee lawyer Fabian Nilsson. J&J LLP is the law firm and Clarissa Porterfield is the lawyer representing Autologica. Clarissa will be joined by her associate Brent Riley.
b. RB Motors is a top ten global car manufacturer which will start manufacturing electric vehicles. It was founded in 1905 in Sweden. Autologica manufactures electric batteries. The parties want to enter into an agreement where RB Motors will purchase batteries from Autologica.
c. A supply of goods agreement is being negotiated.

2.5 Suggested answer:

It could be helpful to know some information about the company because it will help you to understand what it may want and why in the negotiations. It could be helpful to know if the lawyer representing the other side is a native or non-native speaker and where they are from. This allows you to practise your listening comprehension of a specific accent and consider culture before the negotiations.

2.6 Suggested answers:

Payment terms: RB Motors as the customer could want long payment terms so that they have more time to pay Autologica's invoices. Autologica as the Supplier could want short payment terms so that they receive payments quickly from RB Motors.

Force majeure: RB Motors could want to limit the scope of force majeure to reduce the likelihood that Autologica could stop performing under the contract. Autologica could want a broad force majeure clause so that it could stop performing under the contract if problems arise which are outside its control.

Warranty: RB Motors could want to include warranties to ensure the quality of goods being supplied and to have remedies if this quality is not met. Autologica could want to avoid including warranties, or limit them, to reduce their liability if goods are not of a certain quality.

The reasons behind these positions could be that each party wants to run a profitable business without cash flow problems and protect themselves from legal risks.

2.7 Suggested answers:

a. Jakob changed clause 7.2 so that RB Motors could inspect the goods and reject the goods if they exceed a certain volume. Jakob changed clause 7.3 to make it clear that delivery on time is a strict obligation.

b. RB Motors wants these changes because late delivery can cause financial losses and because they have previously had late delivery issues with another supplier.
c. Autologica could want more flexibility with the delivery clause to avoid liability for problems arising.

2.8

a. True.
b. True.
c. False, when long-term relationships are important, non-negotiables should be kept to a minimum.
d. True.

2.9

a. The first goal is to negotiate the contract quickly. The second goal is to establish a long-term business relationship with Autologica.

Suggested answers:

b. Jakob will need to be flexible with alternative solutions to clause amendments. He will need to reach a solution which works for both parties. He will need to be polite and reasonable.
c. Autologica may have similar big-picture goals because they are a growing company with long-term plans.

3.1 Suggested answers:

Opening stage: e. ask questions; h. make small talk; m. introduce agenda; g. review agreed points (if there have been some prior negotiations).

Negotiating stage: i. make counterproposals; f. accept proposals; c. reject proposals; e. ask questions; k. clarify positions; a. make compromises; d. make concessions; n. strengthen proposals.

Closing stage: j. discuss next steps h. make small talk.

3.2

a. False, the lawyers will use first names.
b. True.
c. False, the lawyers are under time pressure.
d. True.

3.3

a. looking forward
b. long-lasting relationship
c. time constraints
d. point by point

3.4 a. 2; b.3; c.4; d.1

3.7 Clarissa and Jakob use: b; d; g

3.10

a. False, Jakob consults with his client, Eymen.
b. True.
c. False, this point is important for both parties.
d. False, the lawyers decide to take a quick five-minute break.

3.11

a. absolutely
b. quite
c. huge
d. totally
e. little bit
f. pretty

3.12

a. Clarissa uses upgraders such as *absolutely* and *huge*. Jakob used downgraders such as *a little bit* and *pretty*.

3.13

Upgraders, adjectives: g. big; h. major
Upgraders, adverbs: k. really; l. incredibly; m. strongly; n. totally
Downgraders, adjectives: c. minor; e. small
Downgraders, adverbs: d. quite; f. just; i. probably; p. perhaps

3.15

a. The lawyers decided to avoid this clause and take a break. They will deal with it later.

3.16

a. False, the competing strategy could damage relationships.
b. True.
c. True.
d. False, in a compromise parties meet in the middle and do not get exactly what they want.
e. True.

3.17

a. 31–180 days.
b. 30–120 days.
c. 31–120 days.

3.18 Suggested answers:
Alex Hamilton makes the point that when a company takes extreme positions in negotiations it has two negative effects: it may slow down negotiations, and it may result in losing a deal.

3.21 a; e; h

3.22 a. hear you out
b. shoes
c. mutual
d. both of us
e. same page

3.24 You may reach a solution where you agree to resolve disputes through ADR. If you choose to resolve a dispute through litigation, some potential solutions are:

If Autologica uses a competing strategy:

12. Jurisdiction
Any dispute arising out of or in relation to this Agreement shall be subject to the exclusive jurisdiction of the New York Courts to which the parties to this Agreement hereby submit.

If RB Motors uses a competing strategy:

12. Jurisdiction
Any dispute arising out of or in relation to this Agreement shall be subject to the exclusive jurisdiction of the courts of Sweden, with the District Court of Stockholm as the court of first instance, to which the parties to this Agreement hereby submit.

If the parties use a compromising strategy:

12. Jurisdiction
Any dispute arising out of or in relation to this Agreement shall be subject to the exclusive jurisdiction of the Courts of England and to which the parties to this Agreement hereby submit.

If the parties use an avoiding strategy:

12. Jurisdiction
[*To be decided at our next meeting*].

If the parties use a collaborating win–win strategy:

12. Jurisdiction
Any dispute arising out of or in relation to this Agreement shall be subject to the exclusive jurisdiction of the New York Courts for cases brought by the Customer to which the Parties hereby submit. Any dispute arising out of or in relation to this Agreement shall be subject to the exclusive jurisdiction of the courts of Sweden, with the District Court of Stockholm as the court of first instance for cases brought by the Supplier to which the parties to this Agreement hereby submit. Counterclaims shall be brought in the same court as the original claim.

As neither party wants to travel for litigation, writing a clause which obligates a party to travel if they want to start litigation may discourage them from bringing a case and encourage them to settle by other means. This is what both parties wanted.

3.25 a. True
- b. False, there are some clauses outstanding.
- c. True.
- d. False, Clarissa will draft the final agreement.
- e. True.

3.26 b. 1; c. 7; d. 3; e. 6; f. 5; g. 4

Test yourself

1. To prepare for contract negotiations you can research the other side; understand what your client wants, needs, and why; prioritise which terms to negotiate.
2. See answer to Exercise 3.1.
3. Upgraders are words which exaggerate the disagreement, such as *totally, completely, absolutely*. Downgraders are words which downplay the disagreement, such as *partially, a little bit, maybe*.
4. Possible strategies:
   - competing: strengthen your argument to convince the other side to agree to your point
   - accommodating: accept the other side's proposal
   - avoiding: take a break and deal with this point later
   - compromising: find a fair solution where parties meet in the middle
   - collaborating: work together to find a win-win solution
5. See answers to 2.2 and 3.4 for possible idioms.

Chapter 10: Alternative dispute resolution

1.1

b. See Exercise 1.2 for answers.
Other methods include company grievance procedures; public grievance procedures such as an ombudsman; a mixture of methods such as meditation followed by arbitration.

1.2 a. 2; b. 1; c. 3; d. 4; e. 6; f. 5

1.3

a. Adjudicative methods: Arbitration, Adjudication, Expert determination
Non-adjudicative methods: Negotiation, Mediation, Conciliation

1.4

a. cheaper b. faster c. private

1.5 Suggested answer:
Parties may prefer ADR instead of litigation because they have more control over the ADR procedure compared to litigation. For example, in arbitration they can appoint an arbitrator with specific expertise, whereas in litigation parties cannot choose the judge. Non-adjudicative methods of ADR also allow parties to work together to resolve the dispute, which can help protect their relationship.

1.6

a. precedent b. vindication c. quasi-criminal; criminal

1.7 Suggested answer:
Parties may prefer litigation instead of ADR because if they have not agreed on ADR methods before the dispute arises and there are high levels of animosity, it may be difficult to agree on an ADR method. If there is an urgent need for interim measures such as an interim injunction, litigation may provide this; however, some methods of ADR also allow for emergency measures and orders.

2.1

a. False, an oral agreement is not valid. An arbitration agreement must be in writing.
b. False, *to refer a dispute to arbitration* is a synonym.
c. True.
d. False, parties may enter into an arbitration agreement before or after a dispute arises.
e. False, party autonomy means that parties have a lot of choice over how arbitration will be conducted.

2.2

a. In institutional arbitration an arbitration institution administers the process. In ad hoc arbitration the arbitral tribunal administers the process.
b. One arbitrator is faster and cheaper, but three arbitrators offer more varied experience.
c. Parties should consider if they and the arbitrators have sufficient knowledge of the language. Not using the parties' native language carries time, cost, and accuracy implications. However, choosing the native language of only one party will put that party at an advantage. Parties may choose more than one language, but this will increase the cost and length of proceedings.

2.3 a. 4; b. 6; c. 1; d. 2; e. 3; f. 5

2.4

a. The seat is the jurisdiction whose arbitration law will govern the arbitration whereas the venue is the physical or virtual location of the hearings.
b. Parties should consider choosing jurisdictions with effective national arbitration laws, a high-quality judiciary, and those which are signatories to international arbitration agreements.

c. The governing law of the contract is the law applied to determine the dispute. The governing law of the arbitration agreement is the law applied to determine the existence of the arbitration agreement and its interpretation.
d. It is not necessary to include a governing law clause of the arbitration agreement if the seat and governing law of the contract are the same.

2.5

a. Institutional arbitration b. Ad hoc arbitration

2.6

Nouns: b. 3; c. 4; d. 1
Verbs: a. 3; b. 1; c. 2
Collocations and phrases: a. 3; b. 4; c.1; d. 5; e. 2

2.7

a. 'If any dispute arises a Party *may* ...': May does not show a commitment to arbitrate.
b. 'London Court of *Arbitrage*': Arbitrage does not have a meaning related to arbitration in English.
c. 'The *venue* of the arbitration is Rotterdam, the Netherlands or otherwise as agreed by the Parties': Venue is not the seat.
d. The governing law of the arbitration agreement is not stated. If the seat is the Netherlands and the governing law of the contract is Dutch law, then there is no reason to also write the governing law of the agreement. However, the seat is ambiguous, it could be London or the Netherlands, and therefore it causes problems.

2.8 Suggested answers to Finn's questions:

Is the governing law now Dutch law?

PetroFirma's amendment changes the governing law of the contract to Dutch law. This means that if a dispute arose, the dispute would be determined by Dutch law.

The governing law of the arbitration agreement is not mentioned. Normally there is only a need to state the governing law of the arbitration agreement if the seat and governing law of the contract are different. This clause is currently ambiguous as to what the seat is.

What's the London Court of Arbitrage?

The London Court of Arbitrage does not exist. *Arbitrage* in Dutch means *Arbitration* in English. Perhaps they mean *The London Court of International Arbitration*. This is an institution which administers arbitration, and which would take control of administrative matters if a dispute under this contract went to arbitration. It is important that the clause correctly states the name of the institution.

Is one arbitrator enough?

If you appoint three arbitrators there will be greater expertise but greater cost. If money is not an issue, it may be more appropriate to have three arbitrators.

Will you have to travel to the Netherlands for arbitration hearings?

The clause is currently ambiguous on this issue. It states that '*The venue of the arbitration is Rotterdam, the Netherlands*'. Normally venue means the physical or virtual location where proceedings take place. It is not necessary to write the venue in the clause as it can be decided by the parties if a dispute arises. If they mean the physical location, parties would have to go to the Netherlands.

However, it is more likely that they mean '*The seat of the arbitration* ...' The seat refers to the jurisdiction whose arbitration laws govern the arbitration procedure. It is important that the clause states the seat.

How can you deal with proceedings if the language is Dutch?

PetroFirma is proposing that the language of proceedings be Dutch. This means that your arbitration communications would need to be translated into Dutch and you would need to hire an interpreter to be present at hearings to translate for you. This would put PetroFirma at an advantage in proceedings as it would be using their native language not yours. Using English is more neutral.

Are there problems with this clause?

Yes. There is ambiguity over the seat and the governing law of the arbitration clause. The clause also does not show an unambiguous commitment to arbitrate because of the wording 'If any dispute arises a Party *may* ...'

2.9

Suggested answer:

Dispute resolution

Any dispute arising out of or in connection with this contract, including any question regarding its existence, validity or termination, shall be referred to and finally resolved by arbitration administered by the London Court of International Arbitration in accordance with its Arbitration Rules, which are deemed to be incorporated by reference into this clause.

The number of arbitrators shall be three. Each Party shall appoint one arbitrator and the two party-appointed arbitrators shall appoint the third arbitrator as the chair.

The seat, or legal place, of arbitration shall be England. The language to be used in the arbitral proceedings shall be English.

The governing law of the contract shall be the substantive law of England and Wales.

2.10

a. The parties must use mediation first then arbitration.
b. A party cannot submit a dispute to arbitration before first attempting mediation. If this happened, the arbitrator would not have jurisdiction over the dispute. If arbitration went ahead and the arbitral tribunal rendered an award, a party may challenge the validity of this award.

c. Changing *shall* to *may* or *should* may result in the clause being interpreted to mean that following an unsuccessful mediation, arbitration is optional not mandatory. It is important that the clause shows an unambiguous commitment to arbitrate; otherwise, a party may start proceedings in litigation.

2.11 Suggested answers:

a. Videoconferencing, hearing room technologies, cloud-based storage, and virtual hearing rooms are currently being used in arbitration. AI is being used to identify relevant documents to support legal proceedings in the e-discovery process.
b. AI could be used in the future to predict the outcome of arbitration, create a fully immersive realistic hearing experience, and create robot arbitrators.

3.1 a. 3; b. 1; c. 2

3.2 Suggested answer:
In facilitative mediation the mediator helps the parties to reach their own resolution. In evaluative mediation the mediator recommends a resolution. In transformative mediation the mediator empowers the parties to improve their relationship and communication.

3.3 Suggested answer:
Sofia was an employee and probably wants to deal with this dispute quickly. Mediation offers a fast and cheap way to deal with disputes and is commonly used in employment disputes. If she brings proceedings before the Employment Tribunal she may not get a judgment in her favour, and it may take longer and cost more than mediation. In mediation she may be able to get an innovative solution that she could not get in court, such as an apology and a letter of recommendation to help her find a new job.

3.4

a. The parties are under a duty to act in good faith. This means that they must be honest. This is stated in clause 1.
b. The mediation is confidential. Parties are not allowed to share information with anyone else. This is stated in clause 2.
c. You can meet the mediator in a private session. The mediator will only disclose this information to the other side with your permission. This is stated in clause 2.
d. No, you do not have to sign it. If you sign the settlement agreement, you will have to follow it. This is stated in clause 3.
e. Sometimes parties get upset when trying to resolve a dispute. If you get upset, you can take a break. However, if you want to end the process, you can talk with the mediator about it. You will not be forced to continue as mediation is a voluntary process. This is stated in clause 4.
f. No. The mediation is without prejudice. This means that any communications made in relation to the mediation, for example, any suggestions for settlement, will remain private and cannot be used in future court proceedings if the mediation is unsuccessful. This is stated in clause 2.

3.5

a. False, parties will use first names.
b. False, the parties have already signed the *mediation agreement*. They may sign the *settlement agreement* at the end of the day or on a later date.
c. True.
d. True.
e. False, Sofia the claimant, represented by Luca her lawyer, will begin.

3.6

b. parties opening statements
c. exploring solutions in plenary and caucuses
d. parties may hit a deadlock
e. parties reach a solution
f. lawyers draft the settlement agreement
g. parties may sign the settlement agreement
h. mediator reviews achievements

3.8

b. A facilitative mediator should listen at level one. It is important that the mediator does not give their own opinions on the matter or judge the parties. It is also important that the mediator makes the parties feel like they are truly being listened to and understood. This helps the parties trust the mediator. It is also important for the mediator to listen deeply and uncover the hidden motivations behind what parties say. This will help the parties to better understand each other and can help them reach a solution.
c. A facilitative mediator listens to different parties who are in conflict explain their issue from different perspectives. The mediator's aim is to help them communicate and understand each other better so that they can reach a solution together. A lawyer listens to their client explaining an issue from their perspective. The lawyer's aim is to give the client advice.

3.10

a. Scenario 1: level 3
   Scenario 2: level 2
   Scenario 3: level 1

3.11

a. The first statement blames the other party, whereas the second statement focuses on the state of the speaker.
b. The second statement is more helpful for resolving conflicts. When a party blames the other party, it can lead to an unwillingness to cooperate. Moving the focus away from blame can encourage the other party to see things from a different perspective and can lead to cooperation.

3.12

a. Framing refers to the way each party views and describes the dispute. Reframing refers to a technique used by mediators where they reword what a party has said in a more constructive way without changing the meaning.

b. Reframing can be helpful when a party talks about the past, states what they want, or makes an accusation.

3.13

b. Focusing on the past → focusing on the present or the future.
c. Stating what a party wants → stating the reason why they want it.

3.14 Suggested answers:

b. So you're saying that the hotel has high standards which it expects staff to meet?
c. So you're saying that the hotel is now facing ongoing financial difficulties?
d. So you're saying that saving time and money is important to you?

3.16 Suggested answers:

a. What do you understand the legal duties of an employer to be on this matter?
b. You previously mentioned that saving time and money was important for you. How much time do you think it will take to get a judgment on this matter? What are the main strengths of your defence? If she wins, how much do you think it will cost you?
c. What do you think Sofia could do in response to that? What impact could that have on the Kiplington Hotel as an employer?

3.17 There is no correct answer. As an example, one possible solution could be to connect to the main sewer and divide the costs between the parties.

Test yourself

1. See the answer to 1.3 a.
2. See the answer to 1.4.
3. See paragraph 1 of Text 10.1.
4. See the answer to 3.6.
5. Reframing is where the mediator rewords what a party says in a more constructive way without losing the fundamental meaning. In contrast, reality testing is where the mediator asks questions about what the party has said to help them understand whether they are being realistic or not.

Chapter 11: Advocacy

1.1

a. In general English, *advocacy* has a broad meaning, whereas in legal English *advocacy* has a narrow meaning and refers to a lawyer preparing for or representing a client in court or arbitration.
b. A lawyer needs oral communication skills to present a case, question witnesses, and argue a case. They need research, analytical, interviewing and writing skills to prepare court documents.
c. No. *Advocate* and *lawyer* are not synonyms.
d. In England: barristers, solicitors, and solicitor-advocates.
   In the USA: lawyers/attorneys who may refer to themselves as litigators.

2.1 b. 1; c. 5; d. 3; e. 4; f. 7; g. 6

2.2 a. complaint
b. request to arbitrate; notice to arbitrate
c. answer
d. answer; answer to the request; defence; statement of defence
e. pleadings
f. statement of case; pleadings
g. no equivalent
h. witness statement
i. brief; memorandum of law
j. skeleton argument
k. motion
l. motion; application notice

2.3 a. different from
b. in contrast
c. likewise
d. as well
e. similarly
f. while
g. the same
h. not the same
i. closest thing to
j. similar to

2.6

a. The parties are: EgyptLux Ltd (claimant) and Cheapomart Ltd (defendant).
b. The case will be heard in the High Court of Justice, Business and Property Courts, Intellectual Property List (CHD), Intellectual Property Enterprise Court.
c. The causes of action are trade mark infringement and passing off.

2.7

a. 2. e; 3. f.; 4. h.; 5. a.; 6. d.; 7. c.; 8. g.
b. 1, 2, 3, 4, 8 are appropriate. 5, 6, 7 are not appropriate as the parties are not parties to a contract or legal document.

2.8

a. injunction
b. delivery up or destruction
c. account of profits
d. damages
e. Costs

2.9

a. False, the claimant expects the amount of damages to be *substantial*, in other words, *a lot*.

b. False, the *quantum*, in other words the *amount of damages*, will be determined after establishing the defendant's liability.
c. True.

2.10
a. seeks:
b. restrain
c. Delete phrase: ~~An order granting an award of punitive damages~~
d. split trial

2.11 Suggested answer:
A story needs characters, a start, middle, end, and something bad which happens and is resolved.

2.15
a. has
b. incorporated
c. EgyptLux Ltd
d. designing, manufacturing, and selling
e. specifically
f. under
g. at
h. carries
i. Claimant's
j. it

2.16 a. Adjectives
well-known; many; leading; following; recognisable; luxurious; gold; white; minimalist; central; well-spaced; impressive; beautiful; gorgeous; rectangular; powerful; triangular; upper; front; distinctive; recurrent; average; magnificent
Adverbs: continually; extremely; effortlessly; marvellously

b. Adjectives
Objective: leading; following; gold; white; central; rectangular; triangular; upper; front; distinctive; recurrent
Subjective: well-known; many; recognisable; luxurious; minimalist; well-spaced; impressive; beautiful; gorgeous; powerful; average; magnificent
Adverbs
Objective: continually
Subjective: extremely; effortlessly; marvellously

c. You could delete some of the subjective adjectives and adverbs or try to replace them with more objective ones:

One of EgyptLux Ltd's products is Puraque. For over ten years, Puraque has been the leading sea salt scrub brand by sales and reputation in the UK.

The following elements have been used continually on the packaging of Puraque since 2012:

(i) a gold colour scheme contrasting with a white box
(ii) a minimalist layout comprising central fonts and 1.5-spaced text
(iii) an illustration of a woman's face in the centre and L-shaped frames on the four corners of the rectangular box; and
(iv) the brand name with a triangular logo on the upper part of the front of the packaging

These recurrent elements indicate to the consumer that the product is Puraque.

2.17

a. 1. b. Damage, loss, and relief; 2. c. Passing off; 3. a. Public impression; 4. d. Trade mark infringement; 5. e. The Defendant's acts of infringement
b. Order of paragraphs: 5; (4; 2 or 2; 4); 3; 1

3.1

b. The judge; the parties; the parties' lawyers

3.2

a. Also called Opening statement/Opening submissions
b. Examination-in-chief/Direct examination
c. Cross-examination
d. Re-examination/Re-direct
f. Closing speeches/Closing statements/Closing submissions

3.3 a. exactly; same
b. whereas
c. rather than
d. comparing; one hand; other hand
e. like this; too
f. quite similar
g. more; less; same
h. alike; as opposed to

3.6 Suggested answers:

a. Following court etiquette shows respect to the court and the judge views you as a credible lawyer.
c. Standing up may not be appropriate for online proceedings as participants may not be seen properly on camera. Interrupting may be necessary in online proceedings to alert participants of technical problems.

3.7 Suggested answers:

Examples b and e show lawyers using poise to appear confident and persuasive.

3.8 Suggested answers:

Do: stand up straight; relax shoulders; keep feet slightly apart; use eye contact with the judge

Don't: act in a nervous and agitated way; ignore the judge; dress untidily; slouch; keep hands in pockets; fiddle with things

3.9 Suggested answers:

Do: Doing these points will ensure that the judge understands you and makes you sound confident and more persuasive.

Don't: Doing these points will make it difficult for the judge to understand you. You will also sound nervous and less persuasive.

3.10 Suggested answers:

Mr Dixon follows all the 'dos' from the checklist and sounds confident and credible.
Mr Lee hesitates, uses fillers, speaks too quietly, and uses a rising inflection.
Ms Wilson speaks too fast.

3.11

a. my Lord; learned friend; friends
b. appear with
c. please the court; I'm an attorney; have here with me; we're joined by

3.14

a. Open questions and closed questions.
b. Leading questions are not allowed in examination-in-chief because the witness must have freedom to tell their own version of the facts.
c. Leading questions are encouraged in cross-examination because the lawyer can control the witness to get an anticipated answer which supports their case.

3.15 Non-leading: a.; d.; e.; f.

Leading: b.; c.

3.16 Suggested answers:

a. What is your name?
b. Where do you live?
c. What is your highest level of education?
d. Where do you work?
e. When did you first become interested in automated communications?

3.17 a. trial bundle; tab

b. witness statement
c. signature
d. true
e. exhibit

3.19

a. This morning you showed some slides to explain how Bespeak works?
b. You heard Jasper Johnson yesterday discuss the source code for Talkomate?
c. Your patent application in Egypt was rejected?
d. You first met Jasper Johnson in 2019?

3.20 Suggested answers:

a. Do you agree with me that the videos you made contained information about the process used in Bespeak?
b. I'm right when I say that the AI for Progress Group was a group of computer hackers?
c. You did not invent android, right?
d. At that point you didn't think he had infringed your patent, correct?

Test yourself

1. See answers to 2.1 e.
2. A skeleton argument is a document used in English litigation and arbitration which briefly sets out the main points to be orally argued in proceedings. The closest thing to a skeleton argument in the USA is a brief or memorandum of law. In the USA, you submit a brief in support of a motion. A brief sets out the arguments in favour of the motion.
3. Persuade with character (ethos); emotion (pathos); logic (logos).
4. See answer to 3.2.
5. Leading questions can be used in cross-examination.

Glossary

Index

This glossary contains key words used in the book. The default language is BrE and where there is another word used in AmE this is given. If nouns are not countable, they are marked with *u* for *uncountable* and for *p* for *plural*. If verbs are not regular, they are marked with *i* for *irregular* and the conjugation is given. There is space for you to fill in a translation of each word in your own language.

Word	Definition	Translation	Page
Accrue (verb)	To accumulate over time.		148
Act (noun)	1. A law, synonym: *statute*. 2. An action, Antonym: *omission*.		183, 215, 216
Act for (phrasal verb)	To represent someone such as a client.		27, 28, 46, 209
Adjudicator (noun)	Someone who makes an official decision in a disagreement.		178, 208
Advice (noun)	A formal recommendation about what to do. Note the verb is spelt: *advise*.		27, 37, 43–4, 64–5, 74, 92, 111, 122, 190
Allegation (noun)	An assertion that someone has done something illegal or wrong.		179, 209, 210, 216, 222
Allege (verb)	To claim or assert that someone has done something illegal or wrong.		192, 216
Amend (verb)	To change a document.		154, 187
Amendment (noun)	A change to a document, especially a contract.		153, 156, 160, 186
Annul (verb)	To declare a legal document invalid.		183
Anti-competitive (adjective)	Reducing competition in an unfair or illegal way. Also written: *anticompetitive*.		see Competition
Appeal (noun)	A legal proceeding challenging a previous decision.		70, 209, 211
Assault (verb)	To harm someone through an act or threat of violence.		71

Word	Definition	Translation	Page
Asset (noun)	A valuable item, characteristic, or property. A company's assets can include real estate, office equipment, and intellectual property. Antonym: *liabilities*. A *digital asset* is content that is stored digitally, such as photos or videos, or cryptocurrency, such as bitcoin.		81, 82, 113, 140, 172
Assign (verb)	To transfer ownership of a right to someone else. Collocation: *assign a right*.		28, 149
Assignment (noun)	The transfer of a right or property by an *assignor* to an *assignee*. Also, a contract clause.		147, 149
Associate (noun)	A junior or senior lawyer who is not a partner in the law firm.		19, 27, 76, 110, 132, 152
Award (noun)	The *judgment* of an arbitrator, also called an *arbitral award*.		178, 183
Bailiff (noun)	A court officer who enforces court orders such as by seizing assets. In AmE, a *bailiff* is a court officer who maintains order during court proceedings, equivalent to an *usher* in BrE.		see Usher
Bear (verb; i)	*Bear, bore, borne/born*. 1. To take on an obligation or duty. 2. To endure.		34
Bill (noun)	1. A written request for payment of money owed for goods or services. Synonym: *invoice*. 2. A proposed law.		46, 197
Binding (adjective)	Must be followed.		43, 178–9
Business (noun)	1. (c) A person or organisation that sells goods or services. Unincorporated businesses include sole traders, ordinary partnerships, limited partnerships. Incorporated businesses include limited liability partnerships, and companies such as private limited companies, and public limited companies. 2. (u) The work related to buying and selling goods and services.		12, 62–4, 76, 80–4, 88, 115, 130, 152, 158

Word	Definition	Translation	Page
Case law (noun; u)	Law made by the courts in common law systems, synonym: *precedent.*		63
Cease (verb)	To stop.		148
Civil law (noun; u)	1. The law which governs matters excluding criminal law. 2. The legal system which is codified. Antonym: *common law.*		177, 207
Claim (noun)	A legal assertion in a civil matter made by a person seeking a remedy. Collocations: to *file/start/bring a claim.*		32, 49, 66, 69, 147, 177, 209–11
Clerk (noun)	A person who assists the court with tasks such as legal research, writing, and filing.		222
Commercial lease (noun)	A contract where the owner of land or buildings, the *landlord*, grants to the other party, the *tenant*, the right to use the property for a business use for an agreed period of time. Another word for landlord is *lessor* and another word for tenant is *lessee.*		130, 138, 170
Common law (noun)	1. Law made through the courts. Synonym: *case law* or *precedent*. 2. A legal system which developed through judicial decisions.		213
Company (noun)	An incorporated business structure which can be a private limited company or a public limited company.		79–80, 83
Compensation (noun; u)	1. A sum of money awarded to the winning party in a civil case to try to compensate for damage. 2. Salary, wages, and work benefits.		142, 144, 201
Competition (adjective)	Related to preventing anti-competitive behaviour such as creating monopolies and fixing prices. AmE: *antitrust.*		5
Competitor (noun)	A person or company that competes with another.		213
Complaints procedure (noun)	A formal way to complain within a company. Synonym: *grievance procedure.*		46

Word	Definition	Translation	Page
Compliance (noun; u)	The following of a requirement. Antonym: *non-compliance.*		91, 100, 122–3
Comply (verb)	To follow a requirement. Collocation: to *comply with.*		63, 98, 183
Confidential (adjective)	Private and not for disclosure.		8, 62, 149, 192
Confidentiality (noun; u)	The state of being private.		98
Construction contract (noun)	A contract made between the *owner* of land and a *contractor* in which the contractor agrees to carry out works on the owner's land.		132
Contentious (adjective)	Related to disputes. Antonym: *non-contentious.*		13, 110, 123
Contractor (noun)	An independent professional who provides services, defined in a contract, to a company for a set period and price.		132, 138, 146, 202–4
Copyright (noun)	An intellectual property right to copy creative work such as writing, music, and art.		see intellectual property
Counsel (noun)	Synonym: *lawyer.*		55, 75, 111, 208
Counterproposal (noun)	An offer made by one party to a negotiation in response to an unacceptable proposal made by the other side. Synonym: *counteroffer.*		66, 159, 162
Court of Appeal (noun)	An appellate court that hears appeals after they have been tried at first instance. AmE: *Court of Appeals*		70
Court reporter (noun)	A person who records in writing oral submissions and testimonies given in court.		222
Damage (noun; u)	Harm, loss, or injury.		173, 213
Damages (noun; p)	A sum of money which is paid by one party to another as compensation for a tort or a breach of contract.		146, 158, 200, 214
Deem (verb)	To consider, to interpret.		148–9, 184, 185, 215

Word	Definition	Translation	Page
Defamation (noun; u)	The publication of a false statement about a person that damages their reputation. There are two forms: *libel* (noun; c/u) in permanent form, such as writing and *slander* (noun; c/u), not in permanent form, such as spoken.		101
Defect (noun)	Problem, imperfection.		74, 139, 142
Defined term (noun)	A word or words in a contract which are capitalised and are given a specific meaning.		see Defined terms
Defined terms (noun; p)	A clause which gives meanings to words used in a contract. Synonym: *Definitions.*		133, 147, 161
Director (noun)	A senior position in a company, responsible for management.		55, 71, 75
Disciplinary (adjective)	Related to enforcing rules and behaviour, especially at work.		
Disclose (verb)	To reveal private information.		148, 192, 210
Discretion (noun; u)	Choice.		175, 192
Discrimination (noun; u)	The prejudicial treatment of people on specific grounds such as race, age, or sex.		74
Dispute (noun)	Conflict, especially of a legal nature.		131, 149, 157, 158, 169, 177
Distribution agreement (noun)	A contract between a *supplier* or manufacturer of goods and a business, called the *distributor*, which will sell those goods to retailers or customers in a particular territory. Also called a *Distributorship Agreement.*		130
Due (adjective)	1. Expected at a certain time. 2. Of suitable quality. 3. Owed 4. Caused by.		139, 157, 172, 203, 215, 234
Due diligence (noun; u)	A process to check the risks involved in taking a particular action. Collocation: *to carry out due diligence.*		5, 123
E-discovery (noun; u)	A digital investigation to find electronic evidence to be used in legal proceedings.		189

Word	Definition	Translation	Page
Elicit (verb)	To obtain information or a response.		230
Employee (noun)	The person who works for an employer.		63, 66, 141, 196
Employer (noun)	The person providing employment for someone.		63, 71, 72, 92, 116, 120, 131, 191
Employment contract (noun)	A contract between an *employer* and an *employee*, which sets out the terms on which the employee will work for the employer.		54, 130, 141
Enforceable (adjective)	Capable of making something applied or carried out. Antonym: *unenforceable*.		62
Entire agreement (noun)	A clause which sets out that this contract contains the whole agreement between the parties and other documents cannot be relied on.		149
Equity partner (noun)	Owner of a law firm who has contributed capital to the company and who receives a share of profits. Antonym: *non-equity partner* or *salaried partner*		111
Evidence (noun; u)	Proof. Collocations: *to give evidence, to elicit evidence.*		182, 192, 210, 230
Expenses (noun; p)	Money a person spends to carry out a job which will be paid back by the customer or employer.		46, 173
Expert witness	A type of witness who can provide a specialised opinion on an issue in a court case due to their expertise.		222
Expiration (adjective)	The end of a fixed period of time during which something can be used.		140
Fee (noun)	An amount of money charged for a service.		6, 46, 100
File (noun)	A lawyer may refer to a *file* to mean a client they are representing.		25, 46, 230
Fine (noun)	An amount of money paid by a person who did not follow the law.		71
Fixed-fee (adjective)	A set amount of money which is paid for a service.		46

Word	Definition	Translation	Page
Force majeure (noun)	The situation in which parties to a contract are excused from performing their contractual obligations. Also, a clause in a contract.		144, 156, 161
Franchise agreement (noun)	A contract where one party, a *franchisor*, grants another party, a *franchisee*, the right to use the franchisor's business model or brand name.		130
Fraud (noun)	A misrepresentation made recklessly or intentionally that results in personal gain.		91
Freeze (verb; i)	*Freeze, froze, frozen.* 1. To stop moving. 2. To prevent money or assets from being used or moved.		35
Full-time (adjective)	Taking up the whole of the working week. Antonym: *part-time.*		6, 93
Good faith (adjective)	Done in an honest way. Antonym: *bad faith.*		169, 192
Governing law and jurisdiction clause (noun)	A clause which sets out the law that will govern the contract (governing law) and which courts will hear disputes arising (jurisdiction).		149, 186
Grant (verb)	To give someone permission to use your rights. Collocation: *grant a licence.*		28, 131, 170, 233
Harm (noun; u)	See *Damage.*		247
Harassment (noun; u)	Unwanted offensive behaviour which intimidates or humiliates someone.		74
Hearing (noun)	An appearance of a case before a court to decide an issue of fact or law.		31, 226
Illegal (adjective)	Contrary to civil or criminal law.		149
In-house lawyer (noun)	A lawyer who is an employee of a company and that company is their single client. Also written: *inhouse lawyer.*		6, 112, 131, 152

Word	Definition	Translation	Page
Incorporate (verb)	To register a company as a corporation and establish a separate legal personality.		see incorporated
Incorporated (adjective)	1. Included into something. 2. Formed as a legal corporation. Antonym: *unincorporated*		81–2, 133
Infringe (verb)	To disobey the law or interfere with someone's rights. Collocation: *to infringe copyright, to infringe a trade mark.*		217–8, 232, 233
Infringement (noun)	The use of intellectual property rights without the owner's permission.		28, 35, 213, 234
Injunction (noun)	A court order restraining party from doing something, *prohibitory injunction*, or obligating them to do something, *mandatory injunction.*		27, 63, 210, 214
Insolvency (noun; u)	The state of being unable to pay debts.		111
Invoice (noun)	See *Bill.*		166
Joint and several liability (noun; u)	In the context of a partnership, this means that each partner has liability for the full amount of the partnership's debts.		82
Joint venture agreement (noun)	A contract where two or more businesses agree to work together on a specific task or project.		130
Jurisdiction (noun)	1. (c) A geographical area with its own set of laws. 2. (u) The power of a court or tribunal to decide a case.		98, 149, 169, 177, 212, 221
Last resort (noun; u)	A final option to solve a problem.		44, 46, 177
Lawsuit (noun)	See *Proceedings.*		201
Lease (verb)	To use property in return for paying rent.		27, 130, 138, 170
Legal action (noun)	See *Proceedings.*		35, 37
Legal tech (noun)	An abbreviation of legal technology. It refers to the use of technology and software in providing legal services. Also called law tech.		91, 126, 143
Legislation (noun; u)	Written laws passed by a legislative body.		123, 136

Word	Definition	Translation	Page
Lending (noun; u)	The action of giving money to someone on condition that they will pay it back.		111
Letter before claim (noun)	A letter sent by a claimant to a potential defendant before starting court proceedings. Synonym: *letter before action*.		28, 32, 203, 222
Liabilities (noun; p)	The outstanding debts a company owes.		
Liability (noun; u)	Legal responsibility.		81, 142, 148, 157, 215
Licence (noun)	Official permission to do or use something that would otherwise not be allowed. Collocation: *To grant a licence*. AmE: *license*.		
Licence agreement (noun)	A contract where one party, a *licensor*, grants another party, a *licensee*, the right to use the licensor's property, for example, the licensor's intellectual property. AmE: *License agreement/Licensing agreement*		130
Licensee (noun)	See *Licence agreement*.		
Licensor (noun)	See *Licence agreement*.		
Liquidated damages (noun)	Damages agreed by the parties in the contract. Also, a contract clause.		146, 158
Liquidation (noun; u)	The process of closing a company and distributing its assets to its creditors.		202
LLP (noun)	Acronym for *limited liability partnership*. An incorporated structure made up of partners who are members of the LLP. A typical structure for law firms and accountancy firms.		81, 93
Loan agreement (noun)	A contract where one party, a *lender*, provides money to the other party, the *borrower*, setting out how the money is to be repaid.		130
Loss (noun)	See *Damage*.		158, 221

Word	Definition	Translation	Page
Ltd (noun)	Acronym for *private limited company*. A company which is limited by shares and not listed on the stock exchange.		234
Managing partner (noun)	Manages the running of a law firm.		18, 114
Material (adjective)	Important, significant. Antonym: *minor*.		140, 174–5, 219
Memorandum (noun)	Plural form: *memoranda*. A brief written report on a specific matter. Do not confuse with the AmE *memorandum of law* which is a document in support of a motion.		43, 66
Merger and acquisition (noun)	A transaction related to the ownership of companies and their assets. Often abbreviated to M&A or M&As. Plural: *Merger and acquisitions or mergers and acquisitions*. A *merger* (noun; c) is when two entities combine to form a new entity. An *acquisition* (noun; c) is when one entity takes over the ownership of another entity.		5, 112, 131
Merits (noun)	The grounds of a claim or defence used to decide a case. Collocation: *On its/the merits*.		178
Niche law firm (noun)	Boutique law firm.		93
Non-competition clause (noun)	Prohibits an employee from working for a competitor within a defined time period. A synonym: *non-compete*. AmE: *noncompetition/noncompete*.		54, 62, 144
Non-contentious (adjective)	See *Contentious*.		110
Non-disclosure agreement (noun)	A contract where the parties promise not to share confidential information which they have received from the other party. It is often referred to by its acronym *NDA*. Also called a *Confidentiality Agreement*.		80, 130

Word	Definition	Translation	Page
Non-solicitation clause (noun)	Prohibits an employee from doing business with the employer's customers or from employing other employees. AmE: *nonsolicitation.*		62
Outstanding (adjective)	1. Impressive. 2. Unresolved, incomplete, or unpaid.		170
Owe (verb)	To be in debt to someone.		192
Parental leave (noun; u)	Time off work for parents to look after their baby. Also categorised as *maternity leave* for mothers and *paternity leave* for fathers.		258
Partner (noun)	The most senior position in a law firm. There are different types of partners.		18, 28, 91, 111
Partnership (noun)	Two or more people who own and run a business together.		82
Penalise (verb)	Antonym: *Reward.*		70
PLC (noun)	Acronym for *public limited company.* A company which is limited by shares, and which can sell its shares on a stock market.		234
Proceedings (noun)	Synonym: *Lawsuit, case, legal action.*		50, 169, 185, 223
Proprietor (noun)	Owner		28, 81, 216
Registered design (noun)	A registered design gives a product owner exclusive rights over the product's shape and appearance so that competitors cannot copy it		28
Restriction (noun)	Something, for example, a law or a contract clause, that limits what you can do.		63
Right of audience (noun)	A right of a lawyer to appear in court and argue a case.		208
Sale of goods contract (noun)	A contract where a *seller* sells goods to a *buyer.* In a one-off transaction this is usually called a *Sale of Goods Contract* or *Sale of Goods Agreement.* A contract where a *supplier* provides goods on a regular basis to a *customer* may be called a *Supply of Goods Contract* or *Supply of Goods Agreement.*		6, 130, 134, 184

Word	Definition	Translation	Page
Seek (verb; i)	*Seek, sought, sought.* To look for. Collocations: *To seek redress/a remedy/relief.*		183, 188, 214
Seize (verb)	To take possession of something by a legal process. Collocation: *To seize assets.*		81–2
Serve (verb)	To officially deliver documents for legal proceedings.		27, 149, 186
Services agreement (noun)	A contract where a business supplies services to another business. Also called a *Supply of Services Agreement*. The party supplying the services may be called a *supplier* or a *service provider*. The other party is usually called the *customer*		130, 139
Set up (verb)	To establish. Collocations: *To set up a company/business.*		54, 84
Settle (verb)	To resolve, to reach a solution.		59, 149, 169, 177, 185
Settlement agreement (noun)	An agreement between disputing parties setting out the terms on which they have agreed to end the dispute.		130, 153, 178, 192, 193
Share (noun)	A unit of ownership of a company.		147
Share purchase agreement (noun)	A contract where a *seller* sells shares in a company to a *buyer*. AmE: *Stock Purchase Agreement*.		130, 147
Sign (verb)	To officially write one's name on a document to agree to its contents.		42, 170, 178, 193
Sole trader (noun)	A person who owns and runs a business alone. Synonym: sole proprietor		79–81
Sovereign investment fund (noun)	A state-owned investment entity.		242
Statute (noun)	See *Act*.		213
Statutory (adjective)	Relating to statute.		68
Subsidiary (adjective)	Less important than but connected to something.		209–10
Subsidiary (noun)	A company owned or controlled by another company.		117, 133, 147

Word	Definition	Translation	Page
Sue (verb)	To take legal action against someone in a civil matter.		44, 200–1
Sum (noun)	Amount of money. A *lump sum* is an amount paid all at once. *Instalments* is an amount divided into smaller parts and paid on a regular basis over a defined time period.		146, 214
Supervising partner (noun)	Oversees the work of associates.		28, 153, 179
Supreme Court (noun)	The highest appellate court in the English and American court system.		53
Tenant (noun)	A person who rents property for a set period.		138, 170
Terminate (verb)	To end, especially a contract.		140, 172
Termination (noun; u)	The end, especially of a contract. Also, a contract clause.		139, 140, 141, 158, 172, 184, 192
Testimony (noun)	Evidence presented by a witness orally and under oath in court.		209, 230
The press (noun; u)	Journalists who work for news organisations.		221, 222
The public (noun; u)	People in general.		213, 222
Third party (noun)	A person other than the two main parties involved in a legal matter.		142, 178
Tort law (noun)	An area of law which regulates relationships between persons who are not in a contract together.		213
Trade secret (noun)	Intellectual property owned by a company consisting of private information about a process or product.		149
Trade union (noun)	An organisation that represents workers and protects their rights.		66
Transaction (noun)	The buying and selling of goods and services.		123, 229
Transactional lawyer (noun)	A lawyer who works on deals involving the buying and selling of goods and services.		110, 208
Trial (noun)	A legal proceeding where parties present evidence before a court or tribunal.		50, 207, 222–3

Word	Definition	Translation	Page
Unfair dismissal (noun)	The dismissal of an employee by the employer without a valid reason.		66
Uphold (verb; i)	*Uphold, upheld, upheld.* 1. To decide that a previous decision was correct. 2. To support a law or principle.		70
Usher (noun)	A person who assists the court with tasks such as swearing in jurors and witnesses and calling the court to order. AmE: *bailiff.*		222
Vacation scheme (noun)	Synonyms: *Legal internship, legal work experience, legal work placement.* AmE: *summer associate program.*		110
Valid (adjective)	Legally or officially accepted. Antonym: *invalid.*		148, 183, 185
Variation (noun)	A change/modification, for example, to a contract. Also, a contract clause.		149
Waive (verb)	To choose to not have a right or rule.		137, 148
White-collar crime (noun)	Financial offences such as corruption and fraud.		91
Witness (noun)	Someone who sees or knows something about a matter in a court case and who gives a written or oral testimony under oath or affirmation as evidence.		22, 99, 192, 208–11, 228–9
Works (noun; p)	Construction project. Distinguish from *work*, which is an activity that you are paid for, like a job.		30, 132, 138, 140, 146, 173

For Product Safety Concerns and Information please contact our EU representative GPSR@taylorandfrancis.com Taylor & Francis Verlag GmbH, Kaufingerstraße 24, 80331 München, Germany